THE GERMAN PEASANTRY

THE GERMAN PEASANTRY

Conflict and Community in Rural Society from
the Eighteenth to the Twentieth Centuries

EDITED BY
RICHARD J. EVANS AND W. R. LEE

CROOM HELM
London & Sydney

© 1986 Richard J. Evans and W. R. Lee
Croom Helm Ltd, Provident House, Burrell Row,
Beckenham, Kent BR3 1AT
Croom Helm Australia Pty Ltd, Suite 4, 6th Floor,
64–76 Kippax Street, Surry Hills, NSW 2010, Australia

British Library Cataloguing in Publication Data

The German peasantry: conflict and community
  in rural society from the eighteenth to the
  twentieth centuries.
  1. German — Rural conditions
  I. Evans, Richard, J. II. Lee, W. R. (William
  Robert)
  943'.009'734   HN445

ISBN 0-7099-0932-2

Typeset in English Times by Patrick and Anne Murphy,
10 Bracken Way, Walkford, Christchurch, Dorset, England

Printed and bound in Great Britain by Mackays of Chatham Ltd, Kent

CONTENTS

FIGURES

TABLES

This book brings together eleven essays, none of which has previously appeared in English, and only one of which has been published anywhere before, on the history of rural society in Germany from the eighteenth century to the present day. Almost to the very end of the nineteenth century, the majority of Germans lived and worked in the countryside. It was only in the 1890s that the urban population became numerically dominant, and a substantial farming sector in the economy continued to provide a livelihood for many millions of men and women for many decades after this. Yet, for reasons explored by Ian Farr in his introductory essay to this volume, the social history of this large and important area of the German population has been neglected until very recently. There has, it is true, been a good deal of work on German peasant politics, not least in view of the fact that the rural population provided perhaps the greatest single reservoir of support for National Socialism in the late Weimar Republic. But much of this work has tended to treat the German peasantry as a more or less undifferentiated mass. Historians have argued fiercely about the nature and consequences of social differentiation among the working class and the *Mittelstand*, but there has been a marked absence of comparable debates on the equally important area of rural society. Some historians have regarded the peasantry as uniformly susceptible to manipulation by unscrupulous aristocrats and demagogues from the towns. Others have suggested that, on the contrary, there was a degree of political self-mobilisation among the rural population in the late nineteenth and early twentieth centuries, without, on the whole, going beyond this to root their analysis in a more precise delineation of the rural social structure.

A major focus of this book, therefore, is on social divisions in rural society. All the contributions concentrate on one aspect or another of this problem. Broadly speaking, four kinds of social division emerge: first, and most obviously, between landlord and serf, the subject of the essays by Hartmut Harnisch and William Hagen; secondly, between large, middling and small peasants, discussed in the contributions by Hainer Plaul, Cathleen Catt, Gerhard Wilke and Christel Heinrich; thirdly, between peasant farmers and others (notably landless labourers and worker-peasants employed in the town but continuing to live in the village), the focus of attention in the essay by Wolfgang Kaschuba as well as many of the contributions already mentioned; and finally, between men and women, the subject in particular of Regina Schulte's contribution, as well as a number of others, notably the essays by Gerhard Wilke and Utz Jeggle. In this way, the volume as a whole aims to convey something of the complexity of rural society, and the ways in which it was structured by many different kinds of social inequality.

This focus necessarily involves a critical 'deconstruction' of the problematical term 'peasant'. As Ian Farr notes, the concept owes much of its power to mythical notions of the sturdy independent farmer as the repository of all that was most solid and wholesome in nineteenth-century German society. Nationalist myths of this kind derived much of their power from widespread anxieties brought about by the rapid social changes of the nineteenth century. A second thread of argument running through this book is the contention that these social changes did not leave rural society untouched. This was perhaps most obvious in the north and east, where, as the contributions by Hartmut Harnisch, William Hagen, Hainer Plaul, Gisela Griepentrog and Christel Heinrich show, the impact of capitalist development through agricultural improvement and, later on, the growth of sugar beet cultivation, had a profound effect on social relations in the countryside. Equally, however, in the south and west, where small farms rather than larger estates were the rule, change also took place, as industrialisation had an increasing impact on rural society. As Cathleen Catt demonstrates in her essay on the village of Maudach, in the Palatinate, the different layers of rural society responded in different ways, and as a result rural society itself underwent a number of important changes.

These changes were not merely the product of outside forces, but were rather the outcome of the ways in which the various elements in rural society sought to exploit these forces for their own benefit. Rural society is often seen not only as unchanging but also as passive, and correspondingly there has been a tendency in the literature on the German peasantry to regard small farmers as victims or dupes, caught in a web of unchanging traditional values of which deference was not the least important. A third aim of this book is to reinstate the peasant as an agent of history, to stress the ways in which peasants acted themselves in defence of their own interests. Strategies of peasant self-defence and resistance form another theme that runs through a number of the contributions, from William Hagen's portrayal of striking serfs in eighteenth-century Brandenburg, to Utz Jeggle's account of the mechanisms through which present-day villagers defend the integrity of their community against interlopers.

As Jeggle shows, however, the unanimity with which villagers close ranks against interference from outside serves as an effective smokescreen behind which the real conflicts and tensions that characterise village life can be concealed. And, indeed, a fourth major purpose of this book is to analyse conflict in rural society, to show that beneath the apparently untroubled surface of village life, social tensions and antagonisms of many kinds divided the village community. These could be expressed in ways not immediately obvious to the outsider — for example, as Gerhard Wilke shows, in the treatment of sickness and health within the village. Nineteenth- and early twentieth-century ethnographers descended upon the peasantry to record their customs in the belief that they represented ancient traditions that bound the village community together; but as Gerhard Wilke and Christel Heinrich show, peasant customs could also serve as tokens of social inequality in the village, even, on occasion, as weapons in the struggles of different groups and factions. Like so many other aspects of life in the countryside, they too were in reality malleable and mutable, changing in function, even changing in form, with the demands of the times.

As well as deconstructing the concept of the peasant, therefore, this book also seeks to deconstruct the notion of 'community'. Several of the contributions present the results of long-term research into the history of village communities, notably the work of Cathleen Catt on Maudach, Gerhard Wilke on Körle in Hesse, and Wolfgang Kaschuba and Utz Jeggle on Kiebingen in Swabia. There are still very few such projects in progress compared with the wealth of local-community studies on France, but they are adding immensely to our knowledge of rural society in the small farming districts of the south and west. For the East Elbian region, dominated by aristocratic Junker landowners, however, different research strategies are called for, and in the present book two of these are represented: first, William Hagen's study of the Stavenow estate in Brandenburg, based on the complete archive of its Junker landlords; and second, the collaborative study in progress at the

Academy of Sciences of the German Democratic Republic on the fertile region near Magdeburg, known as the Magdeburger *Börde*, from which the contributions by Hainer Plaul, Gisela Griepentrog and Christel Heinrich are drawn.

The social history of Germany as it is being communicated to an English-speaking audience is too often the social history of the regions covered by the present-day Federal Republic. It is another aim of this book to do a little to redress the balance by including five essays on areas now within the borders of the German Democratic Republic. East German historians are particularly active in the field of rural social history; their pioneering research, and the important debates and controversies which it has generated among historians in the GDR, are too little known among the English-reading public. As Hartmut Harnisch notes, historians in the GDR are still divided over the origins of the crucial Prussian agrarian reforms of the early nineteenth century, and his contribution serves as a valuable introduction to the debates which this question has generated.

The contributors to this volume are not only drawn from a number of different countries, but also from a variety of academic disciplines. Particular mention should be made of the contribution of social anthropology, ethnography and folklore studies in this respect. As Ian Farr points out, these subjects — subsumed under the concept of *Volkskunde* — have had a chequered history, but they have undergone dramatic changes in recent years, and are now playing an important part in research into the history of popular culture in urban and rural society. The contributions by Gisela Griepentrog, Christel Heinrich and Hainer Plaul, of the Department of Cultural History and *Volkskunde*, at the Central Institute for History in the Academy of Sciences, GDR, by Wolfgang Kaschuba and Utz Jeggle of the Ludwig Uhland Institute for Empirical Cultural Studies, at the University of Tübingen, and by Gerhard Wilke, an anthropologist trained at the University of Cambridge, illustrate not only the theories and methods used in present-day anthropological and cultural studies — including especially oral interviews and 'participant observation' which form the basis for the essays by Griepentrog, Heinrich, Jeggle and Wilke — but also the variety of possible approaches, perhaps too some of the differences in the way the discipline of *Volkskunde* is currently practised in the FRG and the GDR.

The present volume has its (now very remote) origins in the third meeting of the SSRC (now ESRC) research seminar on Modern German Social History, held at the University of East Anglia in July 1979, when the topic discussed was rural society. Although only one of the papers presented at that meeting is published in this collection (by Ian Farr, now, of course, substantially revised and updated), and only two of the contributors to this volume were actually present, it was always the intention of the editors — both of whom attended the research seminar — to publish a collection of essays arising out of the discussions. That it has taken over six years to appear is due to a variety of circumstances, most of them entirely within our control. It was initially very difficult to detect any general theme or thesis emerging from the seminar; it took a great deal of time to assemble a collection of articles which could serve as the basis for one volume; and even longer to edit them, and to translate the seven contributions originally written in German.

As with the previous publications in this series,[1] gratitude is owing to the ESRC for providing the initial support for the seminars (under grant No. HG 113/6/7), and to the participants in the July 1979 seminar for their contributions to the discussion and for helping to shape our ideas on the subject. We would also like to thank Cathleen S. Catt, Eric Clare, Bernd Feldmann and William W. Hagen for their translations, Lynn Abrams for her proof-reading, and Marjan Bhavsar for her typing. To all our contributors, and to Richard Stoneman and David Croom of Croom Helm, we owe a further debt of gratitude for the exemplary patience with which they have borne the protracted editorial process to which we have submitted them. We hope they find the final product has been worth waiting for.

Norwich   RICHARD J. EVANS
Liverpool   W. R. LEE

Note

1. Richard J. Evans and W. R. Lee (eds.), *The German Family: Essays on the Social History of the Family in Nineteenth- and Twentieth-Century Germany* (Croom Helm, London, 1981); Richard J. Evans (ed.), *The German Working Class 1888–1933: The Politics of Everyday Life* (Croom Helm, London, 1982); Richard J. Evans (ed.), 'Religion and Society in Germany', *European Studies Review*, special issue, Vol. 12, No. 3, June 1983.

1 'TRADITION' AND THE PEASANTRY
On the Modern Historiography of Rural Germany

Ian Farr

I

Over the last generation, intellectual and scholarly study of the peasantry has become a sizeable and flourishing industry. In the 20 or so years since the 'paradoxical rediscovery' of the peasantry by the social sciences,[1] countless economists, sociologists, anthropologists and development theorists have become engaged in the business. Moreover, their appreciation of the role played by rural populations in shaping the contemporary world has come to be shared increasingly by historians of modern Europe. With the aid of more sophisticated methodologies and more intensive research, particularly into specific regions and localities, historians of both Western and Eastern Europe have helped to foster a much wider appreciation of the complexities and subtleties within peasant society, as well as of the sympathy and rigour required to study them. It is certainly true that social history remains generally more preoccupied with urban life and the condition of the industrial working class. None the less, recent advances in the social-historical study of the European peasantry lend some weight to Tony Judt's conclusion that 'it is pleasingly rare these days to find rural society consigned to the historical wastebin, with the peasantry wrapped up in their potato-sack, ready for distribution to the real world of the city.'[2]

One country where such welcome trends are regrettably less apparent is the Federal Republic of Germany.[3] The writing of modern German history often continues to incorporate a set of deeply-entrenched and wide-ranging assumptions about the lifestyle, economy, behaviour, culture and political disposition of the German peasantry, which, though superficially plausible, urgently require closer empirical and theoretical scrutiny. These presumptions are reinforced, on the one hand, by the apparent reluctance of specialist agrarian historians to consider wider theoretical issues and, on the other, by the relative indifference of social historians.

1

to the problematics of rural society in the age of industrialisation. Probably the most powerful and persistent of these assumptions is that the peasant-producer in the second half of the nineteenth and first half of the twentieth centuries represented one of the most significant of those 'traditional' or 'pre-industrial' sections of society, whose continued and increasingly anachronistic survival in a rapidly industrialising nation acted as a bulwark against progress, retarded socio-economic change and inhibited Germany's transition to a modern pluralist democracy.

The pervasiveness of such notions can be illustrated at this stage by one example. In some prefatory remarks to his detailed study of the lobbying activities of the *Deutscher Bauernverband* (German Peasant Federation) in West Germany, Paul Ackermann confidently proclaims that the peasantry and their representatives had great difficulty in adapting to the process of industrialisation and rejected its implications. The peasant was to a great extent 'rooted' in the past in a tradition of self-perpetuating conservatism, resignation and mistrust. Industrial society was fundamentally alien to a peasant existence moulded by backward and 'corporate' (*ständisch*) values. The industrial laws of rationalisation, concentration and co-operation were supposedly in diametrical opposition to the intrinsic attitudes of the peasantry.[4] Such comments are by no means untypical of the way in which preconceptions about the peasantry can be presented as self-evident truths, deserving of no further critical analysis or genuinely historical explanation.

The first part of this essay attempts to show how this situation has arisen. This requires, first, a brief assessment of the work produced by those branches of scholarship, notably agrarian or agricultural history (*Agrargeschichte*) and folklore/ethnology (*Volkskunde*), which traditionally have been most involved in the study of the German peasantry. One result of their activity has been to make historical investigation of rural society a largely peripheral exercise, held in narrow confines by inherited academic traditions, and frequently isolated from many of the mainstream historiographical changes of the last generation.

Secondly, it necessitates some appreciation of the way in which the recent flowering of social history in the Federal Republic has, if anything, served only to consolidate this situation. Because of its methodological and conceptual priorities, and because of its often justifiable aversion to *Agrargeschichte* and *Volkskunde*, this newer social-scientific history has generally been either unwilling or unable to enter into any meaningful dialogue with agrarian historians and folklorists. Neither has it encouraged any systematic research into the history of rural Germany since the early nineteenth century. In the absence of any sustained intellectual interchange between these various types of history, their respective prejudices and presumptions have survived relatively intact, a process helped in no small measure by the fact that some of the more important of these presuppositions complement rather than contradict each other.

Certainly there have been indications recently that historical research into the peasantry is beginning to review some of these preconceptions more critically. Nevertheless, the essential task of restoring the peasantry and the rural population to a more central place in history has only just begun. It stands little chance of success unless crucial theoretical perspectives are addressed more openly and more frequently. The final part of this essay will therefore offer some more tentative suggestions about the problems which an effective social history of the German peasantry will have to confront, if future research is to be more incisive in its methods and findings than much of the existing literature.

II

The most substantial contribution to that body of literature has undoubtedly come from the long-established tradition of agrarian history (*Agrargeschichte*). We are certainly indebted to this branch of historiography for providing us with a wealth of information and data on Germany's agrarian and agricultural past. The immense store of knowledge accumulated by agricultural historians, particularly at the local and regional level, is an indispensable foundation for further study. It has to be acknowledged, however, that many works of conventional *Agrargeschichte* fall increasingly short of the quality demanded by current social-historical practice. They tend to be characterised by a high degree of empiricism, a restricted field of inquiry, a methodological conservatism, and a conspicuously legalistic emphasis.[5] Although its previous and sometimes uncomfortably close identification with more reactionary political persuasions had to lapse after 1945, agrarian history in the Federal Republic has continued to exhibit considerable caution in the face of a rapidly changing intellectual climate. It still appears reluctant to conduct a serious examination of its own objectives and methods, and to embrace potentially helpful initiatives from the social sciences. It continues to pay less attention to the history of rural society since 1850 than to developments in the preceding century. Thus many of the critical analytical problems raised by the relative and then absolute contraction of agriculture and the rural population in a period of social change remain unresolved.[6]

The preoccupation of *Agrargeschichte* with developments in the late eighteenth and early nineteenth centuries can be traced back to the pioneering work of Georg Friedrich Knapp.[7] It was his study which made the protracted process of *Bauernbefreiung* ('peasant emancipation', from the contrasting types of feudal and seigneurial obligation to be found in eighteenth-century Germany) a fundamental concern for subsequent agrarian historians.[8] Furthermore, it was Knapp's interest in property rights, laws of inheritance, and in the changing legal basis of the relationship between peasant and lord, which helped to give agrarian history its crucial juridical bias and made the study of Germany's 'agrarian constitution' (*Agrarverfassung*) the 'real core' of *Agrargeschichte*.[9] Although his influence waned somewhat in the 1930s, the essential thrust of Knapp's work continued to be represented — not least by Friedrich Lütge, who devoted a lifetime to clarifying the complex mosaic of laws, obligations, customs and inheritance patterns which was Germany's *Agrarverfassung*.[10]

Lütge's work and, by implication, that of other historians within the same school or tradition of agrarian history, has been subjected to a sustained and perceptive critique by Hans Rosenberg.[11] Rosenberg is inevitably and justifiably hostile to the excessively Germanocentric outlook evident in Lütge's brand of *Agrargeschichte*, and to its close alignment with the outlook and priorities of nationalist politics in Germany. His major criticism, however, is of Lütge's concentration on the *written* rather than on the *real* *Verfassung*. At the heart of many studies by more conservative agrarian historians is an examination of the legal formalities of landholding, of the purely juridical dimensions of peasant emancipation, and of the admittedly awesome technicalities of legalistic terminology. Descriptions of the legal framework of tenure, inheritance, landownership and feudal relations are rarely accompanied by an equally detailed assessment of the practical realisation and functions of these regulatory codes. Consequently, the real social impact of different forms of exploitation and domination seems rarely to be appreciated. Behind a comprehensive and sophisticated knowledge of Germany's *Agrarverfassung*, built up over almost a century of research, lies a social reality which deserves urgent and more intensive scrutiny, irrespective of the undoubted difficulties that would be involved.

This is not to deny, of course, the contribution which a juristic approach can make, for example, towards an understanding of the socio-economic basis of seigneurial and feudal relations, or of the recomposition of peasant—lord relations in the process of peasant emancipation.[12] No analysis of the levels and forms of exploitation experienced by the peasantry, either before *Bauernbefreiung* or as a direct result of the way in which that reform was implemented, would be complete without this legal dimension; a fact appreciated more readily perhaps by Knapp than by some of his successors.[13] What is at issue here is not the value of the legalistic emphasis *per se*, but the inordinate concentration on that aspect of Germany's rural history, particularly given the abundant evidence from elsewhere of the dangers of interpreting peasant behaviour in excessively legalistic terms.[14]

The need to incorporate other factors into the study of rural society was recognised half a century ago by Wilhelm Abel, when his classic work on agrarian crises implicitly challenged the influence of the Knapp school.[15] There is now a much wider appreciation of Abel's work, his understanding of agrarian dynamics, and his determination to explain some of the deeper ramifications of major shifts in agricultural production, such as the incidence of mass poverty in the pre-industrial area. This admiration is reflected in the appearance in 1980 of an English translation of his pioneering study.[16] While remaining sensitive to localised variations, as well as to short-term changes, Abel showed how one could chart demographic trends, the movements back and forth between arable cultivation and animal husbandry, and the conjunctural shifts in grain prices, wages, rents, land values and feudal obligations, without losing sight of their social and political consequences. The value of such perspectives was certainly realised by Abel's own students, whose viewpoints have continued to inform the writing of agrarian history. Equally, a good deal of such writing carried on as before, betraying regrettably few signs of those influences, and frequently failing to heed Abel's salutary warnings that historians should be constantly sceptical of naively romanticised portrayals of peasant life in the pre-industrial era. It is only quite recently that Abel has received fuller recognition in the Federal Republic for his undoubted contribution to our knowledge of rural society in Germany and Europe.

Two qualifications do, however, have to be entered at this point. In the first place the major thrust of Abel's work was to establish the statistical series which, in turn, would facilitate broad comparative analysis of the interrelationships between population movement and agrarian production. He thus provided some of the essential materials for the construction of a more sophisticated rural social history without becoming too closely involved in the process of construction itself. Secondly, the form of quantification produced by Abel was much more appropriate to the study of medieval and early modern conditions than to the examination of the modern countryside, for which the initial data were and are more readily available, and where the types of interdependencies revealed by Abel no longer operated to anything like the same degree. The demographic and agricultural revolutions of the nineteenth century were thus in one sense a postscript to the developments in which he was primarily interested.

Nevertheless, there remains a striking contrast between Abel's work and much of the standard literature on this later period. The further one moves into the nineteenth and early twentieth centuries, the more one is struck by the methodological conservatism of the basic texts on rural society available in West Germany. Many tend to favour that style of agricultural history exemplified by Haushofer's contribution to the representative series of *Deutsche 'Agrargeschichte'*;[17] in such works the history of agriculture is not seen in terms of the people who worked on the land, nor in terms of their economic, social and political relationships to each other and to other sections of German society. The emphasis rather is on the influence of important men, such as agricultural theorists, reformers and rural notables, or on macroeconomic shifts in the structure of rural production. Descriptions of technological changes are rarely related to the changing work patterns of peasants, their families and dependent labourers, but are generally slotted into a narrative framework still redundantly tied to the chronology of political events. Notions of change and conflict are rarely allowed to break through the thick veneer of empiricism, producing descriptions of agriculture which bear little relation to the social and economic realities of peasant existence. Again, the point to stress is the restricted conception of agrarian history evident here. Few would doubt the need for the sort of information provided by Haushofer, but many would now criticise the reluctance to set those details into a much wider theoretical context, capable of illuminating the transformation of rural society brought about by the agricultural and industrial revolutions in Germany.[18] It is only with consideration of the quite profound structural changes in agriculture and rural life that have occurred in post-war West Germany that one notes a higher level of conceptualisation, and that is due primarily to the fact that analysis of this period has largely been the province of agrarian sociology.[19] Surprisingly, not even the co-operation between sociology and agrarian history institutionalised in the important journal, *Zeitschrift für Agrargeschichte und Agrarsoziologie*, has encouraged the adoption by agrarian historians of wider terms of reference. Coexistence rather than mutually beneficial interchange appears to be the order of the day, even within the periodical itself.

The narrow focus and limited theoretical ambition of much conventional *Agrargeschichte* compares distinctly unfavourably at times with some of the corresponding literature produced over the last generation in the German Democratic Republic. While both continue to show significant traces of their common pre-war inheritance, East German scholarship has clearly been invigorated by its unequivocal location within Marxist-Leninist orthodoxy.[20] There may still be a signal preoccupation with the process of peasant emancipation and its consequences, but here the emphasis is on the role played by agrarian reform in the overall transition from feudalism to capitalism in Germany. This immediately draws discussion out of the juristic confines which inhibit too much of West German historiography on the subject, but not necessarily at the cost of being reconfined within the bounds of dogmatic Marxism. One notes first the determination of East German historians to refine Lenin's conception of the particularly 'Prussian path' of agriculture by elucidating what they see as the important 'variations' to be found on Prussia's road to capitalism.[21] The result of intensive research since the later 1960s has been a major advance in our understanding of the advance of capitalist production in German agriculture, and a decisive redefinition of socio-economic structures in East Elbian Prussia. Hartmut Harnisch's essay (Chapter 2) in this volume bears eloquent testimony to the progress he and his colleagues have made in recent years by dint of dense empirical research within a challenging theoretical framework.[22] A further beneficial product of Leninist ideas has been the study by East German scholars of class differentiation within the peasantry in the wake of the dissolution of feudalism and the emergence of capitalist agriculture.[23] As Hainer Plaul's contribution (Chapter 4) illustrates, Lenin's arguments can stimulate fruitful analysis of class conflict and changing social relations in the countryside — issues which are much too infrequently broached in West German historiography.[24]

Some indication of what might be achieved for our knowledge of rural society in modern Germany by a more open exchange of views between Marxist and non-Marxist historians is provided by recent studies of peasant protest in early modern Germany, and of the German Peasant War of 1525 in particular. Much of the value has come out of the need of West German historians to come to grips with the interpretations of the *Bauernkrieg* offered by historians of the DDR, for whom, of course, Engels' study is the necessary starting point in their advocacy of the Peasant War as an 'early bourgeois revolution'.[25] The resulting interchange has, for example, helped towards an understanding of peasant political outlooks in early modern times, and of the influence on them of class, community, culture and religion, that is often clearer and more subtle than that usually found in discussion of peasant politics in the modern era.

This only tends to confirm the main points of the preceding discussion. These are threefold. First, historical study of the German peasantry has been monopolised until recently by a conventional agrarian history which is ill-equipped to offer a more wide-ranging and rigorous social history of rural Germany. This requires the sensitive use of analytical techniques which have traditionally stood outside the narrow scope of *Agrargeschichte*. Secondly, few of the studies which have successfully transcended those limitations, whether those on the Peasant War or those by Abel and by historians in the German Democratic Republic, are centrally concerned with interpreting the structure and character of peasant society in the period from 1848 to 1945. This means, finally, that there has not been a sufficiently coherent challenge to the essentially conservative view of the peasantry which is ingrained in traditional agrarian historiography. Still prominent are notions, whether implicit or explicit, of the peasant as an object of history, a mere recipient of reform, technical change and political guidance, and above all, as a person with a particular set of enduring socio-economic and cultural attributes which distinguished him fundamentally from other groups in a rapidly changing society.

III

The conception of the countryside as a reservoir of traditionalism, and of the peasantry as an arsenal of pre-modern characteristics, has been historically reinforced by another branch of study dedicated to the examination of peasant life, *Volkskunde*. This discipline, which falls somewhere between folklore, ethnology and cultural anthropology, was born over a century ago, after public perception of the peasantry in Germany had undergone a profound transformation. The 'moral image' of the German peasant which evolved during the first half of the nineteenth century attributed to him a collection of personality traits — notably humility, piety, natural wisdom, simplicity and goodness — which were deemed to be a product of his noble labour and frugal life-style. These traits were invoked as positive virtues in contrast to what was seen as the moral and social degeneration of industrialisation. A peasant's freedom, stamina, solidity, simplicity, piety and loyalty were deliberately contrasted with the corrupt and immoral existence of the urban proletariat with its attendant political threat.[26] Contemporary handbooks and encyclopedias reinforced this image of a retarded, conservative and tradition-conscious group. This prototype in turn inspired many investigations into rural and village life which themselves bequeathed a set of assumptions which do not stand up well to more complex theoretical perspectives.[27] This stereotypical peasant also began to pervade popular reading matter. After a period before 1848, when the rural novel (*Bauernroman*) could be seen attacking the last vestiges of feudalism, this form of fiction became increasingly conservative in orientation: a long-lost *Mittelstand* paradise was presented as an alternative to the exploitation and alienation of the capitalist process. From the end of the nineteenth century onwards, a succession of bourgeois writers churned out novels highlighting the supposed virtues of the independent peasant family.[28]

This was the climate which nurtured *Volkskunde*. Its practitioners looked back reverently to the work of Wilhelm Riehl, a writer largely ignored by other academic disciplines in Germany. Successive generations of *Volkskündler* consciously cultivated a nationalist ideal which aggrandised the social and cultural importance of the peasantry within German society. Emphasis was laid on the passage from one generation to the next of a specific cultural inheritance (*Kulturgut*) of ritual, custom, food, fairy-tales and folk-songs. Even the period of the Nazi dictatorship failed to make some *Volkskündler* aware that the very legitimacy of their profession had been undermined by its incorporation into the political and racial priorities of National Socialism. The post-war years have seen a slow but increasing realisation of *Volkskunde*'s limitations, and criticism of its methods and values has become more strident and effective.[29] Historically, however, *Volkskunde* has seen as its main priority the cataloguing of the minutiae of everyday peasant life, thereby accumulating a mass of evidence which it has tried to relate to a specific local or regional *Kulturgut*.

Thus most introductions to the ethnology of a particular area followed a prescribed pattern. Description of the peasant dwelling was followed by detailed — yet superficial — descriptions of furniture, implements, clothing and other material possessions, and details of diet, the calendar rhythm of rural life and customs, popular beliefs and oral cultural transmissions, such as sayings, puzzles and folklore. Underlying this compilation was a very pervasive concept of the continuity or persistence of norms, customs and behaviour. This continuity, which was usually conceived in terms of centuries rather than decades, was not considered a problem requiring investigation: it offered a superficial answer which rendered further analysis redundant.[30] No attempt was undertaken to question the *function* of popular customs. Similarly, the inordinate preoccupation with the material remnants *(Überreste)* of peasant existence precluded any attempt to set findings in their social and historical context. *Volkskunde* was thus interested only in how a plough was made, not in how and when the plough was used, and with what productive result. 'Objects' were not related to either producers or consumers.[31] *Volkskunde*'s preoccupation with the external manifestations of peasant life excluded any conception of the peasant as a thinking and acting person.[32]

It is scarcely surprising, therefore, that *Volkskunde* maintained an intellectual and institutional existence quite separate from history, and this again served to marginalise historical study of the peasantry. It was only rarely that a bridge between the disciplines was erected, and then with mixed results.[33] In the German

Democratic Republic, meanwhile, *Volkskunde* was obviously able to make a much cleaner break from past traditions, largely by trying to find a *niche* for itself in the cultural history of the working class.[34] The last few years have, however, witnessed a distinct convergence of *Volkskunde* and history in the Federal Republic. This has come about because of the growing interest in the 'history of everyday life' (*Alltagsgeschichte*) and because of the strength of the work produced by a new generation of *Volkskündler*, including Utz Jeggle and Wolfgang Kaschuba, who have freed their discipline from some of its previous assumptions and fixations.[35] It is becoming clear that the material accumulated by generations of folklorists, once discriminatingly set in a different ideological and conceptual framework, can yield meaningful insights into rural popular culture. The contributions to this volume from the East German scholars, Christel Heinrich and Hainer Plaul, which are representative of other work in the interdisciplinary Magdeburg project, are good examples of how some of the staple fare of *Volkskunde* — dress, housing, festivals, diet — can be related much more intelligently to the means of production and to dynamic shifts in social relations than they can to the dubiously static typologies employed by traditional *Volkskündler*.

The intellectual rehabilitation of *Volkskunde* in the eyes of historians might have occurred sooner but for the absence in West Germany of any substantial tradition of social anthropology. Until very recently the application of anthropological techniques to historical problems tended to be limited to socio-psychological dimensions, with little appreciation of how social-anthropological perspectives might bring social history and *Volkskunde* closer together in the study of mentalities and popular culture, as they have done in France.[36] Work on the early modern German peasantry is beginning to profit from this realisation,[37] but equivalent progress on the recent past has come more from enlightened folklorists than from historians. One notes, also, how much of the initiative in this direction has come from foreign scholars who are more attuned to the potential benefits of an anthropological input into a broadly conceived social history.[38]

A similar tendency is discernible in the growing interest of West and East German historians in historical demography, a discipline which was central, for example, to the major and pioneering studies of the pre-revolutionary French peasantry by Goubert, Le Roy Ladurie and others. In this volume the contribution to peasant history made by this discipline is exemplified in the work of Gisela Griepentrog (Chapter 8), drawn once more from the multi-disciplinary project on the Magdeburger *Börde* in progress at the Academy of Sciences of the German Democratic Republic. For reasons which are more conveniently outlined elsewhere,[39] it has taken some time for West German historians to become accustomed to the use of demographic data. Again, a lead has been given by non-Germans, including, for example, Robert Lee, whose demographic research has provided a springboard for a more wide-ranging analysis of peasant society and economy in Bavaria in the first half of the nineteenth century.[40]

So far, therefore, we have found a set of interrelated factors which help to account for the relative absence of a rigorous social history of the modern German peasantry. Certainly, the monopoly on the historical study of peasant life exercised for so long by traditional agrarian history and, to a lesser extent, by *Volkskunde*, is beginning to break down. There have been notable advances in our understanding of early modern peasant protest and of some of the broader ramifications of *Bauernbefreiung*, as well as a growing recognition of what might be achieved by careful recourse to demography and anthropology. But the legacy of that monopoly, evident above all in the survival of deeply-entrenched presuppositions about the essential characteristics of the German peasant, is still very much in evidence.

IV

One would have anticipated some challenge to these assumptions by the more theoretically-conscious social history which emerged in the Federal Republic in the 1960s.[41] This has not, however, taken place. Systematic examination of modern rural history has been a low priority for the newer social history, particularly of the 'critical' or 'social-scientific' history which has led the revolution in West German historiography that has occurred over the last two decades. Furthermore, the principal interests and the preferred methodologies of this 'historical social science' have fostered basic preconceptions about the place of the landholding peasantry in an industrialising society which have tended to complement, rather than counteract, those cultivated by the more conservative traditions outlined above.

The dearth of studies on the peasantry by younger social historians can be explained by a number of factors. In the first place, such work would have required a considerable engagement with precisely those disciplines, such as *Agrargeschichte*, whose ideological predispositions and theoretical impoverishment had first helped to trigger the interest in social history. It appeared more promising to investigate new areas with the help of different tools than to go over ground already well tilled, however unsatisfactorily, by others. Secondly, there was an understandable commitment from social historians to the study of those social groups such as the working class, unduly neglected in previous historiography. This was reinforced by the extent to which many of these historians identified with the social and political order which had emerged in West Germany by the later 1960s. The implicit legitimising function of the new social history entailed, thirdly, an explicit rejection of Marxist ideas, for these were associated, somewhat erroneously, with the supposedly rigid dogmatism of East German historiography.[42] This encouraged an undue reliance on models appropriated from sociology and political science, particularly on those which derived initially from Max Weber and which were then fashionable in certain branches of American scholarship.[43] Few of these models were immediately amenable to the more discrete analysis of rural society, politics and culture. In this respect it is surely no coincidence that many of the works on rural Germany which have been produced by the social-scientific history relate directly to one of Weber's principal concerns, the estate economy of the East Elbian Junker and its role in the political evolution of Prusso-Germany.[44]

Of the more general, non-Marxist, sociological concepts available to West German social historians, perhaps the most widely deployed has been that of modernisation. As we shall argue in more detail below, this concept tends to encourage stereotyped views of social groups such as the peasantry, rather than further investigation of the same. It also influences the choice of subjects which are deemed important for future study. Thus one finds that one of the few books dealing specifically with modernisation in Germany embraces only those problems considered the most crucial by social theorists. Issues such as urbanisation, social conflict, political participation and social mobility are, therefore, comprehensively discussed.[45] When confronted with questions of social mobility, however, the authors readily concede their ignorance of how classes were recruited in the agrarian sector:

> Such gaps in our knowledge are particularly serious for historical studies, for there are no concrete indications of which avenues and opportunities for upward mobility were created by industrialisation, the contraction of agrarian society and the steady erosion of the petty-bourgeoisie. Nor do we know whether *our assumptions about the immobility of agrarian society* [my emphasis] and the exclusivity of the petty-bourgeoisie are historically correct.[46]

Another example of the way in which certain theoretical preferences could help to reinforce assumptions, or determine whether or not the peasantry received more detailed historical analysis, particularly given the existence of an established agrarian historiography, can be seen in Jürgen Kocka's assessment of the state of West German social history in the mid-1970s. Emphasising the deficiencies in our knowledge which made West German social history relatively backward by international comparison, he catalogued as areas requiring further scrutiny: historical demography, family history, modern urban history, social stratification and mobility, the working class (as distinct from socialism and the labour movement), social protest, problems of youth and age, female emancipation, professionalisation, and many others.[47] While analysis of the peasantry would clearly have profited from such work, the history of rural society in its own right is conspicuous by its absence from the list.

One should perhaps stress at this point that the development of the peasantry in other countries since the early nineteenth century is also inadequately understood. The most notable exception in this respect is Russia, whose recent history is, in more senses than one, a history of the agrarian problem. The difficulties faced by the Tsarist autocracy in effecting a workable abolition of serfdom and in promoting agricultural modernisation, the massive research undertaken to support different strategies of reform, the role of the peasantry in the revolutions of 1905 and 1917, the dilemma for socialists of achieving and maintaining a Marxist revolution in an overwhelmingly peasant society, and the Bolsheviks' brutal collectivist solution to that dilemma, are all inevitable and indispensable topics for historical discussion.[48] By contrast, the most pressing question for the modern historian of Germany, and the one to which the newer style of history in the Federal Republic was intended to provide the most persuasive answers — to explain the rise and triumph of National Socialism — was not one that appeared to necessitate sustained study of the peasantry.

The concentration on the longer-term origins of the failure of German democracy in 1933 by this more self-consciously problem-solving approach to German history has, however, resulted in an interpretation of Germany's past in the FRG which involves distinctive ideas about the peasantry. The inability of Germany to match the normative model of socio-political development implicit in the concept of 'modernisation' is attributed by many West German historians to the preservation of 'pre-industrial' élites and their malevolent political influence. The adoption of functionalist models leads to an emphasis on the politics of 'system stabilisation' or 'conflict resolution' in which it is often unquestioningly implied that social groups such as the 'independent' peasantry acted as unconscious agents or supporters of élite machinations. The idea of 'traditional' sections of German society being left behind by the rapidity of social and economic change has become deeply embedded in historiography in the Federal Republic. The resultant hostility of these groups to modernity, as expressed in their economic interests, values, behaviour and ideological prejudices, is thereby seen as an essential prerequisite for the rise of German fascism. Correspondingly, it is argued, Nazism and the circumstances of its collapse created the structural preconditions for a society to develop in West Germany that is 'relatively free from pre-modern relics',[49] one relieved of the archaic or anachronistic survivals that had handicapped Germany until 1933.

This emphasis on Germany's deviant path to modernity incorporates certain conceptions of the peasantry — and particularly of its political conduct — which at times come disturbingly close to the moral image of the loyal and conservative peasant so sedulously cultivated in the later nineteenth century.[50] The peasantry also tends to be accorded an essentially passive function which does not differ substantially from that presumed in more conventional accounts of agrarian politics.[51] It is suggested that the political behaviour of German peasants was conditioned by their traditionality, their adherence to pre-industrial norms, and by their subsequent inability or unwillingness to come to terms with the transformation of German society. The resentment and hostility they felt towards industrialisation and the irrevocable erosion of their social status could be exploited by other more powerful interests, such as the Junker aristocracy, to service reactionary aims which conflicted with the real needs of the small farmer. Before 1914 peasants were mobilised behind the popular pre-fascist agrarianism of the Agrarian League (*Bund der Landwirte*), whose activities not only postponed a modernisation of German agriculture, but also prevented the emancipation of German society from the baleful influence of the large landowner.[52] After 1918 the traumatic impact of revolution, inflation and world economic crisis only deepened the peasants' intrinsic aversion to democracy. The direct lineage of anti-modern and reactionary authoritarianism dating back to the Empire thus culminated in the widespread support given by the peasantry, especially in Protestant Germany, to the Nazi Party.

Since the crucial work of Gerschenkron, the issue of tariff protection has been pivotal to most studies of German agrarian politics from the 1870s onwards.[53] The support given by the bulk of the peasantry to the protectionist cause is seen as symptomatic of its presumed role as an agent of élite designs. In the return to protectionism in 1879, as reinforced in the tariff law of 1902, and in the political bargaining over tariff protection in the later Weimar Republic, the objective interests of the smaller peasant-producers, it is argued, were sacrificed to the sectional objectives of the landowning aristocracy of East Elbia. The degree of protection afforded to domestic producers against imported foodstuffs has therefore been interpreted as a critical measure by which to gauge Germany's progress towards democracy.[54]

The analysis of rural politics, so briefly schematised here, constitutes one element in a comprehensive rethinking of Germany's immediate past undertaken by West German social historians of German politics, as well as by influential scholars outside West Germany. This reassessment has inevitably been subject to constant criticism from the numerically stronger but intellectually much less powerful ranks of conservative historiography in West Germany. More recently, however, the stress on Germany's modern history as a *Sonderweg*, or peculiar path to modernity, the insistence on explaining the rise of Nazism primarily in terms of pre-industrial traditions and pre-modern social strata, and the consequential definition of fascism as a product of political backwardness, have come in for more vigorous attack from other quarters.[55] This is not the place to enter the ensuing controversy. It is, however, the place to reflect critically on those conceptual and empirical shortcomings in this reinterpretation of modern German history which bear directly on our understanding of the peasantry in this period.

V

Some of these limitations stem from an occupational habit of many social historians (not just those of Germany) of treating the existing sociological literature as 'an academic potting shed containing a set of handy tools'.[56] Despite an apparently continuous discussion in the 'critical' historiography about how to utilise these tools for explanatory and heuristic purposes,[57] there is still an underlying tendency 'to slake the thirst for more theory by scooping up mouthfuls of unpurified concepts from the waters of conventional sociology'.[58] Consequently, these historians operate with a set of preconceptions which emerge only as 'a fine network of concealed preferences'.[59] This is evident from the continued reliance in West German historiography on terms such as 'pre-industrial', 'traditional' and 'pre-modern', notwithstanding their origins in the increasingly criticised 'theory' of modernisation.

It is now widely recognised that the notion of modernisation embodied a self-confident ethnocentrism, with the American polity being offered as the paradigm of modernity to which newly-developing nations should aspire. The attempt to aggregate in a single concept disparate and complex processes of social change involved the substitution for Marxist historical materialism of a 'functional-technological determinism', which imposed an obvious 'imperialism of categories' on industrialising societies. It was increasingly appreciated that 'tradition' could not be empirically observed, because it existed only as a hypothetical antithesis to an observed 'modernity'. The analytical value of 'tradition' must therefore be seriously in question until traditionality can be demonstrated, rather than assumed.[60] Certainly, it ought not be used loosely as a synonym for resistance to change or stubborn backwardness.[61] As Tony Judt has reminded us, to

be modern is where the historical process intended you to be. (It follows that all evidence of a willingness to adapt to the demands of modern society is a confirmation of the modernised nature of the person or group in question.) Conversely, those who so fail to adapt, who protest against the changes in question are backward-looking and the subject of much properly puzzled investigation.[62]

Because traditional culture is credited with a capacity for independent endurance, traditional features are relegated to the historical wastebin, residual categories that fail to yield to the prescribed imperatives of modernisation. Through the pervasive dichotomies of modernisation, the past is strung out along a linear continuum 'which prevents accurate historical analysis by explaining phenomena in terms of a pre-selected number of variables. Too little thus explains too much.'[63]

We have already seen the extent to which historical analysis of the German peasantry by West German historians and others is couched in a vocabulary which derives directly from the questionable teleology of modernisation. The identification of the city or urban labourer with modernity, and of the peasant with tradition, is ultimately to confuse *labels*, which fit neatly into conceptual packages of dubious theoretical paternity, for serious historical investigation, say, of the similarities, differences and interrelationships between urban and rural life.[64] There is no denying, for example, that both in the *Kaiserreich* and in the Weimar Republic, agrarian politics was suffused with a variety of defensive, anti-industrial and anti-modern reactions, which appear to make the peasant a resentful victim of modernisation and thus all too easy a prey to the illusory promises of the Nazis. Again, however, an uncritical acceptance of modernisation concepts encourages a monocausal interpretation of the direction and function of this agrarian ideology.[65] It also invites too static a view of rural politics, with more emphasis on the structural continuity of 'pre-modern' outlooks than on the perhaps more decisive conjunctural shifts in the character and direction of peasant political action, such as that which occurred in the 1890s.[66] Above all, modernisation concepts suggest a relatively uncomplicated relationship between the peasantry and fascism, a relationship which, on the evidence of some impressive recent research on the regional basis of Fascism in Italy, is a good deal more nuanced than most present studies on Germany seem to indicate.[67]

In this respect it is worth noting that, of the few historical studies devoted specifically to explaining the connection between rural society and the expansion of the NSDAP, three of the best known continue to be those on Schleswig-Holstein, a region where the

Nazis gained early and massive support in the areas of predominantly small and medium-sized peasant farms.[68] The authors are united in showing the vulnerability of the Geest peasantry to the appeal and programme of the Nazis, but they disagree about the political affiliations of the same peasants in the earlier years of the Weimar Republic. However, this concentration on Schleswig-Holstein highlights our limited knowledge of other rural constituencies which either did or did not vote in large numbers for the NSDAP. Overall it seems clear that the Nazis gained a disproportionate degree of allegiance, particularly in election votes, from the peasantry.[69] But we know surprisingly little else apart from that elementary observation, and the possibility that the poorer and more socially marginal peasants may have been recruited in larger numbers by the Hitler movement. We are now rather better informed about the impact on the peasantry of the First World War and the ensuing inflation, and this has allowed some important modifications of previous suppositions.[70] The absence of comparable work on the effect of the economic crisis of 1928 onwards in different regions of Germany[71] further hinders the formulation of more challenging interpretations about the agrarian roots of fascism.

We still need to pursue the lines of research opened up by Horst Gies, who has shown how rapidly the Nazi Party expanded its 'radius of action' from 1930 onwards.[72] Only after the electoral success of that year, and with the emergence of Darré as the principal Nazi theorist on agrarian problems, did the party begin a determined campaign to erect a network of political organisations capable of winning over further peasant votes to the party.[73] The divisions which plagued rival groupings enabled the Nazis to infiltrate and undermine them, while their own peasant organisations became some of the most successfully co-ordinated and reliable in the whole apparatus of the NSDAP. Recent studies emanating from the 'Bavaria project' on Nazism demonstrate the value at a more local level of the perspectives suggested by Gies.[74] Other findings, both from that project and from elsewhere, which suggest how deepening disillusionment, mounting material grievances and the survival of pre-Nazi values made the peasantry increasingly impervious and ultimately hostile to ideological penetration by the Nazi regime itself,[75] should make us yet more cautious of easy generalisations about Nazism and the 'traditional' peasantry. Oversimplified assumptions, which fit neatly into conceptual frameworks of questionable validity, are an inadequate replacement for meaningful historical investigation which takes due account of the manifold complexities and relationships within modern rural society.

VI

The time has come, therefore, when historical study of the modern German peasantry has to free itself more decisively from the seductive but ultimately unhelpful categories of 'modernisation', as well as from the stale formulations of traditional *Volkskunde* and *Agrargeschichte*. Only by posing different questions of the peasantry can there emerge a more systematic and theoretically rigorous understanding of rural society, itself a precondition for the urgent task of integrating the study of rural developments much more successfully into the wider social history of modern Germany.

That task will not be delayed by any dearth of sources. Statistics on types of cultivation, harvest yields, animal stocks, mechanisation and co-operatives have been collected for over a century.[76] Combined with the increasingly comprehensive censuses on occupations and enterprises, they afford some helpful insights into the local and regional contrasts in peasant farming, and into the scope of technical and social change in the countryside. The quantitative evidence is complemented by the large number of official surveys into the state of German agriculture conducted in response to the difficulties faced by peasant-producers during the agricultural crises of the late nineteenth century and the 1920s. Although these reports have to be used with some caution, because of the varying motives and expertise of those compiling them, they do provide further starting points for research. In addition to these more general sources, there is a vast array of local and parish records, land registers, village genealogies and administrative surveys, as well as the abundance of detail bequeathed by generations of folklorists, all of them capable of illuminating conditions and processes in different communities.

A more effective incorporation of the peasantry into the social-historical study of modern Germany will not, however, come about solely through a fuller and more critical exploitation of such sources. It will also depend quite crucially on winning much wider acceptance of the view that peasants in nineteenth- and twentieth-century Germany are better understood as an integral part of an emerging and ultimately mature capitalist society, than as a closed form of existence isolated from the rest of society. Too often historians of Germany, as well as of other countries, have judged the peasantry's relationship to modernising societies primarily on the basis of the clearly defensive character of modern agrarian politics.[77] In doing so, they have tended to ignore equally convincing evidence of the peasantry's determination to be part of capitalist market structure, whether through significant increases in agricultural production and productivity, crop specialisation and commercialisation, through the more efficient use of labour, or through the increasing adoption of co-operative arrangements for the acquisition of credit, machinery and services and for the greater co-ordination of commercialised production. As Hobsbawm has emphasised, the 'classical' paths to capitalist agriculture, involving the radical elimination of the peasantry (Scotland, England and parts of Prussia, for example) are as exceptional in the history of capitalism as internal transformations of the peasantry into fully capitalistic commodity producers, such as occurred in Denmark. This leaves much of Germany sharing with many other societies a middle path, with the surviving peasant being made compatible with and subservient to the capitalist economy, as a commodity producer increasingly geared towards the market and working with a mix of family and hired labour — a process which, incidentally, posed obvious dilemmas for socialist theory and practice before 1914.[78]

Once one accepts the premise that capitalism and peasant-producers are compatible rather than mutually exclusive, certain consequences inevitably follow for the way in which the modern German peasantry should be studied. The first is that future analysis of the peasantry must beware of notions of peasant 'culture' which treat the peasantry as a cohesive, stable and separate social formation, only capable of being examined through the household or the community. Such a perspective, which derives above all from the work and theoretical presumptions of Robert Redfield, can lead too easily to the view that any profound changes in peasant culture must come from the intrusion of exogenous variables into an otherwise immutable way of life, and that it is therefore only these factors which require explanation.[79] This assumption of an essentially autarchic peasantry underpins Weber's fascinating but highly problematical study of how, in the years up to 1914, 'undeveloped France was integrated into the modern world and the official culture — of Paris, of the cities'.[80] The limitations of such a dualistic conception of the peasantry provide Weber's critics with their most penetrating line of criticism,[81] thereby mirroring in many respects the critique that has emerged of Shanin's equally influential work on the Russian peasantry in the era before collectivisation.[82] In both cases the outcome of the ensuing debate has been the elaboration of a cogent and fundamental challenge to excessively culturalist representations of the peasantry, a challenge which future historians of rural Germany should take fully into account.

The controversy especially over the character of the Russian peasantry has also provoked a more general discussion about the overall concept of the peasantry, a dialogue in which few German voices have been heard. This is scarcely the place to review the extensive literature on the problems of defining peasantries. It is important, however, to note the criticism which has been levelled against that general typology — so influentially summarised by Shanin — in which the peasantry is seen to be characterised by the family farm as the basic unit of social organisation, by land husbandry as the principal means of livelihood, by a specific traditional culture related to the way of life in village communities, and by the subordination of the peasantry to outsiders.[83] This criticism has centred on the tendency for the term 'peasant' to incorporate many contrasting forms of production and social organisation. The diversity of peasant types indicated by anthropological and historical research has not, it is argued, led to any reconsideration of the pre-given notion of peasantry, but rather to ever more generalised definitions of the concept. The resulting lack of precision leads to a glaring deficiency of theoretically useful distinctions, thereby obscuring social dynamics and distorting actual historical sequences.[84] As Leeds has emphasised, the term peasant involves the implicit or explicit search for essences — the essence of peasants, peasantries or peasancy. This search 'asserts not only the inherentness, but also, especially, the separateness of some quality or substance of some reified thing — here the "peasantry".'[85] Given the extent to which the German term *Bauer* has repeatedly represented a specific ideological construct, it is obviously imperative for German historians to address themselves more openly and frequently to these issues.

Indeed, there is a strong case for asserting that a major priority for any historian of the modern German peasantry must be to deconstruct the whole notion of *a* German peasantry. This would involve a much more rigorous analysis of the scale and nature of social differentiation in the German countryside, and a full evaluation of the varying ways in which the complex gradations in German rural society might satisfactorily be conceptualised. The 1895 census, for example, registered some 5.6 million 'agricultural enterprises' in Germany, ranging from small garden plots to extensive latifundia. Over three-quarters were less than 5 hectares in size, but these occupied only about 15 per cent of agricultural land, whereas more than half of the available land was taken by properties ranging in size from 5 to 50 hectares, and almost a quarter by the 25,061 large farms and estates of over 100 hectares.[86] A more precise understanding of the size of holdings and their distribution in various parts of Germany is clearly important, but it constitutes only one rather crude method of differentiation.[87] As the work of East German historians and many of the essays in this volume demonstrate, property size alone does not determine levels of prosperity or commercialisation, the extent of any reliance on extra-familial labour, or the socio-economic status of the owner or tenant. We need to know how far the model of class differentiation used so effectively in the study of Magdeburg can be applied to other parts of Germany, where the transition to capitalist commodity-production of crops such as sugar beet may not have been quite so pronounced.[88]

Similarly, too much of our admittedly still limited knowledge of the rural proletariat is based on a long tradition of research into the more capitalised farms and estates of north-eastern Germany.[89] How did the landless labourers of this part of Germany fare in comparison to the large number of smallholders who sold their labour, but also had access to land, and therefore to means of auto-consumption and the production of marketable surpluses? As Regina Schulte indicates (Chapter 6), many larger 'peasants' were employers of non-family labour, frequently the sons and daughters of fellow peasants. The implications of this for class structure and social relations require further exploration, as too does the increasing dependence on seasonal and migrant labour at periods of peak agricultural activity, a trend by no means exclusive to the East Elbian estates. These and many other points need to be clarified if we are to achieve a firmer grasp of the dynamics of social differentiation in rural Germany, itself an indispensable prerequisite for dissecting the convenient but flawed notion of a unitary or autonomous German peasantry.

A stronger emphasis on the processes of change and differentiation in the countryside will, in turn, permit a much more nuanced assessment of peasant agriculture in Germany. The transition from subsistence[90] to commodity production by many peasants has often been inadequately understood, especially in some political histories of modern Germany. First, there is a tendency to rely on over-simplified contrasts between East and West Elbian Germany which simply do not concur with the economic and social geography of the country. Secondly, there is frequent reference to the 'failure' of the German peasant to match the paradigmatic progress of his Danish counterpart,[91] but insufficient allusion to the fact that by the 1900s 'German agriculturalists could claim with some justification that farming in their country was the most advanced in Europe, with the possible exception of that in Denmark.'[92] The great advances made in the agricultural sector during the nineteenth century[93] tend also to be obscured from view because of the inordinate preoccupation with the support many peasants gave to the cause of tariff protection, a course of action which may have been much more 'rational' than has been all too commonly supposed.[94] Instead of treating the peasant family form as a social anachronism and form of production resistant to change, there is a pressing need to understand and explain the decisions made by a peasant-producer.

Once again we can see the necessity of constructing more sophisticated processual models which will adequately explain the socio-economic transformation of the German peasantry, and the varying relationships between different types of commodity-producers and the capitalist market at a time when peasants were increasingly reliant on income from agriculture.[95] Such models would also allow more revealing insights into the structure of social and political relations in the individual village community, and how these were transformed with the advent of commercialised agriculture and industrial capitalism. We already have a good indication of the communal pressures generated by economic and demographic shifts in the years up to 1848, and of the way in which the resulting conflicts were resolved in favour of specific groups in the community.[96] Our understanding of comparable developments in later periods remains, by comparison, seriously deficient. This is all the more regrettable given the need to question received preconceptions about the place of the 'community' in the lives of the peasantry, and to understand how far the functions of the community were changed by socio-economic differentiation, shifts in religious values and practices,[97] the growth of educational opportunities, and by the extension of state and bureaucratic competence.

Finally, these and many other considerations have to be integrated into interpretations of rural politics that are much more broad-ranging than those with which we customarily operate. A fuller appreciation of the processes of commercialisation and differentiation, of the structures of power and control in communities and regions, of the manifold ways in which political conflicts could be mediated,[98] and, above all, of the extent to which politics *did* matter to peasants, will help to bring closer the day when the political behaviour of the peasantry is analysed with the same subtlety and sensitivity that is automatically expected of histories of urban politics. That day will come all the more quickly if more historians realise the importance of releasing historical study of the modern German peasantry from the conceptual confines in which it has been trapped for too long. The processes of economic, social and political change in the German countryside were too uneven and too complex to be accommodated within inflated typologies of peasantry, whether these stem from the ideological inheritance of the nineteenth century or from their latter-day counterparts in modernisation theory and cultural anthropology. Instead of reducing the peasantry to some form of 'essence', characterised by an assumed traditionality, the time is surely ripe to study peasants as an integral part of the class structure of modern German society.

Notes

1. The phrase is Teodor Shanin's in the introduction to his important edition of readings, *Peasants and Peasant Societies* (Harmondsworth, 1971). Other valuable introductions include E. Wolf, *Peasants* (Englewood Cliffs, N.J., 1966), and J. Potter, M. Diaz and G. Foster (eds.), *Peasant Society* (Boston, Mass., 1967).

2. Tony Judt, 'The Rules of the Game' (review article), *Historical Journal*, 23 (1980), p. 181.

3. It will become clear from the text that the main thrust of this bibliographical essay is to review the way in which the modern peasantry is studied in West Germany, but in the context of work on German rural society published in the German Democratic Republic (GDR), Britain and the United States. An earlier

version of this paper was presented in July 1979 as a conference paper to the SSRC research seminar group in modern German social history at the University of East Anglia. Account has been taken of work published in the interim, but it was felt desirable to retain the somewhat polemical character of the original to prevent the essay from becoming a mere catalogue of relevant titles, as well as to encourage further debate and research.

4. P. Ackermann, *Der deutsche Bauernverband im politischen Kräftespiel der Bundesrepublik* (Tübingen, 1970), pp. 1–3, 23–5.

5. G. G. Iggers, *New Directions in European Historiography* (Middletown, Conn., 1975), pp. 112–13.

6. This criticism applies to some extent to the history of other countries in Western Europe.

7. G. Knapp, *Die Bauernbefreiung und der Ursprung der Landarbeiter in den älteren Teilen Preussens,* 2 vols. (Leipzig, 1887).

8. Perhaps the most useful introduction now is C. Dipper, *Die Bauernbefreiung in Deutschland 1750–1850* (Stuttgart, 1980). See also W. Conze, 'Die Wirkungen der liberalen Agrarreformen auf die Volksordnung im Mitteleuropa im 19. Jahrhundert', *Vierteljahrschrift für Sozial- und Wirtschaftsgeschichte*, 38 (1951), pp. 2–43; English translation in F. Crouzet *et al.* (eds.), *Essays on European Economic History 1789–1914* (London, 1969); W. Conze, *Quellen zur Geschichte der deutschen Bauernbefreiung* (Göttingen, (1957). More recent specialised studies include: E. Schremmer, *Die Bauernbefreiung in Hohenlohe* (Stuttgart, 1963); Wolfgang von Hippel, *Die Bauernbefreiung im Königreich Württemberg*, 2 vols. (Boppard, 1977); F. Hausmann, *Die Agrarpolitik der Regierung Montgelas* (Bern, 1975). For English readers much of this research is summarised in Jerome Blum, *The End of the Old Order in Rural Europe* (Princeton, N.J., 1978), passim.

9. R. Berthold, H. Harnisch and H.-H. Müller, 'Der preussische Weg der Land-wirtschaft und neuere westdeutsche Forschungen', *Jahrbuch für Wirtschafts-geschichte* (henceforth *JbWG*) (1970), IV, p. 265.

10. F. Lütge, *Geschichte der deutschen Agrarverfassung vom frühen Mittelalter bis zum 19. Jahrhundert* (Stuttgart, 1963); idem., *Die bayerische Grundherrschaft* (Stuttgart, 1949).

11. H. Rosenberg, *Probleme der deutschen Sozialgeschichte* (Frankfurt am Main, 1969), pp. 87 ff. See also Harnisch's comments, Chapter 2 below.

12. Representative studies include: F.-W. Henning, *Dienste und Abgaben der Bauern im 18. Jahrhundert* (Stuttgart, 1969); idem., *Bauernwirtschaft und Bauerneinkommen in Ostpreussen im 18. Jahrhundert* (Würzburg, 1969); idem., *Bauernwirtschaft und Bauerneinkommen im Fürstentum Paderborn im 18. Jahrhundert* (Berlin, 1970); idem., *Herrschaft und Bauernuntertänigkeit* (Würzburg, 1964); D. Saalfeld, *Bauernwirtschaft und Gutsbetrieb in der vorindus-triellen Zeit* (Stuttgart, 1960); W. Steitz, *Feudalwesen und Staatssteuersystem. Band 1 — Die Realbesteuerung der Landwirtschaft in den süddeutschen Staaten im 19. Jahrhundert* (Göttingen, 1976); J. Karbach, *Die Bauernwirtschaften des Fürstentums Nassau-Saarbrücken im 18. Jahrhundert* (Saarbrücken, 1977); H. Winkel, *Die Ablösungskapitalien aus der Bauernbefreiung in West- und Süddeutschland* (Stuttgart, 1968).

13. Berthold, Harnisch and Müller, p. 266.

14. L. Berkner and F. Mendels, 'Inheritance Systems, Family Structure and Demographic Patterns in Western Europe, 1700–1900', in C. Tilly (ed.), *Historical Studies of Changing Fertility* (Princeton, N.J., 1978), pp. 209–24; L. Berkner, 'The Stem Family and the Developmental Cycle of the Peasant Household: An Eighteenth-Century Austrian Example', *American Historical Review*, 77 (1972), pp. 398–418.

15. W. Abel, *Agrarkrise und Agrarkonjunktur* (Hamburg, 1966^2). See also:

idem., *Geschichte der deutschen Landwirtschaft vom frühen Mittelalter bis zum 19. Jahrhundert* (Stuttgart, 1967²); idem., *Massenarmut und Hungerkrisen im vorindustriellen Deutschland* (Göttingen, 1972); idem., 'Die Lage der deutschen Land- und Ernährungswirtschaft um 1800', in F. Lütge (ed.), *Die wirtschaftliche Situation Deutschlands und Österreichs um die Wende vom 18. zum 19. Jahrhundert* (Stuttgart, 1964), pp. 238–54.

16. W. Abel, *Agricultural Fluctuations in Europe* (London, 1980).

17. H. Haushofer, *Die deutsche Landwirtschaft im technischen Zeitalter* (Stuttgart, 1963). See the critical appraisal by Rosenberg, *Probleme, op. cit.*, pp. 111 ff. Other introductory surveys displaying similar shortcomings include: E. Klein, *Geschichte der deutschen Landwirtschaft im Industriezeitalter* (Wiesbaden, 1973); R. Krzymonski, *Geschichte der deutschen Landwirtschaft* (Berlin, 1961); H. W. Finck von Finckenstein, *Die Entwicklung der Landwirtschaft in Preussen und Deutschland 1800–1930* (Würzburg, 1960); F.-W. Henning, *Landwirtschaft und ländliche Gesellschaft in Deutschland, Band 2 — 1750–1976* (Paderborn, 1978); W. Achilles, 'Die niedersächsische Landwirtschaft im Zeitalter der Industrialisierung 1820–1914', *Niedersächsisches Jahrbuch für Landesgeschichte*, 50 (1978), pp. 7–26.

18. There is little of note in W. Achilles, 'Die Wechselbeziehungen zwischen Industrie und Landwirtschaft', in H. Pohl (ed.), *Sozialgeschichtliche Probleme in der Zeit der Hochindustrialisierung* (Paderborn, 1979). More fruitful are: M. Haines, 'Agriculture and Development in Prussian Upper Silesia, 1846–1913', *Journal of Economic History*, 42 (1982), pp. 355–84; and the essays by H.-J. Teuteberg, 'Die Einfluss der Agrarreform auf die Betriebsorganisation und Produktion der bäuerlichen Wirtschaft Westfalens im 19. Jahrhundert', pp. 167–276; and H. Kiesewetter, 'Agrarreform, landwirtschaftliche Produktion und Industrialisierung im Königreich Sachsen 1832–1861', pp. 89–138, in F. Blaich (ed.), *Entwicklungsprobleme einer Region* (Berlin, 1981).

19. See G. Wurzbacher, *Das Dorf im Spannungsfeld industrieller Entwicklung* (Stuttgart, 1954); G. Spindler, *Burgbach. Urbanisation and Identity in a German Village* (New York, 1973); U. Planck, *Der bäuerliche Familienbetrieb zwischen Patriarchat und Partnerschaft* (Stuttgart, 1964).

20. For a general introduction, see R. Berthold, *Agrargeschichte. Von der bürgerlichen Reformen zur sozialistischen Landwirtschaft in der DDR* (Berlin, 1978).

21. See G. Heitz, 'Varianten des preussischen Weges', *JbWG*, 1969/III, pp. 99 ff.; H. Bleiber, 'Zur Problematik des preussischen Weges der Kapitalismus in der Landwirtschaft', *Zeitschrift für Geschichtswissenschaft* (henceforth *ZfG*), 13 (1965), pp. 57–73; G. Moll, 'Zum preussischen Weg der Entwicklung des Kapitalismus in der deutschen Landwirtschaft', ibid., 26 (1978), pp. 52–62; Berthold, Harnisch and Müller, *op. cit.*, pp. 259–89. From a different perspective, see also A. Winson, 'The "Prussian Road" of Agrarian Development: A Reconsideration', *Economy and Society*, 11 (1982), pp. 381–408.

22. See especially H. Harnisch, *Kapitalistische Agrarreform und Industrielle Relvolution. Agrarhistorische Untersuchungen über das ostelbische Preussen zwischen Spätfeudalismus und bürgerlich-demokratischer Revolution* (Weimar and Cologne, 1984); G. Moll, 'Bürgerliche Umwälzung und kapitalistische Agrarentwicklung', *ZfG*, 30 (1982), pp. 943–56. Important earlier work by the same authors includes: H. Harnisch, *Die Herrschaft Boitzenburg. Untersuchung zur Entwicklung der sozialökonomischen Struktur ländlicher Gebiete in der Mark Brandenburg vom 14. bis zum 19. Jahrhundert* (Weimar, 1968); idem., 'Statistische Untersuchungen zum Verlauf der kapitalistischen Agrarreformen in den preussischen Ostprovinzen (1811 bis 1865)', *JbWG*, 1974/IV; G. Moll, *Die kapitalistische Bauernbefreiung im Klosteramt Dobbertin (Mecklenburg)* (Rostock, 1968). For an indication of the

debate aroused in the GDR by Harnisch's interpretation of the agrarian reforms in East Prussia, see the discussion, reported in *JbWG*, 1978/I, pp. 199–210, of H. Harnisch, 'Die Bedeutung der kapitalistischen Agrarreform für die Herausbildung des inneren Marktes und die Industrielle Revolution in den östlichen Provinzen Preussens in der ersten Hälfte des 19. Jahrhunderts', ibid. (1977), IV, pp. 83 ff.

23. J. Solta, *Die Bauern der Lausitz. Eine Untersuchung des Differenzierungsprozesses der Bauernschaft im Kapitalismus* (Bautzen, 1968); R. Berthold, 'Der sozialökonomische Differenzierungsprozess der Bauernwirtschaft in der Provinz Brandenburg während der industriellen Revolution (1816 bis 1872/82)', *JbWG* (1974), II, pp. 13–50; idem., 'Zur Herausbildung der kapitalistischen Klassenschichtung des Dorfes in Preussen', *ZfG*, 25 (1977). See also the references in note 24.

24. The most important contributions have come from the large-scale research project on Magdeburg, in which Plaul and many others have been engaged. See especially: H. Plaul, *Landarbeiterleben im 19. Jahrhundert* (Berlin, 1979); H.-J. Rach and B. Weissel (eds.), *Landwirtschaft und Kapitalismus. Zur Entwicklung der ökonomischen und sozialen Verhältnisse in der Magdeburger Börde vom Ausgang des 18. Jahrhunderts bis zum Ende des ersten Weltkrieges* (Berlin, 1978); H.-J. Rach and B. Weissel (eds.), *Bauer und Landarbeiter im Kapitalismus der Magdeburger Börde* (Berlin, 1982).

25. A helpful introduction to the differing interpretations is Bob Scribner and Gerhard Benecke (eds.), *The German Peasant War of 1525 — New Viewpoints* (London, 1979). Essential works include the renowned studies of F. Engels, *Der deutsche Bauernkrieg* (Berlin, 1979); and G. Franz, *Der deutsche Bauernkrieg* (Darmstadt, 1975). See also: D. Sabean, *Landbesitz und Gesellschaft am Vorabend des Bauernkrieges* (Stuttgart, 1972); R. Wohlfeil, *Reformation oder frühbürgerliche Revolution?* (Munich, 1972). The anniversary in 1975 also yielded a fresh crop of studies, including: J. Bak (ed.), *The German Peasant War* (London, 1976); H.-U. Wehler (ed.), *Der deutsche Bauernkrieg* (Göttingen, 1975); R. Wohlfeil (ed.), *Der Bauernkrieg 1524–1526* (Munich, 1975); P. Blickle, *Die Revolution von 1525* (Munich, 1975), now available as *The Revolution of 1525* (Baltimore, 1981). For a comprehensive review of the newer literature, see Tom Scott, 'The Peasants' War: A Historiographical Review', *Historical Journal*, 22 (1979), pp. 693–720, and (Part II) pp. 953–74. On the wider problematics of peasant protest, see P. Blickle, 'Peasant Revolts in the German Empire in the late Middle Ages', *Social History*, 4 (1979), pp. 223–40; P. Blickle, *et al.*, *Aufruhr und Empörung. Studien zum bäuerlichen Widerstand im Alten Reich* (Munich, 1980); W. Schulze, *Bäuerlicher Widerstand und feudale Herrschaft in der frühen Neuzeit* (Stuttgart, 1980), with an excellent bibliography, revealing the extent to which West and East German scholars have profited from the wider European historiography on peasant protest. Note also Hagen's essay, Chapter 3 below, for further insights.

26. J. G. Gagliardo, *From Pariah to Patriot. The Changing Image of the German Peasant* (Kentucky, 1969). See also: J. Ziche, 'Kritik der deutschen Bauerntumsideologie', *Sociologia Ruralis*, 8 (1968), pp. 105–41; H. Muth, '"Bauer" und "Bauernstand" im Lexicon des 19. und 20. Jahrhunderts', *Zeitschrift für Agrargeschichte und Agrarsoziologie* (henceforth *ZAA*), 16 (1963), pp. 72–93; W. Conze, 'Bauer, Bauernstand, Bauerntum', in O. Brunner *et al.*, *Geschichtliche Grundbegriffe*, Vol. 1 (Stuttgart, 1972), pp. 407–39; and, very unsatisfactorily, H. Haushofer, 'Die Idealvorstellung vom deutschen Bauern', *ZAA*, 26 (1978), pp. 147–60.

27. W. Jacobeit, '"Traditionelle" Verhaltensweise und konservative Ideologie', in H. Bausinger and W. Brückner (eds.), *Kontinuität?* (Berlin, 1969), pp. 67–75.

28. Of 344 such authors, 209 were teachers, journalists or workers. See

P. Zimmermann, *Der Bauernroman* (Stuttgart, 1975), pp. 70 ff., 180–3; and J. Hein, *Dorfgeschichte* (Stuttgart, 1976).

29. A useful introduction to the history of *Volkskunde* is I. Weber-Kellermann, *Deutsche Volkskunde zwischen Germanistik und Sozialwissenschaften* (Stuttgart, 1969). The best critical perspectives are to be found in: H. Bausinger, *Volkskunde. Von der Altertumsforschung zur Kulturanalyse* (Berlin, 1971); W. Emmerich, *Germanistische Volkstumsideologie* (Tübingen, 1968); idem., *Zur Kritik der Volkstumsideologie* (Frankfurt, 1971). Important initiatives towards a more self-critical approach were: H. Moser, 'Gedanken zur heutigen Volkskunde', *Bayerisches Jahrbuch für Volkskunde*, 1954, pp. 208–34; K.-S. Kramer, 'Zur Problematik historischer Volkskunde', *Zeitschrift für Volkskunde*, 67 (1971), pp. 51–62; and G. Heilfurth, 'Volkskunde jenseits der Ideologien', *Hessische Blätter für Volkskunde*, 53 (1962), pp. 9–20.

30. H. Bausinger, 'Zur Algebra der Kontinuität', in Bausinger and Brückner, *op. cit.*, pp. 9–30. See also A. Gerschenkron, 'The Concept of Continuity in German Anthropology', *Comparative Studies in Society and History*, 13 (1971), pp. 351–9.

31. W. Jacobeit and H.-H. Müller, 'Agrargeschichte und Volkskunde', *JbWG*, 1977, pp. 141–55.

32. This point is stressed by H. Wunder, 'Zur Mentalität aufständischer Bauern', in Wehler, pp. 9–37 (a shorter version of which is in Scribner and Benecke, pp. 140–59).

33. The studies of K.-S. Kramer attempt to combine *Volkskunde* with historical research in local archives; they tend to be limited in approach and subject-matter. See his *Bauer und Bürger im nachmittelalterlichen Unterfranken* (Würzburg, 1957), and *Volksleben im Fürstentum Ansbach und seinen Nachbargebieten 1500–1800* (Würzburg, 1961). The work of Rudolf Braun on the Zürich *Oberland* remains the classic example of how to combine history and *Volkskunde*.

34. See E. Engelberg, 'Zur Frage der Volkskunde und Kulturgeschichte', *ZfG*, 21 (1973), pp. 970–81.

35. U. Jeggle, *Kiebingen — eine Heimatgeschichte* (Tübingen, 1978); A. Ilien and U. Jeggle, *Leben auf dem Dorf* (Wiesbaden, 1978); W. Kaschuba and C. Lipp, *Dörfliches Überleben. Zur Geschichte materieller und sozialer Reproduktion ländlicher Gesellschaft im 19. und frühen 20. Jahrhundert* (Tübingen, 1982). For an evaluation of the place of *Volkskunde* in West German historiography, see M. Scharfe, 'Towards a Cultural History: Notes on Contemporary *Volkskunde* [folklore] in German-speaking countries', *Social History*, 4 (1979), pp. 333–43.

36. Illustrative here are W. Lepenies, 'Probleme einer historischen Anthropologie', in R. Rürup (ed.), *Historische Sozialwissenschaft* (Göttingen, 1977), pp. 126–59; idem., 'Geschichte und Anthropologie', *Geschichte und Gesellschaft*, 1 (1975), pp. 325–43. Note particularly the lack of any significant response to the much more suggestive article by T. Nipperdey, 'Die anthropologische Dimension in der Geschichtswissenschaft', in idem *Gesellschaft, Kultur, Theorie* (Göttingen, 1976), pp. 33–58. See also R. Braun, 'Probleme des sozio-kulturellen Wandels im 19. Jahrhundert', in G. Wiegelmann (ed.), *Kultureller Wandel im 19. Jahrhundert* (Göttingen, 1973); O. Köhler, 'Versuch einer historischen Anthropologie', *Saeculum*, 25 (1974), pp. 129–246.

37. See the penetrating observations of Wunder, pp. 15 ff.

38. Typical in this respect is the influence of David Sabean, with *Landbesitz und Gesellschaft* and, from a later project, 'Verwandtschaft und Familie in einem württembergischen Dorf 1500 bis 1700', in W. Conze (ed.), *Sozialgeschichte der Familie in der Neuzeit Europas* (Stuttgart, 1977), pp. 231–46. Sabean was instrumental in establishing a working group at the Max Planck Institute, Göttingen, on links between ethnology and history, one product of which is R. Berdahl *et al.*,

Klassen und Kultur. Sozialanthropologsiche Dimensionen in der Geschichtsschreibung (Frankfurt am Main, 1982). See especially the essays by Sabean, Berdahl and Hans Medick. Medick provides the introductory essay, 'Missionäre im Ruderboot. Ethnologische Erkenntnisweisen als Herausforderung an die Sozialgeschichte', pp. 295–319, to an edition of *Geschichte und Gesellschaft* (Vol. 10: 3: 1984) on social history and cultural anthropology. In conjunction with the anthropological emphasis at the 1984 conference of West German historians, this could be seen as a seal of approval for a more ethnologically oriented social history. It is worth noting, however, the relative lack on both occasions of major contributions on modern rural society, as well as the discernible backlash against what are seen as positivist elements in this emerging cultural history.

39. A. Imhof, 'Bevölkerungsgeschichte und historische Demographie', in Rürup, *Historische Sozialwissenschaft*, pp. 16–58; W. R. Lee, 'Germany', in idem. (ed.), *European Demography and Economic Growth* (London, 1979), pp. 144–6.

40. W. R. Lee, *Population Growth, Economic Development and Social Change in Bavaria 1750–1850* (New York, 1977); idem., 'Primary Sector Output and Mortality Changes in Early XIXth Century Bavaria', *Journal of European Economic History*, 6 (1977), pp. 133–62; idem., 'Zur Bevölkerungsgeschichte Bayerns 1750–1850: Britische Forschungsergebnisse', *Vierteljahrsschrift für Sozial- und Wirtschaftsgeschichte*, 62 (1975), pp. 309–38; idem., 'Bastardy and the Socioeconomic Structure of South Germany', *Journal of Interdisciplinary History*, 7 (1977), pp. 403–25; idem., 'Family and "Modernisation"': The Peasant Family and Social Change in Nineteenth-Century Bavaria', in R. J. Evans and W. R. Lee (eds.), *The German Family* (London, 1981). Useful complements to Lee's work include W. Hartinger, 'Zur Bevölkerungs- und Sozialstruktur von Oberpfalz und Niederbayern in vorindustrieller Zeit', *Zeitschrift für bayerische Landesgeschichte*, 39 (1976), pp. 785–822; G. Hanke, 'Zur Sozialstruktur der ländlichen Siedlungen Altbayerns im 17. und 18. Jahrhundert', in *Gesellschaft und Herrschaft. Festgabe für Karl Bosl* (1969), pp. 219–69. For other parts of Germany where demographic insights have proved instructive, see A. Imhof, 'Ländliche Familienstrukturen an einem hessischen Beispiel: Heuchelheim 1690–1900', in Conze, *op. cit.*, pp. 197–230; D. Sabean, 'Household Formation and Geographic Mobility: A Family Register Study for a Württemberg Village 1760–1900', *Annales de Demographie Historique* (1970), pp. 275–94; A. Goldstein, 'Aspects of Change in a German Village', *Journal of Family History*, 9 (1984), pp. 145–57; and Cathleen Catt's contribution, Chapter 5 below.

41. The following comments are deliberately brief and generalised. For fuller and more differentiated surveys of historiographical trends in West Germany, see e.g. Iggers, pp. 80–122; W. Mommsen, 'Gegenwärtige Tendenzen in der Geschichtsschreibung der Bundesrepublik', *Geschichte und Gesellschaft*, 7 (1981), pp. 149–88; J. Kocka, 'Theory and Social History: Recent Developments in West Germany', *Social Research*, 47 (1980), pp. 426–57; H.-U. Wehler, 'Geschichstwissenschaft heute', in J. Habermas (ed.), *Stichworte zur geistigen Situation unserer Zeit* (Frankfurt am Main, 1979), Vol. 2, pp. 709–53.

42. See the comments of D. Groh, 'Le "Sonderweg" de l'histoire allemande: mythe ou realité?', *Annales ESC*, 38 (1983), p. 1183.

43. G. Iggers, 'Federal Republic of Germany', in G. Iggers and H. Parker (eds.), *International Handbook of Historical Studies. Contemporary Research and Theory* (Westpoint, Conn., 1979).

44. M. Weber, 'Developmental Tendencies in the Situation of East Elbian Rural Labourers', *Economy and Society*, 8 (1979), pp. 177–205. The most important studies include those by Puhle (see note 52 below) and H. Schissler, *Preussische Agrargesellschaft im Wandel* (Göttingen, 1978); J. Flemming, *Landwirtschaftliche Interessen und Demokratie. Ländliche Gesellschaft, Agrarverbände und Staat*

1890–1925 (Bonn, 1978); K. Saul, 'Der Kampf um das Landproletariat. Sozialistische Landagitation, Grossgrundbesitz und preussische Staatsverwaltung 1890 bis 1903', *Archiv für Sozialgeschichte*, 15 (1975), pp. 163–208; idem., 'Um die konservative Struktur Ostelbiens. Agrarische Interessen, Staatsverwaltung und ländliche Arbeiternot', in D. Stegmann *et al.*, (eds.), *Deutscher Konservatismus im 19. und 20. Jahrhundert* (Bonn, 1983), pp. 129–98. English summaries of work by Puhle and Schissler are in R. Moeller (ed), *Peasants and Lords in Modern Germany* (New York, 1985). For further insights, see the East German literature already cited and Winson, 'The "Prussian Road"', passim.; R. Berdahl, 'Conservative Politics and Aristocratic Landholders in Bismarckian Germany', *Journal of Modern History*, 14 (1972), pp. 1–20; F. Tipton, 'Farm Labour and Power Politics: Germany 1850–1914', *Journal of Economic History*, 34 (1974), pp. 951–79.

45. H. Kaelble *et al.*, *Probleme der Modernisierung in Deutschland* (Opladen, 1978).

46. Ibid., p. 326.

47. J. Kocka, 'Sozialgeschichte–Strukturgeschichte–Gesellschaftsgeschichte', *Archiv für Sozialgeschichte*, 15 (1975), pp. 31–2.

48. A representative cross-section would include W. Vucinich (ed.), *The Peasant in Nineteenth-Century Russia* (Stanford, 1968); L. Haimson (ed.), *The Politics of Rural Russia 1905–1914* (Cambridge, 1979); T. Shanin, *The Awkward Class. Political Sociology of the Peasantry in a Developing Society* (Oxford, 1972); M. Perrie, 'The Russian Peasant Movement of 1905–1907: Its Social Composition and Revolutionary Significance', *Past and Present*, 57 (1972), pp. 123–55; G. J. Gill, *Peasants and Government in the Russian Revolution* (New York, 1979); E. Kingston-Mann, *Lenin and the Problem of Peasant Revolution* (Oxford, 1984); M. Lewin, *Russian Peasants and Soviet Power* (London, 1968); A. Husain and K. Tribe, *Marxism and the Agrarian Question*. Vol. 2 *Russian Marxism and the Peasantry 1861–1930* (London, 1981). The Russian peasantry figures prominently in comparative works such as E. Wolf, *Peasant Wars of the Twentieth Century* (London, 1969); T. Srocpol, *States and Social Revolutions* (Cambridge, 1979).

49. The phrase is H.-A. Winkler's in his 'Stabilisierung durch Schrumpfung. Das gewerbliche Mittelstand in der Bundesrepublik', in W. Conze and M. R. Lepsius (eds.), *Sozialgeschichte der Bundesrepublik* (Stuttgart, 1983), p. 208.

50. In this regard, see especially D. Blackbourn, 'The *Mittelstand* in German Society and Politics, 1871–1914', *Social History*, 4 (1977), pp. 409–33.

51. Examples include F. Jacobs, *Deutsche Bauernführer* (Düsseldorf, 1958); idem., *Von Schorlemer zum Grünen Front* (Düsseldorf, 1957); G. Franz (ed.), *Bauernschaft und Bauernstand* (Limburg, 1975).

52. Indispensable here are: H.-J. Puhle, *Agrarische Interessenpolitik und preussischer Konservatismus im wilhelminischen Reich (1893–1914)* (Hannover, 1966); idem., *Politische Agrarbewegungen in kapitalistischen Industriegesellschaften* (Göttingen, 1975), esp. pp. 28–122; idem., *Von der Agrarkrise zum Präfäschismus* (Wiesbaden, 1972); idem., 'Der Bund der Landwirte im wilhelminischen Reich', in W. Ruegg and O. Neuloh (eds.), *Zur soziologischen Theorie und Analyse des 19. Jahrhunderts* (Göttingen, 1971), pp. 145–62. Still valuable is S. R. Tirrell, *German Agrarian Politics after Bismarck's Fall* (New York, 1951). A major study of the Agrarian League is due shortly from the East German historian, Dieter Fricke.

53. A. Gerschenkron, *Bread and Democracy in Germany* (New York, 1943).

54. Among the many works the more important are: H. Rosenberg, *Grosse Depression und Bismarckzeit* (Berlin, 1967); H. Böhme, *Deutschlands Weg zur Grossmacht* (Cologne, 1966); K. D. Barkin, *The Controversy over German Industrialization 1890–1902* (Chicago, 1970); M. Kitchen, *The Political Economy of Germany 1815–1914* (London, 1978); K. Hardach, *Die Bedeutung wirtschaftlicher Faktoren bei der Wiedereinführung der Eisen- und Getreidezölle in Deutschland*

(Berlin, 1967): H.-H. Herlemann, 'Vom Ursprung des deutschen Agrarprotektion-ismus', in E. Gerhardt and P. Kuhlmann (eds.) *Agrarwirtschaft und Agrarpolitik* (Berlin, 1969), pp. 183–208. See also the works cited in note 52 above. For the Weimar Republic see: D. Gessner, *Agrarverbände in der Weimarer Republik* (Düsseldorf, 1976); idem., *Agrardepression und Präsidialregierungen in Deutschland 1930–1933* (Düsseldorf, 1977); idem., 'Agrarprotektionismus und Welthandelskrise 1929/32', *ZAA*, 26 (1978), pp. 161–87; idem., 'Agrarian Protectionism in the Weimar Republic', *Journal of Contemporary History*, 12 (1977), pp. 749–78; idem., 'The Dilemma of German Agriculture during the Weimar Republic', in R. Bessel and E. Feuchtwanger (eds.), *Social Change and Political Development in Weimar Germany* (London, 1981), pp. 134–54; also the essays by Gessner, 'Industrie und Landwirtschaft 1928–1930', D. Stegmann, 'Deutsche Zoll- und Handelspolitik 1924/5–1929 unter besonderer Berücksichtigung agrarischer und industrieller Interessen' and T. Koops, 'Zielkonflikte der Agrar- und Wirschaftspolitik in der Ära Brüning', in H. Mommsen *et al.* (eds.), *Industrielles System und politische Entwicklung in der Weimarer Republik* (Düsseldorf, 1974).

55. The critique is at its most blunt and controversial in G. Eley and D. Blackbourn, *Mythen deutscher Geschichtsschreibung* (Frankfurt am Main, 1980), available now in a revised English edition, *The Peculiarities of German History* (Oxford, 1984). Among the more considered responses, see Groh, *op. cit.*, R. Moeller, 'The *Kaiserreich* Recast? Continuity and Change in Modern German Historiography', *Journal of Social History*, 17 (1984), pp. 655–84; Wolfgang Mommsen's review in the *Bulletin* of the German Historical Institute, London (No. 8, 1981), pp. 19–26.

56. D. Smith, 'Social History and Sociology — More than Just Good Friends', *The Sociological Review*, 30 (1982), p. 287.

57. Of the countless examples, see especially Kocka, Sozialgeschichte, H.-U. Wehler, 'Vorüberlegungen zu einer modernen deutschen Gesellschaftsgeschichte', in D. Stegmann *et al.* (eds.), *Industrielle Gesellschaft und politisches System* (Bonn, 1978), pp. 3 ff., and the references which they both cite.

58. G. Eley, 'Some Recent Tendencies in Social History', in Iggers and Parker, p. 59.

59. Ibid., pp. 60 ff.

60. For an introduction to the debates on 'modernisation' see R. Bendix, 'Tradition and Modernity Reconsidered', *Comparative Studies in Society and History*, 9 (1967), pp. 292–346. Critics include Dean C. Tipps, 'Modernization Theory and the Comparative Study of Societies: A Critical Perspective', ibid., 15 (1973), pp. 199–226; I. Weinberg, 'The Problem of the Convergence of Industrial Societies: A Critical Look at the State of a Theory', ibid., 11 (1969), pp. 1–15; J. Gusfield, 'Tradition and Modernity: Misplaced Polarities in the Study of Social Change', *American Journal of Sociology*, 72 (1966), pp. 351–62; L. F. Rudolph, *The Modernity of Tradition* (Chicago, 1967) (source of the quotation on p. 17). Many of the criticisms are acknowledged by H.-U. Wehler, *Modernisierungstheorie und Geschichte* (Göttingen, 1975), but, like many of his colleagues, he insists on the value of 'modernisation' as a conceptual tool.

61. R. M. Bell, *Fate and Honor, Family and Village. Demographic and Cultural Change in Rural Italy since 1800* (Chicago, 1979), p. 23.

62. T. Judt, 'A Clown in Regal Purple: Social History and the Historians', *History Workshop*, 7 (1979), p. 69.

63. Weinberg, p. 12.

64. The essays in this volume by Hainer Plaul (Chapter 4) and Cathleen Catt (Chapter 5) demonstrate the dangers of static typologies when studying a period of social transition. Recent research, for example, on migration back and forth between cities and the countryside in industrialising Germany reinforces this point.

See D. Langewiesche, 'Wanderungsbewegungen in der Hochindustrialisierungs-periode. Regionale, interstädtische und innerstädtische Mobilität in Deutschland 1880–1914', *Vierteljahrsschrift für Sozial- und Wirtschaftsgeschichte*, 64 (1977), pp. 1–40; P. Borscheid, 'Schranken sozialer Mobilität und Binnenwanderung im 19. Jahrundert', in W. Conze and U. Engelhardt (eds.), *Arbeiter im Industrialisier-ungsprozess* (Stuttgart, 1979), pp. 31–50; idem., 'Saison- und Etappenwanderung im Münsterland 1880–1900', in Blaich, pp. 9–46.

65. See the interesting, though still flawed, comments of G. Lewis, 'The Peasantry, Rural Change and Conservative Agrarianism. Lower Austria at the Turn of the Century', *Past and Present*, 81 (1978); pp. 119–43; and K. Holmes, 'The Forsaken Past: Agrarian Conservatism and National Socialism in Germany', *Journal of Contemporary History*, 17 (1982), pp. 671–88.

66. D. Blackbourn, 'Peasants and Politics in Germany, 1871–1914', *European History Quarterly*, 14 (1984), pp. 47–75; idem., *Class, Religion and Local Politics in Wilhelmine Germany* (New Haven, Conn., 1980); J. C. Hunt, *The People's Party in Württemberg and Southern Germany 1890–1914* (Stuttgart, 1975); G. Eley, *Reshaping the German Right: Radical Nationalism and Political Change after Bismarck* (New Haven, Conn., 1980), esp. pp. 9–40; idem., 'The Wilhelmine Right: How it Changed', in R. J. Evans (ed.), *Society and Politics in Wilhelmine Germany* (London, 1978), pp. 116–21; I. Farr, 'Populism in the Countryside: The Peasant Leagues in Bavaria in the 1890s', ibid., pp. 136–59; idem., 'Peasant Protest under the Empire: The Bavarian Example', in Moeller, *op. cit.*

67. See especially: A. Cardoza, *Agrarian Elites and Italian Fascism* (Princeton, N.J., 1982); P. Corner, *Fascism in Ferrara 1915–1925* (Oxford, 1975); and the essays by Cardoza, 'Agrarians and Industrialists: the Evolution of an Alliance in the Po Delta, 1896–1914', pp. 172–212, F. Snowden, 'From Sharecropper to Prole-tarian: The Background to Fascism in Rural Tuscany', pp. 136–71, and A. Lyttleton, 'Landlords, Peasants and the Limits of Liberalism', pp. 104–35, in J. Davis (ed.), *Gramsci and Italy's Passive Revolution* (London, 1979). Note also as a seminal work on the agrarian roots of the Spanish Civil War in E. Malefakis, *Agrarian Reform and Peasant Revolution in Spain* (New Haven, Conn., 1970).

68. R. Heberle, *From Democracy to Nazism* (Baton Rouge, 1945); G. Stoltenberg, *Politische Strömungen im schleswig-holsteinischen Landvolk 1918–1933* (Düsseldorf, 1962); T. A. Tilton, *Nazism, Neo-Nazism and the Peasantry* (Bloomington, ill., 1975). See also H. Beyer, *Die Agrarkrise und die Landvolkbewegung in den Jahren 1928–1932* (1962).

69. C. Loomis and J. Beegle, 'The Spread of Nazism in Rural Areas', *American Sociological Review*, 11 (1946), pp. 724–34. See also O. Poppinga, *Bauern und Politik* (Frankfurt am Main, 1975), pp. 208–30.

70. R. Moeller, 'Dimensions of the Social Conflict in the Great War: The View from the German Countryside', *Central European History*, 14 (1981), pp. 142 ff.; idem., 'Winners as Losers in the German Inflation: Peasant Protest over the Controlled Economy, 1920–1923', in G. Feldman *et al.* (eds.), *Die deutsche Inflation: Eine Zwischenbilanz* (Berlin, 1982); pp. 255–88; J. Osmond, 'Peasant Farming in South and West Germany during War and Inflation, 1914 to 1924: Stability or Stagnation?', ibid., pp. 289–307.

71. In this respect, see G. Eley, 'What Produces Fascism: Preindustrial Traditions or a Crisis of the Capitalist State?', *Politics and Society*, 12 (1983), pp. 53–82, for a re-emphasis on the conjunctural crisis as a crucial determinant in the Nazis' success. See also R. Bessel, 'Easterm Germany as a Structural Problem in the Weimar Republic', *Social History*, 3 (1978), pp. 199–218.

72. H. Gies, 'NSDAP und landwirtschaftliche Organisationen in der Endphase der Weimarer Republik', *Vierteljahreshefte für Zeitgeschichte*, 15 (1967), pp. 341–376; idem., 'Die nationalsozialistische Machtergreifung auf dem agrar-

politischen Sektor', *ZAA*, 16 (1968), pp. 210–32. More generally, see J. Farquharson, *The Plough and the Swastika* (London, 1976).
73. For an alternative view, see J. H. Grill, 'The Nazi Party's Rural Propaganda Before 1928', *Central European History*, 15 (1982), pp. 149–85; idem., *The Nazi Movement in Baden, 1920–1945* (Chapel Hill, 1983), Ch. 4.
74. Z. Zofka, *Die Ausbreitung des Nationalsozialismus auf dem Lande* (Munich, 1979); idem., 'Dorfeliten und NSDAP. Fallbeispiele der Gleichschaltung aus dem Kreis Günzburg', in M. Broszat, *et al.* (eds.), *Bayern in der NS-Zeit*, Vol. 4 (Munich, 1981), pp. 383–423; E. Fröhlich and M. Broszat, 'Politische und soziale Macht auf dem Lande. Die Durchsetzung der NSDAP im Kreis Memmingen', *Vierteljahrsheft für Zeitgeschichte*, 25 (1977), pp. 546–72.
75. See especially I. Kershaw, *Popular Opinion and Political Dissent in the Third Reich: Bavaria 1933–1945* (Oxford, 1983). For further insights see: A. von Saldern, *Mittelstand im 'Dritten Reich': Handwerker–Einzelhänder–Bauern* (Frankfurt, 1979); K. Wagner and G. Wilke, 'Dorfleben im Dritten Reich: Körle in Hessen', in D. Peukert and J. Reulecke (eds.), *Die Reihen fast geschlossen* (Wuppertal, 1981), pp. 85–106; idem., 'Family and Household: Social Structures in a German Village Between the Two World Wars', in Evans and Lee, *op. cit.*, pp. 120–147. Other works of importance include: F. Grundmann, *Agrarpolitik im 'Dritten Reich'. Anspruch und Wirklichkeit des Reichserbhofgesetzes* (Hamburg, 1979); H. Gies, 'Die Rolle des Reichsnährstandes im nationalsozialistischen Herrschaftssystem', in G. Hirschfeld and L. Ketternacker (eds.), *Der 'Führerstaat': Mythos und Realität* (Stuttgart, 1981), pp. 270–303.
76. Particularly helpful here are: S. Dillwitz, 'Die Struktur der Bauernschaft von 1871 bis 1914 dargestellt auf der Grundlage der deutschen Reichsstatistik', *JbWG*, 1973, pp. 47–127; idem., 'Quellen zur sozialökonomischen Struktur der Bauernschaft im deutschen Reich nach 1871', *JbWG*, 1977, pp. 237–69.
77. H. Gollwitzer (ed.), *Europäische Bauernparteien* (Stuttgart, 1977), p. 2.
78. E. Hobsbawm, 'Scottish Reformers of the Eighteenth Century and Capitalist Agriculture', in E. Hobsbawm *et al.* (eds.), *Peasants in History* (Calcutta, 1980). The best introduction to the relationship between the SPD and the peasantry in Husain and Tribe, *Marxism and the Agrarian Question*. Vol. 1, German Social Democracy and the Peasantry 1890–1907. See also the same authors' *Paths of Development in Capitalist Agriculture: Readings from German Social Democracy* (London, 1983); and H. G. Lehmann, *Die Agrarfrage in der Theorie und Praxis der deutschen und internationalen Sozialdemokratie* (Tübingen, 1970); W. H. Maehl, 'German Social Democratic Agrarian Policy, 1890–1895, Reconsidered', *Central European History*, 13 (1980), pp. 121–57.
79. S. Silverman, 'The Peasant Concept in Anthropology', *Journal of Peasant Studies*, 7 (1979), pp. 56–7.
80. E. Weber, *Peasants into Frenchmen: The Modernization of Rural France 1870–1914* (London, 1977).
81. See P. McPhee, 'A Reconsideration of the "Peasantry" of Nineteenth-Century France', *Peasant Studies*, 9 (1981), esp. pp. 18–19; and R. Magraw, *France 1815–1914: The Bourgeois Century* (London, 1983), Ch. 9. Note the phrasing of Weber's reply to some of his critics in E. Weber, 'Comment la Politique vint aux Paysans: A Second Look at Peasant Politicization', *American Historial Review*, 87 (1982), pp. 357–89, which still sees the peasantry in receipt of change. In similar vein is the none the less interesting E. Wallner, 'Die Rezeption stadtbürgerlichen Vereinswesens durch die Bevölkerung auf dem Lande', in Wiegelmann, *Kultureller Wandel, op. cit.*, pp. 160–73.
82. Shanin's, *The Awkward Class*, has met powerful criticism from G. Littlejohn, 'The Peasantry and the Russian Revolution', *Economy and Society*, 2 (1973), pp. 112–25; T. Cox, 'Awkward Class or Awkward Classes? Class Relations

in the Russian Peasantry before Collectivisation', *Journal of Peasant Studies*, 7 (1979), pp. 70–85; M. Harrison, 'Resource Allocation and Agrarian Class Formation. The Problem of Social Mobility among Russian Peasant Households, 1880–1930', ibid., 4 (1977), pp. 127–61; Husain and Tribe, *Marxism, op. cit.*, vol. 2, passim.

83. Shanin, *op. cit.*, pp. 14–15.

84. See especially J. Ennew, P. Hirst and K. Tribe, ' "Peasantry" as an Economic Category', *Journal of Peasant Studies*, 4 (1977), pp. 295–322; G. Littlejohn, 'Peasant Economy and Society', in B. Hindess (ed.), *Sociological Theories of the Economy* (London, 1977), pp. 118–56.

85. A. Leeds, 'Mythos and Pathos: Some Unpleasantries on Peasantries', in R. Halperin and J. Dow (eds.), *Peasant Livelihood*, pp. 227–56. See also Silverman, *op. cit.* Shanin's reply to these criticisms has been disappointing; see T. Shanin, 'Defining Peasants: Conceptualisations and De-Conceptualisations — Old and New in a Marxist Debate', *Sociological Review*, 30 (1982), pp. 407–32.

86. *Statistik des deutschen Reiches*, Vol. 112 (Berlin, 1898), p. 11.

87. See Dillwitz, *op. cit.*

88. A helpful introduction to the issues raised originally by Lenin is D. F. Ferguson, 'Rural/Urban Relations and Peasant Radicalism: A Preliminary Statement', *Comparative Studies in Society and History*, 18 (1976), pp. 106–18.

89. In addition to the works already cited, especially in note 44 above, see T. Frhr. von der Goltz, *Die Lage der ländlichen Arbeiter im deutschen Reich* (Berlin, 1875); G. Ernst, *Die ländlichen Arbeitsverhältnisse im rechtsrheinischen Bayern* (Regensburg, 1907); F. Wunderlich, *Farm Labour in Germany* (Princeton, N.J. 1961); J. Perkins, 'The German Agricultural Worker, 1815–1914', *Journal of Peasant Studies*, 11 (1984), pp. 3–27; J. Flemming, 'Landarbeiter zwischen Gewereschaft und Werkgemeinschaft', *Archiv für Sozialgeschichte*, 14 (1974), pp. 351–418; K. Bade, 'Massenwanderung und Arbeitsmarkt im deutschen Nordosten von 1880 bis zum Ersten Weltkrieg: Überseeische Auswanderung, interne Abwanderung und kontinentale Zuwanderung', ibid., 20 (1980), pp. 265–323; J. Nichtweiss, *Die ausländischen Saisonarbeiter in der Landwirtschaft der östlichen und mittleren Gebiete des deutschen Reiches, 1890–1914* (Berlin, 1959).

90. On the need for caution when using the term 'subsistence', see D. Sabean, 'Small Peasant Agriculture in Germany at the Beginning of the Nineteenth Century: Changing Work Patterns', *Peasant Studies*, 7 (1978), pp. 218–24.

91. See, for example, Gerschenkron, *op. cit.*, pp. 38–9; and Gessner, 'Agrarian Protectionism', p. 763.

92. J. Perkins, 'The Agricultural Revolution in Germany, 1850–1914', *Journal of European Economic History*, 10 (1981), p. 114. See also G. Helling, 'Zur Entwicklung der Produktivität in der deutschen Landwirtschaft im 19. Jahrhundert', *JbWG* (1966), pp. 129–41.

93. For a useful comparison, see the comments by McPhee, *op. cit.*, pp. 13–19.

94. A reassessment of the peasantry's relationship to tariffs has been led by R. Moeller, 'Peasants and Tariffs in the *Kaiserreich*: How Backward were the *Bauern*?' *Agricultural History*, 55 (1981), pp. 370–84; J. Hunt, 'Peasants, Grain Tariffs and Meat Quotas: Imperial German Protectionism Re-examined', *Central European History*, 7 (1974), pp. 311–31; S. Webb, 'Agricultural Protection in Wilhelminian Germany: Forging an Empire with Pork and Rye', *Journal of Economic History*, 42 (1982), pp. 309–26.

95. On this process of re-agrarianisation, see the essays in H. Kellenbenz (ed.), *Agrarisches Nebengewerbe und Formen der Reagrarisierung im Spätmittelalter und 19/20. Jahrhundert* (Stuttgart, 1975).

96. See E. Bucholz, *Ländliche Bevölkerung an der Schwelle des Industriezeitalters: Der Raum Braunschweig als Beispiel* (Stuttgart, 1966): and J. Mooser,

'Gleichheit und Ungleichheit in der ländlichen Gemeinde', *Archiv für Sozialgeschichte*, 19 (1979), pp. 231–62. For a later period, see also R. Schulte, 'Feuer im Dorf', in H. Reif (ed.), *Räuber, Volk und Obrigkeit* (Frankfurt, 1984), pp. 100–52.
97. The best study so far here is R. Marbach, *Säkularisierung und sozialer Wandel im 19. Jahrhundert* (Göttingen, 1978). See also H. Hörger, *Dorfreligion und bäuerliche Gesellschaft* (Munich, 1978).
98. This can be seen in the crucial role played by poaching. See H.-W. Eckardt, *Herrschaftliche Jagd, bäuerliche Not und bürgerliche Kritik* (Göttingen, 1976). In similar vein, J. Mooser, ' "Furcht bewahrt das Holz". Holzdiebstahl und sozialer Konflikt in der ländlichen Gesellschaft 1800–1850 an westfälischen Beispielen', in Reif, *op. cit.*, pp. 43–99.

2 PEASANTS AND MARKETS
The Background to the Agrarian Reforms in Feudal Prussia East of the Elbe, 1760–1807*

Hartmut Harnisch

I

In England and the Netherlands the ancient feudal order of the countryside gradually vanished in a slow process of disintegration and disruption which led to the gradual transition into modern capitalist agriculture; in France it was abolished by the powerful revolutionary forces which operated between 1789 and 1793. In Prussia, as in the other German states east of the River Rhine, and indeed in most of the European continent, feudal bonds and burdens were, by contrast, removed by way of agrarian reforms, consisting of legislation combined with compensations to the old feudal lords. In these lands, by contrast to England, France and the Netherlands, traditional feudal agrarian structures changed, at varying speeds and with varying completeness, into capitalist agricultural systems which eventually dispensed with all the old legal and economic ties between peasants and lords, once the latter had received their indemnities. Clearly, this procedure allowed a greater continuity between the old and the new orders than was the case when feudal agrarian structures were destroyed through revolutionary activities: essential features of the old order were either preserved or only modified a little. In practice, for example, the landowning families stayed in full possession of their large estates as well as of their often extensive forests.

Even the considerable losses of land that peasants in the eastern provinces had to suffer as part of the compensation to the feudal lords did not fundamentally change the overall distribution of land in those regions. The stress shifted a little in favour of large estates at the cost of the peasants, and indeed, in some smaller regions — as in parts of East Prussia and Pomerania — this shift was

---

*Translated by Bernd Feldmann and Richard J. Evans, with assistance from William W. Hagen.

considerable. But Prussia east of the River Elbe was already a land of large estates and large holdings, both before and after the reforms. It can also be assumed that the class of large and middle peasants were able to withstand the enormous burdens imposed on them by the agrarian reforms. Only the landless and the poor farmers from the villages, whose numbers increased rapidly after the agrarian reforms (and to a large extent because of them) underwent significant changes. In East Elbian Prussia their numbers rose at such a fast rate, not least because of a major labour shortage after the abolition of serfdom, that within a few decades, by about 1840, a structural over-population had developed.

It is by no means true to say that there has been little research into the agrarian reforms of the German states. Indeed, so much has been published that one person can hardly read it all now. This also applies to the period from the sixteenth to the beginning of the nineteenth centuries. But the great bulk of this research follows the fundamentally juridical approach pioneered by Georg Friedrich Knapp in his renowned *Die Bauernbefreiung und der Ursprung der Landarbeiter in den älteren Theilen Preussens* [*The Emancipation of the Serfs and the Origins of the Rural Labourers in the Older Parts of Prussia*]. Knapp's work, published as long ago as 1887, was continued by his pupils, and in many respects still prevails, having dominated the historiography of the subject for some 60 to 70 years. This school of learning focused above all on the legal status of the peasant, and in particular on the relationship between the peasantry and their feudal lords. By contrast, the management of the farms, holdings and estates, their relations with the market, and the effects of the market on them and the agrarian order, have received little attention.[1]

It was only in the 1930s that Wilhelm Abel began stressing the importance of this long-neglected complex of problems. Yet in spite of numerous valuable studies by Abel and his pupils, many aspects of the relations of the peasantry to rural market structures during the last stages of feudalism still remain to be investigated. While we know a good deal about the large estates, for example, the development of peasant agriculture on the eve of the bourgeois agrarian reforms certainly deserves closer scrutiny than it has so far received. There can be no doubt that the course and the results of the bourgeois agrarian reforms, bringing as they did a complete legal and economic rupture between peasant and lord, were of the utmost importance to demographic development, to the growth of the domestic market and, not least, to the industrial revolution in Germany as a whole. There is an urgent need, therefore, to determine how and in what ways these developments were determined by pre-reform structures in feudal agrarian society. As Gerhard Heitz of Rostock University stressed some time ago, agrarian history has a special contribution to make to research into the transition from feudalism to capitalism, above all by delivering a precise analysis of agrarian structures on the eve of the agrarian reforms.[2]

This paper, therefore, focuses on the last phases of feudal agrarian society in East Elbian Prussia; on the question of whether the traditional relation between peasant and feudal lord was already being undermined even before the reforms. Two closely connected processes have to be examined. First, I shall look at the changes in the prevailing economic situation of the peasant holdings in East Elbian Prussia. These changes must, of course, be seen in the context of the overall macroeconomic development of Central and Northern Europe during the last three to four decades before the beginning of the agrarian reforms in Prussia in 1807. In the final analysis this amounts to research into the relations of peasant holdings with the market. This in turn means that we have to examine changes in market structures during this period, and the position of the market within the overall system of the late feudal economy. Secondly, I shall argue that the peasants gained in self-confidence as they gained in importance to the market. The omnipresent antagonism between peasant and lord quite often led to protracted conflicts even before this period. Now it was raised to a higher level. It eventually became so pronounced that the Prussian government had to accept the necessity of far-reaching steps towards reforms.

This chapter draws its data mainly from the Mark Brandenburg, not only because I have devoted many years to a thorough study of this province, but also because significant historical developments are often best shown through the example of a single region. And since the effects of the market on peasant holdings are of central importance to this study, Brandenburg is particularly appropriate because of its proximity to Berlin, which was already functioning as the one outstanding market within the near and far surrounding countryside in the second half of the eighteenth century, far outweighing the importance of the Baltic ports in this respect. First of all, therefore, we require a description of the agrarian order that had developed in that region since the sixteenth century.

II

Estate agriculture (*Gutsherrschaft*) predominated in the German territorities east of the River Elbe, as well as in larger areas of Eastern Central Europe and in the eastern Baltic regions, from the sixteenth century to its abolition in the first half of the nineteenth century. It has long figured as the main topic of research in the agrarian history of Germany; the term *Gutsherrschaft* was in fact introduced by Georg Friedrich Knapp in 1891.[3] Under this system the lords ran their own large estates, aiming to enlarge them and have them worked completely, or to the largest possible degree, by enforced serf labour. Knapp used this term to discriminate between the agrarian structure that had developed east of the Elbe in the sixteenth century and the older peasant agriculture (*Grundherrschaft*), predominant in western and central Germany, The characteristic socio-economic features of this latter system were that serfs were liable to dues in kind and rents to their lords, but the lords themselves had no or only small estates.

For a long time the main features of the estate system and the reasons for its emergence in the sixteenth century were matters of controversy in German historical research.[4] Today, partly under the additional influence of the results of research in Poland,[5] it seems to be commonly accepted that the decisive impulses for the enlargement of the fedual estates and the increase of the peasants' enforced labour were provided by the market. Only when a stable market to some extent ensured the sale of agrarian products (above all corn, but also wool), were the feudal lords stimulated to enlarge their estates. In Central and Northern Europe the estate system meant an almost exclusive concentration on arable farming; the keeping of sheep and the production of wool were merely of supplementary significance, though they should not be underestimated. In the sixteenth century, therefore, the rising demand for corn acted as the trigger to the enlargement of the feudal estates and the transition to the estate system. However, the vast areas of Northern Europe under the estate system varied in different regions and territories. The parallellogram of (i) forces of ruler, aristocracy and bourgeoisie in each state, (ii) the legal status of the peasants' land, (iii) the position of the rural community in feudal society, and

(iv) the distance to the market for agrarian produce all led to further differentiations.

The different constellations of power between the classes in each state and their effects on the development of agrarian structures are relatively easy to elucidate. The Electors of Brandenburg and the Dukes of Mecklenburg and Pomerania had to give in repeatedly to the demands of the aristocratic Provincial Estates (*Landstände*) to have their debts paid and rents granted — at the cost, of course, of the peasants. The Electors of Saxony, on the other hand, had considerable profits from the rich silver mines of the Erzgebirge mountains through a special tax, the *Bergregal*, and were better equipped to resist the Estates' demands. So the noblemen of the Provincial Estates (*Landstände*) in the Electorate of Saxony were never as important as their counterparts in Mecklenburg and Prussia. In addition, the bourgeoisie in Saxony was powerful enough to act as an ally for the Elector. He had to take them seriously in the political and even more in the economic sphere, but together they were well placed to resist the fiscal demands of the landed aristocracy.

In addition to this, the legal status of the peasants' land was also of great importance,[6] a fact often neglected by historians. From the sixteenth century, if not before, there had been two main legal categories of peasants, though there was of course a great variety of nomenclature and many differences in the area of jurisdiction. We can more or less discount the comparatively small number of peasants who were subject to the sovereign himself and not to any local lord (a minor number of free peasants and above all the so-called *Köllmer* in East Prussia). These were large peasants with especially favourable conditions in the area of the former territory of the Teutonic Knights. They were personally free, were obliged to render only modest feudal dues, and had legal property in their holdings. In the eighteenth century they lived almost exclusively within the sphere of the sovereign demesnes. Apart from these, the two major legal categories into which the great majority of peasants fell were those with property in their holdings, and those without it. Both were subject to lords, but while the former were able to bequeath, mortgage or even sell their farms — albeit, only with the approval of their lords — the latter were granted only a temporary or life-time use, without any right of disposal at all. The regional distribution of these two principal legal categories probably went back to the time of the German feudal settlements in the West. Peasants with property were concentrated in the western parts of the Mark Brandenburg (e.g. in the Altmark west of the River Elbe, and in the Prignitz and the Zauche areas east of the river). In Lower Silesia and in those districts of the Neumark north of Lower Silesia (Kreis Sternberg) peasants with property prevailed as well.

In all other areas — i.e. in the central, northern and eastern regions of the Electorate of Brandenburg, in the districts of the Neumark north of the River Warthe, in Pomerania, in the larger parts of East Prussia and in Upper Silesia — the majority of peasants had no (freehold) property. In this category a further distinction has to be made between hereditary and non-hereditary usufructory holders (*Lassiten*) and leaseholders (*Zeitpachtbauern*). According to the lease the leaseholder could dispose of his holding only for a number of years, whereas the usufructory holders had as a matter of principle no limit of time. (They could, of course, be evicted in case of conflict with their lord.) Their hereditary rights developed as a customary law in some areas of Brandenburg, but did not lead to any legal right to their property. Apart from a few free peasants (the *Köllmer*) and a privileged class of village mayors (*Lehnsschulzen*) all Prussian peasants east of the river were subject to the estate system. They were not allowed to leave their farms; their children were liable to enforced labour on the estates at the fixed wages. This subordination developed in the course of time into hereditary serfdom or bondage in East Prussia and Pomerania, and in the Uckermark of Brandenburg bordering on Pomerania. In those provinces, each inhabitant of a feudal estate was hereditarily subject to his lord from birth. In other provinces, as in most parts of the Mark Brandenburg, this hereditary serfdom did not develop. Instead, the peasant's dependence began when he entered a contract to serve as a smallholder with some arable (*Kossät*) or a cottager with a small plot (*Büdner*) on the estate. It ended when the peasant gave up this position and left, although he had to find a successor acceptable to the feudal lord as a condition of leaving.

In correspondence with the regional distribution of one or the other category of feudal peasants, considerable differences in the size of estates and the amount of enforced labour developed in the course of the establishment of the estate system.[7] Peasants without legal property in their holdings could very easily be forced to perform more labour for the lord, because the landed aristocracy possessed the right of patrimonial jurisdiction, including the right of disposal of enforced labour. Insubordinate peasants were promptly evicted and replaced by more docile ones. Even the much-acclaimed *Bauernschutz* (protection of the peasants) of the absolutist Prussian kings did not lead to anything more than protecting the given holdings. It did not secure their continued use by one peasant, or even one family. Peasants who did possess legal property over their land, on the other hand, could not be evicted so easily. Even if their full power was used — including patrimonial jurisdiction — lords wanting to evict rebellious peasants had to pay the estimated price for the holdings. These cases usually went to a higher court. After the verdict the peasants could not refuse the price that had been fixed. But the peasant communities fought bravely for their rights, not seldom appealing to the High Court (Kammergericht) in order to prevent the imposition of higher feudal duties and increased drudgery by the lord. These lawsuits were protracted and needed considerable money, which the peasants raised by 'collections'. Appeals to the High Court were not very popular with the lords — after all, the result was uncertain, and the lord might well lose his case.[8]

The process of the extension of the big estates at the peasants' expense was undoubtedly slowed down in all those regions in which peasants with property prevailed. The enormous rise in feudal duties — up to five or six days of labour performed with teams of draught animals (*Spanndienst*) each week per farmstead — was quite common for peasants without property, but it was unknown in those areas where peasants were legally in possession of full property rights over their holdings.

If the varying legal status of peasants had important effects, so too did their distance from the markets. Obviously the great plain between the southern Baltic Sea, the east Baltic regions and the central German mountains was well suited for the large-scale cultivation of corn. It is a fact, too, that apart from some far-off areas, the corn could easily be transported to the Baltic ports, often down the major rivers. Still, the importance of the rivers can be overestimated, as in recent work by Rusinsky.[9] The Rhine, Main, Weser and Elbe were all important channels for trade and communication, but the lands of the river basin of the Elbe consisted of peasant holdings as well as fully-developed estates and there was thus no simple correlation between the proximity of a navigable river and the development of feudal estates.

Rusinsky has also argued recently[10] that in the Polish regions the development of an economy based on enforced labour depended strictly on market conditions. The evidence available for Brandenburg does not fully bear this out. Take, for example, a document of 1797 specifying the winter sowing in the Kurmark Brandenburg for large estates and peasant holdings.[11] Among other things, this document provides us with a fairly accurate measure of the share of large, landed property in the important agrarian area. It tells us that a third of the cultivated area in the Kurmark Brandenburg (excluding the Altmark) consisted of large farms (feudal estates, royal demesne farms and those owned by urban boards — *Städtische Kämmereien*). This can be compared with the Prignitz region, east of the Elbe, where communications with the export market in Hamburg were good and there were many peasants with legal property in their land. Here only 27.7 per cent of the cultivated land consisted of large farms. If we turn to a third region, the Uckermark, where most of the peasants were without property rights, 43.8 per cent of the cultivated land belonged to large estates, mostly owned by noblemen. This third region was situated very favourably towards a major market centre and port.

But not only were seaports market centres in the eighteenth century, so too was Berlin, which, thanks to the Spree and Havel, developed into a thriving market during the eighteenth century. In the district of Teltow, south of Berlin, 27 per cent of the cultivated land was held by large landed proprietors, and in the district of Niederbarnim, to the north it was 25.5 per cent. In both districts, it seems, peasants without property prevailed, but a large number of the villages belonged to the sovereign boards of demesnes (*Domänenämter*), and so only a small number of peasants were expropriated and included in the large estates. In Prussian Pomerania, with its very favourable communications with the Baltic ports, a specification that is not fully comparable to the figures from the Kurmark Brandenburg shows that the portion of large, landed property on the eve of the reforms was some 48 per cent. The overwhelming majority of Pomeranian peasants were leasehold tenants.

These figures reveal a complex pattern that cannot be reduced to a simple formula. In discussing the causes of the development of *Gutsherrschaft* and the regional differences in its nature and extent, we have to weigh very carefully the material effects of the overall situation of domestic politics in the territories and states, as well as of the legal status of the peasants' land (including the role of the village commune in feudal society) and their communications with the markets. All three factors played a role and combined in different ways.

In the present state of research it is impossible to be exact about the proportion of large landed property in any one of the territories in question. It is even more difficult to provide precise figures for the whole region. And it is equally hard to estimate even approximately the percentage of landed estates that were still cultivated by serf labour on the eve of the agrarian reforms. Tentatively, we can risk a rough estimate of between 50 and 70 per cent of cultivable land taken up by large landed property. The proportion of land still cultivated by serf labour was most probably quite large also.

III

As a rule of thumb, one can say that enforced serf labour did not exceed 2–3 days a week for peasants with property in their land. As for peasants without property, it depended entirely on the requirements of the estates. There were quite often 4, 5 or even 6 days of enforced labour per peasant-farmstead. As the great majority of the peasants in large parts of the Kurmark Brandenburg, the northern Neumark, Pomerania, East Prussia and in Upper Silesia had no property rights in their land we can quite confidently say that enforced labour for more than 3 days a week was very widespread in these areas.

On estates with enforced labour the highest possible portion of the operating costs was shifted on to the peasants. This included the care of the draught animals, upkeep of the pigsties, cowsheds and stables, and even the lodging, boarding and the pay of the farmhands. This was indeed the major reason for the enormous profitability of these estates and doubtless also a prime cause of their longevity. As the head of the provincial government of Pomerania, *Kammerpräsident* von Ingersleben, wrote in 1799, managing an estate with enforced labour might not lead to the highest possible yields and would certainly cause a lot of irritation and annoyance (especially, one might add, among its reluctant subjects), but it was 'convenient and cheap'.[12] The peasants could only bear such enormous burdens if they kept two teams of draught animals. To simplify feeding and reduce costs there was usually one team of horses and one of oxen. Experts in the higher ranks of the bureaucracy as well as economic theorists knew very well even in the eighteenth century that these peasants had to maintain one team, with a farm servant (*Knecht*) and quite often also a maid, merely to be able to meet their feudal duties.[13] The strain on the peasants' economy is obvious, as their own consumption rose considerably and the goods for the market were substantially reduced. Compared with enforced labour, the other duties — both in payment and in kind — were of minor importance.

But in spite of all this these peasants did produce for the market as well. Indeed, they had to, if only to be able to pay their farm-hands and the taxes. As might be expected, it is far from easy to estimate the average percentage produced for the market. We have to remember that the nucleus of the peasants in the villages east of the Elbe was made up by the full peasants (*Hufenbauern*), who cultivated the biggest area of the peasants' land, running holdings of about 20 to 70 hectares each, and also of course took advantage of the common pastures that were grazed by the whole commune. The classic three-field system, as is well known, involved a threefold rotation of winter crops, spring crops and fallow. But on the North German plain it was by no means possible to cultivate two-thirds at a time. Inferior soil and a chronic lack of fertilisers allowed the regular cultivation of only about a half. Substantial areas of the holding were included in the rotation only every 6, 8, 9 or even 12 years; in the meantime, they were used as pasture. Depending on the amount of land actually cultivated, and on the number of children able to work, these peasants employed about two to five farmhands from outside the family to maintain their farmsteads and to fulfil their feudal duties. Judging from the few taxation records[14] of peasant holdings that have survived, and from the far more numerous accounts of sowing[15] which allow us to assess the extent of the crop, it is possible to estimate that surplus production (after the feudal dues and domestic consumption) came to an average of 0.5–10 tons per holding. According to some taxation records from the area surrounding Berlin 2–4 tons seem to have been an acceptable average. It would seem, therefore, that Jerome Blum, in his book *The End of the Old Order in Rural Europe*,[16] underrates peasant market production considerably when he claims that it was minimal or non-existent. Blum bases his claim on William Jacob's report of 1820 on the marketing of produce by peasants in Frankfurt am Main, in West Germany, but conditions were very different in the area described by Jacob, where small and very small holdings prevailed, from those obtaining further east, which allowed, as we have seen, much more substantial production for the market.

The second group of self-sufficient peasants in the study area were smallholders (*Kossäten*) with holdings of about 5–10 hectares (15 hectares maximum). They too could provide the market with a modest surplus production in years of normal cropping. In the Prussian territories of the Elbe (with the exception of Silesia) the strata below the peasants obtained greater importance only in the course of the eighteenth century. In terms of figures, cottagers with small plots, garden cottagers and day-labourers (*Büdner, Häusler* and *Einlieger*) were the largest sectors of village society almost everywhere by the end of the century. They did, to be sure, owe their existence to the Prussian kings and their endeavours to increase the population of their country. But the growing demand for labour on the estates could no longer be met by enforced labour and so called for the settlement of farmhands. Thus these three groups, each with a smaller amount of land than the last, can, in effect, be regarded as successive phases of the settlement of labourers.

In the villages of the sovereign demesnes (*Domänenämter*) the numerous cottagers with small plots were the first to be established. Each had a farmhouse and 1 to 3 hectares of land. (The aristocracy, on the other hand, established only a very small number of these.) The establishment of garden cottagers instead of smallholders was very often caused by the lack of land for settlement. The lodgers (*Einlieger*) developed as a final group of the village poor. They had no land at all and either lodged with peasants, or rented from the landowners, living in tied cottages on the estates. The noble estates met the additional demand for labour mostly with garden cottagers or lodgers. All three groups only produced part of their own food supply, or even none of it. If they worked as threshers they received a portion of the threshing; those with small plots may occasionally have sold animals for slaughter; the rest had to buy most of their provisions.

Although the full peasants (*Hufenbauern*) produced remarkable quantities for the market, all the relevant sources, including the testimony of contemporary experts, agree that their net proceeds were minimal, which meant that they could only keep their farmsteads going through the utmost exertions.[17] When Friedrich Eberhard von Rochow (1734–1805), a large landowner in the Mark Brandenburg, tried to draw up the balances of a peasant holding in this area on the River Havel in 1798, he remarked that this had 'always been one of the most difficult tasks' which a landowner faced.[18] Like many previous observers, he found it almost impossible to explain how the peasants were able to keep their farms running with all the burdens that the lords and the government put on them. Statements such as these form the economic background to the agrarian historian Wilhelm Abel's instructive phrase that the peasant was always 'balancing on a knife-edge'.[19] In many different ways, therefore, a good number of peasants were anxious for the opportunity to earn extra money outside agriculture. One very popular source of secondary employment, for example, was delivering cart-loads of timber. Records from the wooded areas in the north of Brandenburg state that peasants quite often took on 'cart-loads of Hamburg timber';[20] in other words, they transported tree trunks to the Havel to be rafted to Hamburg and from there delivered to England. Cart deliveries were certainly the most important source of peasants' extra income. Nevertheless it seems quite certain that the average peasant holding was run at a deficit, as is indicated by the few taxation records that have survived. Once he had handed over his feudal duties, rents and taxes, and paid wages and the maintenance of buildings and stock, the average peasant was left without about as much as a farmhand earned in a year, some 15–20 *Reichstaler*.[21] This had important implications for the economy as a whole, for while the peasant could contribute to the market by delivering produce, his part in the circulation of goods was a very one-sided affair, as he himself was not able to act as a purchaser of industrial products.

The peasants struggled desperately against the increase in enforced labour to more than two or three days a week, above all in the sixteenth and seventeenth centuries. The victory of the feudal landowners in the second half of the seventeenth century, with the establishment of feudal absolutist control, can be explained by the precarious economic situation in which the peasants found themselves. As Heitz[22] aptly put it, the point in this struggle was whether the peasants could keep their position as small-scale producers or not. It is also possible to agree with Henning,[23] who some time ago called the income of the peasants a residual quantity and said that especially the peasants under the estate system had 'no latitude for special expenses or investments'.[24] The low purchasing power of the peasant population was most likely the basic reason for the miserable existence to which the majority of the towns in the territories east of the Elbe were condemned. The only exceptions to this general picture of urban misery were a few seaports and a very small number of commercial towns inland (Berlin, Frankfurt an der Oder, and Breslau [Wrocław]).

Those peasants whose enforced labour did not exceed two or three days a week were probably a little better off, as they had to maintain fewer draught animals and farmhands. On the other hand, they had to pay substantial feudal dues in kind. For example, the full peasants of the royal demesne of Dambeck in the Altmark, which belonged to the foundation of the famous Joachimsthal Grammar School in Berlin, only had to give one day of service with a team of animals per week, a small amount of enforced labour compared with the smaller farms under the same demesne. But to compensate for this their dues in grain amounted to 20 per cent of an average harvest.[25] The situation was very much the same on the estates of the Prignitz and the district of Ruppin, where 2−3 days of manorial service with a team of animals was very common. Here too some 10−20 per cent of the crop had to be paid to the lord as feudal rent. It is obvious that the lords had a good idea how to cream off the peasant surplus production in a way most suited to themselves. Nevertheless, as these peasants spent less on wages, the losses to their potential market production caused by dues in kind on the one hand, and the additional costs for wages and home consumption for peasants with 4−5 days of manorial service on the other, most probably balance each other out.

Any more specific research into the regional differences of the overall area of the estate system has to start from the diverse burdens of enforced labour. Such research is still in its beginnings and calls for international discussion. The complete dominance of enforced labour, or its combination with dues in kind or in cash, possibly marked the socio-economic structure of a region much more than all the other factors under consideration. The type and form of the feudal rent not only determined the amount of produce which the peasants could market, it also affected their remaining purchasing power and thus the development of the industrial economy. Only the most extreme elaboration of this late feudal agrarian structure required more than two or three days' service per farmstead per week. This was common above all along the southern shore of the Baltic, from the east of Holstein to East Prussia and inland up to the lower River Warthe and the area round Berlin. In the western parts of the Mark Brandenburg, in the south of the Neumark and in Silesia, the burden tended to be less, with only two or three days a week. Duties of one day of manorial service per week were common the Altmark, in the *Kammderdistrikt* of Magdeburg and that of Halberstadt and up to the River Weser, and in Saxony between the Rivers Elbe and Saale; they were also quite widespread in Thuringia. There were more or less concentrated 'islands' in the last-mentioned areas with two days of enforced labour per peasant per week. Here we can see the development of a transition to the estate system. And at least for a very important group of the dependent rural population — the full peasants (*Hufenbauera*) — quite substantial changes began to take shape and to determine the character of favoured regions by the end of the eighteenth century.

IV

For more than two centuries the estate system had proved to be 'convenient and cheap' for the lords. In the last third of the eighteenth century, however, there were indications that this once solid form of economic dominance was beginning to decay and to outlive its usefulness. Above all the rise in grain prices starting at the end of the 1760s had a lasting effect on agriculture, and on agrarian structures in general. Its general features are shown in Figure 2.1.[26] The price rise was partly caused by the continuous exports of grain to Great Britain that began in the decade between 1766 and 1775. These indeed affected the grain market in the whole Baltic region, not simply in Prussia. A second reason was the immense increase of home consumption due to a very substantial growth in the population. Here attention has to be drawn to the development of important urban centres of consumption. Above all Berlin, whose population rose from 55,000 to 178,308 between 1709 and 1803. Berlin's consumption of grain is calculated at 36,300 tons for 1777 and at 53,400 tons for 1802/3.[27] Indeed, for some time the area around Berlin (the Kurmark Brandenburg) had been unable to supply the growing city on its own. Large amounts of grain had to be transported to Berlin along the waterways from the Altmark and the area around Magdeburg, from the Neumark, Lower Silesia and from West Prussia. A number of other Prussian towns had also grown considerably, including Breslau (Wrocław), Königsberg (Kaliningrad), Potsdam, Stettin (Szczecin), with similar

Figure 2.1: Grain Prices in Prussia, 1766–1865

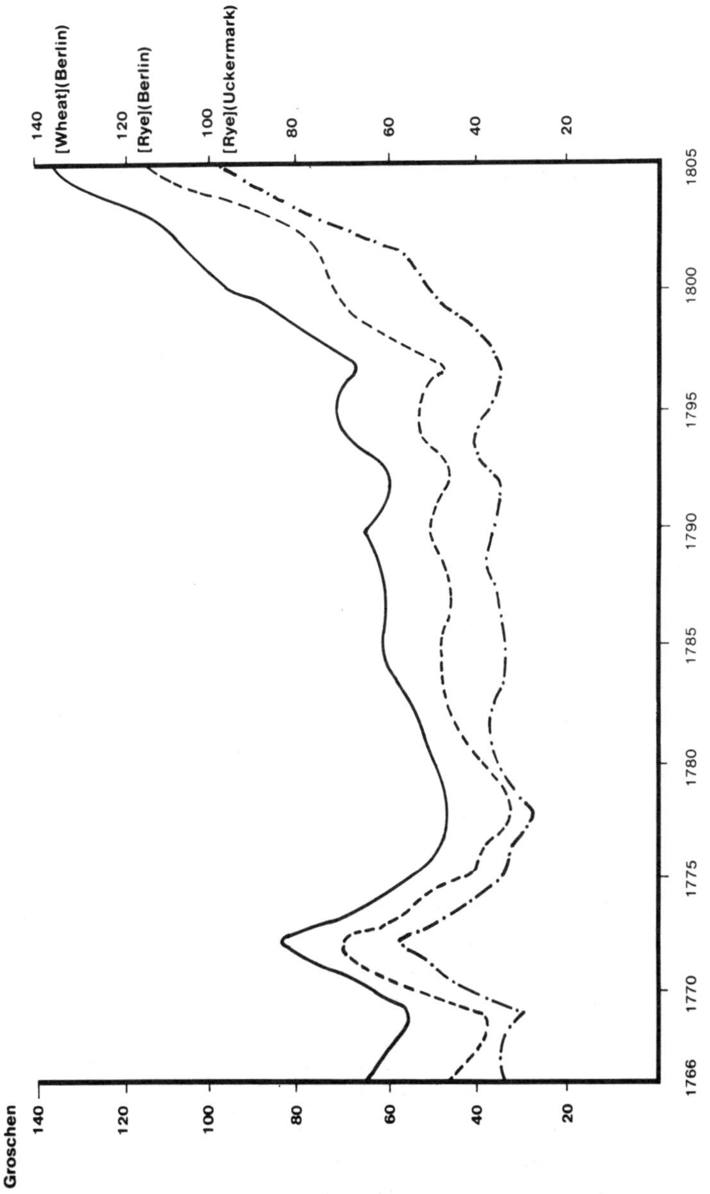

Groschen

140 [Wheat](Berlin)

120 [Rye](Berlin)

100 [Rye](Uckermark)

effects.[28] In some regions a market for agrarian produce had developed in the countryside as well, because of the growing numbers of landless or virtually landless peasants who had to buy a large portion of their provisions. This factor was particularly important in populous areas such as the *Kammerdistrikt* of Halberstadt and that of Magdeburg, and also in parts of the Kurmark Brandenburg. It played a major role in the mountainous regions of Silesia too, where the growth of the linen-weaving industry was already causing a tremendous concentration of the rural population.

Thus rising exports to England as well as growing home consumption stimulated agrarian production. England mostly imported wheat, which always commanded the highest prices. As the cultivation of wheat required rich soils and so high inputs of fertiliser the demand for wheat also had the additional effect of stimulating agricultural improvement. It was, of course, comparatively easy for the large estates to respond to new conditions in the market. They could independently decide on new systems of cultivation in order to improve their yields and to maximise their profitability. They were able to include new crops into their rotations, whether fodder crops such as clover, or fallow crops such as potatoes. (Clover and potatoes had been cultivated in Germany since the end of the seventeenth century, and had been recommended and propagated for a long time, but only became important in the late eighteenth century and then mainly on the large estates). They could thus increase their livestock holdings through the increased production of fodder, thus improving the fertilising of their arable land.[29] The importance of a higher yield of manure to the fertility of the soil at that time was stressed by an expert from the *Börde* of Magdeburg on the Elbe in 1755: 'The increase of cattle and sheep is the soul of agriculture.'[30] Where the estate lands were still interspersed with those of the peasants the lords as often as not succeeded in carrying through evictions, all the more so if the peasants had no legal property in their holdings and were leaseholders or usufructory holders.

Agriculture became more profitable in the decades before the reform. Grain prices rose, more grain was harvested, sheep increased in number, wool was produced in greater quantities, and in some areas potatoes came onto the market as well. The intensification of agriculture, especially in the cultivation of fallow crops, naturally led to a higher demand for labour. But this could no longer be met by increasing the amount of enforced labour under the feudal system. For peasants without property, enforced labour had very often already reached the maximum limit of 5–6 days a week per farmstead. Since the stabilisation of the central authority in Berlin with the rise of absolutism and 'enlightened despotism', peasants with property in their land found it much easier to obtain backing in their lawsuits from the superior courts. So the lords had to resort to paid labour, whether they liked it or not, and they installed peasants who had little or no land, as we have already seen. This of course stimulated an accelerated population growth, thus reinforcing the general trend. More important, the running of large estates without forced labour was now put to the test on a bigger scale than ever before. The productivity of paid labour, as might be expected, was much higher than that of enforced labour. Moreover, a further increase in profitability arose from the fact that wages for manorial servants and day labourers were subject to a legal freeze, and had to be paid according to the Statute of Labourers (*Gesindeordnung*) of 1769, which coincided with the beginnings of the rise in grain prices.[31] In spite of a remarkable growth of estate income because of the price rise, the freeze was again confirmed in 1797. Nevertheless, the high demand for labour meant that it was often disregarded by estate owners, who were forced to pay over the maximum allowed if they wanted anybody to work for them. In the past, it had long been much cheaper for the large estates — in spite of all the well-known shortcomings — to have grain produced by forced labour with their own teams of draught animals instead of paid labour with teams from the estates. But the introduction of new systems of cultivation and the increase of paid labour boosted the production and the productivity of the estates to such a high degree that, considering the development of grain prices, the substitution of enforced labour by paid labour became a viable alternative. It no longer automatically led to financial losses for the landowners. The conversion of the traditional feudal estate into a modern estate based on wage-labour thus became economically justifiable.

It was much more difficult for the peasants to adapt to the new market conditions. Until the agrarian reforms of the nineteenth century every initiative of theirs was constantly shackled by the three-field system, with its obligatory fallow periods, and by the right of pasturage (*Aufhütungsberechtigung*), according to which the estates and the commune were allowed to use the fallow and the arable land as soon as the harvest was finished as pasturage for cattle, sheep or pigs. Berthold[32] and Müller[33] have pointed out that the peasants did try hard to apply agricultural progress to their own family activities. Nevertheless, the sources indicate that, as far as really important innovations, like the large-scale cultivation of fodder plants and fallow crops, were concerned, the possibilities open to the peasant community were limited because of the right of pasturage already mentioned above. Thus for the cultivation of fodder plants and potatoes the peasants were normally only able to use the home meadow or *Wörde* (a grassy orchard of about 0.5−1 hectare next to the farms, with well spaced-out fruit trees). Continuous efforts were made by the peasant community to get the feudal authorities to allow certain parts of the fields to be taken out of the crop rotation and the right of pasturage, so that they could cultivate fodder plants on them.[34] The peasants understood very well the connection between the production of fodder, the possible volume of livestock, the amount of manure and the possibilities and limitations of cultivation on their holdings. The majority of them doubtless knew full well what the obstacles to decisive improvements in their economy were, namely the high costs of the uneconomically large numbers of farmhands and draught cattle that had to be kept to fulfil their feudal duties, and the pressures generated by the collective three-field system and the right of pasturage.

Considering these obstructions inherent in the feudal system, the ingenuity of the efforts of numerous peasant communities in making use of the new market conditions is remarkable. Because of the obligation for all members of the community to act according to the rule of the three-field system, in practice any attempt at improving their situation could only be made if everyone in the commune agreed on it. This agreement could often be best achieved in regions with good market communications, e.g. in the area round Berlin. The commune usually started its efforts in a field where no alterations to the general system of cultivation within the framework of the three-field system and the right of pasturage were needed, i.e. in a field devoted to the cultivation of grain. Thus the concentration of sowing was increased by improving the fertilising of the area sown (the possible yield depended to a large degree on the state of the soil) or by cultivating more frequently the outer fields which, because of the lack of fertilisers, had only been sown every 6, 9 or even 12 years. At the same time the communes also began to introduce a greater degree of specialisation into their cultivation system. Between 1749/55 and 1805, for example, the four villages of the royal demesne of Gramzow (Briest, Federsdorf, Meichow, Lützlow) north-east of Berlin, in the Uckermark, raised the amount of grain sown to 130 per cent of the starting point; while the amount of wheat sown on their most fertile soil was raised to 183 per cent.[35] In 1805 the proportion of wheat in the overall sowing came to 21.2 per cent. The peasants of the village of Lüdersdorf to the north of Berlin in the district of Ruppin, an area of rather poor soil, raised their amount of grain sowing to 140 per cent between 1727 and 1817.[36] In this context it is well worth mentioning that some villages in the district of Ruppin with slightly better soil turned to the cultivation of barley after the Ruppin canal had been built in 1791 — a canal that had been designed for shipping peat to Berlin, but which also offered a cheap means of transport to the capital for other goods; the peasants were clearly quick to take advantage of this.[37]

Some of the best-documented cases of the specialisation of cultivation and thus of the peasant response to the new market conditions are available for the villages of the royal demesne of Löcknitz in the northern Uckermark. There the soil was fertile and the peasants used it mainly for cultivating highly profitable wheat. Between 1794 and 1804 the six villages of Bergholz, Bagemühl, Fahrenwalde, Grimme, Wallmow and Zerrentin increased their sowing of wheat to 158 per cent. The peasants of Wallmow responded most successfully to the market. They concentrated so much on the cultivation of wheat that their production of rye no longer met the requirements for their own consumption, and they had to start buying it in considerable quantities. As rye was cheaper than wheat their calculation would doubtless have been the correct one.[38] The sources only allow us to look at individual examples of the market orientation of grain cultivation such as these, but in the case of crops which did not infringe the traditional system of cultivation and the privileges of the lords, more general observations can be made. In the Prignitz, east of the lower Elbe, and in the district of Lebus, east of Berlin, many peasants increased the cultivation of fruit, and sold it fresh or dried in Berlin and Potsdam. It has also been said that in 1799 the small town of Lübbenau in Lower Lusatia (at that time still belonging to Saxony) was largely engaged in providing Berlin with legumes.[39]

These examples — and more could be given — clearly show the effects that a large market had on the development of agricultural production. Over and above this, they demonstrate these peasants' mature and considered attitude to the market; and these were, it should be stressed, peasants who still lived under feudal dependence. Baron Magnus von Bassewitz (1777–1858), who before 1806 had worked as a young official in the royal demesnes commissioned with carrying through the abolition of feudal duties and who later became the Supreme President (*Oberpräsident*) of the province of Brandenburg, was undoubtedly well placed to judge the condition of the peasants, and in 1805 he wrote in the following terms about the peasants of the royal demesne of Gramzow who had become wealthy by growing wheat: 'This wealth is also a reason for concluding that these subjects would have a notion of a higher form of agriculture if only they had not been hindered by the hitherto existing legal subjection and by the communal cultivation of the land.'[40] This verdict is undoubtedly applicable to all those peasants who tried to improve their holdings by their own efforts.

Of course, not all peasants were proceeding along the road towards agricultural progress and a purposeful market orientation. In large parts of East Prussia (above all in the south and east of that province), Pomerania, the Neumark, in the Polish regions of Silesia and also in the areas in the south of the Kurmark Brandenburg with very poor soil, there was hardly any market orientation or specialisation of production at all. In all areas far removed from the markets there was little innovation or progress. Nevertheless the assumption that only the large estates benefited from the increase in grain exports, while the peasants were allegedly compelled to buy extra grain when the cropping was poor, as Hanna Schissler has recently stated,[41] is incorrect. It is true that the classes with little land, above all those who had been dispossessed, could on occasion be confronted with a situation of this kind; this applies especially to peasants with little or no land of their own, though those with a small plot were certainly much less susceptible. The large and the medium peasants certainly produced enough grain for their own consumption even in lean years. This does not exclude the possibility, however, that after really disastrous harvests (as in 1771/72) seed corn would have to bought or borrowed. But the middle and large peasants, with holdings of between 20 and 70 hectares, could benefit from the rise in grain profits, so the income differentials in the rural population increased and in due course social differences were aggravated.

Table 2.1: Proceeds from Sales of 1 Tonne of Grain for the Periods
1766/70 and 1801/05 in Berlin and in the Uckermark

	Berlin		Uckermark
	Wheat	Rye	Rye
1766/70	48.14.8	42.22.10	27.8.5
1801/5	97.22.0	73.11.4	61.3.0

Sources: See Figure 2.1.
Note: Prices are in *Taler, Groschen* and *Pfennige*, respectively.

All peasants who were able to sell their produce on the market
with any regularity experienced an increase in their income even if
they could not deliver a single additional bushel, simply because of
the rise in grain prices. The actual effect is demonstrated by the
figures in Table 2.1, based on the prices shown in Figure 2.1. For
the peasant-producers this remarkable increase in money income
was to a high degree an increase in real income, as taxes in Prussia
were not raised during the second half of the eighteenth century.
For the peasants on the royal demesnes, the feudal dues payable to
the demesne office were not raised either. The effect of the rise in
grain prices on the tax burden of the peasants is shown by the
example of the village of Briest in the royal demesne of Gramzow in
the Uckermark, which has already been mentioned. The most
important taxes were the *Kontribution, Kavalleriegeld, Metzkorngeld* and *Hufen-* and *Giebelschoss*. The *Kontribution* was the
peasant land tax since the war of 1618–48; *Kavalleriegeld* was
introduced when in 1717 the quartering of the cavalry with the
peasants on the basis of payment in kind was stopped. From that
year the cavalry was quartered in the towns, only moving to the
country for some months in summer. The *Kontribution* and *Kavalleriegeld* were the most important taxes on peasant holdings in
absolutist Prussia. *Metzkorngeld* was introduced when a duty in
kind from the war of 1618–48 was converted into payment in cash
in the eighteenth century. The *Hufen- und Giebelschoss* was a tax
on houses and fields that the Provincial Estates (*Landstände*) again
and again granted the princes from the fifteenth and especially
from the sixteenth centuries to enable them to pay their interest and
to pay off their debts that arose from the underdeveloped financial
administration. Since the establishment of absolutist sovereignty in
Brandenburg-Prussia in the seventeenth century the sovereign
actually disposed of the tax yield. There was good soil at Briest,

Table 2.2: Grain Sales of a Peasant Farm in the Village of Briest (Amt Gramzow/Uckermark) necessary to meet tax demands

	Berlin		Uckermark
	Wheat	Rye	Rye
1766/70	1978	2264	3559
1801/5	987	1324	1591

Note: Figures are in kilograms.

Sources: Cf. Figure 2.1; P. G. Wöhner, *Steuerverfassung des platten Landes der Kurmark Brandenburg*, Parts 1 & 2 (Berlin, 1804).

the village with which we are concerned, and peasants with holdings of about 48 hectares (*Dreihüfner*) there were taxed with a comparatively high total of 97 Taler 6 Groschen (some minor dues payable to the community, alms and fire prevention are not taken into account). To raise this amount of taxes a peasant would have to sell the amount of grain shown in Table 2.2. Of course, the large peasants with 2–5 hands not belonging to the family also profited from the legally-fixed maximum wages for farmhands.[42] The real income of the peasants must have risen substantially in some cases, while the real income of their hands probably fell.

The peasants on the royal demesnes, who have been cited again and again because they are the best documented, were not the only ones to profit from these developments; the peasants on noblemen's land gained substantially as well. For example, in the estate of Boitzenburg, also in the Uckermark, with its markets in Berlin and in the local towns, the peasants were tenants with six-year leases, and apart from a comparatively low burden of enforced labour of about 80 days a year with a team of animals the most important feudal due they owed was the rent. Because of the short lease the lords could usually raise the rents to keep pace with the rise in grain prices. Nevertheless in the decade from 1795 to 1805, during which grain prices rose very quickly, the rent increases did not keep up with the rise in prices. In the village of Thomsdorf, for example, each peasant had to pay a rent of 24 Taler a year from 1743 to 1802,[43] and then 28 Taler a year from 1802 onwards. According to the grain prices in Berlin this equalled 558 kg of rye in 1766/70 and 381 kilograms from 1802 onwards, so that the peasants had in fact gained over the period despite the rise in the rent in 1802. A note of caution has to be sounded here, however, because the present state of research does not allow a definitive statement to be made as to whether the Lordship of Boitzenburg was typical or not: the Counts of Arnim, its proprietors, were very large landlords, whose income for a long time had come mostly from the management and lease of a considerable number of estates.

Still, the peasants in regions favoured by good market conditions took advantage of the situation by increasing their production or by specialising; and it seems beyond doubt that the full peasants (*Hufenbauern*) — especially those on the demesnes — started in these decades to break the cycle of destitution and 'balancing on a knife-edge' which had enslaved them for so long. As one might expect, this breakthrough was most obvious in the regions adjacent to the market. In practice, though, this must also have been the case in more remote regions, so long as the peasant surplus production was not creamed off by the lords through feudal dues in kind. Where this was the case the peasants remained more or less excluded from the intensification of market relations. In large parts of southern, western and central Germany a large portion of feudal dues — sometimes an overwhelming one — was made up of dues in kind, above all in the form of the tithe. It is at least possible, therefore, that the agrarian reforms in Prussia were pushed through quite quickly from 1811 onwards[44] because of the intensification of the market relations of the estates and peasant holdings in the decades before 1807. On the other hand, the comparatively less well-developed market relations of peasant holdings in the western and southern regions may be one of the causes why the agrarian reforms came to a halt after they had started so well during the period of Napoleonic domination.

V

It seems clear, then, that profound changes in the relationship of the economically-advanced middle and large peasant holdings and the market took place during the last decades before the agrarian reforms, especially if the communications with the market were favourable and if the surplus product was not creamed off by the lords by way of feudal dues in kind. For a long time the proceeds from the sale of the peasants' produce had been hardly enough to pay for the taxes, feudal dues, farmhand wages and other costs, fire insurance, alms contributions and other expenses. Their situation had been so miserable that even well-trained observers had not been able to say just how the peasants made ends meet. Now the situation was progressively changing for the better. What was the effect of these developments on the national economy in general? One may suppose that at first many peasants preferred to hoard their increasing receipts than to consume them or invest in their holdings in order to improve them. Naturally enough this was especially so for peasants without real property rights and that meant (Silesia excluded) the vast majority of peasants in East Elbian Prussia. Whether this changed after 1799, when the peasants on the demesnes were able to commute their dues into rents or purchase their property, and whether this had visible effects on trade, awaits further research. It must not be forgotten, though, that grain prices had only begun rising really rapidly from the 1790s, so that the period of major effects on the national economy was not much longer than a decade.

For the region of the Magdeburg *Börde* (black-earth district) west of the Elbe, there is proof that a genuine consumption boom in the countryside started at the end of the eighteenth century. The peasants owned their farms, and most property belonged to large holdings which took advantage of the rich soil to produce large quantities of wheat and barley for brewing. Several observers reported that a small upper class of well-to-do peasants had developed by the early nineteenth century. They spent a much-admired amount on clothes, coffee, sugar, and, above all, beer.[45] In the regions of the estate system, by contrast, practically nothing of this kind was reported in this period. Another effect of the good market for agrarian produce and of the slowly-increasing proceeds of the peasantry was, however, of quite decisive importance in the inevitable supersession of the traditional *Gutsherrschaft* estate system, and that was the growing resistance of the peasants.

There was nothing new about struggles between lords and peasants, of course. Conflicts on questions of feudal duties, rights of tending and driving herds, the use of forests, and so on, were part of the everyday life of the estate system. Quite often peasants ran away from the unbearable pressure; flights of this kind were particularly common among the propertyless, who were the ones with the hardest burdens, of course. Occasionally there were strikes against the feudal dues, in which the peasants refused to render their lords the dues owing to them. Arrest and ill-treatment, especially of the peasants' spokesmen, temporary sequestration of the draught cattle and — the ultimate sanction — eviction, were the usual reactions of the lords to such insubordination. With the establishment of the absolutist state during the seventeenth and eighteenth centuries matters changed somewhat. On the one hand, the feudal lords became so all-powerful that any revolt against them seemed hopeless from the start, but on the other hand, the Crown now took steps to stop the worst excesses of *Junker* imperiousness. On a local scale, though, everyday strife went on as usual. The sources indicate that as grain prices rose, so the peasants became more and more aware of the obvious impediments to a more efficient management of their farms. They knew well enough that there were many ways of expanding their production and their deliveries to the market, but as they had to adapt their economy to the needs of the estate system with its enforced labour (two teams) they could not break out of the narrow confines of minor improvements only. From their own experience they also knew that the majority of the lords would not give up their enjoyment of enforced labour voluntarily. With the prospects of a real increase in their proceeds, all the peasants' hatred was centred on their feudal dues which burdened their economy so heavily and made them exert themselves so much to no profit to themselves.

In 1774 King Friedrich II, who in 1777 went so far as to call feudal duties a 'repulsive arrangement',[46] suggested, by means of a Cabinet Order to the General Directory[47] his supreme ministry of all the administrative authorities responsible for internal affairs, that feudal dues should no longer be fixed in the form of a certain number of days of service. Instead, each peasant should be made responsible for a certain acreage of land on the estates, taking care of all necessary husbandry. Thus the peasants were to be stimulated to fulfil their duties as effectively as possible. Although this attempt came to nothing, it was interesting as a pointer to the future. In this Cabinet Order, Friedrich announced his intention of counteracting 'the continuous urgent complaints of the peasants about much too severe duties, both with teams and in manual labour . . .'[48] The struggle against feudal dues increased in line with the intensification of the peasants' market relations. Very pointedly the President of the Provincial Board of War and Demesnes of the provinces of Pomerania, Herr von Schütz (predecessor of the above-mentioned *Kammerpräsident* von Ingersleben) described the situation that had developed for the peasants, in a memorandum of 1796. Pomerania, of course, did not rank among those well-developed regions in which the problem had already become an urgent one. Still, Schütz wrote:

> Now the peasant feels the inequality he had to live with; he knows the evils that prevent him from cultivating his land more efficiently; he understands that he cannot proceed because of the amount of money needed for feudal dues and because of the time required for labour service, that he is more or less forced to waste. That is why there are now so many complaints by the King's subjects.[49]

At the time when Schütz was putting down these reasons, detailed information about the French Revolution and the peasants' achievements there had already penetrated as far as the remote villages east of the Elbe. There can hardly be any doubt that the pressure from 'the base' against the obsolete system of dominion and economy, the system of *Gutsherrschaft*, was now intensified.

At first, though, leaders of the Prussian state were obviously inclined to keep the old order unchanged. On 4 September 1794, in the reign of King Friedrich Wilhelm II, after some villages in the Altmark had held a meeting to discuss the possibilities of abolishing feudal dues, the Prussian High Court (*Kammergericht*) issued a sharp warning,[50] delivered through the district presidents (*Landräte*) against any repetition of such activities anywhere in the country. Though it was harmless enough, the meeting in the Altmark was evidently taken very seriously indeed by the High Court, which emphasised that the right to levy feudal dues had been legally acquired by the lords, who could 'not do without them if they are to maintain their estates'. All that the villagers of the Altmark had in fact asked for was the right to commute their dues into money rents without obtaining the prior agreement of the lord. This modest demand was explicitly rejected by the High Court, which even at this late stage thus displayed no inclination at all towards reform.

It was only after the succession of King Friedrich Wilhelm III in 1797 that an intensive discussion about the need for agrarian reform began within the higher ranks of the Prussian bureaucracy. The bureaucrats had finally realised that the estate system and its feudal dues had become more and more ineffective. It was also becoming clear that the tensions between the peasants and the feudal authorities were reaching a dangerous crisis point. On

14 May 1798 Baron Friedrich von Schroetter, the provincial minister for East and West Prussia, and one of those who were most active in the reforms after 1807, wrote a long letter to Cabinet Councillor Beyme, one of the most influential of the King's men in Berlin.[51] Schroetter told Beyme that rumours were spreading in his area about the activities of the special financial commission that had been installed by the new king in 1797 to work out proposals for reform. The rural population were particularly excited about the abolition of hereditary serfdom and feudal dues. Schroetter's concerned statement that there was a 'dull rumbling' among the peasants is of particular interest. In East Prussia, where the peasants on the noble estates were still subject to strict hereditary serfdom, the abolition of this condition was the major demand. In other areas, as in the Altmark in 1794, the abolition of feudal dues (in East Prussia called *Scharwerk*) was the main demand.

A little later, on 23 July 1798, Beyme addressed a letter to Grand Chancellor of Justice von Goldbeck,[52] stressing the urgent need to improve the situation of the peasants. He drew Goldbeck's attention to the possible evil consequences of further delays (the Chancellor was obviously hesitating and averse to reforms). Many years later, in 1847, Baron von Bassewitz, whose views on the situation in 1805 we have already encountered, looked back on the mistrust shown by the peasants for landowners and tenants of demesnes before 1806.[53] The much talked-of patriarchal relationship between lord and peasant had, he said, been an exception. The peasants did not feel they were looked after by the lords, they 'felt they were only used by them'. Evidently a deep discontent and 'dull rumbling' were widespread among the rural population in the years preceding 1807. On the other hand there was no ignoring the fact that very many peasants were both willing and able to orient themselves to the market and to modernise their holdings. It might therefore be of interest to recall the highly pessimistic verdict on the peasants under the estate system near the end of the introductory chapter of Georg Friedrich Knapp's masterwork on the old Prussian agrarian state before 1807: 'The peasant', he wrote, 'remained on the same level for ever and ever, confused, gloomy, dissatisfied, rude, servile, obedient only to the steward; an unhappy hybrid of beast of burden and human being.'[54] Maybe things were still like that in remote areas with strictly-managed and legally-fixed serfdom, but the well-considered and purposeful economic behaviour of many peasants and peasant communities in areas with favourable market conditions tells another tale. So too does their evident consciousness of the essential factors that stunted any progress, a consciousness which manifested itself openly in the struggle for the abolition of feudal dues.

Under the conditions of the estate system the modernisation of agriculture was only possible with the abolition of feudal dues. This was the first and fundamental prerequisite of all subsequent steps. Hence the fact that not only the peasants but also an increasing number of noble landowners and bourgeois tenants open to experimentation, as well as theorising economists and philanthropically-minded Secretaries of State, demanded the abolition of feudal duties. Hence also the fact that an influential group among the Prussian leaders of state now realised that it had become an urgent necessity. The increasing profitability of agriculture that had started at the end of the 1760s, and the constant pressure from the base that was obviously increasing rapidly after 1789, created an atmosphere of open-mindedness towards reform among the Prussian leaders. The agrarian political reforms undertaken after 1799[55] not only show how the Prussian authorities viewed the situation in the countryside, but also revealed very quickly the limits of their power. In fact they could only set about improving the economic and legal status of the peasants on the royal demesnes. Efforts to obtain the nobility's consent to the abolition of hereditary serfdom and *Gutsuntertänigkeit* (subjection to the estate) or to commute feudal dues in kind into money rents came unstuck as early as the preliminary negotiations. There are no accurate figures available for the actual number of peasants on the royal demesnes, but depending on whether the smallholders (*Kossäten*) are counted as peasants (an assumption justified in most cases) or not, their number in the Kurmark Brandenburg, the Neumark, Pomerania, West Prussia, East Prussia and Lithuania probably amounted to some 70,000–90,000. In Silesia there were only very few; and for the Netze valley there are no figures. All those peasants on the royal demesnes were given the opportunity to commute their feudal dues into annual money rents. Additionally those peasants in the provinces of Kurmark, Neumark and Pomerania who had no property (usufructory holders and leasehold tenants) — a large percentage of the peasants in those regions — were allowed to purchase their holdings by paying the so-called *Erbstandsgeld*. In other East Elbian Prussian administrative districts this concession was not given. There can be no doubt that these measures were influenced by the distant effect of the French Revolution and the increasing ferment among the peasant population. When the agrarian reforms of Baron vom Stein started with the edict of 14 October 1807 (i.e. after the Prussian defeats at Austerlitz and Jena) the measures begun in 1799 had by no means been completed. For some 30,000 peasants feudal dues had been commuted into annual rents and up to the middle of 1806 some 6000 peasants and 2000 smallholders had gained legal property rights in their holdings.

These measures did not mean the complete abolition of the feudal relationship of lord and peasant. The change to rents necessarily bound the peasants to the market closer than ever before. But the rent was not adjusted to the yields, the situation on the market or the demand for land, i.e. it was no capitalist rent. Rather it was calculated as the sum of the former, minor duties in payment and the new, additional expenditures arising from running the farms of the royal demesnes with paid hands instead of farmhands rendering feudal dues. Those peasants who purchased their farms did not enjoy the unlimited right of disposition over them. They could not cease production, or sell the whole or parts of them without the consent of the demesne office. Thus no free market in real estate developed. Moreover, the peasants' children were not allowed to work outside agriculture without the approval of the authorities. According to the sources, by paying the *Erbstandsgeld* peasants on the demesnes acquired their holdings as hereditary leaseholds (*erbliches Zinseigentum*),[56] a phrase that would seem to describe the legal position very well. Royal peasants gained this new status in many areas, in the districts of Magdeburg and Halberstadt, and also in the Altmark and the Prignitz area, that is, in the western parts of the Kurmark Brandenburg.

The limitation of the reforms of 1799 to the peasants on demesnes was a consequence of the internal relation of power between the authorities and the nobility. It illustrates very clearly just how limited was the effectiveness of the Prussian leaders of state. Yet serious questions about their intentions and about their perceptiveness are raised by the fact that in some districts the peasants were given no opportunity at all to acquire property in their holdings, and elsewhere they could only acquire hereditary leaseholds; and even more by the suppression of a free market in real estate and the continuing obligation of the peasants' children to work on the land. It seems that these measures were not aimed at overcoming the feudal order so much as at stabilising it.

Certainly no Prussian expert or official is known to have suggested that the reforms were supposed to lead in the long run to the complete legal and economic separation of the feudal authorities and the peasants or, in modern terms, a capitalist agrarian system. Nevertheless these reforms, which practically brought the estate system to an end in the royal demesnes, were certainly consistent with the general undermining and disruption of the feudal order.

Until the disaster of 1806/7, however, the Prussian central authorities were unable to progress beyond the steps originally taken in 1799. Considering the favourable macroeconomic conditions and the universally-known 'dull rumbling' among the rural population, this was by no means an impressive performance. The really decisive breakthrough for a final rupture between the peasants (whatever their legal status) and their lords, or in other words a capitalist emancipation of the peasants, took place only after 1807.

Historians in the German Democratic Republic are still divided over the question of whether and how the reforms starting in 1807 were conditioned or determined by the socio-economic development of the preceding years. Jürgen Kuczynski, the Nestor of economic history in the GDR, has recently stressed the backwardness and stagnation of the late eighteenth-century socio-economic system in Prussia as well as in Germany as a whole, in the towns as well as the countryside.[57] On the other hand, Heinrich Scheel pointed out some time ago[58] that the influences and stimuli coming from England and France even before 1806 would have had no effect if there had been no developments in agriculture ready to be positively stimulated and influenced, or in other words if a bourgeois transformation had not been in the making. For the sphere of agriculture Berthold and Müller[59] have argued practically along the same lines as Scheel, and the argument of the present essay has also been that the bourgeois revolution in the country had been prepared by socio-economic developments long before 1807. Of course, Kuczynski's stress on the defeat of 1806/7 as the decisive 'detonator', the triggering-off event, cannot be entirely dismissed. Among other things, this essay has tried to show how slowly the efforts at reform started. In spite of the universally-recognised tensions, all measures actually begun before 1807 still remained within the framework of feudal legality. Any efforts at reform from peasants other than those on the royal demesnes failed. There is no way of finding out whether without the disaster of 1806 there would have been stabilisation and consolidation of the feudal order or whether the pressure from the peasants and the market would have led, in whatever way, to a capitalist solution. In the event, however, it is clear that the events of 1806/7 did indeed open the way towards a bourgeois development.

Notes

1. See the discussion above, pp. 3–8.
2. Gerhard Heitz, 'Die Differenzierung der Agrarstruktur am Vorabend der bürgerlichen Agrarreformen', *Zeitschrift für Geschichtswissenschaft*, Vol. XXV (1977), p. 912.
3. Georg Friedrich Knapp, 'Die Erbuntertänigkeit und die kapitalistische Wirtschaft', in idem., *Landarbeiter in Knechtschaft und Freiheit* (Munich and Leipzig, 1891). The reference is to G. F. Knapp, *Einführung in einige Hauptgebiete der Nationalökonomie (Selected Works*, Vol. I, Munich and Leipzig, 1925), p. 144.
4. Cf. the still instructive report of Georg von Below, 'Der Osten und der Westen Deutschlands. Der Ursprung der Gutsherrschaft', in idem., *Territorium und Stadt. Aufsätze zur deutschen Verfassungs-, Verwaltungs- und Wirtschaftsgeschichte* (Munich and Leipzig, 1900), pp. 1–94. For the later discussions cf. Hartmut Harnisch, 'Die Gutsherrschaft in Brandenburg, Ergebnisse und Probleme', *Jahrbuch für Wirtschaftsgeschichte* (1969), Part IV, pp. 117–47.
5. Cf. summary in Władysław Rusiński, 'Some Remarks on the Differentiation of Agrarian Structure in East Central Europe from the 16th to the 18th Century', *Studia historiae oeconomicae*, Vol. 13, Poznán (1978), pp. 83–95.
6. Hartmut Harnisch, 'Rechtsqualität des Bauernlandes und Gutsherrschaft', *Jahrbuch für Geschichte des Feudalismus*, Vol 3 (Berlin, 1979), pp. 311–63.
7. Ibid., pp. 361–2.
8. We cannot deal with these conflicts in detail here. For the time of their development, cf. Hartmut Harnisch, 'Bauernbewegungen gegen die Gutsherrschaft. Die Mark Brandenburg im Jahrhundert vor dem Dreissigjährigen Krieg', in Winfried Schulze (ed.), *Aufstände, Revolten, Prozesse. Beiträge zu bäuerlichen Widerstandbewegungen im frühneuzeitlichen Europa* (Geschichte und Gesellschaft. Bochumer Historische Studien, Vol. 27 Stuttgart, 1983), pp. 135–48. For later periods, cf. Günter Vogler, 'Probleme des bäuerlichen Klassenkampfes in der Mark Brandenburg im Spätfeudalismus', *Acta Universitatis Carolinae — Philosophica et Historica* 1 (Prague, 1974), pp. 75–94, Studia Historica XI.
9. Rusiński, *op. cit.*, p. 92.
10. Ibid.
11. Staatsarchiv (StA) Potsdam, Pr. Br. Rep. 2A, Regierung Potsdam, I. Kom., No. 558, ff. 1–2.
12. Zentrales Staatsarchiv (ZSA) Merseburg, Generaldirektorium, Generaldepartment, Tit. XLI, No. 10, f. 10.
13. As an example, cf. the most famous German demographer of the eighteenth century, Johann Peter Süssmilch, *Die göttliche Ordnung in den Veränderungen des menschlichen Geschlechts aus der Geburt, dem Tode und der Fortpflanzung desselben erwiesen*, Part 3 (Berlin, 1776, 4th edn), pp. 277–8. Here the uneconomic nature of this kind of organisation is also stressed.
14. *Taxationen* were records of cultivation and yields as well as debits of working costs and duties, and finally the net proceeds of estates and holdings. For noble

estates there are a great many of these records dating from the sixteenth century onwards.

15. See Harmut Harnisch, *Kapitalistische Agrarreform und Industrielle Revolution. Agrarhistorische Untersuchungen über das ostelbische Preussen zwischen Spätfeudalismus und bürgerlich- demokratischer Revolution* (Weimar, 1984), pp. 33 f.

16. Jerome Blum, *The End of the Old Order in Rural Europe* (Princeton, N.J., 1978), p. 171.

17. Harnisch, *Kapitalistische Agrarreform, op. cit.*, pp. 30 f.

18. ZSA Merseburg, Rep. 96A, No. 42A, f. 1.

19. Wilhelm Abel, *Geschichte der deutschen Landwirtschaft vom frühen Mittelalter bis zum 19. Jahrhundert* (Stuttgart, 1967, 2nd edn), p. 107. Here Abel refers to a peasant in the High Middle Ages.

20. StA Potsdam, Pr. Br. Rep. 2, Kurmärkische Kriegs- und Domänenkammer, D 16374, f. 156.

21. Harnisch, *Kapitalische Agrarreform, op. cit.*, pp. 305 f.

22. Gerhard Heitz, 'Zu den bäuerlichen Klassenkämpfen im Spätfeudalismus', *Zeitschrift für Geschichtswissenschaft*, Vol. XXIII (1975), p. 771.

23. Friedrich Wilhelm Henning, *Dienste und Abgaben der Bauern im 18. Jahrhundert* (Stuttgart, 1969) (*Quellen und Forschungen zur Agrargeschichte*, W. Abel and G. Franz (eds.), Vol. XXI), pp. 166–7.

24. Ibid., p. 166.

25. StA Potsdam, Pr. Br. Rep. 32, Joachimsthalsches Gymnasium, No. 1533, Pachtanschlag des Amtes Dambeck 1793–1802.

26. Figure 2.1 shows the growth in the prices of wheat and rye between 1766 and 1805 in Berlin and in the Uckermark (Groschen per 50 kg, annual averages). 24 Groschen = 1 Reichstaler = 16.7039 g. of fine silver.

The sources are as follows: For Berlin *Jahrbuch für die amtliche Statistik des Preussischen Staates,* Vol. 2 (Berlin, 1867), p. 112; for the Uckermark, Staatsarchiv Potsdam, Pr. Br. Rep. 2A, Regierung Preussen, I HG, No. 3635. In this latter source the prices of rye from the clerical lands of the village of Briest on the markets of Angermünde, Prenzlau and Schwedt are given. Wheat was not sold.

27. Hartmut Harnisch and Gerhard Heitz, 'Feudale Gutswirtschaft und Bauernwirtschaft in den deutschen Territorien. Eine vergleichende Analyse unter besonderer Berücksichtigung der Marktproduktion', in *Large Estates and Smallholdings in Europe in the Middle Ages and Modern Times* (International Congress of Economic Historians, Budapest, 1982), National Reports, p. 17.

28. The growth of some towns is demonstrated by the following figures:

Breslau (Wrocław)	1710:	40,000
	1770:	58,215
	1804/5:	69,005
Königsberg (Kaliningrad)	1723:	39,475
	1766:	46,621
	1804/5:	60,701
Potsdam	1722:	2600
	1780:	27,896
	1804/5:	29,355
Stettin (Szczecin)	1720:	6081
	1770:	13,990
	1804/5:	23,469

Deutsches Städtebuch. Handbuch städtischer Geschichte, Vol. 1, Erich Keyser (ed.) (Stuttgart, 1939). The figures for 1804/5 are from Karl Friedrich Wilhelm Dieterici, *Der Volkswohlstand im preussischen Staate* (Berlin, 1846), p. 14. There was, however, little change in the ratio of urban to rural populations. In the Prussian administrative districts more or less dominated by *Gutsherrschaft* (Kurmark, Neumark, West Prussia, East Prussia, Netze) the urban population made up 26.9 per cent of the general population in 1785 and 29.3 per cent in 1802. Cf. Georg von Viebahn, *Statistik des zollvereinten und nördlichen Deutschland*, Vol. 1 (Berlin, 1858), pp. 115, 124. In Silesia the first reliable census giving the numbers of both the urban and the rural populations was not undertaken until 1787. In that year the urban population amounted to only 17.4 per cent (ZSA Merseburg, Rep. 96, No. 249B, ff. 1–6), and in 1802 17.7 per cent (cf. Viebahn, *op. cit.*, p. 124).

29. Cf. Hans-Heinrich Müller, *Märkische Landwirtschaft vor den Agrarreformen von 1807* (Potsdam, 1967) (Veröffentlichungen des Bezirksheimatsmuseums Potsdam, Vol. 13), pp. 108–10.

30. Hartmut Harnisch, 'Produktivkräfte und Produktionsverhältnisse in der Landwirtschaft der Magdeburger Börde von der Mitte des 18. Jahrhunderts bis zum Beginn des Zuckerrübenbaus in der Mitte der dreissiger Jahre des 19. Jahrhunderts', in *Landwirtschaft und Kapitalismus. Zur Entwicklung der ökonomischen und sozialen Verhältnisse in der Magdeburger Börde vom Ausgang des 18. Jahrhunderts bis zum Ende des ersten Weltkrieges*, Vol. I, Part I (Berlin, 1978) (Veröffentlichungen zur Kulturgeschichte und Volkskunde, Vol. 66/1), p. 77.

31. *Corpus Constitutionum Prussico-Brandenburgensium praecipue Marchicarum*, Vol. 9 (1798), No. LXXIX, co. 1173–776.

32. Rudolf Berthold, 'Einige Bemerkungen über den Entwicklungsstand des bäuerlichen Ackerbaus vor den Agrarreformen des 19. Jahrhunderts', in idem., *Beiträge zur deutschen Wirtschafts- und Sozialgeschichte des 18. und 19. Jahrhunderts* (Berlin, 1962), pp. 81–131; Rudolf Berthold, 'Entwicklungstendenzen der spätfeudalen Getreidewirtschaft in Deutschland', in *Bäuerliche Wirtschaft und landwirtschaftliche Produktion in Deutschland und Estland (16. bis 19. Jahrhundert)*, (Berlin, 1982), *Jahrbuch für Wirtschaftsgeschichte* (special edition 1981), pp. 7–134.

33. Müller, *Märkische Landwirtschaft, op. cit.*

34. Cf. the examples in Harnisch, *Kapitalistische Agrarreform, op. cit.*, pp. 55 f.

35. StA Potsdam, Pr. Br. Rep. 2, Kurmärkische Kriegs- und Domänenkammer, D 9818, Generalpachtanschlag des Amtes Gramzow, 1749–1755, ibid., D 9820, 1798–1810.

36. Harnisch, *Kapitalistische Agrarreform, op. cit.*, p. 46.

37. StA Potsdam, Pr. Br. Rep. 7, Amt Ruppin, No. 115, Generalpachtanschlag des Amtes Ruppin, 1798–1804.

38. Harnisch, *Kapitalistische Agrarreform, op. cit.*, pp. 49 ff.

39. Ibid.

40. StA Potsdam, Pr. Br. Rep. 2, Kurmärkische Kriegs- und Domänenkammer, D 9944, f. 11.

41. Hanna Schissler, *Preussische Agrargesellschaft im Wandel. Wirtschaftliche, gesellschaftliche und politische Transformationsprozesse von 1763 bis 1847* Kritische Studien zur Geschichtswissenschaft, Vol. 33 (Göttingen, 1978), pp. 62 ff.

42. Cf. note 31.

43. Hartmut Harnisch, *Die Herrschaft Boitzenburg, Untersuchungen zur Entwicklung der sozialökonomischen Struktur ländlicher Gebiete in der Mark Brandenburg vom 14. bis zum 19. Jahrhundert* Veröffentlichungen des Staatsarchivs Potsdam, Friedrich Beck (ed.), Vol. 6 (Weimar, 1968), p. 215.

44. Hartmut Harnisch, 'Die kapitalistischen Agrarreformen in den preussischen Ostprovinzen und die Entwicklung der Landwirtschaft in den Jahrzehnten vor 1848. Ein Beitrag zum Verhältnis zwischen kapitalistischer Agrarentwicklung und Industrieller Revolution', in *Bäuerliche Wirtschaft und landwirtschaftliche Produktion in*

Deutschland und Estland (16. bis 19. Jahrhundert) (Berlin, 1982), *Jahrbuch für Wirtschaftsgeschichte* (special edn, 1981), pp. 135–253; also Harnisch, *Kapitalistische Agrarreform, op. cit.*, pp. 1–58.

45. Harnisch, 'Produktivkräfte und Produktionsverhältnisse in der Landwirtschaft der Magdeburger Börde', *op. cit.*, pp. 151–2.

46. Cited from Ingrid Mittenzwei, *Friedrich II. von Preussen. Eine Biographie* (Berlin, 1979), p. 157.

47. *Corpus Constitutionum Prussico-Brandenburgensium praecipue Marchicarum*, Vol. 5, 1776, No. XLVII, col. 335–6.

48. Ibid., cols. 335–6.

49. ZSA Merseburg, Rep. 96A, No. 20E.

50. *Corpus Constitutionum Prussico-Brandenburgensium praecipue Marchicarum*, Vol. 9 (1976), No. LXXVI, cols. 3295–400.

51. ZSA Merseburg, Rep. 96A, No. 118C, f. 3.

52. Ibid., Rep. 96A, A 20, 15 f.

53. Anon. [Magnus Freiherr von Bassewitz]. *Die Kurmark Brandenburg, ihr Zustand und ihre Verwaltung unmittelbar vor Ausbruch des französischen Krieges im Oktober 1806. Von einem ehemaligen höheren Staatsbeamten* (Leipzig, 1847), p. 433.

54. Georg Friedrich Knapp, *Die Bauernbefreiung und der Ursprung der Landarbeiter in den älteren Theilen Preussens*, Vol. 1 (Leipzig, 1887), p. 77.

55. Hartmut Harnisch, 'Die agrarpolitischen Reformmassnahmen der preussischen Staatsführung in dem Jahrzehnt vor 1806/07', *Jahrbuch für Wirtschaftsgeschichte*, 1977, Part III, pp. 129–53.

56. Ibid., p. 151.

57. Jürgen Kuczynski, *Vier Revolutionen der Produktivcräfte. Theorie und Vergliche* (Berlin, 1975), pp. 67 ff.

58. Heinrich Scheel (ed.), *Das Reformministerium Stein. Akten zur Verfassungs- und Verwaltungsgeschichte aus den Jahren 1807/08* (Berlin, 1966), Vol. I Introduction.

59. R. Berthold, 'Einige Bemerkungen über den Entwicklungsstand', *op. cit.*; Müller, *Märkische Landwirtschaft, op. cit.*

THE JUNKERS' FAITHLESS SERVANTS
Peasant Insubordination and the Breakdown of Serfdom in Brandenburg-Prussia, 1763–1811

William W. Hagen

I

In July 1787 the Prussian government commanded that a Royal Proclamation be read throughout the kingdom, 'especially to the lower orders [*niedere Volks-Classen*]'. 'We are', said Friedrich Wilhelm II, 'compelled to observe, with the highest displeasure, that in recent times lawsuits and quarrels between landlords and their subject villagers have greatly multiplied in many of Our provinces.' The common people 'very frequently' succumbed to an 'unbridled passion for litigation', no matter how hopeless their case. Shady petition-writers (*Winkel-Schriftsteller*) forced their services on the peasants, and on the 'common burghers' as well, goading them into the courtroom. So too did other third parties, who vented 'hateful insinuations and stir up unfounded mistrust towards higher authority'. The King menaced such troublemakers with 'one, two, or more years of prison'. He ordered the people to present their complaints only to licensed attorneys, who must not allow 'laziness or fear of other people' to subvert their obligation to accept all admissible cases. Persons unable to pay lawyers' fees could have the nearest court take their testimony free of charge, whereupon justice would promptly and fairly be done. Addressing 'our loyal nobility', the King reaffirmed his 'well-founded confidence' that they would not make themselves guilty of 'any illegal oppression of Our subjects'.

But if any estate owner abuses his rights and jurisdictional powers to harass his subject villagers unrightfully with demands for labour services and fees beyond what they properly owe him; or if he in any way encroaches upon their property or their prerogatives; or if he is guilty of other forbidden exactions or violent mistreatment of his subjects; then not only will such wrongful breach of Our trust in the nobility be punished by the laws of

the land, but it will also incur special signs of Our deepest displeasure and disgrace at Our hands.[1]

The 'lower orders' must have relished hearing these words, however much they may have doubted their effect.
Friedrich Wilhelm's proclamation paid unwilling tribute to the
gathering force of peasant unrest in late eighteenth-century
Brandenburg-Prussia. As this paper will show, the subject farmers'
resistance to new seigneurial demands upon them, like their efforts
to free themselves of long-endured feudal burdens, were aspects of
the rural landscape of old-regime Prussia to which contemporary
landlords and officials were far from blind. But the historical
literature, even when it does not ignore the question of peasant
turbulence, casts it only in a subordinate role in the larger drama
that Henri Brunschwig called the 'crisis of the Prussian state', and
that Günter Vogler and Klaus Vetter have recently termed the
'crisis of late-feudal society'.[2]

To some historians, this crisis was essentially political and institutional: the difficult passage from enlightened autocracy, which
expired with Friedrich II in 1786, across the time of troubles of the
French revolutionary and Napoleonic wars, to the renewal of the
Prussian state under the domination of a reforming bureaucracy
after 1806. Accompanying this constitutional transformation was a
change in the reigning socio-economic world-view, from state-
regulated mercantilism to liberal individualism. It followed that the
reformers, once in power, would emancipate the peasantry and
promote capitalism in agriculture. What mattered, in the benign
gaze of Hintze and Meinecke as in the critical glare of Hans
Rosenberg, were ideological and social shifts within the Prussian
governing class, not rumblings in the villages, to which they paid no
attention at all.[3]

Such narrowly political interpretations of the crisis and transcen-
dence of the pre-1806 old regime in Prussia are not typical of the
historical literature. Knapp's exceptionally long-lived work of 1887
on the peasant emancipation in Prussia has led many broader interpretations of the old regime to underscore, deploringly, the
eighteenth-century Junkers' heightening exploitation of their subject peasants, who by 1807 had sunk to the status, as Knapp wrote,
of 'an unhappy middle term between beast of burden and human
being'.[4] The estate-owning Junkers squeezed new profits, in the
form of heavier labour services and other seigneurial rents, from

the peasantry. This thwarted the enlightened autocracy's efforts to invigorate the common people's legal and cultural condition, and so also their economic productivity, tax-paying ability, and patriotism. In this perspective, which represents the view of such able scholars as Brunschwig, Reinhardt Koselleck, Hanna Schissler and Christoph Dipper, the crisis of the old regime possessed an important socio-economic dimension. The absolutist system was foundering both on the abuses and decadence of the manorial/serf system in agriculture, and upon the failure of mercantilist industrial programmes to absorb the labour of the rapidly increasing landless villagers and propertyless towns-people.[5] In the gathering Malthusian gloom, only the Junker landlords profited from the rapid rise in agricultural commodity prices at home and abroad in the decades after 1763. But they did so, as the neoclassical economic historians hold, 'by accentuating the feudal dependence' of the subject peasantry 'rather than adapting the organisation of their enterprises to "capitalist conditions".'[6]

In this historiographical setting, conflicts between manor house and village, such as those that Friedrich Wilhelm II's proclamation of 1787 denounced, would seem to qualify for serious consideration. Yet the stress that this analysis of the old regime lays on the baleful powers of the Junkers — as landlords, local officials (*Landräte*) and military officers — has led some of its proponents to conclude that the peasantry's resistance to their seigneurial overlords was futile, and irrelevant to the resolution of the crisis. Accordingly, village unrest and peasant protest make no appearance in the influential arguments of Knapp, Otto Büsch and Schissler.[7] Brunschwig, Koselleck, and Dipper steer a different course. They perceive an increasing turbulence of rural discontent, but they interpret it as the peasantry's desperate and ineffectual reaction to old-fashioned seigneurial oppression. It was symptomatic of the crisis, and a part of its solution only to the degree that the reform-minded among the governing class added peasant unrest to their reasons for aiming to eradicate the old regime.

There is, finally, yet another way of construing the socioeconomic crisis. Acknowledging the political and institutional obsolescence of the absolutist system, it emphasises the spread in the eighteenth century of capitalist or proto-capitalist forms of production. Merchants and other entrepreneurs built up networks of rural cottage industries and pioneered centralised factory production, especially in Berlin. In agriculture, profit-hungry landlords, especially after 1763, enclosed their demesnes, adopted improved crop rotations, and began to replace enforced with free wage labour. Exploitative terms of employment, and a post-1763 conjuncture unfavourable to real wages, impoverished the workers in these advanced spheres of the pre-1806 economy, which were themselves embedded in the faltering late-feudal social order.[8] From this perspective, the agrarian crisis was one of transition rather than decadence. Its resolution demanded the liberation of nascent capitalist production from feudal bonds, which in turn, as the followers of Adam Smith in the propertied and governing classes understood, required the peasants' emancipation from serfdom. But what part did rural unrest play in the crisis of transition before 1806? And how did peasant protest influence the form and timing of the Prussian emancipation?

Johannes Ziekursch's durable study of Silesia stresses the coincidence, in the second half of the eighteenth century, of modernised estate agriculture, Junker forays into textile and metallurgical production, and steadily intensified, though harshly repressed, peasant resistance to their landlords' demands upon them. The villagers' protests arose in defensive reaction to the estate owners' exploitative innovations, without succeeding in warding them off. The provincial bureaucracy and army stood on the Junkers' side, thwarting all enlightened reform. After 1806, the government in Berlin imposed peasant emancipation on the province only after granting extraordinary concessions to the landlords at the numerically preponderant lesser peasantry's expense.[9]

Hartmut Harnisch weighs the importance of the Junkers' agricultural improvements more lightly than Ziekursch, but the consequences of peasant protest more heavily. Analysing the government's efforts at agrarian reform in the decade before 1806, he argues that widespread peasant resistance to old-fashioned compulsory labour convinced progressive-minded officials that property and labour relations, anticipating liberal capitalism, had to supersede the old regime without delay. This was a precondition not only of social peace in the countryside, but also of meeting the Junkers' clamorous demands for the unimpeded right to export their grain crops. Without immediate productivity gains in estate agriculture, such exports could only accelerate the rise in the domestic price of bread, which was already, in the 1790s, beginning to drive the landless villagers and urban poor into food riots. In Harnisch's view, then, peasant protest spurred the bureaucracy on towards effecting the transition to capitalism in agriculture, especially considering that the substantial improvements the government actually made in the tenures and rents of many peasants on the royal demesnes during the years 1799 to 1805 only heightened the discontent of the noble landlords' subject farmers, still chafing under the old regime.[10]

Harnisch nevertheless holds that, in the Brandenburg-Prussia of 1806, 'widespread dissolution of feudal relations of production' had not yet begun, nor had 'the level of development of the forces of production in agriculture' by itself yet made necessary the liquidation of the old social order in the countryside.[11] But Hans-Heinrich Müller's study of farming in Brandenburg in the half-century before 1807 shows that the Junkers had adopted the techniques of the Western European agricultural revolution on a wide scale. This went hand in hand with commutation of feudal labour rents into cash rents. With this new income the landlords and lessees of royal demesnes paid a growing force of manorial servants and wage labourers, who worked the estate lands with teams and equipment their employers had acquired for themselves, instead of relying, as they had in the past, on those of their subject peasants.[12] Müller does not dwell on the causes of these advances in techniques and productivity, which historians as ideologically unrelated as Robert Brenner, Jerome Blum and Douglass North would not expect to find within a seigneurial order resting on extra-economic coercion.[13] But Müller suggests that the landlords' and the royal demesne tenants' interest in fattened profits underlay their agronomic experiments. He notes the frequency of peasant refractoriness under the unreformed manorial/serf system, but assigns it no special motivating force.[14]

Not so the dissertation of Kurt Wernicke, which stands alone in his exclusive focus upon the East Elbian peasantry's resistance to their seigneurial overlords in the period 1648 to 1789.[15] Without weighing their representativeness, Wernicke adduces a mass of examples of peasant self-defence, from shoddy labour to harvest strikes and minor uprisings. He concludes that the hardships attendant upon the landlords' intensified production for the market goaded the peasantry into increasingly widespread resistance. Though usually ineffective in preventing a worsening of the protestors' conditions at their own pugnacious Junkers' hands, such resistance persuaded other landlords to substitute wage labour for sullen servile *corvées*. Commuting labour services into cash payments hastened the transition to capitalism, while the pervasiveness of peasant protest in the late eighteenth century convinced enlightened officials and *literati* that serfdom should be abolished altogether. Wernicke's study, impressionistic and speculative though it is, has the virtue of suggesting that it was precisely peasant resistance to heightened exploitation that led profit-minded landlords to turn increasingly from feudal to wage labour. If we grant, (as most of the authors discussed above do not), (1) that important proto-capitalist innovations in estate agriculture occurred before 1806, and (2) that peasant protest could effect real change under the old regime, then Wernicke's argument is worth pursuing. It has, indeed, been advanced without further proof in two widely-read surveys, one published in West Germany, the other in the German Democratic Republic.[16]

Wernicke's analysis lacked quantitative underpinning, while his denial of success to most local movements of peasant resistance raises the question why the Junkers turned to commutation of *corvées* and the employment of wage labour, rather than squeezing heavier labour services and other rents from their defenceless subject peasants. These defects are absent from a recent study of the West Elbian Magdeburg region, to which Harnisch contributed the analysis of the agrarian economy and rural social structure in the period 1750 to 1835. Here, Harnisch argues, the peasantry's greater personal freedom and stoutly-defended strong tenurial rights prevented the estate owners from raising rents. This forced the improving landlords to hire wage labour, leaving the landed peasants free themselves to profit from the agricultural conjuncture of the decades before 1807. The peasantry's successful self-defence channelled the forces of production, on manor and farm alike, in a gradual transition to capitalism in agriculture made smoother by a peasant emancipation after 1807 preserving the landed peasantry's large arable holdings intact.[17] Harnisch holds that such a favourable exit from the era of serfdom was denied the East Elbian peasantry, poorer and legally weaker than their Magdeburg counterparts.[18] No doubt, the East Elbian Junkers' subject peasants paid them fuller compensation for emancipation than the West Elbian landlords collected. Nevertheless, the present Chapter will offer an example, drawn from East Elbian Brandenburg, of successful peasant resistance to heightened seigneurial demands. The analysis will show that, in the villages of the noble estate of Stavenow, the subject farmers' efforts at self-defence could indeed shield them from degradation of their circumstances, while simultaneously compelling improving landlords to intensify capital investment and rely increasingly on wage labour.

This result demonstrates concretely the connection Wernicke posited between peasant protest and capitalist development in estate agriculture. But it contradicts his view, shared by Harnisch and the other historians discussed above, that the East Elbian peasantry — and especially the large majority among them with limited tenurial rights — could not effectively resist the seigneurial powers of landlords fully determined to heap new burdens on their subjects' backs.[19] In its conclusion this paper will present some of the grounds for regarding the case studied here as representative of a far wider wave of East Elbian manor/village conflict in the half-century after 1763. If the pattern that prevailed at Stavenow reflected a fundamental trend in Brandenburg-Prussia, the crisis of the old regime will appear in a different light. Peasant protest, no longer only a symptom of the crisis of transition, will emerge as one of its principal causes. The subject peasants will be seen to have played a weighty part in their own emancipation.

II

Stavenow lay near the River Elbe in the Prignitz district of Brandenburg, north-west of Berlin (See Figures 3.1 and 3.2). In the second half of the eighteenth century its four demesne farms, including the home farm of the Stavenow manor house, had some 3300 acres under the plough. Its meadows and pastures spanned 1400 acres, and its forests another 1700 acres.[20] In seven villages the Stavenow Junkers claimed labour services and other seigneurial rents from 60 large and 25 small peasant farms. The largeholding or full peasants (*Vollbauern*) owed the manor in a few cases two but in most cases three days of weekly labour with a team of horses, together with yearly corn rents, payable in bushels of rye, of varying but mostly modest extent. The smallholders (known as *Kossäten*) served three days weekly in manual labour, and the more well-endowed with land among them also paid a not inconsiderable corn rent.[21] The Stavenow landlords levied rents in labour and cash on other smaller villagers, but the full peasants' and smallholders' weekly manorial service (*Hofdienst*) was the jewel in their seigneurial crown. It was by their subject farmers' human

Figure 3.1: East Elbian Germany in the Late Eighteenth Century

Figure 3.2: The Altmark and Mittelmark Districts of Brandenburg

muscle and horsepower that the Junkers expected their broad manorial fields to be cultivated and their harvests hauled to market. In return the full peasants lived from the yields of their own farms, which they occupied by hereditary tenure without the right to mortgage or sell them (see note 19). These holdings, like those of most other full peasants in Brandenburg, comprised some 75–85 acres of arable within an unenclosed three-field system, together with shares of communally-held meadows, pastures and woods. The smallholders' lands lay separate from the full peasants' and, though varying in size, amounted to no more than half of a full holding.[22]

Stavenow was larger than most Junker properties but in other respects, and especially in the manorial obligations of its subject farmers, it was a typical Brandenburg estate. In 1717 it passed into the hands of Lieutenant-Colonel Andreas Joachim von Kleist, a career officer who nevertheless took an active interest in its management until his death in 1738. For the next 20 years his widow ably supervised the estate officials while raising to maturity 10 sons, nine of whom joined the officer corps, and five daughters, all of whom married advantageously. Following her death in 1758, in the midst of the Seven Years' War, her sons agreed that the estate should fall undivided to one of their numbers, Major Friedrich Joachim von Kleist. The Major, after retiring from the army, took command of Stavenow in 1763. He and his brothers had accepted an appraisal setting the net value of the estate's fixed capital, demesne production and seigneurial rights, including peasant rents, at 127,483 pre-war Taler. The inheritance settlement praised Friedrich Joachim's willingness to take possession of Stavenow as a 'brotherly deed'. So it was, for the Major thereby assumed responsibility for paying out at 5 per cent interest from Stavenow's income and his own capital each of his nine brothers' 10 per cent shares in the estate. At their mother's death Stavenow was free of debt, but Friedrich Joachim acquired it heavily mortgaged.[23]

Undaunted, he set out to improve the profitability of his patrimony. In this he followed the example of his parents, who had raised the estate's capitalised value from its purchase price in 1717 of 54,000 Taler to the 127,483 Taler the brothers agreed it was worth in 1763. The gain had been largely real, not inflationary. Average grain prices at Stavenow rose only slightly between 1717 and 1763, while the currency depreciated by only 17 per cent. The elder Kleists had replaced at their two largest demesne farms the

Table 3.1: Demesne Farming at Stavenow, 1694–1808: Grain Sowings and Sales

Year	Rye bushels sown[1]	Rye bushel price[2]	Rye marketable surplus[3]	Barley bushels sown[1]	Barley bushel price[2]	Barley marketable surplus[3]	Oats bushels sown[1]	Oats bushel price[2]	Oats marketable surplus[3]	Sum of Rye, Barley and Oats bushels sown	Sum of Rye, Barley and Oats bushel price[4]	Sum of Rye, Barley and Oats marketable surplus
1694	576	12	288	432	10	180	144	4	24	1152	10	492
1717	576	16	384	252	14	147	408	10	170	1236	14	701
1763	1163	17	824	349	16	233	561	9	210	2073	15	1266
1805[5]	1296	24	3426	168	20	410	2040	16	3297	3504	20	7133

Notes:

1. Current average production levels, as established in estate appraisals. Otto Behre set the following weights of the eighteenth-century Berlin bushel (*Scheffel*): rye — 45 kg; barley — 38 kg; oats — 25.5 kg. *Geschichte der Statistik in Brandenberg-Preussen* (Berlin, 1905), p. 277. William Abel's figures on the Berlin bushel in the year 1800 are lower: rye — 40 kg; barley — 32.5 kg; oats — 24 kg. *Agrarkrisen und Agrarkonjunktur* (Hamburg, 1978), p. 291.

2. In current Groschen, as fixed by estate appraisals.

3. In current Taler, as computed in estate appraisals (1 Taler = 24 Groschen).

4. Average of rye, barley and oats prices, to the nearest Groschen.

5. Figures assume that the seed yield ratios at the smallest of the four demesne farms, leased in 1808 to a tenant farmer, equalled the known average ratios of the three demesne farms under direct seigneurial management.

Sources: GStA. Stavenow, No. 282 (1694): No. 240 (1717); No. 259 (1763): No. 39 (1808).

ancient three-field system with an 11-course rotation of grain crops and pasturage (*Koppelwirtschaft*) that dispensed altogether with fallowing. They also settled a new village of eight full peasants and eight smallholders on the long-uncultivated site of a village deserted in the late Middle Ages. Here their gain lay not only in the colonists' labour services and rents, but in the acquisition of a new demesne farm on the seigneurial share of the new village's fields. By these means they increased, between 1717 and 1763, the sum of rye, barley and oats sown annually by 60 per cent (see Table 3.1). Having also improved their pasturage, they could expand their dairy herd by more than half and thus, since dairy prices rose by a quarter in the period, they doubled their income from this important branch of stock-raising alone.[24]

The cash accounts of the Stavenow estate survive from eight of the years between 1746 and 1759. They show that, on average, cereal cultivation, stock-raising and peasant rents and other seigneurial levies produced a gross yearly income of 5717 Taler. But the annual sum of labour and production costs averaged 1764 Taler, or 31 per cent of income.[25] Under this heading fell the wages in cash and kind as well as the boarding costs of more than 30 regularly employed estate officials, foremen and manorial farm servants. Here too were reckoned the estate's payments in cash and kind to seasonally hired threshers and day labourers, as well as the expenses of seed, livestock, hardware and the 28 draught horses kept for work on the demesne fields. Altogether, wages of all kinds each year cost the estate 1236 Taler, while other operating expenses averaged 528 Taler, of which 313 Taler were spent on the seigneurial draught horses alone.

How did Stavenow's wages bill and production costs compare with the value to the estate of the subject peasants' labour services and other rents? From the beginning of the eighteenth century, nearly all the full peasants faced the choice of serving three days weekly or paying a yearly commutation rent (*Dienstgeld*) of 20 Taler. Most served two days and paid 6.66 Taler for the third day. But in the appraisal of 1760/63, the Kleists agreed that, together with the commutation payments, the labour services were worth only 15 Taler a year, 'because there are many deficiencies' in their performance.[26] Combining this scaled-down assessment of the labour services with the market value in 1763 of the subject farmers' corn rents produces a sum of 1556 Taler, representing the monetarised equivalent of the landed peasantry's principal obligations to their landlords. This credit was almost exactly offset by the average debit of 1549 Taler the estate actually expended in the 1740s and 1750s on wages and manorial teams. In effect, what the Kleists gained in servile dues they spent again on operating costs.

The appraisal of 1760/63 acknowleded this unsatisfactory state of affairs in its estimate of Stavenow's marketable grain surplus. An 11-year average produced seed yield ratios of no more than 1:3.5 for rye and oats, and 1:4 for barley. Reserving 'one kernel' as seed for the next sowing left only one for sale, since wage payments in cash were high, while the grain consumed by the manorial officials and farm servants and as fodder amounted alone to a full kernel. Consequently, the rule of thumb that one kernel represented seed corn, one kernel operating costs, and the remainder profit did not apply.[27] In other words, Stavenow's wages bill and operating expenses were more than half again higher than they should have been. No wonder that Major von Kleist, as he sought to pay his debts and raise his revenues, was tempted to correct the 'deficiencies' of his subject farmers' labour services. To satisfy his brothers' most pressing financial claims and to bring new land under the plough, he began clearing part of the Stavenow forest and selling the timber. In 1766 he commanded his full peasants to haul the wood to the Elbe, 15 miles distant, during their regular weekly manorial service. The farmers refused, charging Kleist with an illegal innovation that would exhaust their horses.[28]

So began an embittered, sporadically violent conflict between the Major and his subject peasants that soon widened into a dispute encompassing virtually the whole range of his claims upon their labour and obedience. At first Kleist tried to enforce his will through his seigneurial court, which ruled in 1766 against the peasants. But still they refused to comply, despite court-ordered impoundment of the 'ringleader's' horses, short-term imprisonments at the Stavenow jail, and beatings, some of which the peasants later charged Kleist with having illegally ordered before the seigneurial court pronounced sentence.[29] His extra-economic coercive powers having failed him, Kleist appealed to the High Court of Brandenburg (*Kammergericht*) in Berlin. The peasants hired a lawyer and a series of lawsuits adjudicated in the royal courts ensued that lasted until 1797. During these 30 years of litigation, the subject farmers refused — for the most part successfully, though often illegally — to carry out the new tasks Kleist sought to impose upon them.

The most important of the strictly economic points he tried to gain in his long struggle with his subjects added up to a dangerous assault. Had he carried the day, it would have shifted many heavy costs of the expanding manorial economy at Stavenow onto the peasantry's shoulders. Because the peasants' labour service commutation fees were fixed by long usage, while the value of payments in kind to manorial servants and the cost of horsepower were steadily rising, Kleist tried to abolish commutation payments and so compel the farmers actually to serve the three full days. Custom permitted service with a team to be performed by a farmer's son or servant alone, except in ploughing and manure-hauling, when two workers were needed. But Kleist demanded the farmer report in person, together with his son or servant, on all days of manorial service. Formerly, the full peasants had served no more than five full days during the manorial rye harvest. Now, as Stavenow's arable expanded, Kleist tried to extend their harvest obligation, without relaxing his demands on them at other seasons. On the contrary, he sought to lengthen the working day and eliminate their slow-footed malingering. 'The peasant', Kleist sermonised, 'does nothing from love or virtue, at least not in manorial service'.[30]

Kleist struggled above all to widen his claims on the full peasants' horsepower so as to reduce his heavy expenditures on manorial teams and occasional hired carters. He tried unrelentingly to increase the number and distance of the peasants' transports of manorial grain, while pressing new cartage on them in connection with his building projects. For other jobs he ordered them to report for work with larger than customary wagons. He even goaded the cottagers into a lawsuit against him by raising new demands on their modest teams.[31] As the conflict wore on, both sides grew more intransigent and radical in their objectives. Kleist's efforts to force long-distance lumber haulage on the peasants stood at centre stage until 1771. By then he had gained three decisions in his favour in the *Kammergericht*, which ordered the peasants to perform the hauls pending their successive appeals. Yet they consistently baulked, despite the jailing of their leaders for terms of several weeks in 1769 and again in 1771. But then, later in 1771, the Royal Court of Appeal (*Ober-Appellations-Gericht*), the final legal power above the *Kammergericht*, ruled definitively against Major von Kleist.[32]

This last-ditch victory of the peasants, which Kleist called 'miraculous', stiffened their resistance to his demands for new grain cartage, construction work haulage, and harvest labour.[33] This led the *Kammergericht* in 1775 to despatch a mediator to Stavenow, whose job was to negotiate a comprehensive settlement. The peasants proving refractory, the court pronounced a compromise by fiat, but the peasants ignored it. In 1777, the *Kammergericht* could offer Kleist no more support than the advice that he should hire additional police officials, and himself enforce its rulings. But Kleist's judge replied, in a proposal that enforcement be entrusted to the Prignitz sheriff (*Landreiter*):

> It does no good to try to hold these stormy people to their obligations by imprisoning them [at Stavenow]. They just sit in jail for a while, letting their farms go to ruin, and then they carry on with their insubordination as before. And there is no end of this in sight.[34]

In 1785, Kleist was still complaining that the full peasants refused the long-distance grain hauls long since ruled enforceable by the *Kammergericht*. Moreover, when in 1780 he ordered them to pay the labour costs of building a new barn for one of the village sextons, they declined, pleading poverty, but more likely in order to flout his powers of church patronage. Another lawsuit flared up during which, in the years 1781–85, the full peasants withheld payment of their labour service commutation fees, depriving Kleist of an income of more than 1000 Taler (although the arrears were later paid).[35] He tried to quell this rent strike by clapping three of its leaders in irons. But they broke out of the ramshackle Stavenow dungeon and rode to Berlin, delivering the irons to the *Kammergericht*. While the High Court later ruled that Kleist had incarcerated his subjects without a proper court order, it proceeded itself to sentence the escapees to brief jail terms for their flight.[36] The Stavenow farmers' refusal to pay the old-established labour service commutation fee suggests that, after 20 years of defiance, they had decided to take the offensive with the aim of reducing the rents they had paid before 1763. Thus, by the early 1780s Kleist's relations with his peasants had escalated into a duel of litigation in which both combatants sought to alter the pre-existing system of rents and labour services in their own favour.

In these same years, a rising flood of manor/village lawsuits and sporadic local uprisings was engulfing the Silesian countryside. In

1783 Friedrich II ordered the provincial bureaucracy to draw up registers (*Urbaria*) for each seigneurial jurisdiction, in which all peasant labours and rents, together with the Junkers' obligations towards their subjects, were to be unambiguously fixed once and for all. In 1784 he extended this policy to Brandenburg 'to prevent and redress the numerous lawsuits and grievances between landlords and their subjects'.[37] The Stavenow farmers immediately petitioned the government for an *Urbarium*, goading Kleist to write an irritated letter to the Crown.

Since the subject farmers' labour services and dues are already fixed, and old estate registers exist in which they are written down, the peasants' only motive in calling for an *Urbarium* was to gain advantages for themselves in the course of its formulation, in which, however, they will not succeed.

Kleist himself had decided not to oppose the *Urbarium*, 'only to avoid drawing upon myself the suspicion that I had set myself against a policy Your Royal Majesty intends to carry out'.[38] In 1790, six years after its appointment, the Stavenow *Urbarium* commission completed its work. In 191 paragraphs it had defined the reciprocal obligations of village and estate 'for all time'. But neither Kleist nor the peasants accepted all the commission's formulations. In 1797 the *Kammergericht* pronounced judgment on the disputed points, compelling both parties finally to sign the revised *Urbarium* into law. The armistice so concluded survived Kleist's death in 1803, though not for long.[39]

The *Urbarium* laid to rest the angry disputes sparked by Kleist's efforts to intensify his subject farmers' labour services. It fixed their hours of work at the manor, defining the extent of a day's labour at their various jobs in the fields. It regulated minutely the vexed question of cartage, specifying what goods they were obliged to haul, the size of the loads, the distance and frequency of the transports, and the time off in lieu from regular manorial service they accrued in making long hauls. These were terms the peasants could accept because they upheld the principle that their regular manorial service should not consume more than two full work days a week, while allowing them, as before, to commute the third day's labour into cash at the rate set at the beginning of the century. The peasants had, it is true, tried during the negotiations to shake off the obligation to serve or, alternatively, to pay for the third day.

But Kleist's ancient legal claims were too strong and his subjects had to concede defeat in their strike of 1781–85 against the third day's commutation fee. To the Major this signified merely the restoration of order. The *Urbarium* had improved within limits his exploitation of his farmers' horsepower, but not in the form of the rent increase he had tried to impose since the 1760s. Instead, he was obliged to trade one claim on his subjects' regular manorial service for another, while translating his demand for unlimited service in construction work and harvesting into four and five days, respectively, of yearly service.

Worse still, the *Urbarium* compelled Kleist to acknowledge that his village adversaries' labour services and dues were now permanently fixed. He had striven to escape this conclusion by insisting during the negotiations that, while the rents of his present tenants and their heirs might not be raised, he had the right to set the obligations of new tenants taking over one of the farms in the villages covered by the *Urbarium* as high as he chose. To make such an eventuality more likely, Kleist also sought to strengthen his right to evict his present tenants. At Stavenow this had been a very rare procedure, which required proof of incompetence (*liederliche Wirtschaft*), demonstrated by a subject farmer's incapacity under normal circumstances to render his dues and services and support his household. A farmer facing eviction (*Exmission*) could appeal against it to a higher court, requiring his landlord to await its verdict on the correctness of the seigneurial court's judgment before vacating the farm. Kleist now claimed the power of eviction in advance of the appeal, so cancelling the right of succession of the deposed farmer's children and collateral heirs and freeing him to settle a new peasant at a new level of rent.[40] In these proposals, Kleist aimed to undermine his subjects' hereditary tenures, the legal source of their powers of resistance to his seigneurial will. By a piecemeal policy of eviction he could replace his refractory peasants with a degraded tenantry, nullifying the *Urbarium* in the process. Inevitably, the *Kammergericht* threw Kleist's aggressive initiatives out of court. But that he launched them at all measures his failure since 1763 to have his way with his subjects.

III

The Major's economic stewardship of the Stavenow estate was

nevertheless strikingly successful. After his death in 1803 his surviving brothers decided, after several years of legal wrangling with his widow, to sell the estate, since they could not afford to assert their right to buy out her claims and keep Stavenow themselves. In 1808 the influential, though soon to be toppled, minister of state and director of the corporate nobility of Brandenburg, Baron Otto Carl Friedrich von Voss, agreed to purchase the estate, taking it under his direct administration in the summer 1809. This acquisition cost him 280,855 Taler, Stavenow's capitalised value as assessed in 1808. This sum represented an increase, at constant currency values, of 120 per cent since 1763.[41]

The appraisal of 1808 surveyed the estate as Kleist left it. In the decades after 1763 he had separated his two still-unenclosed demesne farms from the three-field system in which they had been cultivated together with peasant land. He then adopted improved rotations on all his arable, and so raised his average yields of rye and oats, his main crops, by 40 per cent and more on his better soils. He increased his annual sowings by nearly three-quarters, in response to a price rise registered in the Stavenow appraisals of 1763 and 1808 at 41 per cent for rye, 25 per cent for barley and 180 per cent for oats.[41] Higher yields, heavier sowings and rising prices combined to multiply the estate's average net profit from cereal cultivation, the source of half the estate's annual earnings, nearly sixfold, from 1266 to 7133 Taler. Not content with this, Kleist built up his brewery and distillery to the point where, if grain prices sagged, he could sell as much as one-third of his rye and barley as beer and schnaps.

Because of rising livestock prices, Kleist's net profits on his sizeable, but numerically stable herds of dairy cattle and sheep rose nearly 60 per cent between 1763 and 1808. He could have earned more from stock-raising if he had not supplemented the 28 work horses the estate had kept since before 1763 with 26 plough oxen.[43] This was a heavy production cost forced upon him by his full peasants' refusal to expend more of their horsepower in manorial service. From 1763 the estate employed eight men to drive and tend the horses at the four demesne farms. But three new manorial farm servants were needed to work the oxen, while Kleist's expanded cereal production required him to hire two new field foremen (*Statthälter*) as well. By 1809, among the 54 employees on the payroll of the four demesne farms there were 3 bailiffs, 3 foremen, 13 drivers and ploughmen, 7 animal herdsmen, 6 female farm servants, 3 dairymen working with hired hands, a forester with 2 assistants, a brewer, a gardener and a hunter. In 1808/9 the cost to the landlord of this labour force included large quantities of the estate's produce and a separate herd of 30 dairy cows for the workers' and manorial kitchens. Beyond this, the estate paid out wages of nearly 1350 Taler annually, payments in grain worth 434 Taler, and many other types of wages in kind.[44] Kleist's total wages bill at the beginning of the nineteenth century cannot be precisely quantified. In cash and grain allotments alone, it doubled during his years at Stavenow. But the points to stress here are, first, that rising production costs, including wages, did not prevent him from doubling the estate's average annual profits and so also its market value. Second, his investments in draught animals and the wages of permanent manorial workers resulted in large measure from his failure to press the full peasantry more completely into his service. Third, these investments having once been made, the operation of the demesne farms became more self-sufficient.

To meet his need for labour, Kleist not only hired new supervisors and manorial workers, he also greatly increased his supply of seasonal manual labour by adding seven new families of freely contracted day-labourers (*Tagelöhner*) to the eight households already settled at Stavenow in 1763.[45] In the winter these workers threshed, against payment in shares, the Major's ever-heavier harvests. At other seasons they did, among other tasks, the work the full peasants and smallholders absolved, against Kleist's will, through commutation payments. The day-labourers were also needed in the increasing harvest work that he had initially tried to add to his subject farmers' manorial service. In 1763, the day-labourers paid a yearly cash rent for their houses, gardens and grazing rights, averaging 9.5 Taler per household. They also all rendered the manor six days of unpaid harvest work. Beyond that, the Stavenow estate had first call on their labour, which it hired for cash and/or wages in kind. But Kleist drastically rewrote their contracts, so that by 1808 they each owed 5 Taler yearly for garden land and grazing, but instead of paying house rents they each performed 65 days of compulsory unpaid labour (excluding threshing, ploughing and other heavy work). At a minor loss of cash income, Kleist had increased his annual supply of unpaid manual labour from 48 to 975 days.[46]

Paradoxically, then, he had been more successful in wringing advantages for himself from his day labourers than from his subject peasants, although the cost to him of freely contracted labour was still substantial. But, if this outcome advanced the self-sufficiency of the manorial economy, neither Kleist nor his successor Voss wished to lose the full peasants' obligatory service with teams of horses. Between 1763 and 1803 the assessed value of the Stavenow full peasants' yearly manorial service rose by two-thirds, reflecting the rising market price of horsepower in those years. For this reason above all, the appraisal of 1808 registered the peasants' compulsory labour at a sum representing 14 per cent of the estate's yearly net profit. Yet in 1763 this figure had stood at 21 per cent. The declining importance of non-wage labour to the estate's mounting profitability meant that Kleist, by his capital investments and ever greater reliance on freely-contracted labour, had brought the manorial economy to the threshold of full-scale capitalist production techniques by the eve of the Prussian peasant emancipation. His subject peasants' refractoriness, no less than this search for profit, pushed him in this direction.[47]

To complete the transition, it was necessary to break the Stavenow landlords' lingering dependence on their full peasants' horsepower. This was a blow the peasants themselves soon struck. In the summer of 1808 they stopped rendering labour services and dues, pleading economic exhaustion resulting from the requisition of horses and other exactions of the war of 1806 and the French occupation of Brandenburg that followed. The *Kammergericht* ruled against the peasants, but they refused to comply. In mid-1809 Voss offered to accept commutation fees for all labour service for a period of one year. Unmollified, in December his subjects sent deputies to the town of Pritzwalk, where they joined representatives of many other villages in proclaiming a rent strike throughout the Prignitz.[48] Bassewitz, at the time a high Brandenburg official, later wrote that the local authorities (*Kreis-Direktorium*), by unspecified means, peacefully contained this movement.[49] At Stavenow, the threat of military quartering forced the peasants of one striking village back to manorial service in 1810, but the next year they began paying full commutation fees instead, as the other striking villages had formally agreed to do in 1810. In fact, the two Stavenow villages with the largest numbers of full peasants paid nothing between 1808 and 1817/18, paying off their arrears only after they had negotiated with Voss the terms of the emancipation at Stavenow.[50] For most of the Stavenow peasants, the centuries-old era of labour services at the manor — the heaviest burden of

serfdom — ended in 1808. This happened in spite of the protests of
Voss and his head bailiff, who recognised that a full commutation
fee of 20 Taler, even if actually paid, was no substitute for a full
peasant's labour.[51] After the publication of the Regulation Law of
14 September 1811, which allowed the peasantry of Brandenburg-
Prussia to acquire their farms in freehold and liquidate all feudal
rents upon payment of compensation to their landlords, 'the disposition to want to be free', as Voss's bailiff wrote to him, 'is mani-
festing itself everywhere'.[52] The Stavenow farmers petitioned for
regulation, and in 1812 Voss opened the negotiations.

By 1820 nearly all of Voss's peasants had bought themselves out.
A detailed analysis of the negotiations would require a separate
essay. Here it suffices to say that, while some full peasants and
smallholders paid Voss his compensation in cash, most surrendered
a quarter or a third of their farmland to him. All peasants with
arable holdings of any size gained freeholds. Despite land cessions,
the full peasants emerged from the regulation process with farms of
60 acres and more, and the better-off smallholders with 25 acres of
arable and some meadowland and pasturage as well. These were
holdings capable of self-sufficiency. If some had shrunk in size, they
had also been shorn of one-third of their pre-regulation tax burden
and they no longer needed to reserve part of their manpower and
horsepower for labour at the manor. There is no evidence that the
Stavenow peasants believed they could throw off their old obligations at no cost to themselves. No doubt the Junkers' claims to compensation were shabby. The social and political costs of the enlargement of their estates during and after the peasant emancipation rose
steadily to 1945. Yet the compensation the peasants paid did not
ruin them. On the contrary, at Stavenow the regulated farmers
gained from the emancipation personal freedom and self-sufficient
landholdings of indubitable value.[53]

IV

How representative of manor/village relations throughout Brandenburg-Prussia was the final half-century of serfdom at
Stavenow? In the Prignitz district the frequency of lawsuits over
labour services and communal usages within the three-field system
led the corporate nobility (*Ritterschaft*) as early as 1754 to petition
Friedrich II for permission to separate and enclose their lands

unilaterally, whether the peasants agreed or not. The king assented, and by 1810 virtually all the private estates and royal demesnes in the Prignitz had withdrawn from the three-field system, a process normally accompanied by adoption of fallow-free cereal pasturage rotations and division of ancient grazing commons between manor and village.[54] Some of the Prignitz nobility subverted Friedrich II's colonisation programme by settling day labourers as small-scale cottagers (*Büdner*) on ancient deserted peasant holdings, illegally incorporating most of the land intended for full peasant colonisation into their demesne farms.[55] In 1765, and again in 1770, the corporate nobility sought to degrade the tenures of the numerous Prignitz peasants who possessed full property in their holdings, arguing unsuccessfully for a redefinition of the common law before the Justice Ministry.[56]

Despite such seigneurial aggressiveness, the Prignitz peasantry, as at Stavenow, held their ground. In the second half of the eighteenth century many were financially strong enough to pay half or full labour service commutation fees. Others petitioned for *Urbaria*, ensnaring their Junkers in lengthy negotiations and lawsuits.[57] After the Thirty Years' War, and again at the beginning of the eighteenth century, the Prignitz peasantry had organised regional strikes against seigneurial efforts to exact heavier feudal rents.[58] The movement of 1809–10, which in all probability produced a widespread conversion of labour services into full commutation fees, offers more evidence that the Stavenow peasants' refractoriness was a regional trait. Among its results, again as at Stavenow, was increased hiring of freely-contracted labour on the noble estates. Between 1725 and 1801 the rural population of the Prignitz doubled, while the number of peasant holdings, excluding smallholders, remained roughly constant. In the same years the ranks of landless labourers, dependent primarily on the large estates for hire, swelled sixfold.[59] Finally, like their brethren at Stavenow, the Prignitz peasants petitioned promptly for regulation under the law of 1811. Harnisch found that liquidation of compensation obligations in lump-sum cash settlements — a measure of peasant creditworthiness, if not of savings — occurred 'to an astonishing degree' both in the Prignitz and the neighbouring district of Ruppin.[60]

Elsewhere in Brandenburg the Junkers were also busy after 1763 improving their estates. By the year 1800 an unenclosed demesne farm was becoming a rarity and the employment of wage labour was widespread, either in place of commuted peasant manorial services or, as at Stavenow, as a supplement to the peasants' old-established duties.[61] Of Silesia, Ziekursch wrote that the landlords' 'own draught teams, their life-long manorial servants, and the day labourers settled on the estates' gave the noble demesne farms at the beginning of the nineteenth century 'a thoroughly modern stamp'.[62] In East Prussia, the Junkers commuted labour services into cash and turned to wage labour on a large scale.[63] In Pomerania, too, the Junkers enclosed and rationalised their estates.[64] Even in such regions as the Uckermark in Brandenburg, where peasant tenures were very weak and labour services were, according to local custom, unlimited and therefore redifinable at the Junkers' will, the landlords separated their holdings from their peasants' fields and worked them increasingly with hired labour.[65] No doubt many Junkers clung to the old-fashioned system of unenclosed demesnes worked as exclusively as possible by their subject peasants.[66] Yet the historical literature supports the conclusion that throughout the East Elbian provinces the agronomic improvements, the move to wage labour and the capital investment characteristic of Stavenow represented the dominant trend of estate agriculture in the years after 1763, if not before. As at Stavenow, so elsewhere the transformation of manorial production occurred amidst a rising clamour of conflict between peasants and lords over labour dues and other seigneurial rents. The topography of this antagonism remains to be drawn precisely, but its pervasiveness, especially in Brandenburg and Silesia, is well attested in the literature from which this Chapter has drawn.

It is revealing that in 1787 Friedrich Wilhelm II, soon after ascending the throne, attempted to halt the work of Friedrich II's *Urbarium* commission, saying that its creation 'has led a good part of the peasantry to the wild delusion [*irrigen Wahn*] that the Departed Royal Majesty intended by it to abolish manorial labour services.' False as this was, an open announcement that the *Urbarium* commission was to cease work would cause the peasantry to become 'very ill-humoured, because they would think themselves robbed of the hope of exemption from labour service.' Accordingly, the *Urbarium* programme should simply be quietly shelved. But the king's ministers Hoym and Danckelmann soon persuaded him to rescind his decision, in all likelihood because the *Urbaria* seemed precisely the best way to restrain the peasants' ill-humour.[67]

After the military defeat of 1806, peasant protest pushed the government further down the path of peasant emancipation upon which Stein's ministry had taken the first steps in 1807. Rent strikes of serious proportions broke out in Silesia in 1808, and again in 1811.[68] In November 1809 the Governor (*Oberpräsident*) of Brandenburg, returning from a tour of his province and of neighbouring Pomerania, advocated rapid abolition of labour services, 'for they are performed extremely badly and unwillingly'.[69] Already in 1807 the East Prussian corporate nobility described their subject peasants as 'restless'. In 1813 the official in charge of peasant regulation in Pomerania rejected the idea, aired in conservative circles, that the nobility should not be forced to negotiate a liquidation of feudal rents against their will. The peasants were 'pressing mightily for the speediest regulation possible'. The farmer under arms in the war against Napoleon might, upon his return, fix his weapons upon 'the enemy of his bliss [*Glückseligkeit*]' at home.[70] In December 1812 the peasant deputies in the government's consultative assembly composed a denunciation of seigneurial abuses exclaiming that, 'exposed to such illegal treatment, the peasantry's hatred of the estate owners has grown extraordinarily, indeed has now become almost universal.'[71]

The extent of peasant turbulence after 1806, like its influence on the political history of the emancipation, should not be exaggerated, although both questions deserve further study. It was probably no less important that the Junkers resigned themselves as readily as they did to the loss of the compulsory labour, and especially of the horsepower, of their peasant subjects. Klaus Vetter has shown that, in the *Landtag* assemblies of 1809, the corporate nobility of Brandenburg voiced no principled opposition to the abolition of the full peasants' feudal rents and the conversion of their farms into freeholds. What interested the Brandenburg Junkers was the sum of their compensation for surrendering their seigneurial privileges.[72] As the landlords' ability to compel the full peasants actually and conscientiously to perform their weekly labour services weakened, their claims to those services diminished in value. For the peasants' commutation fees were fixed by custom or even, as at Stavenow, by urbarial law at rates far below the actual cost of the commuted work. Because a full peasant at Stavenow had for a century exercised the option of paying 20 Taler yearly in place of his three days of weekly manorial service, the estate appraisal of 1808 could rate the value of all his dues and rents no higher than 28.5 Taler. But in 1814–15 Voss and his legal counsel reckoned that a freely contracted day's labour with a team of horses cost ½ a Taler. To replace a full peasant's weekly obligation alone would, accordingly, require a yearly outlay of 78 Taler, nearly four times the commutation fee.[73]

If the Junkers gained little more from the full peasants than the commutation payment, it was better to exchange their seigneurial claims for compensation in cash and/or land as they did after 1811.[74] Here is perhaps the best measure of the significance of the peasantry's resistance to new seigneurial demands on their labour in the half-century after 1763. By holding their ground (or giving away as little as possible) the peasants forced the Junkers to foot the bill of expanding their demesne production. The result at estates like Stavenow was that non-wage labour became an economic asset of rapidly shrinking worth. When, after 1806, political circumstances and, here and there, peasant protest compelled its abolition, the improving landlords among the Junkers needed only to increase the numbers of manorial draught horses and freely contracted workers they had already been obliged to employ before the end of serfdom.[75] At the same time, the peasants' defence of their farms against new burdens of seigneurial rent secured the economic margin that enabled them to pay commutation fees. No less important, they had money to spare for the legal fees they incurred in their courtroom duels with the Junkers.

In the summer of 1809, when Baron von Voss ceremonially took possession of Stavenow, his assembled subjects swore the ancient oath to be 'faithful, obedient, and subject' to him, whereupon he treated them to drinks.[76] A few months later, in December, they banded against him in a regional peasant movement. Voss demanded that they return the next spring to actual performance of manorial service. When the time came, they did not report for work. In June 1810 Voss's bailiff, appealing in court for police action against them, declared that Voss had ordered him to do so, 'especially since since leniency only strengthens their unruliness [*Widerspenstigkeit*], which by now has become second nature to them.'[77]

Notes

The research underpinning this Chapter was supported by grants from the University of California, Davis, from the National Endowment for the Humanities, and especially, from the Humboldt-Stiftung. To these organisations, and to the helpful staff of the Geheimes Staatsarchiv in West Berlin, I extend my thanks.

1. 'Publicandum, wegen Bestraffung der muthwilligen Querulanten', 12 July 1787, *Novum Corpus Constitutionum Prussico-Brandenburgensium*, Vol. VIII (1791), No. LXXV, 1497–1508.

2. Henri Brunschwig, *La crise de l'état prussien et la génèse de la mentalité romantique* (Paris, 1947); Günter Vogler and Klaus Vetter, *Preussen. Von den Anfängen bis zur Reichsgründung* (Berlin, 1979), p. 97.

3. Otto Hintze, *Die Hohenzollern und Ihr Werk* (Berlin, 1916), Ch. 8; idem., 'Preussische Reformbestrebungen vor 1806', in *Regierung und Verwaltung* (Göttingen, 1967); Friedrich Meinecke, *Das Zeitalter der deutschen Erhebung 1795–1815* (Leipzig, 1906), Ch. 2; Hans Rosenberg, *Bureaucracy, Aristocracy, and Autocracy. The Prussian Experience 1660–1815* (Boston, 1966), Chs. 8–9. In his *Geschichte der deutschen Agrarverfassung* (Stuttgart, 1963), Friedrich Lütge offers a political interpretation that dispenses with the concept of crisis: after 1807 the Prussian state abolished the eighteenth-century regime of Junker manors worked by servile peasants because it conflicted with the bureaucracy's and progressive landlords' notions of economic rationality. High above the peasantry's head, one 'agrarian constitution' eclipsed another. See pp. 175–9.

4. Georg Friedrich Knapp, *Die Bauernfreiung und der Ursprung der Landarbeiter in den älteren Theilen Preussens*, (Munich and Leipzig, 1927, 2nd edn), I, 77.

5. Brunschwig, *op. cit.*, Ch. 7. Reinhardt Kosselleck, *Preussen zwischen Reform und Revolution* (Stuttgart, 1967), pp. 78–142; Hanna Schissler, *Preussische Agrargesellschaft im Wandel* (Göttingen, 1978), pp. 89–82; idem., 'Die Junker: Zur Sozialgeschichte und historischen Bedeutung der agrarischen Elite in Preussen', in Hans-Jürgen Puhle and Hans-Ulrich Wehler (eds.), *Preussen im Rückblick* (Göttingen, 1980), pp. 98–104; Christoph Dipper, *Die Bauernbefreiung in Deutschland 1790–1850* (Stuttgart, 1980), Ch. 1.

6. Knut Borchardt, 'Germany 1700–1914', in Carlo M. Cipolla (ed.), *The Fontana Economic History of Europe* (London, 1973), Vol. 4:1, pp. 85. Borchardt's judgement is shared by Wilhelm Abel, *Geschichte der deutschen Landwirtschaft* (Stuttgart, 1962), pp. 308 ff; Friedrich-Wilhelm Henning, *Dienste und Abgaben der Bauern im 18. Jahrhundert* (Stuttgart, 1969), pp. 169 ff; Robert A. Dickler, 'Organization and Change in Productivity in Eastern Prussia', in William N. Parker and Eric L. Jones, (eds.), *European Peasants and Their Markets* (Princeton, N.J., 1975), pp. 269–92. Fritz Martiny's influential work, *Die Adelsfrage in Preussen vor 1806 als politisches und soziales Problem* (Stuttgart, 1938), demonstrated the 'proletarianisation' of those among the *Junkers* nobility not secure in the possession of a landed estate or a high post in the government or the military. This aspect of the Prussian crisis underscores its social pervasiveness.

7. See Büsch's *Militärsystem und Sozialleben im alten Preussen 1713–1807* (Berlin, 1962), pp. 42, 47, 154 and passim. Abel and Henning also neglect the question of peasant protest. Robert Brenner's exaggerated emphasis upon feudal landlords' extra-economic coercive powers dovetails his sketchy remarks on the East Elbian German scene with the concept, here under discussion, of a crisis of decadence and heightened seigneurial exploitation of the peasantry ('The Agrarian Roots of European Capitalism', *Past and Present*, No. 97 (November 1982), pp. 66–7, 69–76).

8. On industry, see Horst Krüger, *Zur Geschichte der Manufakturen und der Manufakturarbeiter in Preussen* (Berlin, 1958); and the still useful work of Kurt Hinze, *Die Arbeiterfrage zu Beginn des modernen Kapitalismus in Brandenburg-Preussen 1685–1806* (Berlin, 1963 edn). On agriculture, see text and notes below.

9. Johannes Ziekursch, *Hundert Jahre schlesischer Agrargeschichte* (Breslau, 1927), passim.

10. Hartmut Harnisch, 'Die agrarpolitischen Reformmassnahmen der preussischen Staatsführung in dem Jahrzehnt vor 1806/07', *Jahrbuch für Wirtschaftsgeschichte* (1977), III, pp. 129–53.

11. Hartmut Harnisch, 'Vom Oktoberedikt des Jahres 1807 zur Deklaration von 1816. Problematik und Charakter der preussischen Agrarreformgesetzgebung zwischen 1807 und 1816', *Jahrbuch für Wirtschaftsgeschichte*, Sonderband (1978), p. 232. This important article supersedes Knapp's interpretation of the *Bauernbefreiung* in its political aspect.

12. Hans-Heinrich Müller, *Märkische Landwirtschaft vor den Agrarreformen von 1807. Entwicklungstendenzen des Ackerbaues in der zweiten Hälfte des 18. Jahrhunderts* (Potsdam, 1967), pp. 37–8, 53–62, 79 ff, 115 ff.

13. Brenner, *loc. cit.*, pp. 18, 34; Jerome Blum, *The End of the Old Order in Europe* (Princeton, N.J., 1978), p. 303, Ch. 15 and passim. Douglass C. North and Robert Paul Thomas, *The Rise of the Western World. A New Economic History* (Cambridge, 1973), Part III and passim.

14. Müller, *op. cit.*, 144 ff.

15. Kurt Wernicke, *Untersuchungen zu den niederen Formen des bäuerlichen Klassenkampfes im Gebiet der Gutsherrschaft*, Diss. Phil. (Humboldt Universität, Berlin, 1962).

16. Günther Franz, *Geschichte des deutschen Bauernstandes* (Stuttgart, 1970), p. 196; Vogler and Vetter, *op. cit.*, 97–8.

17. Hartmut Harnisch, 'Produktivkräfte und Produktionsverhältnisse in der Landwirtschaft der Magdeburger Börde von der Mitte des 18. Jahrhunderts bis zum Beginn des Zuckerrübenbaus in der Mitte der dreissiger Jahre des 19. Jahrhunderts', in Hans-Jürgen Rach and Bernhard Weissel (eds.), *Landwirtschaft und Kapitalismus: Zur Entwicklung der ökonomischen und sozialen Verhältnisse in der Magdeburger Börde vom Ausgang des 18. Jahrhunderts bis zum Ende des ersten Weltkrieges*, Vol. I Halbband (Berlin, 1978), pp. 108, 138, 156–9.

18. Harnisch, 'Oktoberedikt', *loc. cit.*, p. 232.

19. In 'Peasants and Markets' (Chapter 2 above), the chacteristically strong essay he contributes to the present volume, Harnisch underscores the importance which his earlier work ascribed to peasant protest as an indirect cause of the emancipation. His chief aim, however, is to show — as he does very well — that those peasants who prevailed in their resistance to new seigneurial impositions profited from their own heightened and increasingly lucrative production for the market. He confines the circle of such peasants to those with full property in their holdings (*Eigentümer* or *Erbbauern*). But, as he acknowledges, most full peasants (*Hufenbauern*) in Brandenburg and elsewhere in East Elbian Prussia possessed only a usufructuary (*lassitisches*) right to their holdings: after payment of seigneurial rent and royal taxes, the residual net product of their labour belonged to them, but they could not sell or mortgage their farms. To these East Elbian *Lassiten* or *Lassbauern* Harnisch's negative judgement, discussed in the text above, still applies.

Granting that the titles of the full proprietors were better than the tenures of the *Lassiten*, there was nevertheless a great difference, which Harnisch appears to neglect, between *hereditary* and *non-hereditary* usufructuary holdings. As Berthold has recently shown in a major re-evaluation of the statistical evidence, about half of all full peasants in Brandenburg were hereditary *Lassiten*, the type of peasant that will occupy centre stage in the text below. See Rudolf Berthold, 'Die Veränderungen im Bodeneigentum und in der Zahl der Bauernstellen, der Kleinstellen und der Rittergüter in den preussischen Provinzen Sachsen, Brandenburg und Pommern während der Durchführung der Agrarreformen des 19. Jahrhunderts', *Jahrbuch für Wirtschaftsgeschichte*, Sonderband (1978), pp. 10–116, and esp. 21–8. The reader of the present paper will see that tenants of such hereditary usufructuary holdings, even if not full proprietors, could very well defend themselves at law against their lords.

In my view, the weakness and vulnerability Harnisch ascribes to *all* usufructuary tenures should be assigned to those that were non-hereditary, which in 1816, according to Berthold, comprised only 10 per cent of all farms exceeding 7.5 hectares in size. The hereditary *Lassiten* should be reckoned as peasants able and willing to resist abusive seigneurial innovations. Together with the full proprietors, they represented 90 per cent of the *Hufenbauern* in Brandenburg. On legal distinctions among the peasantry, see Friedrich Grossmann, *Über die gutsherrlich-bäuerlichen Rechtsverhältnisse in der Mark Brandenburg vom 16. bis 18. Jahrhundert* (Leipzig, 1890).

20. Geheimes Staatsarchiv, West Berlin. Provinz Brandenburg, Rep. 37: Gutsherrschaft Stavenow (hereinafter cited as GStA. Stavenow), No. 258 (survey of 1809), ff. 9–10. The scholarly literature on Stavenow consists principally of the dissertation of Joachim Sack, *Die Herrschaft Stavenow* (Cologne and Graz, 1959). It offers a generally accurate account of the estate's ownership and organisational structure. But it does not present an economic analysis of the eighteenth- and early nineteenth-century estate accounts, nor does it plumb the depth of village/manor conflict after 1763. On these subjects, see the text below. On other questions relevant to the argument of the present paper, see William W. Hagen, 'How Mighty the Junkers? Peasant Rents and Seigneurial Profits in Sixteenth-Century Brandenburg', forthcoming in *Past and Present*; and idem., 'Working for the Junker: Real Wages of Manorial Labourers in Brandenburg, 1584–1810', forthcoming in *The Journal of Modern History*.

21. GStA. Stavenow, Nr. 259 (*Anschlag*, 1760/63) and No. 39 (*Specieller Anschlag*, May 1808), ff. 5–20.

22. Many of the farms in the Stavenow villages were surveyed during the peasant emancipation. See GStA. Stavenow, Nos. 441, 408, 198, 451, 428, 425. (1 hectare equals c. 2.5 acres.)

23. GStA. Stavenow, No. 259 (appraisal of 1760) and No. 58 (inheritance agreement of 1763, including revision of the 1760 appraisal in the light of 1763 commodity prices). Originally each of the brothers left 3000 Taler in the estate as shares in the *Lehn-Stamm* securing their rights of future inheritance, but in 1770 this arrangement was liquidated, so that Kleist was obliged to pay out the shares as well. No. 58, ff. 107–13.

24. Figures for 1717 from GStA. Stavenow, No. 240.

25. GStA. Stavenow, Nos. 265, 207, 208, 229, 270, 233, 262, 261, 237 (*Geldrechnungen*). During these years Kleist's personal household consumed products of the estate averaging 778 Taler in value annually. The estate accounts treat this consumption neither as a profit nor a loss.

26. GStA. Stavenow, No. 259, f. 9. The cottagers' labour services could be absolved by a commutation payment of 10 Taler. But the appraisal rated their actual annual value at 7.5 Taler.

27. GStA. Stavenow, No. 259, ff. 3–4.

28. GStA. Stavenow, No. 343, ff. 3–23.

29. Ibid., No. 343, 25–32, 53–83. ff. This volume contains the full record of Kleist's litigation with his subjects from 1766 to 1777.

30. Ibid., No. 343, f. 187. See also ff. 13–23.

31. GStA. Stavenow, No. 354. See also Nos. 573, 363, 424, 345, 355, 344, 334, 316.

32. The appellate court invoked the common or customary law of Brandenburg prohibiting cartage to market during regular manorial service of products, other than grain, intended for sale (*Kaufmannsgüter*). GStA. Stavenow, No. 343,

ff. 267–9. In its various rulings on the suits Kleist and his peasants brought before it, the *Kammergericht* exhibited a certain bias, where the law seemed open to interpretation, in favour of Kleist's seigneurial interests. But, as the dispute over lumberhauling shows, the Royal Court of Appeal could correct the bias. Undoubtedly, Friedrich II's legal reforms gave the peasants cheaper access to the higher courts and the chance of a fairer hearing. The connection between the reforms and manor/ village litigation deserves exploration, but cannot be pursued in the present essay. On legal developments, see Otto Hintze, 'Preussens Entwicklung zum Rechtsstaat', *Forschungen zur brandenburgischen und preussischen Geschichte*, Band 32 (1920), pp. 385–451; H. Weill, *Frederick the Great and Samuel von Cocceji* (Madison, Wisc., 1964); Friedrich Grossmann, *Über die gutsherrlich-bäuerlichen Rechtsverhältnisse in der Mark Brandenburg vom 16. bis 18. Jahrhundert* (Leipzig, 1890).

33. GStA. Stavenow, No. 343, ff. 260–2, 272.

34. Ibid., f. 344. See also Nos. 573, 363.

35. GStA. Stavenow, No. 719, ff. 71–5.

36. GStA. Stavenow, No. 340, passim.

37. K.O. of 11 September 1784, published in Rudolph Stadelmann, *Preussens Könige in ihrer Thätigkeit für die Landescultur, Vol. 11, Publicationen aus den K. Preussischen Staatsarchiven* (Leipzig, 1882), p. 619. See also Stadelmann, *op. cit.*, pp. 112–13. On Silesia, ibid., pp. 605–6, 621, 632; and Ziekursch, *op. cit.*, 206 ff. Frederick later decreed that.*Urbaria* were to be compiled in East Prussia, but the nobility of that province, like their brethren in Silesia, contrived to evade the order. See Stadelmann, *op. cit.*, pp. 637–8.

38. GStA. Stavenow, No. 719, f. 71.

39. GStA. Stavenow, No. 353, *Urbarium* of the village Premslin, and No. 51, revisions of the *Urbaria* of Premslin, Glövzin, and Karstädt. These were the villages in which 44 of Kleist's 60 full peasants lived. It was against them that his offensive had principally been aimed, since the other full peasants were either new settlers with recently and unambiguously-defined labour obligations and rents, or residents of a village in which Kleist's seigneurial powers were limited by those of other noble landlords and the Crown.

40. GStA. Stavenow, No. 353, ff. 67–9.

41. On Voss's purchase of Stavenow, see GStA. Stavenow, Nos. 122, 65, and 39, ff. 61–3. The appraisal of 1808 is cited in note 21 above. On Voss, see *Allgemeine Deutsche Biographie* (Leipzig, 1896), Vol. 40, pp. 352–61.

42. Behre's series of average prices in Brandenburg shows that between 1755–66 and 1796–1805 rye rose by 42 per cent, barley by 60 per cent and oats by 50 per cent. But wartime demand and post-1806 requisitioning drove the price of oats up rapidly, which explains the great rise in the value of this grain at Stavenow between the appraisals of 1763 and 1808. Otto Behre, *Geschichte der Statistik in Brandenburg-Preussen bis zur Gründung des Königlich Statistischen Bureaus* (Berlin, 1905), p. 277. Magnus Friedrich von Bassewitz, *Die Kurmark Brandenburg im Zusammenhang mit den Schicksalen des Gesamtsaats Preussen während der Zeit vom 22. Oktober 1806 bis zu Ende des Jahres 1808* (Leipzig, 1852), Vol. II, pp. 401–2.

43. Before 1809, one of the four Stavenow demesne farms was regularly leased to a tenant farmer, who supplied his own draught animals. The figures in the text refer only to the estates's own inventory.

44. GStA. Stavenow, No. 62.

45. The legal status of day labourers and their families differed markedly from that of the full peasants (*Hufenbauern*) and smallholders (*Kossäten*), upon whose households the law of serfdom (*Untertänigkeit*) was based. Legal serfdom at Stavenow, as (with some exceptions) elsewhere in Brandenburg, was tied to the landed peasant holding, rather than being an hereditary state of personal

unfreedom. Occupancy of such a holding above all bound the peasant to perform labour service on his lord's demesne land, while his mature but unmarried children, if expendable in the operation of the family holding, could be compelled to work as farm servants at the manor for a period of three years (*Gesindezwangsdienst*). The sons of such peasants could also be compelled to succeed their fathers in running the family farm or to take over a vacant tenancy in the lord's jurisdiction. If such farmers or their sons could present the lord with an acceptable substitute, they were free to quit their holdings, whereupon they ceased to be subject to the legislation of serfdom. Their status then became that of a day labourer and all other unprivileged residents of the local seigneurial jurisdiction, such as artisans, small-scale cottagers, and the majority of manorial workers who were not in compulsory service. All such persons could depart from their seigneurial jurisdiction upon payment of a statutory fee, which at Stavenow, however, was seldom levied. Otherwise, they were bound by the terms of their labour or rental contracts, subject to cancellation at will, or upon notice by either party, which they had voluntarily concluded with their lords. In this sense they were a 'free' labour force, though princely legislation (notably the statutes of labourers [*Gesindeordnungen*] and of guilds) attempted to fix all wage-earners' pay. But because of the great importance of unregulated wages in kind in the countryside, workers such as Stavenow's day labourers in effect negotiated their own terms of settlement and employment on an early form of the modern free labour market.

46. A fuller discussion of the manorial servants and day labourers will be found in my article on real wages, cited in note 20 above. Under Kleist's regime, day labourers were paid for all harvest work except for six days of labour by a man and woman from each household during the rye harvest.

47. The preceding analysis, except as otherwise noted, rests on the inventories and appraisals of 1763 and 1808, cited in note 21 above.

48. GStA. Stavenow, No. 202, ff. 178–9, 211–15; No. 314, ff. 1–9 and passim; No. 342, ff. 1–9.

49. Bassewitz, *op. cit.*, Vol. III, p. 675.

50. GStA. Stavenow, Nos. 352, 423. The descendants of the farmers settled by Major von Kleist's parents in the village of Dargard alone stood aloof from the strikes that broke out in 1808.

51. GStA. Stavenow, No. 202, f. 211,; No. 191, ff. 162–3,; No. 314, ff. 1–3; No. 341, ff. 1–6.

52. GStA. Stavenow, No. 409, f. 5: 'Die Neigung äussert sich überall frei werden zu wollen.'

53. The main documentation of the emancipation at Stavenow is located in the following dossiers of the estate archive: Nos. 448, 449, 441 (Premslin); 408, 409, 198 (Mesekow); 390–3 (Karstädt); 433, 453, 483, 427, 451, 428, 425 (Glövzin); 520, 474–5, 405, 513 (Blüten); 440 (Sargleben). The emancipation of the *Erbzinsbauern* in the settlers' village of Dargard under the law of 1821 appropriate to their legal status remains to be studied. On the peasant emancipation in general, see, in addition to the works of Knapp, Harnisch and Dipper cited above, Erich Langelüddecke, 'Zum Grundsatz der Entschädigung und des Loskaufs bei den Eigentumsregulierungen und Dienstablösungen der ostelbischen Bauern Preussens im 19. Jh.', *Zeitschrift für Geschichtswissenschaft*, 1960:4, pp; 890–908; Dietrich Saalfeld, 'Zur Frage des bäuerlichen Landverlustes im Zusammenhang mit den preussischen Agrarreformen', *Zeitschrift für Agrargeschichte und Agrarsoziologie*, 11:1 (1963), pp. 163–71; Hartmut Harnisch, 'Statistische Untersuchungen zum Verlauf der kapitalistischen Agrarreformen in den preussischen Ostprovinzen (1811 bis 1865)', *Jahrbuch für Wirtschaftsgeschichte*, 1974:4, pp. 149–83; and especially Rudolf Berthold, 'Die Veränderungen im Bodeneigentum und in der Zahl der Bauernstellen, der Kleinstellen und der Rittergüter in den preussischen Provinzen

Sachsen, Brandenburg und Pommern während der Durchführung der Agrarreformen des 19. Jahrhunderts', *Jahrbuch für Wirtschaftsgeschichte*, Sonderband
(1978), pp. 10–116. On the Junkers' social and political fortunes after 1806 see,
inter alia, Kosselleck, *op. cit.*, pp. 487–559; and Hans Rosenberg, 'Die
Pseudodemokratisierung der Rittergutsbesitzerklasse', in H.-U. Wehler (ed.),
Moderne deutsche Sozialgeschichte (Köln and Graz, 1968), pp. 287–308.

54. Gerhard Albrecht, *Die Gutsherrschaft Freyenstein*, Dissertation (Pädago-
gische Hochschule Potsdam, Historisch-Philologische Fakultät, 1968), p. 137;
Bassewitz, *op. cit.*, Vol. III, pp. 676–7; Johannes Schultze, *Die Prignitz. Aus der
Geschichte einer märkischen Landschaft* (Colgne and Graz, 1956), pp. 238 ff., 277.

55. Schultze, *op. cit.*, pp. 233–5.

56. Albrecht, *op. cit.*, p. 170.

57. Ibid., p. 184; Müller, *op. cit.*, p. 37; Ulrich Wille, *Das Urbarium von
Abbendorf und Haverland 1786* (Goslar, 1938), pp. 5–6 and passim. The energetic
and hard-bargaining Major von Kleist negotiated this *Urbarium* in his capacity as
ward of the von Saldern children.

58. Chr. O. Mylius, *Corpus Constitutionum Marchicarum*, VI Theil, I
Abteilung, No. CXXVI (1656); V Theil, Abt. II, No. XV (1702).

59. F. W. A. Bratring, *Statistisch-Topographische Beschreibung der gesamten
Mark Brandenburg* (Berlin, 1968; reprint of the original text of 1804–09),
pp. 395–7. Since the number of peasant farms remained constant, so too must the
numbers of retired farmers and their wives (*Altsitzer*), with whom the numbers of
day-labourers (*Einlieger*) are combined in Bratring's statistics. Another sign of the
rationalisation of manorial production in the Prignitz was the decline in the number
of noble families presiding over their estates in person — from 141 in 1750 to 63 in
1801. The number of estate administrators, bailiffs and lessees rose correspondingly
from 85 to 233. Ibid., p, 395.

60. Harnisch, 'Statistische Untersuchungen', *op. cit.*, p. 158.

61. Müller, *op. cit.*, 61. But Bratring's somewhat vague descriptions of the
various districts of Brandenburg suggest that there were numerous pockets of
unimproved estate agriculture within a larger setting of considerable progress. See
Vol. I, pp. 12, 83, 230, 397; Vol. II, p. 7; Vol. III, pp. 41–2. Between 1767 and 1798
the combined sowings of wheat, rye, barley, oats, peas, lentils and potatoes
throughout the Mark Brandenburg rose by about 50 per cent from 79,000 to 119,000
Wispel (1 Wispel = 24 bushels). The sowings of potatoes alone rose from 1653
Wispel in 1765 to 21,188 in 1801. Behre, *op. cit.*, pp. 234–7.

62. Ziekursch, *op. cit.*, p. 154.

63. Wernicke, *op. cit.*, pp. 187 ff; Dipper, *op. cit.*, p. 57; Henning, *op. cit.*, p. 26;
Abel, *op. cit.*, p. 192.

64. Knapp, *op. cit.*, Vol. I, p. 60.

65. Hartmut Harnisch, *Die Herrschaft Boitzenburg* (Weimar, 1968), pp. 158,
170, 229–33; Günter Vogler, 'Die Entwicklung der feudalen Arbeitsrente in
Brandenburg vom 15. bis 18. Jahrhundert', *Jahrbuch für Wirtschaftgeschichte*
(1966) I, pp, 155 ff; Vetter, *loc. cit.*, pp. 455–7; Carl Brinkmann, *Wustrau* (Leipzig,
1911), p. 83 ff; Siegfried Passow, *Ein märkischer Rittersitz* (Eberswalde, 1907),
Vol. I, pp. 155 ff.

66. For example, see Christoph Freiherr Senfft von Pilsach, 'Bäuerliche
Wirtschaftsverhältnisse in einem neumärkischen Dorf (Land Sternberg) vor der
Regulierung der gutsherrlich-bäuerlichen Verhältnisse und der erste dortige
Regulierungsversuch', *Forschungen zur brandenburgischen und preussischen
Geschichte*, XXII:2 (1909), pp. 127–91.

67. Stadelmann, *op. cit.*, Vol. III, Urkunden 9–10, pp. 169–70. See also Vol.
IV, p. 30.

68. Harnisch, 'Vom Oktoberedikt', *loc. cit.*, pp. 247–8, 275–9; Vogler and

Vetter, *op. cit.*, p. 151.
  69. Sack, quoted in Bassewitz, Vol. III, *op. cit.*, p. 674.
  70. Quotations in Knapp, *op. cit.*, Vol. II, pp. 159, 348. See also the report of 1814 on peasant demands for regulation in Upper Silesia, pp. 349–51.
  71. Quoted in Harnisch, 'Vom Oktoberedikt', *loc. cit.*, p. 266.
  72. Vetter, 'Kurmärkischer Adel', *loc. cit.*, pp. 440–6 and passim.
  73. GStA. Stavenow, No. 341, ff. 1–6.
  74. It is well known that the Junkers fought successfully after 1811 to limit regulation to *spannfähige* holdings, (i.e. to those maintaining draught teams) so as to retain their rights to the small-scale cottages' unpaid manual labour services. But Berthold has shown Knapp's argument that the Declaration of 1816 doomed the smallholdings to eventual absorption into the Junker demesnes to be untenable. In fact, the numbers of smallholdings increased very rapidly throughout the nineteenth century. See *idem* 'Die Veränderungen', pp. 74, 108–9.
  75. In the year following the outbreak of the Stavenow peasants' strike against manorial service, Voss's bailiff added at least 8 horses and 19 oxen to his work teams. GStA. Stavenow, No. 202, 35–42, 52–3, 63–7, 92–3 ff.
  76. '*Treu, gehorsam, und unterthänig*', ibid., No. 27, 23–6 ff.
  77. Ibid., No. 314, f. 14.

4 THE RURAL PROLETARIAT
The Everyday Life of Rural Labourers in the
Magdeburg Region, 1830–80*

Hainer Plaul

I

The Magdeburg black-earth region (Magdeburger *Börde*) is one of the most favoured agricultural areas of Central Europe. Its exceptionally high fertility generally guarantees crop yields well above average. To these natural characteristics were added favourable conditions of ownership and inheritance. The peasants in this region were freer than the serfs further east, and enjoyed a system of impartible inheritance. By the late feudal period this combination of circumstances had already led to a situation where the peasants could produce significant surpluses. Furthermore, they had also managed to retain most of the agricultural land themselves. The portion of the surplus that remained to them after payment of feudal land dues was decisive in fostering the development of a stable regional market. The area's advantageous geographical position, close to the commercial centre of Magdeburg, which lay on the navigable River Elbe, also meant that it formed close ties with other markets fairly early on. This led at first to a modest, then later to a growing, accumulation of capital. We can estimate the extent of this accumulation from the fact that as early as the last quarter of the eighteenth century the majority of peasants wanted to commute their feudal dues into money rents. This development facilitated and stimulated the growing tendency of the more well-to-do peasants to employ day-labourers on their farms. All these factors laid the foundations for the later transformation of the peasants into capitalist farmers.

As time went on, three main groups of impoverished or completely landless agricultural labourers emerged in the Magdeburg region: farm servants (maids, cowherds, stable-hands); full-time farm workers (usually employed as harvesters or threshers, and

---

*Translated by Cathleen S. Catt, Richard J. Evans and W. R. Lee.

known as *Deputatlandarbeiter*); and day-labourers. In a sense, a fourth group, the smallholders, could be added, as they owed their independence to their grazing rights on common land. Like the peasant farmers, the various groups of rural poor in the late feudal period were subject to a system of non-economic feudal ties and restrictions. However, in the Magdeburg region this was not derived from a system of actual serfdom, but was connected with the legal form of feudalism (*Gerichtsherrschaft*) which had developed. Feudal ties included forced labour and *Vormietsrecht*, statutory limits to the wages of servants and day labourers, payment of a protection tax, and the performance of services on the basis of the traditional relationship between a feudal lord and a dependent peasantry. They also involved the obligation to offer labour first to the local feudal lord, the right of the lord to deal with the non-performance of labour services by corporal punishment or monetary fines, and the obligation to ensure that the education and training of their children accorded with seigneurial interests.

This system of non-economic restrictions was abolished in 1807, when the Magdeburg region was incorporated into the newly-created Napoleonic kingdom of Westphalia. It thus became subject to the progressive French legislation on agriculture. At the Congress of Vienna, when Prussia obtained large parts of the former kingdom of Westphalia, and thus also acquired the Magdeburg region, it agreed in principle to recognise all the constitutional legislation passed by Westphalia, including the agricultural legislation. Prussia then attempted to bring the agricultural reforms which had taken place under French rule into line with its own reform programme in this sector by promulgating a series of special laws. For the rural poor (with little or no land) who were dependent on their wages for their subsistence, the chief significance of all these land reforms lay in the fact that henceforth they were free in law to dispose of their own labour. Thus the fundamental change in character of these labourers into capitalist rural workers can be seen to be part of a comprehensive social process, which ended feudal agriculture and brought about the development of capitalist farming. However, this process did not create a unified or homogeneous agricultural proletariat and the rural workforce continued to be differentiated on the basis of those with little or no land, in a manner typical of late feudalism. Two main factors influenced the composition of the rural workers in the capitalist system: the extent of integration into the employer's economy, and the existence, or not, of property and land.

As the nineteenth century unfolded, four main social groups became distinguishable within the rural proletariat, according to their degree of integration into their employer's farming enterprise and the amount of land and property they owned. First were the rural workers without any land or other property, who were very closely integrated into the economy of the peasant farm where they worked. This included in the first place farm servants, who were, by this time, more or less free from feudal restrictions. There were important distinctions to be made between single male and female farm servants on the one hand (*Knechte, Enken, Mägde*) and married farm servants on the other. The single farm servants represented the group within the rural proletariat most strongly integrated into their employers' farm economies. Single farm servants did not usually have their own separate households, whereas the married farm servants usually did. Even if these latter households were not economically entirely independent of the farmer, they were usually physically separate. Thus the married farm servants were already less closely integrated into the economy of the peasant-producer than the single farm servants were. Both married and single farm servants, however, had in common the fact that they had voluntarily entered into a legal contract with their employer, which bound them to work for him for a stipulated, and often long period of time. This contract also bound them to a series of laws governing the conditions and duties of farm servants, the *Gesindeordnung*, which were in force in various forms all over Germany until 1918. These laws laid down the extent and the manner of their integration into the farm's economy, and meant, in effect, that even under the new capitalist mode of production they remained under some form of non-economic regulation.

Secondly we can distinguish rural labourers with property (houses and/or land), who were nevertheless integrated into someone else's farm economy. Here we are talking about those rural labourers who had a more or less permanent contract to work for a particular farmer, and who either received a certain proportion of the farm's production, or specific payments in kind (so-called allowances) as part of their wages. They were also usually granted an allotment of land for their own use by the farmer. Their wages were further supplemented by the produce of the patch of land they actually owned. In the Magdeburg region, as in other parts of

Germany, these permanent farm workers were generally employed as mowers (*Schnitter*) and threshers (*Drescher*). If they worked on the estates of nobles or great landlords, they usually lived either as estate workers in housing which the landowner rented out to his labourers (rather in the manner of tied cottages in England), or, as manorial cottagers, in their own house built on estate land for which they had to pay a ground rent and render certain services. If they worked for peasant farmers, they would generally live in their own houses on common land. In some instances (which became more frequent with increasing labour shortages) even some of the large- and middle-sized peasant farmers began to offer their permanent workers tied accommodation. As with the laws governing the conditions of employment of farm servants, employers could only exercise their non-economic forms of exploitation if the labourer — driven it is true by economic circumstances — voluntarily entered into a legal contract with them.

Thirdly, there were non-integrated, 'free' day-labourers with no property, or only a small plot of land. These were the historical descendants of the tenant agricultural producers of the late feudal period. They did not own their houses, but rented living quarters. These 'free' labourers were the most mobile sector of the rural proletariat.

A fourth group consisted of free (i.e. non-integrated) labourers owning a house and perhaps some outbuildings affording the possibility of keeping some livestock. The majority would also have some land which, however, seldom amounted to more than a vegetable plot. Their historical origin lay in the cottagers and smallholders who had depended for their existence on the common land grazing rights. After the enclosure of common land they lost their relative independence, and had been forced into a complete reliance on wage labour.

Apart from these four categories within the indigenous rural proletariat, there was also a further important social group: the seasonal migrant workers. In the Magdeburg region they first appeared in large numbers following the change from extensive to intensive farming methods in the 1840s. They only achieved real significance in this area however after 1870.[2]

II

The system of non-economic coercion, ties and dependencies, to which the poor and landless as well as the peasant farmers were subjected during the feudal period, included a particular framework of social relations, which, above all, was characterised by the dependence of both the peasants and the rural poor on the feudal lord. In the face of this major opposition of class interests the larger and middling peasants and the rural poor were very much in the background. The low level of production, feudal oppression and, initially, an underdeveloped market, did not allow a very great difference in the levels of prosperity within the agricultural population to develop. In the second half of the eighteenth century, clear indications of a significant change in this respect can be seen. As early as the end of the eighteenth century the continued development of a stable market economy induced many peasants, particularly those living near the commercial centre of Magdeburg, to begin producing cash crops for the market, in particular chicory.

The really decisive changes however only really took place from the mid-1830s onwards, with the introduction of beet cultivation for sugar production, and as a result of the agricultural reforms. Significantly, this new area of production did not remain concentrated in the hands of the great landowners. Peasant farmers — and to some extent even smaller peasant-producers — were involved both in the cultivation of sugar beet and, as shareholders in sugar-refining companies, in the actual production of sugar.[3] The introduction and development of this area of production was responsible for the specific features which characterised the process of the development and consolidation of capitialist agriculture in the Magdeburg region from about 1830 to 1880. The newly-awoken and rapidly-increasing desire for profit on the part of the large landowners and large sections of the peasantry could be efficiently and satisfactorily met by the cultivation and processing of sugar beet. Not only could large profits be made from the beet and sugar trade, but ground rents and land prices also soared. Thus the area around Magdeburg represented a special case in comparison with other rural areas of 19th-century Germany. Here, capitalism penetrated extraordinarily early into agriculture and transformed it with astounding rapidity. The effect of this transformation on social relations was momentous. Within the peasant class the process of differentiation into large, middle and small farmers continued. Important developments appeared in connection with the partition and enclosure of common lands. As a result of losing their rights to use communally-owned land, a large proportion of the smallholders (*Kleinkossäten*) entirely lost their economic independence and became either permanent farm workers or 'free' day-labourers who nevertheless owned their own cottage. Enclosure also destroyed the communally-agreed three-field system of agricultural production which had predominated until then.

This whole development not only sharpened the social contradictions between the great landowners and the rest of the population; it also heightened the differences between the peasant farmers and the rural workforce. The desire for profit on the part of the peasant landowners, no longer limited by feudal constraints, and the effects of this on the rural labourers who worked for them, together with the attempts of these labourers to satisfy their growing needs, led to an increasingly irreconcilable clash of interests between farmers and labourers. This class antagonism was expressed in various ways. Communications between the two groups became restricted; marriage between the two groups became increasingly rare; contacts outside the workplace at social gatherings were reduced to a minimum; and even in the religious sphere — for example, with the foundation of choral societies — attempts to bring the two sides together foundered. There were even communes where the well-to-do peasant farmers went to the extreme of setting up separate cemeteries for their own kind. They also tried to introduce new methods of exploitation to meet the changed conditions, for example by using written, often discriminatory, employment contracts, or, in addition to the enforcement of the *Gesindeordnung* (which controlled wage levels), by using the work book, and introducing piecework. All these measures were designed to keep the amount paid for labour below its real value — one of the fundamental laws of capitalism.

The rural labourers, for their part, developed new forms and methods of resistance and opposition. Demands for higher wages and greater independence became more frequent as the demand for labour increased dramatically with the introduction of labour-intensive sugar-beet cultivation and the parallel establishment of numerous sugar refineries. The labour shortage was exacerbated from about the middle of the nineteenth century by the industrial development of Magdeburg and its environs. Increased mining production and road and railway construction in this region from 1850 onwards created more jobs. Rural employers often responded to this demand for industrial labour — which was naturally tempting to their servants — with harsh counter-measures, including a strict interpretation of the law governing servants, with threats, by forbidding them to go out, by forcing them to accept poor food and lodgings, and even with actual physical violence. They also introduced 'servant books' (*Gesindebücher*) which meant that the behaviour of a servant could be monitored over a much longer time period than the previous system of employers' references had allowed. So-called Servant Improvement Societies (*Dienstbotenverbesserungsvereine*) were founded towards the end of the 1830s in neighbouring regions, and quickly spread over the whole of Prussia and even further afield, the purpose of which was to keep labourers in line by public commendations and prizes for good work and loyal service. However, the early shortage of farm workers in the Magdeburg regions because of the high local demand for labour, meant that they failed to take root there.

The only way that a male or female farm servant could achieve a genuine improvement was to leave farm service altogether and become part of another social group — for example, by becoming either a 'free' day-labourer or by joining the industrial proletariat in the mining, factory, or railway and road construction industries. The result of this was that, apart from an obvious shortage of farm workers, there was also a marked shift in the average age of farm workers. Previously it had not been uncommon to find a farm hand thirty years old. It now became usual, as soon as he came of age, to leave farm service altogether.

At the same time, production on the large estates and larger peasant farms became increasingly mechanised and geared to sugar beet while other branches of agriculture, such as cereal production and livestock, became less important. As a result these farms became more and more seasonal concerns. This tendency became very evident in the Magdeburg region after 1850, during the consolidation phase of capitalist agriculture. As seasonal-based farms only require large numbers of workers at particularly critical times of the year, farmers and estate owners increasingly replaced permanent-contract farm workers by 'free' day-labourers and, after 1880, by seasonal migrant workers. By 1880 these farms were employing virtually no permanent farm workers. Where other branches of farming continued, the farmers increasingly employed specialised agricultural workers for ploughing and keeping livestock. These were generally more likely to be married men employed on a permanent contract, rather than being bound by the old farm servant regulations. And in place of the dairy maids, farmers increasingly employed female domestic servants (house-keepers, etc.).

The shift towards seasonal production had implications for other sectors of the rural proletariat too, namely the permanent farm workers. In the Magdeburg region the majority of these workers were employed as threshers. The introduction of threshing machines, in particular steam-threshers from the end of the 1850s, was a decisive turning-point for them. Mechanisation considerably reduced the amount of labour required for cereal production. For the farmers this was an additional reason to dispense with permanent farm labourers, and to replace them with 'free' day-labourers. Where possible, these permanent farm workers attempted to find other work with similar contractual arrangements, and many moved into specialisation, such as looking after livestock. However, the majority, who owned their own house and perhaps a little land, began to commute to work in the nearby industrial centres.

Underpinning these developments was the continual process of differentiation and increasing social division between the larger and middle-sized farmers on the one hand and the rural workforce on the other. As in other areas of Germany, in the Magdeburg region the relationship between the threshers and large-scale farmers was characterised initially by a residual feudal arrangement in which the thresher was granted an allotment to grow his own staple foods, and was guaranteed a certain proportion of the harvest. At the beginning of the 1830s the agricultural crisis, which had lasted for nearly a decade, began to recede. Against the background of a general increase in population and a disproportionate rise in those engaged in non-agricultural work — the result of industrialisation — there was a constant expansion of the market, which in turn led to a general increase in agricultural production. The great landowners and larger peasant farmers therefore became increasingly reluctant to allow their labourers a fixed proportion of their increasing harvest. From the first they attempted to replace this method of payment, which was now disadvantageous for them, with money wages. In the first instance they got rid of most payments in kind — a process which was more or less complete in the Magdeburg region by 1845. They carried on paying a proportion of corn to the threshers until the 1860s though, for the simple reason that, while hand-threshing was still the rule, this was a guarantee that the work would be carried out carefully and waste kept to a minimum. Stopping this method of payment would also have provoked stiff resistance in the threshers themselves, who, after the abolition of other payments in kind, certainly meant to maintain this one.

However, as soon as the farmers were able to do the threshing just as reliably and more profitably by machine, with all the other advantages this entailed, they began increasingly to reduce the proportion of corn to which the threshers were entitled, and finally did away with it completely. Even middle and small farms were able to use steam-threshers, as farmers developed a system of jointly hiring or purchasing a machine, which was then sent round the farms on a rota system. Alongside this, the farmers introduced a new way of paying for the threshers which enabled them to break the threshers' resistance. In this steam-threshing machine owners worked hand in glove with the farmers who hired their machines. What happened was that the proportion of the corn that had previously been paid to the threshers was now paid to the owner of the steam-threshing machine instead, as payment for its hire, and the farm workers were paid wholly in cash — not by the farmer, but by the machine owner. The net result of this manoeuvre was that the threshers were often paid half as much in cash as the value of the corn they had formerly received. As a result the status of the permanent farm workers suffered a significant deterioration. Previously they had been relatively closely integrated into the farms they worked on — not only through their contact with the farmer, but also economically, through their portion of the gross yield of the farm. Now this relationship was broken and replaced by a cash relationship. In the developmental stage of capitalist agricultural production they had lost most of their payments in kind, and in the consolidation phase they lost their right to a proportion of the corn threshed. Although the permanent workers were still employed by farmers, they were no longer entitled to a share in the produce of the farm, and the proportion of wages paid in cash had been considerably increased.

With the change in the social status of permanent farm workers and servants, a further and more comprehensive process was initiated, which became increasingly evident in the later phase of capitalist development. There was an increasing tendency towards a unified rural labour force. The increasing importance of a cash wage in the remuneration of permanent farm workers removed an important distinction between this group and 'free' day-labourers. As a result the feudal distinction between agricultural producers with little or no land was lost and a unified and homogeneous labour force emerged, characterised by 'free' wage labour.

Differences between the various social groups of the agricultural proletariat diminished, and the social antagonism between estate holders and large- and medium-sized peasant producers, on the one hand, and the agricultural proletariat on the other hand, became very evident. However, increasing capitalist production also meant greater differentiation between large-, medium- and small-scale peasant producers.

The trends in the social composition of the agricultural labour force also facilitated increased mobility between the different categories and between rural and industrial employment. In particular farm servants frequently became 'free' day-labourers and members of both these groups tended to seek factory employment in the developing sugar refineries after 1836, and from the 1850s onwards in the metal-working factories which sprung up in and around Magdeburg. This contributed to an intensification of contact between the rural proletariat and the city. The breakthrough of capitalist production in agriculture did not lead to a diminution in social communication, but was accompanied by an expansion and intensification, although only within each individual class and group.

III

The enclosure and division of common land and the abolition of feudal dues had also deprived the peasant farmers of much of their economic power, although this varied according to individual groups. The early profits from their involvement in the sugar industry were used, by and large, to pay off outstanding debts and to retain their land. Thus at first, for these farmers, mechanisation and the use of chemical fertilisers was out of the question. However the early completion of the agrarian reforms and the retention of land by the peasantry enabled large- and medium-sized peasant-producers to benefit from the economic boom in Germany between 1853 and 1857, which continued unabated after 1859. This was reflected particularly in their increased participation in sugar beet production, which by now was one of the most profitable agricultural sectors. Between 1850 and 1867 the number of sugar beet factories in the Magdeburg region increased from 40 to 70, by which time approximately a quarter of all Prussian sugar beet production was concentrated in this area. Competition for maximum profit and market shares became particularly intense and led to a severe deterioration in the living conditions of the indigenous agricultural labour force.

Eventually there came a point when traditional methods of sugar beet cultivation no longer realised the profit expectations of the Junkers and the large- and middle-sized farmers. By the 1840s the so-called 'beet farmers' (*Rübenbauer*) had moved over to a system of continuous rotation, and by the end of the 1850s a much freer system of cultivation without a set pattern of rotation had developed in the Magdeburg region. The tenant farmers figured particularly in the switch to monoculture. The proportion of fallow land declined to a minimum. In 1878 in the district of Wanzleben, the main area of beet cultivation in the Magdeburg region, only 0.3 per cent of arable lay fallow compared with 8.8 per cent for Prussia as a whole. As a result the use of chemical fertilisers had become common as early as the late 1850s. The introduction of machinery dates from the same time. Formerly the ground had been dug by hand, but this was increasingly replaced by deep ploughing with the 'Wanzleben' plough developed in the area. The former practice of sowing the beet seed by hand was rapidly replaced by the use of seed drills. A little later hand and mechanical (gin) threshing machines appeared, along with clover- and rape-sowing machines, and then seed drills for the other crops. There were also beet-cutting machines and hand-sowing machines. Towards the end of the 1850s came the steam-threshing machines and at the beginning of the 1860s fully mechanised beet-harvesting machines, horse-hoes, and — only on the large estates, however — steam ploughs. From the end of the 1860s on the Junker estates there were also mowing machines to be found. As a result of their participation in the sugar industry even fairly small farmers had access — albeit to a limited extent — to agricultural machinery.

The greater use of machinery meant that the amount of time necessary to complete some agricultural tasks was significantly reduced. The net result of this was to enhance the seasonal nature of agricultural employment. The machines also released labour. It should not be overlooked, however, that the introduction of machinery also meant a reduction in the amount of hard physical labour agricultural workers had to perform and an increase in the intellectual skills that were demanded of them. Not only did they have to master new techniques and skills, but mechanisation led also to the appearance of specialised, skilled workers. The education of technical agricultural workers had its origin in this development.

Yet, in general, mechanisation and the increased seasonal character of agricultural work reinforced the levelling process within the rural workforce. The payment of a proportion of corn to the permanent workers was abolished, wages were paid increasingly in cash instead of in kind, and in the Magdeburg region payment in kind had virtually disappeared by 1880. The previous relationship between peasant farmers and farm hands was dissolved and the permanent farm worker was increasingly replaced by the 'free' day-labourer and seasonal migrant worker. The latter were generally employed on contract, from April to November by large estate owners and larger farmers. The farmers, naturally enough, were concerned to make sure these workers were fully employed before hiring any additional labour, so that local labourers were only hired when economically necessary. The seasonal worker, who came from the eastern provinces of Prussia and later from Poland, were recruited not only to work in the beet fields, but also to help with the cereal harvests. They were not only cheaper than local workers and did not demand an allotment, but farmers also found it profitable to use them in the wheat fields, where there was much to do during the slack period in sugar beet cultivation between hoeing and harvesting. Their contracts therefore kept them from spring until late autumn. In particular, it was the local female farm workers who suffered most from the use of seasonal workers. Now they could often only find employment during the hoeing and harvesting of the beet; the introduction of seed drills for sowing the beet destroyed what had once been an exclusively female occupation. Finally, the employers used seasonal workers to depress wages. They constituted a reserve army of agricultural labour whose origins lay in the different pace of regional industrial development characteristic of capitalism. The seasonal workers were willing to accept wages regarded as insufficient by indigenous labour, and the employers used this as a way to depress wages in general.

This process, together with mechanisation, facilitated the introduction of piecework, which further heightened the seasonal character of agricultural production. For the workers this meant an immediate and immense increase in the physical effort they were required to put into their work. The opportunity of earning more money, despite the extra physical effort involved, was an effective incentive to use working hours to the full, or even to increase them.

In agriculture, where it was usual at critical times of the year to have a 17-hour working day, an increase in the time worked could only be achieved by reducing the number of rest periods. As the employers became aware of the effectiveness of the piecework system in getting the most out of their workers, they began, as the English manufacturers had done before them, systematically to reduce the amount paid per job.

The lust for profit and increased competition pushed the employers to further measures which also had a direct effect on the living standards of their workers. In the middle of the nineteenth century it was still usual for permanent farm workers and servants to be granted a small allotment of land by their employer on which they grew potatoes or flax. Even the day-labourers who owned no land were often able to rent an allotment. With the expansion of sugar beet cultivation in particular, the farmers became increasingly reluctant to rent out any land. The maximum they would allow their farm servants or permanent workers to cultivate was a small patch for potatoes, and as sugar beet production became more lucrative, so land rents soared, making it impossible for the labourer to rent anyway.

A labourer who is paid entirely in cash is naturally much more vulnerable to price rises, which certainly occured in the early 1870s, when inflation hit him harder than a labourer who received at least part of his wages in kind. On the other hand, payment in kind restricts the labourer's mobility and makes him dependent on his employer. Furthermore a rural worker employed in a village, perhaps some miles from a main road, was often dependent on the village storekeeper, who, with no competition, could generally charge higher prices for food and clothing, etc. than his town counterpart. On top of all this, the employers used the change to payment in cash as an excuse to depress the real value of the rural worker's labour, by not making up in cash the true value of earlier payments in kind.

The deterioration in the living conditions of rural labour was also reinforced by the gradual change in the cycle of the agricultural year. It was impossible to talk of the continuity of agricultural work; the annual agricultural cycle was broken, and shortened by at least two or three months. Even those labourers who managed to find employment in the sugar factories after the beet harvest were not fully employed. Despite increased sugar beet cultivation, new technological developments in the last third of the nineteenth century meant that production was usually over by the end of January. In the winter months, therefore, until well into April, there was virtually no regular work to be found in this area. The working year of local male and female labourers was now differentially structured, as women could only find employment later in the year than men. Even with an increase in real wages, this meant that wages were below the real value of labour, as 'within the family the number of wage-earners was reduced, while the cost of reproducing labour within the family remained the same'.[5]

The rural workforce could not be regarded as well-off even before the decline in living standards in the 1860s. There were, however, certain differences in the standard of living of specific social groups, particularly between integrated farm workers (farm servants and permanent workers) and 'free' day-labourers. The threshers, being permanent farm workers, were generally able to make ends meet. In addition to their money wages, they received certain payments in kind, were able to maintain some livestock, and received an adequate amount of land (1–1½ *Morgen*) for their own needs. Even unmarried farm servants who received board and lodgings from their master, and who often also had a small patch of land for growing flax or potatoes, were relatively secure, although the only way they could achieve their legitimate demands for better wages or more personal freedom was to leave farm service. However, as the employers came under more pressure from the increasing scarcity of labour, brought about by the transition to more intensive agriculture and the onset of industrialisation, the farm servants began to realise some of their demands.

The social position of the 'free' day-labourers was much worse. But even between the indigenous day-labourers and the seasonal migrant workers there were certain differences. Thus most of the day-labourers who owned a house and/or a little land were able to keep small livestock or cultivate their own vegetables. The most vulnerable were those day-labourers who owned neither land nor property, or only a tiny patch of land. They were in practice completely dependent on their uncertain money wages, and if they were able to rent a little additional land for flax and potato cultivation, it meant parting with some of their hard-earned wages. We must assume that, in general, these families lived on the very margin of subsistence, and at certain times of the year fell below the subsistence minimum. They could only increase their income significantly by taking on continual piecework. It is no coincidence that this group constituted the most mobile section of the rural proletariat. As payment in kind became more rare, as farmers ceased to employ permanent workers and came to rely increasingly on day-labourers and seasonal migrant workers, and as renting or buying more land became increasingly impossible, the general poverty of the rural proletariat became not only more acute, but also more widespread. The levelling process within the rural workforce was expressed in a trend towards a common experience of poverty.

IV

This process of general impoverishment was reflected in concrete changes in living conditions, diet and clothing. However, despite the gradual levelling process within the rural proletariat, there still remained very substantial differences between the various social groups, particularly in housing conditions. Above all the degree of integration into the employers' economy, and the ownership of some property (which generally included accommodation) continued to be significant. Living quarters for farm servants, without exception, displayed two major characteristics: farm servants did not form separate households; and their sleeping and living quarters were physically separate from each other. Both were provided by the master. Servants who were very strongly integrated into the economy of their masters had very little say over the standard of their living quarters. This was true both of farm servants employed on the large estates and those employed by peasant farmers. There was very little to choose between the sleeping quarters of these two groups, but their living quarters differed considerably. On the estates of the large estate owners and nobles, each of whom on average employed between 18 and 30 male farm servants and about as many maids, there was no possibility of a personal relationship between employer and employee developing. Here, therefore, special servants' quarters had traditionally been provided.

On peasant farms it was different; where only one or two male farm servants and the same number of maids were employed. Servants on these farms were not only a part of the farming economy, but also of the farmer's family. They not only ate with them — if not at the same table, then at least in the same room — but also spent their free time in the farmer's company. In the Magdeburg region, where most farms were of the peasant type, this was the predominant form of social organisation. During the development of the capitalist mode of production, however, it was destroyed. Two specific processes contributed to this: first, the dissolution of feudal ties and their replacement by a contract of work; and secondly, the development of class antagonism between the peasant farmers and the labouring classes. The relationship between the farmer and his farmhands developed into one of overt exploitation, without the mitigating influence of personal ties. One direct and logical result of this was to exclude the maids and other workers from the farmer's family. The larger peasant farmers, with between four and six servants, took the lead. Following the example of the great estate owners, they began to provide separate servants' quarters: peasant farmers with only two servants followed suit rather later, and only if they had the necessary space available. However, it should be emphasised that the segregation from the farmer's family was welcomed by the servants themselves, as they were glad to escape their employer's constant surveillance, and in many instances it seems that the exclusion took place as a result of pressure from the servants themselves for greater independence and more personal freedom.

From the 1860s, with the increasingly seasonal nature of agricultural work, the larger beet farms kept on only a bare minimum of permanent farm workers. In practice this was usually the married stable hands and livestock men. This group of farm servants gained a similar status to the other permanent farm workers, the threshers. They usually lived in tied cottages, provided contractually by their employers; but former threshers, who had managed to find employment as grooms and already owned their own houses, continued to live in them; and a smaller number of these married farm servants rented accommodation, either from small farmers or from those labourers who owned their own houses. One common characteristic of the married servants' mode of living, in contrast to that of single farm servants, was the fact that they constituted independent households, with adjacent living and sleeping quarters. In so far as single farm servants were still employed — usually on middle-sized farms — either their living and sleeping quarters were still separate, or they lived at home with their parents. Thus the levelling process within the rural proletariat can be seen in this respect as well.

Tied cottages were often located on estate land, and therefore subject to certain ground rents and dues. Other cottages, like those of the day labourers, were built on common land. Until the 1860s, against a general background of rising population, there was disproportionate increase in the number of permanent farm workers (threshers) living in their own houses in comparison with those living in tied housing. This trend was clearly only possible for as long as they received a portion of the harvest as part of their wages. With the disappearance of this method of payment, and with the transition to cash wages and the general reduction in the amount of allotment land, building activity declined. This factor, together with increasing labour shortages, which reflected the impoverishment of the rural workforce and increasing urban migration, forced the larger peasant farmers and sugar factory owners to begin building houses for their permanent workers. By the turn of the century in the Magdeburg region there were no permanent farm workers who did not live in tied housing. The vast majority of former permanent farm workers who owned their own homes had become commuters, working in local sugar refineries or in the metalworking industry.

Under the pressure of a rural exodus, the employers also found themselves compelled to improve the living quarters provided for their workers. However, as they also took every possible opportunity to reduce their capital outlay to a minimum, overcrowding was the principal characteristic of most tied housing. Lack of space and sparse furnishing were also common characteristics of many of the houses owned by the permanent farm workers and day-labourers, although here the overcrowding was not as severe as in the tied housing. Similarly, overcrowding was common throughout this period in the rented accommodation of the day-labourers.

At the beginning of the nineteenth century, rented accommodation was usually in the houses of smaller peasant farmers. However, these farmers increasingly wanted the extra rooms themselves, for example to provide separate accommodation for aged parents. Evidently, the gradual loosening of family ties which had taken place earlier in the larger peasant families, was also becoming evident in this group. As a result, day-labourers now had to rent accommodation either with other labourers who owned their own houses, or perhaps with a village craftsman. As very few of these 'free' day-labourers would have been able to become home-owners themselves, they thus constituted the most vulnerable section of the agricultural proletariat.[6]

Evidence of the continuing levelling-down and impoverishment of the rural workforce can also be found in their diet. In the Magdeburg region in this period, as in other parts of Germany, the largest part of an agricultural worker's family budget went on food: the proportion of annual income spent on food was approximately 60 per cent, a figure which corresponds well with the general average for working families in pre-monopolistic Germany.[7] However, the daily diet of the different social groups within the rural proletariat displayed certain variations which derived from their differing social and economic status. So long as part of a labourer's wages were paid as a portion of the corn harvested — a thresher received every 16th bushel for hand threshing, and every 20th bushel for machine threshing — the threshers were not only provided with sufficient corn for bread for their own consumption, but often had a surplus which could either be sold or traded for other goods. In contrast, the 'free' day labourer would only receive a payment of corn if he had been employed to harvest both the winter and summer cereal crops. Moreover, the amount he received by itself would scarcely have been enough to meet his own needs. In these cases he would have to buy additional corn, flour or bread. Permanent farm workers, with allotments or rented strips of land, generally had adequate supplies of potatoes and other vegetables. This was seldom the case for 'free' day labourers, unless they owned their own houses with a kitchen garden.

Meat consumption was determined almost exclusively by the weight of the family pig. This would have been supplemented at the most by one or two goats. Extra meat was rarely purchased, and then only during periods of hard physical labour, and for feast days. However, only those rural labourers who had outbuildings and enough land to grow animal feed could keep a pig or goat. This factor also determined the consumption of goat's milk and cheese. Other products, such as butter, and to a large extent eggs (poultry-keeping was not allowed everywhere), salt, sugar, lard, fish, rice, barley, beer, coffee, spirits, etc. all had to be bought.

Thus the agricultural labourer's diet was basically dependent on the extent and quality of land available for cultivation; the amount of wages paid in kind; the livestock kept; but also inevitably on the level of real income.

The continual increase in the cost of living from about 1851 had drastic consequences. From about 1845, when payment in kind ceased apart from the portion of the crop paid to the threshers, only the latter had enough cereals for their own subsistence. The increase in the price of rye was accompanied by a marked decline in bread consumption, and a corresponding increase in the consumption of potatoes. Significantly, farmers continued to allow their permanent workers enough land to grow their own potatoes, despite the general reduction in the provision of allotment land. As the size and availability of allotments and rented land decreased, the possibility of keeping livestock declined. This led to a general decrease in the consumption of meat, milk and dairy products. Finally, this process contributed to a reduction in the consumption of fruit and vegetables other than potatoes. Thus the standard of nutrition for rural labourers of the Magdeburg region during the period of the consolidation of agrarian capitalism was characterised by a diet poor in meat and fat, with potatoes constituting the main source of nourishment. More bread was eaten during the summer months, both because the availability of piecework meant that families could afford it, and also because potato stocks were then at their lowest point.

While estate servants frequently complained about the poor quality and quantity of their food, servants on peasant farms generally received at least adequate food as long as they continued to eat in the same room as the farmer's family. Where they were provided with separate quarters the quality of food generally deteriorated, which once again reflected the increasing social antagonism between farmers and servants. This development was generally confined to larger peasant families; on the middling farms, servants continued to eat in the same room as the farmer's family, and so did not experience a similar deterioration in their diet.

During the 1860s the large capitalist estates began commuting the part of a servant's salary paid as board into cash payments. Just as exclusion from the farmers' families had in some ways been in the interests of the servants, to some extent they also welcomed the replacement of payment in kind by cash payments. Justified grievances about the poor quality of food provided were added to other specific provocative complaints, as servants realised that more cash led to greater personal freedom and independence. The same development occurred with married servants who were later employed by farmers and estate owners in place of farm servants. Thus in the Magdeburg region from the middle of the 1860s there was a general levelling of the differences in nutrition, particularly between permanent workers and day-labourers.

Clothing styles also reflected this levelling process. In the first instance the differences had been mainly those of quality and durability. All peasant farmers wore a traditional costume (*Tracht*) until at least the middle of the nineteenth century. But there is no evidence that the labourers of the Magdeburg region ever wore a distinctive costume. The only uniformity was the degree of shabbiness. The labourers neither tried to emulate the *Tracht*, nor did they develop a costume of their own. Their clothing, more than anything, reflected what was on offer in the towns. One of the typical features of their mode of dress was the careful distinction between work clothes and Sunday clothes, which were for church and feast days and festivals: a distinction that was maintained as far as possible. Sunday clothes had not only to be decent, but also, if possible, of a better quality than working clothes.

As far as work clothes were concerned the cheaper they were the better. In crisis years — for example, 1848 — clothes could even form part of payments in kind. Other sources of clothing were secondhand clothes dealers and hand-outs from charitable gentry. In this manner even quite smart 'town' clothes found their way into the village. Next to cheapness, labourers were concerned with the durability and hard-wearing quality of the clothes they bought, in particular as their work clothes were subjected to a great deal of wear and tear. With the increase in sugar beet cultivation from the 1840s in the Magdeburg region the amount of cultivated flax declined sharply, at the same time as cotton in particular became generally more available. Thus in place of the sturdy, hard-wearing homespun linen clothes that former generations had worn, cotton garments became the rule. This was another area where the position of the rural labourers deteriorated. They now not only had to buy their clothes in the first place, but, as cotton was less hard-wearing, they had to replace them more frequently. This development constituted an additional and continual drain on the household budget.

V

How did the labourers respond to increased exploitation and declining living standards? Their response was characterised by three elements: (i) family self-help, (ii) different forms of solidarity, and (iii) particular methods of economic class warfare.

Family self-help frequently took the form of avoiding any

unnecessary expenditure and trying wherever possible to reduce outgoings by making things at home. In particular in the Magdeburg region labourers obtained their own supply of coal, which was dug from local pits. Self-help also included the careful preservation of clothing and household linen (by constant mending and careful washing, the handing on of children's clothes down through the family, altering clothes at home, etc.) and saving on lighting and heating costs by going to bed early. Where the family engaged in supplementary activities, like spinning or quilting, they often spent the evening working with neighbouring families; this also enhanced social life and communication.

Rural workers and their families also gleaned the fields after they had been harvested, and in times of crisis — for example, in the late 1840s when the living conditions of labourers seriously and dramatically declined — raids on fields, orchards and grain stores became exceptionally common and widespread. In winter even the sugar beet clamps were forced open and raided: 'We're going out into the beet fields' became a common expression. In November 1847, the Prussian administration passed a police law which prohibited these practices and laid down suitable penalites. But the labourers continued their understandable thieving forays, while the farmers vocally but unsuccessfully demanded that only people with a licence signed by the village authorities should be allowed into the harvested fields. When the Prussian and then the Imperial Criminal Law Code (passed in 1872) exempted children under 12 from the penal code, many labourers sent their children to steal from the fields.

Another illegal form of self-help was the insurance fraud, for example deliberately starting fires in one's own home. (This obviously could only be practised by labourers who owned their own homes.)

Mutual self-help within families consisted mainly in all family members working the family plot of land, in the older children or grandparents looking after smaller children, the aged, ill or handicapped members of the family, and in the elderly helping with the housework. With the general and increasing impoverishment of the labourers, family aid became increasingly important in the search for new and more profitable work opportunities. Of course, increasing or supplementing the family income took a high priority. Idleness was simply not justifiable, and was actively scorned by the labourers in the Magdeburg region.

Perhaps this is most clearly expressed in the restraint they showed in the consumption of alcohol, an astonishing phenomenon in view of the fact that average *per capita* consumption of spirits in Germany increased steadily from the early nineteenth century. Temperance had not always been the rule even in the Magdeburg region, and in the early 1830s local clergy had frequently complained of increasing drunkenness. The trend towards restraint coincided with the introduction of sugar beet cultivation and the change to payment by piecework. A contributory factor may have been the introduction of coffee, which had the added attraction that it could be 'stretched' by the addition of coffee substitutes such as chicory, roasted rye, barley kernels and beet skins. As these substitutes grew locally and were cheap, they thus provided a further opportunity for savings, and from the early 1840s labourers drank coffee substitutes instead of the traditional, and expensive, beer to slake their thirst and to accompany their meals. This trend began at exactly the same time as spirits, particularly potato schnaps, were being offered as a cheaper and stronger alternative to beer, and when employers began to use intensive methods of exploitation, in particular piece-rate payments for specific agricultural tasks, such as digging over the beet fields and harvesting cereal crops.

This coincidence was certainly not a chance occurrence. In comparison with other foods it was cheaper to produce a meal based on coffee (with bread, or potatoes), and the time factor was also clearly important. Now the rest periods which the labourer had been accustomed to when he was paid by the day, needed to be voluntarily reduced to a minimum by the labourer himself so that he could maximise his working day and realise a higher wage. Nothing proved so suitable for this purpose as the relatively cheap coffee substitute. It could be quickly prepared in the morning, and also be taken into the fields in jugs and cans, which made returning home to the village at lunchtime unnecessary. It should be noted, however, that the disappearance of the practice of eating a hot midday meal — and this not only at harvest time — represented a significant deterioration in the labourer's daily nutrition.

From the 1860s in the Magdeburg *Börde* spirits were increasingly displaced as a stimulant and tonic by beer, which was now considerably cheaper. The introduction of mechanisation certainly contributed to this development. Looking after a machine did not demand crude muscle power enhanced by schnaps, but rather, greater care and skill. Employers, therefore, often wrote specific clauses into work contracts which forbade the consumption of spirits before and during working hours, as they were now concerned with the maintenance of expensive machinery. In addition particularly the younger labourers regarded beer-drinking as a kind of status symbol, and its consumption was regarded as more refined than drinking spirits. Despite the fact that it was clearly unnecessary, the clergy in the Magdeburg region tried to set up temperance unions as their counterparts in the United States and Britain had done. They had no success.

Indigenous labourers also attempted to maximise their earning capacity through the skilful utilisation of specific mechanisms of the capitalist labour market, often depending on the assistance of family members, friends and acquaintances. If they still had a little land for growing flax, they could earn some supplementary income by the sale of linen thread, but keeping livestock was more significant. Even when the employers reduced the amount of allotment and rented land, and thus limited the possibility of growing animal feedstuffs, the labourers held on to their livestock, resorting largely to field raids to feed them. This was not of course viable in the long term, and the largest and most useful source of supplementary income was derived from the remaining cultivable allotment or plot, whether owned or leased by the labourer.

During the working week the labourer was supposed to work only on the farmer's land. This meant that the labourer could only cultivate his own patch on Sundays and feast days, and even this was restricted during harvest time. In addition there were numerous religious restrictions about working on Sundays. At a time when there were no legal limits to the amount of time a man could work, the ban on Sunday working could have been to the labourers' advantage, as it limited the working week to six days. However, as it did not take account of the real situation of the working population, in practice this measure worked against their interests. While employers had the whole week, day by day, from morning till evening, with 10, 12 and even 17 hours a day to cultivate their land with others' labour, the labourer had only Sundays and feast days to cultivate his own patch. A genuinely humane and Christian attitude — and the most vociferous advocates of banning Sunday working claimed to represent such an approach — would have taken into acount the real needs of the working population. Along with banning work on a Sunday they should also have advocated a regulation of working hours, which would have enabled the labourer to cultivate his own patch of land at certain times during the working week. Only then would labourers have been able to enjoy Sundays as a day of rest. But this was not the case, as the economic interests of the farmers precluded such a regulation of working hours. As it was also in the farmers' interests to maintain a healthy working population they enforced the ban on Sunday working and made their labourers observe Sundays and feast days as rest days. The farmers were also concerned to leave open a possible channel for ideological influence by the ruling class, namely through church-going. The state was also interested in this context in maintaining a relatively healthy rural population for conscription purposes. However despite repeated threats and actual punishments, the rural labourers continued openly to defy all laws forbidding Sunday work.

In addition to putting the cultivation of their own patch of land on a regular basis, the indigenous rural labouring families resorted to another method of increasing the family labour force, apart from using the labour of family members and friends. In order to provide the family with additional labour they encouraged their adult sons and daughters to marry early, although this met with opposition from the children themselves, particularly from those in service, who wanted greater personal independence. This ploy also relieved the problem of overcrowding in the parental home. The trend was further strengthened by the fact that women's wages in particular were declining in the 1860s: they were now unemployed for longer periods during the year due to mechanisation and the increasing use of seasonal migrant workers. Therefore it is not surprising that parents should have favoured early marriage to relieve the burden on the parental home. Easy relations between the sexes were not only silently tolerated by the parents, but in very many cases actively encouraged. It was also usual that where a couple had engaged in sexual relations, they both recognised a moral obligation to marry. Under these circumstances it is no wonder that premarital sex evoked no moral indignation on the part of the indigenous rural proletariat. If disapproval was voiced, it was usually on economic grounds, though if the daughter became pregnant marriage was certainly the most economic course.

The spirit of family self-help, typical of the relatively high moral code of rural labourers in the Magdeburg region, was also evident in their readiness to help others. In the crisis years of 1846/47 they collected substantial donations for workers suffering in other parts of Germany.

For a long time the acquisition of a sufficiently large plot of land to ensure a degree of security seemed to the labourers of the Magdeburg region a worthy goal, and one that was worth saving and making sacrifices for. The demand for land was the main issue in their conflict with the great landowners and employers of the region. But they did not have the remotest chance of realising these demands through legal means — for example, by influencing village policies. This remained true even after the introduction in 1850 of progressive legislation governing local political structures, a result of the struggles of the bourgeois-democratic revolution. In any case, it was rescinded three years later by the victorious forces of the counter-revolution. They were thus forced to resort to illegal methods. They were particularly incensed by the measures connected with enclosure, in particular by the inequity of the distribution of former common land. In two villages collective arson resulted, and two other parishes joined in the public disturbances during the revolutionary year of 1848. In addition to the burning of property, setting fire to wheat fields was also popular. However the majority of these violent acts were isolated incidents and were partly acts of revenge, or attempts at intimidation.

But collective actions stopped at the village boundaries. The indigenous rural workers did not join together to form larger regional associations. Their failure to increase their power and thus improve their chances of success was a result of an undeveloped class-consciousness and their geographical isolation. Of great significance was the fact that in the Magdeburg region west of the Elbe (in contrast to the situation to the east) class conflict had developed very early between the peasantry and the rural proletariat. On the one hand this tended to increase the development of class-consciousness both of the rural proletariat and of the peasant farmers. On the other hand, it also produced a feeling of isolation on the part of the rural labourers within the framework of the disintegration of the village community. Their earlier alliance with the peasantry, in particular with the more prosperous sections of it, which was basically a non-feudal one, broke down as soon as the peasantry were freed of their feudal restrictions. The increasingly prosperous 'sugar beet peasants' were no longer their partners but increasingly their class enemies, who now openly sided with the great landowners.

This conflict, which reflected the class antagonism between the Junkers and the rural proletariat, even affected the relationship between farm servants and permanent farm workers and their employers. It was particularly apparent in the struggle of these workers for better working and living conditions. Again, however, individual action was the rule in these struggles. Some of the most widely used methods to improve or shorten the period of service preferred by servants, and which were occasionally successful, included deliberate damage to equipment, provocation, bad behaviour, frequent changes of master, negotiating short-term contracts, breaking contracts, and in the case of male farm servants refusing to enter into a new contract after their period of compulsory military service. After the defeat of the 1848/49 revolution, most of the methods of resistance which had been used previously — for example, general disturbances or uprisings, or acts of individual or collective terror — were no longer possible due to the changed political situation. However, rapid industrialisation allowed the more frequent use of one particular method, which formerly had only been one among several, namely the actual or threatened breach of the employment contract. In the case of the day labourers this mostly involved quitting employment early — for example during harvest time, or at least threatening to do so. The most significant legal measure set in motion by the forces of political reaction in the interests of the large estate owners was a law 'pertaining to the negligence of farm servants and labourers', passed in 1854. This law was characteristic of the counter-revolution's method of protecting its own interests, and one can imagine how unpopular it was with the Prussian rural proletariat.

The employers however could never achieve the success they hoped for. So in the Magdeburg region, at least, they resorted to other methods. Even the Anti-Socialist Law of 1878–90, which made it easier to punish contract-breakers, failed to satisfy them. The only method remaining to them was to bind their servants by offering small concessions, while at the same time reducing customary favours in their own interest. Thus the possibility of higher earnings through piecework had to be paid for by the labourers by enormous physical effort; the little potato allotment was set against the impossibility of renting additional land; the small improvements in living conditions were offset by the binding terms of the written contract; and so on. However, the most profitable and efficient method that the employers found to combat the effects of the flight from the land was the massive employment of seasonal migrant workers. In some places this might have made it easier to break contracts, but its major significance lay in the fact that it seriously undermined the position of the indigenous rural labourers in their continuing struggle for a direct improvement in their living and working conditions.

Notes

1. This article is a summary of the author's monograph: *Landarbeiterleben im 19. Jahrhundert. Eine volkskundliche Untersuchung über Veränderungen in der Lebensweise der einheimischen Landarbeiterschaft in den Dörfern der Magdeburger Börde unter den Bedingungen der Herausbildung und Konsolidierung des Kapitalismus in der Landwirtschaft. Tendzen und Triebkräfte* (Akademie der Wissenschaften der DDR. Zentralinstitut für Geschichte. Veröffentlichungen zur Volkskunde und Kulturgeschichte, Band 65, Berlin, 1979). Detailed source references can be found in this book.

2. For a comparison see, for example, Christel Heinrich, 'Lebensweise und Kultur der in- und ausländischen landwirtschaftlichen Saisonarbeiter von der Mitte des 19. Jahrhunderts bis 1918', in *Bauer und Landarbeiter im Kapitalismus in der Magdeburger Börde. Zur Geschichte des dörflichen Alltags vom Ausgang des 18. Jahrhunderts bis zum Beginn des 20. Jahrhunderts* (Akademie der Wissenschaften der DDR. Zentralinstitut für Geschichte. Veröffentlichungen zur Volkskunde und Kulturgeschichte, Band 66/3, Berlin, 1982), pp. 117–62.

3. For an extensive commentary see the article by Hans-Heinrich Müller, 'Zur Geschichte und Bedeutung der Rübenzuckerindustrie in der Provinz Sachsen im 19. Jahrhundert unter besonderer Berücksichtigung der Magdeburger Börde', in *Landwirtschaft und Kapitalismus. Zur Entwicklung der ökonomischen und sozialen Verhältnisse in der Magdeburger Börde vom Ausgang des 18. Jahrhunderts bis zum Ende des ersten Weltkrieges*, 2 (Akademie der Wissenschaften der DDR. Zentralinstitut für Geschichte. Veröffentlichungen zur Volkskunde und Kulturgeschichte, vol. 66/2, Berlin, 1979), pp. 9–61.

4. For a comparison, see Siegfried Graffunder, *Die gesetzmässige Verelendung der werktätigen Volkschichten unter den Bedingungen der landwirtschaftlichen Produktionssteigerung in Deutschland des vormonopolistischen Kapitalismus*, Landwirtschaftswissenschaftliche Dissertation (Berlin, 1960).

5. Jürgen Kuczynski, *Die Theorie der Lage der Arbeiter* (Die Geschichte der Lage der Arbeiter unter dem Kapitalismus, vol. 36, Berlin, 1968), p. 73.

6. On living conditions for the rural labourers in this area, see Hans-Jürgen Rach, *Bauernhaus, Landarbeiterkaten und Schnitterkaserne. Zur Geschichte von Bauen und Wonhen der ländlichen Agrarproduzenten in der Magdeburger Börde des 19. Jahrhunderts* (Akademie der Wissenschaften der DDR. Zentralinstitut für Geschichte. Veröffentlichungen zur Volkskunde und Kulturgeschichte, vol. 58, Berlin, 1974).

7. Cf. Gaffunder, *op. cit.*, p. 128.

8. Cf. Weyhe, 'Vortrag über die Rübenzuckerfabrikation und deren Besteuerung, gehalten in dem zu Frankfurt a.M. in November 1848 versammelten Congress deutscher Landwirthe', in *Zeitschrift des landwirtschaftlichen Central-Vereins der Provinz Sachsen*, vol. 6 (1849), p. 91.

5 FARMERS AND FACTORY WORKERS
Rural Society in Imperial Germany: the Example of Maudach

Cathleen S. Catt

I

For a number of reasons which have been well rehearsed elsewhere[1] the immediate post-war generation of German historians was pre-occupied with the study of high politics in the conservative scholarly tradition. During the 1960s a younger generation successfully challenged this conservative interpretation of recent German history both intellectually and institutionally.[2] The overall thesis that this new interpretation generated has been extremely fruitful in terms of the research it has inspired, and it has become widely accepted — so much so that it has been referrred to as a 'new orthodoxy'. It sees Wilhelmine Germany as a basically pre-industrial society suddenly catapulted into the industrial age.[3] German industrialisation certainly occurred much later than in Britain or France, where the origins of industrialisation are often traced back to the 1750s.[4] Germany cannot be regarded as partially industrialised even as late as the 1820s (although a convincing case has been made for regarding the period 1800–50 as a period of 'proto-industrialisation' in certain parts of what was later the German empire).[5] It is also claimed that German industrialisation was partial, in that some sectors of the economy industrialised very rapidly, while others lagged behind. Again there is certainly a great deal of evidence to back up this view, although the evenness of British and French industrialisation should not be overemphasised. Finally, it is claimed, industrialisation in Germany was much more rapid than was the case in Britain or France. As a result of these three factors a series of stresses and strains was set up within the social fabric, and the pre-industrial ruling élites were obliged to come to terms with new social forces without the time for adjustment which Britain and France had supposedly enjoyed. This set of circumstances is sometimes referred to as 'synchronous anachronism' (*gleichzeitige Ungleichzeitigkeit*).[6] This notion helps

129

account for both the reaction of the pre-industrial élites (regarded by some as social imperialism)[7] and their (later) attempts to use Nazism. It also helps explain the political reaction of the middle classes to the threat posed by the working-class movement, and eventually, the underlying appeal of Nazi ideology.

The newer generation of historians, both in Britain and in West Germany, have been widely influenced by this persuasive interpretation of the history of Wilhelmine Germany. Nevertheless, for some time it has been apparent that this view of German history sees the immense social upheavals that were taking place in the second half of the nineteenth century mainly from the point of view of the élite circles of government and socially-privileged groups. By simply stressing the continuity of German society through to the 1930s, it largely ignores the complexities of the changes that were certainly taking place. So it is clearly in need of some revision. Thus younger historians have increasingly stressed the importance of 'history from below' in illuminating this immensely complex process of change.

Within this general context, the study of rural society has been largely neglected — though this is now being rectified, as the contributions to this volume show.[8] The same basic dichotomy is reflected here: earlier studies of rural society stressed the traditionalism and conservatism of the German peasantry, and went on to discuss in depth the way in which agrarian élites manipulated the peasantry through various interest groups.[9] More recent work has stressed the extent to which the peasantry themselves became politicised, through particular economic pressures, and has argued that this politicisation was by no means a straightforward, conservative one. Indeed, Ian Farr has stressed that it was peasant radicalism that pushed the Centre Party into introducing more radical policies,[10] and David Blackbourn's study of the Centre Party in Württemberg backs up the idea that to some extent the grassroots of politics were as important in shaping policy as any national criterion.[11]

Within the general debate, there are very few detailed local studies of rural society on which to base more wide-ranging conclusions.[12] It was for this reason that I undertook a study of one particular village — Maudach, in the Bavarian Palatinate. The Palatinate belonged to the Bavarian state during the nineteenth century, but it was economically and politically very different from Bavaria. For a start, the Palatinate had been under the direct

Figure 5.1: Map of the Palatinate

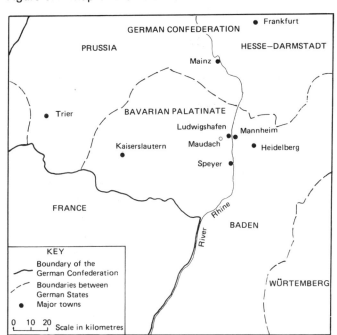

control of the French during the Napoleonic wars. It retained throughout its association with Bavaria its right to the *Code Civil*. This affected many aspects of social and political life. The Palatinate is a small region (5927.96 sq. km)[13] with a diverse climate and soil. The strip of land (some 10–15 km wide) running alongside the Rhine is some of the most fertile farming soil in Central Europe. In the nineteenth century it supported many prosperous farming villages.[14] It was on this fertile strip that cash crops were first grown extensively, particularly tobacco and flax. These crops were later replaced largely by market gardening, which still flourishes today.[15] Further west are the famous wine-growing regions of the Palatinate, and westwards of these the impoverished hilly region of the Westrich which stretches to the French border (see Figure 5.1).

Maudach is situated in the fertile farming land approximately 4 km from what is now the large industrial conurbation of Ludwigshafen/Mannheim. To a large extent the social history of Maudach has been shaped by the meteoric growth of the town of

Ludwigshafen. In 1840 there were only 90 inhabitants of the town's predecessor, the settlement called the Rheinschanze. These were mainly farmers, dockers and warehousemen, as there was a landing place on the river bank. By 1905 the population had risen to 72,286:[16] an increase by a factor of 83 in 65 years. The growth of Ludwigshafen was associated with its increasing importance as a port, but also with the development of the chemical and light engineering industries. In particular the siting of the *Badische Anilin- und Sodafabrik* (BASF) just to the north of the town in 1865 contributed to its growth.[17]

This meteoric population growth was not reflected in Maudach. Its population only doubled in 60 years, rising from 828 in 1835 to 1521 in 1895. However, during this time Maudach changed from an essentially rural community (some 70 per cent of the population derived their living from agricultural pursuits in 1840) to a community split between those who still gained their living from agriculture and those who subsisted on industrial employment.[18] Thus Maudach represents an interesting context for a study of the stresses within rural society caused by the rapid industrial growth of Germany in the nineteenth century.[19]

Within the context of a comprehensive social and economic study of the village, based on a family reconstitution, I have focused on one question in particular: Does the evidence support the idea that rural society remained essentially traditional and conservative throughout the Wilhelmine period? Can we talk about the unchanging nature of that society, in contrast to the changes taking place in the urban environment? Or did the profound social changes taking place directly affect the rural population in a fundamental way before 1900?

If local studies are to illuminate wider historical questions then it is imperative that they should at least attempt to reflect adequately the complexities of the societies they seek to represent. Some earlier rural studies ran into the problem of an oversimplified analytical structure which represented a rather static picture of village life which 'responded' to changes which were generated outside the village.[20] From here it was a short step to seeing rural groups as the dupes of outside manipulative forces. In order to overcome this problem it has been the main aim of this study to seek out the differing and sometimes conflicting experiences of the various social groups within the village of Maudach. In doing this, I hope to answer the question as to whether village life was vitally affected in the period 1840–1900 by the social tensions attendant on rapid industrialisation, and to explore the problem of how far those changes in village economic relations, power structure and underlying attitudes were generated within the village itself. In this way we can question the myth of an unchanging rural society dominated by peasant conservatism, and ultimately help explain why some sections of the rural population turned so readily to conservative and finally fascist ideologies.

II

Any attempt at classifying a population in the past runs immediately into problems. What categories should be used, and what relation do they bear to social reality? Historians can either set up their own categories and, using various socio-economic indices, slot individuals into socio-economic categories of their own devising,[21] or they can use the classifications current at the time and investigate the socio-economic reality behind the labels. Both methods have certain methodological and theoretical problems associated with them: any classification system cuts across what is essentially a continuum of human activity.

The classification system used here is the result of a compromise, arrived at empirically. During the initial stages of data-collection it became clear that the registrar of births, marriages and deaths was dealing with — or thought he was dealing with — people who belonged mainly to three occupational groups: farmers (*Ackerer*), day-labourers (*Tagner*) and factory workers (*Fabrikarbeiter*). The great majority of Maudach residents were listed under these three occupations throughout the period. However, there were also a great many other occupations listed, particularly from 1880 onwards, such as innkeepers, smiths, carpenters, tailors, builders, bricklayers, and so on. Many of these occupations could be regarded either as petty-bourgeois or as artisan occupations. However, there were not, in any of the three 20-year periods between 1840 and 1900, enough of these 'other' occupations to be analysed statistically if the group was broken down further. There were, however, too many to leave out of the picture entirely. Thus I have included those whose occupation did not fall into the other three occupational categories in a miscellaneous group referred to throughout as the 'self-employed', as the majority certainly were. I make no claims for these to be regarded as a cohesive social group. This certainly represents an oversimplification of the social situation in Maudach, and elsewhere[22] I have looked at the group in more detail, but it does have the advantage that it leaves three substantial and clear-cut occupational groups within the village which can then be analysed to discover the social reality behind the labels used at the time.

In the following, then, it should be remembered that the terms 'farmers', 'labourers' and 'workers' refer to those classified as such by the registrar of births, marriages and deaths. It may be that the social reality behind the term was rather different from our expectations, and that the term was used to cover a wider range of activities than might at first be expected (this is particularly true of the farmers). It does not seem reasonable, however, to set up, at this stage, another, essentially arbitrary classification system. Throughout I have used the term 'farmers' as a translation for *Backerer* rather than peasant, as from the late eighteenth century at the latest large sections of the Palatinate farming community had ceased to be peasant farmers in the usually accepted sense of the word,[23] although to regard them as fully capitalist farmers would be equally mistaken.

Figure 5.2 shows graphically the changes in occupation that had taken place in Maudach by 1900. Before discussing the changes in more detail it is necessary first to introduce a note of caution about the figures. The statistics on which this graph are based have been compiled from a variety of sources — a family reconstitution,[24] land tax records,[25] and some unpublished statistics of the Bavarian administration in Speyer.[26] Each set of figures has its own biases and pitfalls. In particular unmarried men and women who owned no land are hard to identify. This is borne out by an examination of the 1851 Bavarian government survey, which shows a slightly larger percentage of labourers than appears from the family reconstitution, and a number of farm servants who do not appear at all in the other sources, apart from the occasional mother of an illegitimate child. The proportion of farm servants in the Bavarian government survey is approximately 3 per cent of Maudach's total population. The discrepancy between the number of labourers shown in the survey and the results of the family reconstitution is approximately 4 per cent. So in all, the single, landless element of the population may have accounted for about 7 per cent in 1851. However, bearing in mind the fact that the figures for the farmers in particular might

Figure 5.2: The Social Structure of Maudach, 1840−1900

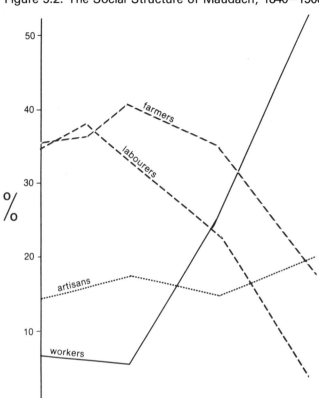

Sources: St. A. Lu. Bes. Mau., pp. 631−848; L. A. Speyer Präsidialakten H3 220 n-x.

be a little inflated because of this, the general trend of the changing occupational structure of Maudach is clear enough.

In the decade 1840−50 roughly one-third of the population were farmers and their families, one-third labourers, and the remaining third either fell into the category of 'self-employed' or were weavers. By 1860 the situation had changed. The number of farmers had actually increased slightly, as had the proportion of the 'self-employed'. However the proportion of labourers had decreased slightly and there were now a few factory workers in the village. By 1880 the trend had become clear. The proportion of farmers in the village was declining, although it is important to remember that this does not mean that the absolute number of farmers was declining. In fact, there were slightly more farmers in 1880 than there had been in 1840; it was their numerical importance in relation to the rest of the village, whose population had been gradually increasing since 1860, which had declined. However, as far as the labourers were concerned both their relative numerical importance and their absolute number had declined considerably since the 1860s, while the proportion of the 'self-employed' remained at approximately the same level. By 1900 the workers were by far the most important group statistically in the village, comprising over 50 per cent of the population. The numerical importance of the farmers had declined even further, although there were still more farmers in 1900 than there had been in 1840. The labourers were by now a numerically almost insignificant group, while the proportion of the self-employed had increased.

Thus the occupational profile of the village in 1900 was radically different from the profile for the village in 1840. It is tempting to conclude that what happened was that labourers left their work on the land and took jobs in factories, changing their old masters for new. However, the situation was far more complex than this. A look at people's life histories reveals that although most (80 to 90 per cent) farmers remained farmers throughout their lives, labourers lived in a more precarious situation, drifting from labouring to factory work and back again. Some managed to save enough of the money they earned as factory workers to set up as farmers, while some farmers, unable to survive the agricultural depressions of the 1870s and 1880s became factory workers themselves. Certainly, many farmers' sons also took work in the factories either before inheriting their portion of the family farm or as an alternative, leaving the farm intact to another brother.[27]

III

Maudach lies on some of the best farming land in the Palatinate, on the fertile soil of the Rhine plain. Although its position has meant that it has in the past been liable to serious flooding, and although the presence of stagnant pools of surface water was detrimental to the general health of the population throughout the nineteenth century, this privileged position meant that it could support a fairly large farming population on a relatively small amount of land.

Here, according to Mang and Zink,[28] a farming family could live reasonably well on 2 hectares of land, provided it was farmed efficiently. Two hectares may seem at first sight rather an underestimation, particularly as contemporaries writing about other areas, notably Bavaria, seem to have regarded 10 hectares as the minimum requirement. However two points must be remembered. First, the land in this area was regarded by contemporaries as among the most fertile in Germany[29] — Mang and Zink themselves stress that further west on the hilly land of the Westrich even 10 hectares could be insufficient to keep a family. Secondly, the main crop in the Palatinate was, by the 1840s at the latest, potatoes, which grew particularly well in the fertile loam of the Rhine plain. Other areas with similar conditions (for example the Black Fens of East Anglia) have also been reported as producing enough food for a family from 2 hectares.[30]

All the farmers who lived in Maudach throughout the second half of the nineteenth century owned some land, so we are not dealing with a situation where there were large numbers of tenant farmers, although there was a large area of council land which was regularly leased out, and which farmers could use to supplement their own land if it was insufficient.[31] In 1840, when a new land tax register was drawn up, nearly 40 per cent of the men classified as farmers (*Ackerer*) owned under 2 hectares of land. Just over 35 per cent owned between 3 and 5 hectares, while just under 20 per cent owned between 6 and 10 hectares. Only 4 per cent owned over 10 hectares. In 1880 this pattern was even more pronounced, and 45 per cent of the men calling themselves farmers owned under 2 hectares of land. By 1900 however the proportion had dropped to 35 per cent, and the proportion falling into the 2–5 hectare category had risen accordingly. The proportion of farmers in the other size categories remained much the same throughout the period, as we can see from Figure 5.3.

These figures are interesting for, on the face of it, they mean that over one-third of the men in the village calling themselves farmers owned insufficient land to feed themselves and a family. Furthermore the number, absolutely and relatively, of these men increased between 1840 and 1880, although it thereafter declined. How can this be accounted for? First, some may have had a supplementary means of income. Petersen remarks[32] that the most widespread form of supplementary income in the Palatinate was distilling spirits from potatoes, and it is likely that some of the farmers were

Figure 5.3: Amount of Land Owned by Farmers in Maudach, 1840–1900

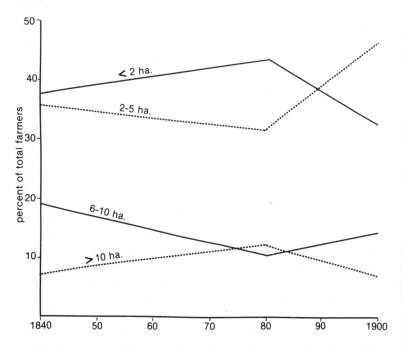

involved in this. Other supplementary forms of income for the Maudach farmer ranged from peat-cutting (there was an abundant supply in the nearby peat bog formed by the Rhine) to the cash-cropping of tobacco, flax or, in the later period, the production of milk and fresh vegetables for the nearby town of Ludwigshafen.

Secondly, and more importantly, the amount of land a farmer owned changed over his lifetime. In this region a son rarely inherited a farm intact. In the first place, the area was governed by the French *Code Civil*, which made it illegal for the father to hand over the farm intact to one son; each child was entitled to an equal share. What often happened was that when a son reached a certain age — this varied from family to family, and does not appear to coincide very exactly with marriage plans — the farmer would hand over a small amount of land to his son to farm. Two hectares might be necessary to feed a family, but less than 1 hectare would be sufficient to keep one man in food. The son would almost certainly eventually marry a girl who would bring some land with her as her marriage portion, and thereafter he would strive to increase his land through purchase, and if necessary rent some land either from the village council or an absentee landowner (of whom there were several). Clearly the nature of the local land market is crucial. Petersen suggests[33] that throughout the Palatinate it was buoyant between 1850 and 1880. Certainly the farmers of Maudach were able to increase their land, as the land records clearly show.[34] This can be partly accounted for by the amount of cash in the economy as a result of cash-cropping, sales of local peat and timber, and the proximity to Ludwigshafen. Thus there was a lively land market in the Palatinate, and this pattern of acquisition of land over a life-time was widespread.[35] Finally the farmer would begin settling land on his sons and daughters as they married or became old enough to set up for themsleves, and at the age of 70 he might well be left with a plot of land about the size he started out with. Thus the fact that about one-third of the men calling themselves farmers did not own enough land to keep themselves and a family reflects as much this cycle of landholding, as it indicates a growing impoverishment through the vicissitudes of partible inheritance. Certainly this large proportion of farmers owning under 2 hectares of land does suggest that Maudach, in line with other villages in areas of partible inheritance, did suffer from land morcellisation. Many could in fact be classified as 'smallholders' and in economic terms there may have been little difference between farmers at this end of the scale and those labourers who managed, through the manipulation of the local land market, to achieve a similar level of landholding. However it would be a mistake to overemphasise the extent of morcelisation, as many of those with land under 2 hectares did have either a genuine expectation of more land through marriage (which few labourers could aspire to) or had only themselves to keep in old age — a very different situation from a labourer with 2 hectares and seven children to provide for.

Yet the fact that the proportion of farmers owning less than 2 hectares of land increased between 1840 and 1880, coupled with the fact that the absolute number of farmers also increased in these years, does seem to indicate that increasing competition made it more difficult for a young farmer to increase his land. The fairly dramatic drop in the proportion of farmers owning under 2 hectares between 1880 and 1900 on the other hand, coupled with a slight decrease in the absolute number of farmers, seem to indicate that the weakest went to the wall. Those with some advantage, perhaps better land or marketing sense, or who chose to diversify and serve the growing population of Ludwigshafen, did well, and the proportion of farmers in the 2–5 hectare category certainly increased in the last two decades of the nineteenth century. A process of rationalisation seems to have taken place in Maudach's farming in these years. Petersen highlights this development by remarking that it was the small farmers rather than the large estates that were maximising productivity by growing cash crops increasingly from the 1870s.[36] In particular tobacco, flax and onions were grown in increasing quantities. Rather than the number of impoverished farmers continuing to rise, as one could expect in an area of partible inheritance, the numbers dimished as the weaker, smaller farmers found other occupations in the growing industrial and service sectors. It seems reasonable to conclude that although many of the farmers in Maudach owned less than 2 hectares of land, many were able, during their lives, to increase the amount of land they owned. Their proximity to a large industrial town from the 1870s meant that even smaller farmers in the late nineteenth century could be assured of a certain level of income from market gardening and cash crops — an assurance which did not extend to wheat and cereal growers elsewhere, adversely affected by foreign competition.[37] There were opportunities of raising money to buy extra land. However, it is also reasonable to suppose that some who began farming in the 1870s and 1880s were not able to compete successfully and chose other ways of earning a living, leaving a smaller number of more successful farmers who may have maintained a higher standard of living in the late nineteenth century.[38]

Far more numerous, however, were the agricultural day-labourers. There were in general a considerable number of day-labourers on the land in the Palatinate in the nineteenth century; in Maudach they accounted for about one-third of the population until the 1860s. Thereafter their numbers began to decline, and they quickly became a minority within the village. In Maudach the day labourers were not landless, and until 1900 and beyond, almost all day labourers owned some land. (The figures range from 95–7 per cent, although this is probably an overestimation, due to the difficulty of identifying the unmarried landless section of the population.) The amount of land they owned was of course very small, and usually insufficient to keep a family. In 1840 only 3.5 per cent of day labourers owned over 2 hectares of land, in 1880 3.1 per cent; in general these were labourers descended from weaving families. However in 1900, although the absolute number of day-labourers had fallen to under half the number there had been in 1840, 17 per cent owned over 2 hectares of land. Most of the day-labourers throughout the period, however, owned less (often considerably less) than 0.34 hectares (1 *Tagwerk*) of land, and the absolute necessity of labouring to obtain the basic necessities of life cannot be seriously disputed. The fact that there were labourers owning more than 2 hectares and that the proportion of these increased can perhaps also be accounted for by reference to bureaucratic registration procedures, and the traditional nomenclature of holdings, which may not have taken into account the way in which holding size could fluctuate. This means that there may well have been some overlap between the economic position of those at the bottom of the scale in the occupational group of farmers, and those at the top of the scale in the labouring group. A degree of overlap is however, inevitable in any classification system, and as long as it is remembered that labels specify groups along a continuum, this should not be an insuperable problem.

The day-labourers generally worked for the larger farmers, and for the one large estate owner, Count von Waldkirchen, who owned a large estate in Maudach until 1849. They also found work in the summer months as peat-cutters, working either directly for the village council or again for one of the larger farmers. There were other jobs offered by the village council as well; while they meant a steady income, there were several problems attached to these. There were two field watchers, whose job was to prevent theft from the fields, report the first signs of pest problems such as beetles and mice, and whose job it was to keep the paths and walkways clear of weeds. There was also a nightwatchman, a cowherd, a gooseherd and a man who looked after the horses which were grazed on the council meadow land. In the 1830s these council workers were still paid partly in kind, and this continued right up to the 1890s, although the money part of the wages became increasingly important.

How adequate was the wage paid to the agricultural labourers? Of course this is a particularly difficult question to answer. For the period 1840–60 it is very difficult to say with any certainty what the standard of living of an agricultural worker might be. Wages were still paid at least partly in kind, so that in a bad year a labourer or council employee would at least be sure of a certain amount of grain, irrespective of price. However this was seldom enough to feed a family on, and the labourer had to supplement this grain both with the produce of his own plot and by buying in necessary staples. Food prices varied enormously, depending on the weather, pests and crop diseases, and when food prices were high this was often when the produce from the labourers' own patch of land was inadequate too. What was an adequate wage one year might be pitifully inadequate the next. For the 1840s particularly there is evidence of widespread poverty and distress in Maudach, as all over Germany. In 1840 Maudach's council had to pay out 84 florins from the poor relief fund. This rose to 130 florins in 1842 and 210 in 1847.[39] In 1843, 490 loaves of bread were distributed to the poor,[40] and in the same year the council petitioned the Bavarian administration to be allowed to let 36 debtors to the council postpone payment[41] 'because there is no possibility of any work for the lower classes'. The potato famine in 1847/48 struck the Palatinate particularly hard, as for many years the poorer classes of the population had subsisted almost entirely on a diet of potatoes and sour milk.[42] In Maudach the village council had to set up a vigilante group to prevent thefts from the fields, which threatened to overwhelm them.[43]

The 1850s were better in some respects, and there was no repeat of the terrible failure of the potato crop. Yet the problem of poverty did not disappear. Contemporary reports all agree that the poorer classes in the Palatinate lived on simple, unvaried fare, in overcrowded, poorly-lit and poorly-heated accommodation, and were frequently exhausted by long hours of hard work outside and wore ragged inadequate clothing.[44] In the late nineteenth century the labourers were consistently paid less — often considerably less — than the unskilled factory workers, whose wages were often well below the level considered by contemporaries as the minimum possible to keep a family on[45] although payments in kind continued for council workers until well into the 1880s. For example in 1886 the nightwatchman was paid 120 Marks p.a. and 10 hectolitres of grain. During this period the average general wage for an adult male agricultural labourer was around 200 Marks p.a. They were paid from 50 pfennigs to 1 Mark less per day than the average worker in the chemical industry.[46] They did of course have the produce of their own plots of land. Thus the evidence suggests that the day labourers continued throughout the nineteenth century to subsist on the threshold of poverty. However, the day labourers of Maudach were certainly in a better position than the entirely landless labourers further east.[47]

A third occupational group in the village consisted of the self-employed. Fewer people in this group owned land in the village but even so, throughout the period, between 68 and 73 per cent of them owned some land. The amount of land they owned varied tremendously. The village smiths were by far the largest landowners, closely followed by innkeepers. Carpenters and bricklayers, tailors and shopkeepers, if they owned land at all, owned less than 2 hectares.[48] The tax paid by this group bears out this estimate of relative wealth, the innkeepers and smiths emerging as wealthy village characters.[49] The position of this group in relation to other groups in the village seems to have remained fairly constant over the 60 years from 1840–1900, although contemporaries claim to have noticed an increase in the prosperity and respectability of the craftsmen and shopkeepers in rural villages over the Palatinate as a whole.[50]

Finally, from 1859 the number of factory workers living in Maudach increased continually. The growth was gradual at first, but accelerated after the founding of the BASF works in Ludwigshafen in 1865. The vast majority of factory workers who lived in Maudach had to commute to nearby towns every day for their work. Most went on foot until 1890, when a narrow-gauge railway connecting Dannstadt, Mutterstadt, Maudach and Mundenheim with Ludwigshafen was opened. An idea of the numbers involved in commuting can be obtained from looking at the sale of tickets: in December 1890 over 9000 workers' season tickets (*Arbeitermonatskarten*) were sold for this stretch of line, and over 500 single tickets were issued daily.[51] Conditions in the factories in this area have been fully described elsewhere.[52] They were, of course, far from pleasant, and the workers in the chemical industry had to face the additional hazards of working with toxic chemicals with minimal safety procedures.[53] Breunig concluded that the average wage paid to an unskilled worker was not adequate to support him and his family in the town.[54]

The workers from Maudach were in a slightly better position as rents were far lower in Maudach than in the city, and if they owned a little land there was always the possibility that food grown on that land could supplement the family diet. However, the proportion of factory workers in this position should not be overemphasised. In 1880 only about one-fifth owned any land, although this figure rose to one-third by 1900. This is an interesting development, open to a number of interpretations. The first and perhaps most obvious interpretation is that, given partible inheritance and the increasing employment prospects in the factories, day labourers were increasingly attracted to industrial employment. And this certainly partly accounts for the phenomenon. However, many of the factory workers who owned land in the village were in fact immigrants into the village. Presumably this group moved to the village first of all, attracted by the job opportunities in the area, and then used their industrial wages to buy land, later marrying into settled Maudach families — a source of possible conflict with farmers, who were also attempting to purchase land. Selective migration would then account for the rise in the proportion of factory workers owning land, as those with no stake in the village would tend to move out, particularly as firms in the area increasingly offered their own accommodation to their workers. Overall, however, the number of workers living in Maudach continued to rise until after 1900.

In summary, then, the picture that emerges from a detailed statistical examination of the village of Maudach between 1840 and 1900 is not one of a homogeneous 'peasant' village, although from 1840−60 the overwhelming majority of the population were employed in the agricultural sector. There were considerable differences in the amount of land owned, the amount of tax paid, and the kinds of work undertaken by the different occupational groups, and there was a considerable gap between the expectations and the possibilities open to those who were reasonably secure and sure of being able to cover their basic needs and those who were not. Nor did the relative positions of the groups remain the same over these 60 years. The farmers as a group seem to have experienced increased difficulty in obtaining land during the 1870s and 1880s, and some of the smaller farmers were probably squeezed out during this period. By the 1890s, however, the farmers seem to have solved this problem, and as a group appear more prosperous than before. This point should not be overemphasised, since there were certainly in 1900, as in 1840, a number of smallholders within this occupational group who were struggling to make a living. The day-labourers, subsisting throughout the 1840s and 1850s on the threshold of poverty, and hit by a series of crises, the most serious being the potato famine, continued in much the same way throughout the later years of the century, although perhaps marginally more prosperous than before. However their numbers declined as work became more freely available in the factories. Certainly the kind of lives they led, with the constant possibility of being laid off by the factories in accordance with market pressures, meant that a good many drifted from day-labouring to factory work and back again as the circumstances demanded.

The position of the craftsmen and shopkeepers included in the 'self-employed' group seems to have remained relatively stable throughout the 60 years, although it must be remembered that this group covers a wide variation in wealth and social standing. The workers from the 1860s gradually became numerically the most important group in the village. The majority of them lived on their wages from the factories, and thus were dependent on outside forces for their livelihood. However some did have land in the village, and the proportion of them increased quite substantially in the 20 years between 1880 and 1900. This meant that what was originally an essentially rootless immigrant group (though some indigenous former day labourers were also included) increasingly had a stake in the economic and social life of the village.

IV

In some ways the farmers (bearing in mind that this label covers a wide range of people) constituted a privileged group within the village. This is borne out by an examination of the registrar's records, which show clearly that the farmers as a group differed in important ways from the other groups in the village. For example, an examination of age-specific fertility patterns reveals that farmers' wives married younger (often as young as 17), had their children at younger ages, and stopped producing children at a younger age than the labourers' wives. The highest rate of marital fertility is found for farmers' wives aged 15–19, while for labourers' wives, their peak of fertility is not reached until 20–24 in the period 1840–69, and 25–29 in the period 1870–99.[55] Farmers were certainly a privileged group in terms of mortality, and farmers and their families on average lived longer, and enjoyed a lower infant mortality rate (although overall infant mortality in Maudach was high in comparison to other villages). The mortality rates also reveal that although farmers maintained their relatively privileged position as regards mortality, the 1860s and 1870s — the years of progress and expansion in nearby Ludwigshafen — were years of increasing mortality for all groups in Maudach. Poverty and hardship seem to have increased in these years. The study of differential mortality according to socio-economic status is still in its infancy,[56] but differences in mortality should not be simplistically seen as a direct reflection of differences in income. The standard of housing, extent of overcrowding, sanitary arrangements, availability of medical care, levels of nutrition, work patterns, attitudes towards and care of the sick and elderly, breast-feeding and general standards of education all affected mortality. Certainly, however, the farmers of Maudach, their wives and their children enjoyed an advantage over labourers and workers with regard to mortality rates.

The 1880s and 1890s, however, were characterised by general improvements in health and mortality, and the introduction of new regulations for public hygiene and better medical care was reflected in the clear overall decline in mortality for all the groups in the village towards the end of the nineteenth century. From the council records it is clear that there was an increasing awareness about public hygiene from about 1880 onwards, particularly with regard to the public water supply and waste disposal. Regulations regarding sanitation in public houses, butchers' shops and food processing were also enforced, and the introduction of sickness insurance meant that the groups in the village least able to afford medical assistance had at least minimal cover.[57] Thus the data from statistics bear out the thesis that the farmers were a privileged group within the village in the context of a situation which deteriorated gradually from 1840 to 1880 and then improved quite rapidly.

By this time, however, the proportion of factory workers living in the village was increasing dramatically. The farmers had been the most powerful group within the village in the 1840s. At that time the lower classes had been financially dependent on them, and they had thus exerted both political and economic power over the labourers. However, factory workers were not financially dependent on the farmers as employers. How then did the farmers cope with a situation where their economic ascendancy over the rest of the village was being undermined by changing employment patterns? To examine this question we need to look carefully at the changing political constellations in the village. Who were the most powerful people? What was the nature of the power they enjoyed? How successful were they in maintaining their power in the 60-year period 1840–1900?

In Maudach[58] the most important governing body was the

council (*Gemeinderat*) which enjoyed a considerable degree of autonomy over certain areas of village life. It was responsible for the way agriculture was carried out in the village, and appointed the animal inspectors, the weights and measures officials, and organised pest control, all within the guidelines laid down by the regional government, based in Speyer. It was responsible for law and order in the village, and to this end appointed nightwatchmen and a police officer (whose appointment nevertheless had to be ratified by the regional government). It was in charge of education, and appointed the teachers of the schools (there was both a Protestant and a Catholic school in Maudach). It decided how much money the poor relief committee should have, and determined who was entitled to aid in disputed cases. It was in charge of public health and fire-fighting, though again initiatives in this area usually came from the regional government. It also constituted the link between the village and the regional government in Speyer, which in turn was responsible to Munich, and it was obliged to put into practice what the regional government decided was necessary in terms of road-building and maintenance, and the quartering of troops and provision of foodstuffs for the army when its manoeuvres took it to the region.

The mayor (*Bürgermeister*) and his assistant (*Adjunkt*) and 14 councillors (*Gemeinderatsmitglieder*) were elected by the citizens (*Bürger*) of Maudach every five years. Council members were drawn from a restricted number of families, basically the larger farming families; this continued throughout the nineteenth century. The position of mayor was almost hereditary in Maudach: from 1818 to 1863 the post was held successively by Peter Gruner (1818–33), Johann Gruner (1833–48), Michael Amberger (1848/9), Anton Gruner (1849–59), and Johann Gruner again (1859–63). After this the schoolteacher, Johann Adam Anton Ginkel (who also owned a 10-hectare farm) was mayor until 1872, followed by Georg Kummermehr (1872–85) and Johann Kummermehr (1885–99), both of whom owned over 10 hectares of land. Essentially this is a list of the most substantial farmers in Maudach. The council members too were drawn from the larger farming families, although during the 1850s and 1860s three innkeepers served on the council, and in the 1890s the teacher Heinrich Bossong and the barber and farmer Hieronymus Rosenkranz also served. There was a remarkable degree of continuity. In 1874, 9 of the 14 council members had fathers or uncles who had served on the council elected in 1849; in 1895 there were 10 council members whose fathers or uncles had served on previous councils.[59]

The only people entitled to vote in a local council election were those who were formally registered as citizens. (This category did not include women, who did not have a right to vote.) The electoral roll in March 1848 shows that 80 per cent of the farmers living in Maudach at that time were registered as voters, while 92 per cent of the self-employed, and 74 per cent of the labourers were registered. There is only one other roll that has survived, and that is for 1874. This list shows 72 per cent of farmers, 65 per cent of labourers, 65 per cent of self-employed, and 42 per cent of factory workers were entitled to vote. In the earlier period, then, the majority of men in Maudach from all groups were entitled to vote for the council, although there were more labourers than farmers who did not have a vote. By 1874 there had clearly been important changes. For all groups the proportion of voters had fallen. It had fallen least for the farmers: on the other hand, less than half the workers had the vote at this time. The reasons for the fall in numbers of voters are fairly obvious. Those who were born in Maudach were citizens by right. But it cost 100 florins for a person moving into Maudach to become a citizen. Furthermore, the request had to be submitted to a higher authority through the council, and ratified by the Bavarian government. With wages at about 200 florins p.a. for an agricultural labourer in the 1860s buying citizenship was certainly beyond the means of most. For men marrying women from Maudach the charge was reduced to 50 florins but even so this was a considerable sum of money for most. As more people from outside moved into the village, the electoral base of the council became more heavily weighted in favour of those with property, and in favour of the old established families. This then is the first part of the answer to the question of how the farmers maintained their position of power over an increasingly diverse population. The restricted franchise certainly operated in their favour.[60]

Nevertheless, the story is not as simple as this. For the meaning and nature of political power at this level changed during the period we are considering. There are two facets to power at any intermediate level: its relation to the higher authority and its relation to those below. The relationship between the council and the regional government (ultimately the central Bavarian government) changed during the second half of the nineteenth century. In some respects this was as a direct result of the increasing centralisation of state power,[61] but the council's attitude towards its own role also changed. Until about 1860 there are numerous examples in the local council records[62] of instances where the council refused to put into effect decisions taken by the regional authority before a lengthy debate had taken place. The most striking example is over the question of building a road between Neustadt and Mannheim.[63] Maudach's council regarded the road as a matter for the regional government and did not agree that it should pay part of the maintenance and construction costs. The dispute continued for over a year, and several strongly-worded messages passed between the council and the regional government. The local council eventually lost the battle. By the 1890s, however, a different spirit was abroad. For a start, the job of being a mayor, or even simply a council member, had become a much more complicated affair. There were abundant forms and questionnaires from the regional and central government to fill in. For example in August 1882 a whole meeting was devoted to setting out the average agricultural wage for the different sexes and age-groups for sickness insurance purposes. Then again, the council's finances had become much more complex as they had sums invested in the railways and several companies, as well as money loaned out to individuals, and to other villages, on which the interest had to be collected. Alongside this increasing bureaucratisation of the local council's tasks went a decrease in its areas of jurisdiction. Education, planning, even matters of law and order came increasingly under the control of the regional government. Thus there was ever more work and ever less power. The council became less and less representative of their village, and more and more like a band of civil servants. This was a parallel development to their loss of economic power over their fellow villagers.

The council's relationship to those below its members on the social scale (and the majority of the villagers fell into this category) was at all times an ambivalent one. On the one hand council workers such as the nightwatchmen and even the police officer were drawn from the labourers of the village, and on the other it was the labourers by and large who threatened the peace and order of the village. This tension can clearly be seen if we trace the relations between the council and its employees. The post of field-watcher[64] was a continuous problem. In 1848 half the council, led by the mayor, wanted to dismiss Martin Mohr and Johann Sosser because they had allegedly been partisan in their work. Sosser often stays overnight or for several days in other villages, and has been fined for drunkenness in Oggersheim. He often works his own land. Michael Müller and Georg Mohr both agree that Martin Mohr incited them to steal from Philip Gebhardt's fields. Furthermore he lives with his son who has been convicted for stealing. Neither of them reports daily to the mayor as he is supposed to do.

They were both dismissed.[65] In January 1849 two new field-watchers were appointed: Georg Adam Scheibel, formerly a Bavarian soldier who had left the army with a good reference, and Jakob Borstler IV, who also had a good reputation.[66] Two years later more problems had arisen. Forty-five landowners complained to the council officially about the way the field-watchers were carrying out their job. The council was split. Some thought the only thing to be said against them was that in the previous winter the theft of potatoes had got out of control and someone had destroyed the young trees on the parish meadow, but this had all been cleared up and it certainly had not been the fault of the field-watchers. Others thought they were guilty of gross negligence and should certainly be sacked. This affair caused a great deal of bitterness and in September of the same year we discover that the council was again discussing whether to dismiss Scheibel, but this time because the mayor had taken court proceedings against him for uncouth behaviour.

There are similar instances in the council records up until the end of the century, and the nightwatchmen too could not always be relied on to perform their duties conscientiously. Until the 1860s the main problems in terms of law and order that the council — or, more accurately, the council employees — had to deal with were drunkenness and theft from the fields. But as the number of workers in the village increased other tensions surfaced, although the problems of order and drunkenness continued.[67] It became increasingly difficult over the last two decades of the nineteenth century for the council to maintain its authority. We find incidents where council members had their hayricks burned, and they took court proceedings against other members of the community who publicly expressed their disapproval of the council.[68] These tensions were most clearly expressed in the growing rift between the Catholic and Protestant communities in Maudach. Most of the farmers and the village council members were Catholics (although in the 1880s there was one Protestant farmer on the council). From the 1880s onwards there were increasing signs of tension both between the two religious communities and within the Catholic community. In 1882 for example the council issued a proclamation to the effect that

All possible steps must be taken to settle the present unrest in the village, and to avoid further disturbances. The police are ordered to carry out their duty with the utmost severity, and those in the village who object to the Catholic priest should seek redress for their grievances through the proper channels.[69]

There are no details about the causes of the disturbances, but the priest in question, Konrad Reith, was removed from Maudach the following year.[70]

Friction between the two communities came to a head when the council funded the building of the new Catholic priest's house in 1890. It cost 28,000 Marks, and caused a great deal of ill-feeling in the village. For example the council noted in 1891 that

many refuse to enter the inn of Johann Jakob Gruner 'zum bayerischen Hof', because of differences with the landlord, who was an active agitator in the council election and when the new Catholic priest's house was built. [Johann Jakob Gruner was a staunch Catholic, and at his death in 1903 his religion was recorded as 'altcatholisch'.][71]

The feeling was widespread, and resulted in an incident which made clear the delicate nature of the situation that the council had to deal with. The incident began in July 1893 when the Protestant teacher, Eduard Theobald, made insulting remarks about the council in the hearing of the Catholic teachers, Heinrich Bossong and Heinrich Stauber. The council took legal proceedings against him, despite the fact that Theobald made a public apology. In November of the same year the council recommended that Theobald be removed from his post.

Teacher Theobald is not respectful. He insulted the council, saying 'I'll put an end to this pig's mess; the council is a band of robbers; the mayor is a rascal, etc.' He has been fined by a court for this. At school committee meetings he often swears, particularly at the two priests, calling them lazy pigs, which undermines their respect and effectiveness. This is a religiously mixed community but he has continually complained that the Catholics are exploiting the Protestant minority, and he said that the new Catholic priest's house is a proof of this, despite the fact that the council had proper authority to build it. He has also neglected his duty [. . .] in view of the delicate social situation in this village, a teacher who consistently undermines temporal and spiritual authority must have a detrimental effect on the children he teaches. We recommend that he be moved to another school.

This lengthy petition to the regional government highlights both the tension between the two religious communities in the village, and the way in which national issues impinged on village life. The *Kulturkampf* of the 1870s did not end with a piece of Bismarckian legislation, but continued to divide rural Germany long after official approval for harassment of Catholics ceased. Clearly a Protestant teacher in a Catholic village would be at odds with the prevailing authority. Probably a liberal, he would have had powerful ideological weapons at his disposal to withstand the authority of the Catholic council.

This is partly a reflection of the fact that during the 1880s and 1890s the various groups in the village became increasingly politicised. This can be seen in the proliferation of clubs and societies (there is no evidence of any of these existing before the 1880s) and in increased police surveillance of political activities. Most of the social and sporting clubs in Maudach had a clear political division. There was, for instance, a workers' choir (*Arbeitergesangverein*) and a village choral society; there was a workers' gymnastic club and a '*Kriegerverein*' (veterans' club) whose members practised shooting.[72] As regards national politics, the voting behaviour of Maudachers is rather difficult to disentangle, particularly support for the Catholic Centre Party. There seems to have been a fairly constant hard core of about 70–80 voters for the Centre Party, although in 1890 this rose to 143. This is considerably below the number of farmers in Maudach, or for that matter the number of Catholics, so it is reasonable to conclude that for many voting in national elections appeared irrelevant. The percentage poll for Maudach was rather lower than the *Reich* average: in Reichstag elections it was 52.7 per cent in 1878, 51.3 per cent in 1881 and 80.5 per cent in 1898. In 1886 there were 60 votes for the National

Liberals. Support for this party declined steadily until, in the 1903 election, there were only seven Maudachers who voted for them The vote for the SPD, on the other hand, consistently increased — from 56 in 1887 to 195 in 1898, although this figure dropped back to 150 in the 1903 elections. In the end, the voting pattern reflects the social composition of the village fairly accurately, with a majority of workers mostly voting for the SPD, and a sizeable minority of Catholic farmers and shopkeepers voting for the Centre Party.[73]

VI

I began this paper by focusing on the question of whether or not a detailed empirical study of a German village would reveal it as a traditional peasant society left behind by the developments in the town, and characterised by conservative, traditional attitudes, or whether the village itself changed dramatically over the 60 years. The answer is of course, something of both. The farmers of Maudach certainly constituted a group who maintained traditional behaviour norms in their marriage patterns and retained their positions of power over the rest of the village. However, the nature of that power changed radically. In the 1840s and 1850s the village oligarchy of substantial farmers had had greater autonomy from central government. It was thus able to exercise greater control over what went on in the village. The larger farmers had been in a position of economic ascendancy over the poorer strata of the village and had thus been able to exert their power more effectively. In the 1880s and 1890s this was no longer the case. The economic divisions within the village had radically altered, and the workers were no longer financially dependent on the ruling farming group. Nevertheless the farmers retained a good deal of their traditional position of power over the village, through the structure of the local franchise to some extent, but also through their increasing role as administrators rather than as representatives of the village to a higher authority. Thus as their real economic power over the village waned their importance was bolstered by the power of an increasingly bureaucratic state (Bavaria in the first instance, and later the German empire). The few signs of social integration of the workers into the farming community were not mirrored by corresponding changes in the power structure of the village. It is tempting to conclude that such integration that did take place was with the poorer section of the farming community rather than with the village oligarchy. There were no workers on the village council until after the end of the First World War.

These changes in the position of the farmers of Maudach may be taken as symptomatic of changes that were taking place all over Germany. There were certainly villages where this change did not take place as quickly, and where the substantial farmers continued to be the main employers in their villages. But equally, recent research is uncovering more villages where a large proportion of the population found work outside the village in nearby towns while continuing to live in the village. The nature of German industrialisation — late, rapid, but above all, much more evenly spread out geographically than was the case in Britain or France — coloured the nature of changes within rural society. Within the context of great changes in the position of farmers in rural society, questions about peasant political affiliations become more comprehensible. The lure of *Mittelstand* ideology for the farmers of Germany was probably not its inherent conservatism, but the fact that it offered an ideological rationale for their continued prominence in their own communities at a time when the economic basis of their power was declining. For the farmers of rural Germany in the nineteenth century the threat posed by the Social Democratic Party appeared frighteningly real, directly rooted as it was in their own everyday experience within the village.

There are certain parallels to be drawn with what was happening to other traditional groups in German society. In some important respects the peasant farmers faced the same forces that were undermining the power of the traditional élites and this makes their alliance at certain junctures with those élites far more comprehensible. All this is not to stress the continuity of rural society. The first point to underline is that at no time during the second half of the nineteenth century could rural society in this area be regarded as an essentially 'peasant' society. There were within every village other groups of people with whom the farmers had to deal. Secondly, the relative positions of these groups changed dramatically during the century, and it was the stresses and tensions generated by those changes that informed the political attitudes and actions of the farmers, day labourers and workers who constituted the rural population.

Notes

1. See the discussion in R. J. Evans (ed.), *Society and Politics in Wilhelmine Germany* (London, 1978), pp. 1–5; Geoff Eley, 'Memories of Underdevelopment: Social History in Germany', *Social History*, Vol. 2, No. 3 (September 1977), pp. 785–91; J. Kocka, 'Recent Historiography of Germany and Austria', *Journal of Modern History*, Vol. 47, (1975), pp. 57 ff.

2. For an account, see John A. Moses, *The Politics of Illusion* (London, 1975). Various viewpoints in the debate are expressed in H. W. Koch, *The Origins of the First World War* (London, 1972). See also F. Fischer, *War of Illusions. German Politics from 1911–1914* (London, 1975); and V. R. Berghahn, *Germany and the Approach of War in 1914* (London, 1973).

3. See H.-U. Wehler, *Das deutsche Kaiserreich, 1871–1918* (Göttingen, 1973) (Eng. transl. *The German Empire, 1871–1918* (Leamington Spa, 1985).

4. T. S. Ashton, *The Industrial Revolution* (London, 1964); M. W. Flinn, *An Economic and Social History of Britain since 1700* (London, 1975).

5. P. Kriedte, H. Medick and J. Schlumbohm, *Industrialisation before Industrialisation* (Cambridge, 1981).

6. The phrase is Ernst Bloch's. For a sustained exposition, see A. Gerschenkron, *Economic Backwardness in Historical Perspective* (Cambridge, Mass., 1962).

7. Cf. Berghahn, *op. cit.*; Wehler, *op. cit.*

8. In the past 8–10 years there have been several studies of German rural society. For example, W. R. Lee, *Population Growth, Economic Development and Social Change in Bavaria, 1750–1850* (New York, 1977); A. E. Imhof, 'Ländliche Familienstrukturen an einem hessischen Beispiel: Heuchelheim 1690–1900', in Werner Conze, *Sozialgeschichte der Familie in der Neuzeit Europas* (Stuttgart, 1976), A. Ilien and U. Jeggle, *Leben auf dem Dorf. Zur Sozialgeschichte des Dorfes und Sozialpsychologie ihrer Einwohner* (Opladen, 1978); Kriedte *et al., op. cit.*; D. Sabean, 'Unehelichkeit: Ein Aspekt sozialer Reproduktion kleinbäuerlicher Produzenten. Zur Analyse dörflicher Quellen um 1800', in Robert Berdahl *et al., Klassen und Kultur. Sozialanthropologische Perspektiven in der Geschichtsschreibung* (Frankfurt, 1982), pp. 54–76. These are just a few of the new publications. For a very good bibliography see W. Kaschuba and C. Lipp, *Dorfliches Überleben* (Tübingen, 1982), pp. 610 ff.

9. The classic work is H. J. Puhle, *Agrarische Interessenpolitik und preussischer Konservatismus im wilhelminischen Reich, 1893–1914* (Hanover, 1966).

10. Cf. Ian Farr, 'Populism in the Countryside: The Bavarian Peasant Leagues in Bavaria in the 1890s', in Evans (ed.), *op. cit.*

11. D. Blackbourn, *Class, Religion and Local Politics in Wilhlmine Germany. The Centre Party in Württemberg before 1914* (London, 1981); G. Eley, *Reshaping the German Right* (London, 1980), Ian Farr and David Blackbourn, *European History Quarterly* (1984); and other chapters in the present volume.

12. See note 8.

13. Brockhaus, *Konversationslexikon* (Berlin and Vienna, 1898), Vol. 13, pp. 41 ff.

14. Aug. Becker, *Die Pfalz und die Pfälzer* (Neustadt an der Haardt, 1857), p. 79.

15. W. Weidmann, *Die pfälzische Landwirtschaft zu Beginn des 19. Jahrhunderts* (Saarbrücken, 1968), pp. 54 ff; H. Petersen, 'Bäuerliche Verhältnisse Zustände in der Pfalz', *Schriften des Vereins für Sozialpolitik* (Leipzig, 1883), Vol. 1, pp. 237–73.

16. W. Breunig, *Socialverhältnisse der Arbeiterschaft und sozialistische Arbeiterbewegung in Ludwigshafen am Rhein, 1869–1919* (Ludwigshafen am Rhein, 1976), pp. 376 ff.

17. J. Esselborn, *Geschichte der Stadt Ludwigshafen* (Ludwigshafen am Rhein, 1887): S. Fauck, *Ludwigshafen am Rhein in Daten* (Speyer, 1972).

18. I compiled the statistics from a family reconstitution using the birth, marriage and death registers for Maudach. The relevant references are: Stadtarchiv Ludwigshafen, Bestand Maudach, pp. 631–848 (Hereafter referred to as St.A.Lu.Bes.Mau.).

19. The question of typicality should perhaps be raised at this point. Maudach certainly cannot be regarded as a 'typical' German village. However present research is uncovering a number of villages which share many of Maudach's characteristics. See in particular Kaschuba and Lipp, *op. cit.*, pp. 610 ff.

20. Examples of literature using a rather static model include: R. Thabault, *Education and Change in a Village Community. Mazières en Gatine 1848–1914* (London, 1971). An explicit exhortation to adopt this model can be found in H.-U. Wehler, *Modernisierungstheorie und Geschichte* (Göttingen, 1975).

21. For example, Kaschuba and Lipp, *op. cit.*, have attempted their own classification system, which runs into some serious problems. See H. Rosenbaum, *Formen der Familie. Untersuchungen zum Zusammenhang von Familienverhältnissen, Sozialstruktur und sozialem Wandel in der deutschen Gesellschaft des 19. Jahrhunderts* (Frankfurt, 1982), pp. 5–49, for a discussion of this.

22. More detailed results are contained in C. S. Catt, *Family, Land and Occupation. German Rural Society in the late Nineteenth Century. The example of Maudach in the Lower Palatinate, 1840–1900*, Ph.D. dissertation (University of East Anglia, forthcoming).

23. There is a good discussion of what constitutes a peasant in T. Shanin, *Peasants and Peasant Societies* (Harmondsworth, 1971), pp. 6–12.

24. Figures from the family reconstitution. See note 18.

25. St.A.Lu.Bes.Mau., 247–250.

26. Landesarchiv Speyer (La. Sp.), Präsidialakten H3 220 n-x.

27. Fam.'y reconstitution, see note 18.

28. L. Mang and Th. Zink, *Das Wirtschaftsleben der Pfalz in Vergangenheit und Gegenwart* (Munich, 1913), p. 12.

29. Brockhaus, *op. cit.*, p. 41; Becker, *op. cit.*, p. 67; Weidmann, *op. cit.*, pp. 52 ff.

30. W. Cobbett, *Rural Rides* (London, 1830).

31. St.A.Lu.Bes.Mau, *Gemeinderatsprotokolle*, 1840 ff.

32. Petersen, *loc. cit.*

33. Ibid.

34. St.A.Lu.Bes.Mau, 247–250.

35. Petersen.

36. Ibid., p. 262. Petersen suggested that peasant indebtedness was far lower in the Palatinate than elsewhere in the empire, particularly Bavaria. He provides many details about the crop rotation used in the lower Palatinate. In particular he notes the increase in the cultivation of onions and early potatoes for the market, the increase in tobacco and the introduction of sugar beet cultivation.

37. There are parallels here with the situation on the Magdeburger *Börde*. See H. Plaul, *Landarbeiterleben im 19. Jahrhundert* (East Berlin, 1979), p. 38; Petersen, *loc cit.*; J. Kermann, 'Die gesundheitliche Lage der pfälzischen Landbevölkerung in der Mitte des 19. Jahrhunderts nach Berichten der Kantonsärzte und des Kreismedizinalrats', in *Mitteilungen des Historischen Vereins der Pfalz*, Vol. 74 (Speyer, 1976), pp. 101 ff.

38. Petersen, p. 173.

39. St.A.Lu.Bes.Mau, 282.

40. St.A.Lu.Bes.Mau, Gemeinderatsprotokolle, 1843.

41. St.A.Lu.Bes.Mau, Gemeinderatsprotokolle, 1843.

42. Petersen, p. 271; Kermann, p. 103.
43. St.A.Lu.Bes.Mau, Gemeinderatsprotokolle, 1848.
44. Kermann, p. 109.
45. Breunig, p. 60.
46. St.A.Lu.Bes.Mau, Gemeinderatsprotokolle, 1881, 1887, 1890; Breunig, *op. cit.*, p. 387.
47. cf. Plaul, *op. cit.*, p. 38.
48. St.A.Lu.Bes.Mau, 247–250.
49. St.A.Lu.Bes.Mau, 282.
50. Petersen, p. 209.
51. Breunig, p. 386.
52. Breunig; J. Queva, 'Auf geht die Saat', *Bei uns Daheim, Heimatsbeilage der 'Pfalzischen Post'* (Ludwigshafen am Rehein, 1928).
53. In particular the aniline dyes, which have now been proved to contain certain active carcinogens.
54. Breunig, pp. 380 ff.
55. Space forbids a comprehensive survey of the figures. See Catt, *Family, Land and Occupation, op. cit.*
56. R. Spree, *Soziale Ungleichheit vor Krankheit und Tod* (Göttingen, 1981).
57. The Palatinate enjoyed a privileged constitutional position within the Bavarian state. It retained the *Code Civil* granted by Napoleon during the French occupation of the left bank of the Rhine, and the retention of the Code was one of the provisions of the Congress of Vienna.
58. A citizen (*Bürger*) was a member of the village entitled to vote.
59. St.A.Lu.Bes.Mau Gemeinderatsprotokolle; St.A.Lu.Bes.Mau, 631–848.
60. St.A.Lu.Bes.Mau. Wählerlisten, 1848–1874.
61. Ibid.
62. St.A.Lu.Bes.Mau Gemeinderatsprotokolle.
63. Ibid.
64. The field-watchers' main task was to ensure that no produce from the fields was stolen. They were also responsible for keeping paths clear and undertook routine maintenance.
65. Gemeinderatsprotokolle, 1848.
66. Ibid., 1849.
67. There was a definite degree of ambivalence on the part of the council towards the question of drunkenness. On the one hand, it was certainly the largest problem in terms of law and order the village had to deal with. On the other, the farmers produced a lot of the spirits (*Branntwein*) sold, and moreover many were related to the village's innkeepers; thus they had a vested interest in keeping the inns open for as long as possible.
68. Gemeinderatsprotokolle, 1882.
69. K. Kreuter, *Maudach im Wandel der Zeiten* (Ludwigshafen, 1955).
70. Gemeinderatsprotokolle, 1891.
71. Ibid., 1885.
72. St.A.Lu.Bes.Mau, Verzeichnis der Vereine, 1890.
73. Cf. Breunig, *op. cit.*

6 PEASANTS AND FARMERS' MAIDS
Female Farm Servants in Bavaria at the End of the Nineteenth Century*

Regina Schulte

Of course, the best that could happen was to have some money and get married to someone, and she had soon worked out who that someone could be. About a quarter of an hour's walk from Kolbach there stood a small house close by a wood, where a thousand Marks cash would be very welcome. The house belonged to a widow who owned two cows. She had one son. During the winter months he worked as a forester, and during the summer, when he had finished working their own land (which didn't take long), as an agricultural day-labourer.

During the previous harvest season he had worked for Schormayer for a while, and she had often sat by him at lunchtime on the edge of a field or under the shade of a hazel hedgerow. He was a cheerful lad, who enjoyed a joke with any girl. Now she thought of it, he had said something to her. Once, while she was on her way to the farm, she had seen him in the distance. He had put down his axe and told her that if he knew for certain that she could raise a thousand marks, perhaps they could talk.[1]

I

Many young women from the agricultural lower classes left home to work as farm servants in order to earn the money they needed to marry and set up home. For these women, however, going into service was more than merely a means of earning money. The work they performed and the social situation in which the work was carried out formed a distinctive way of life. It was shared by many young women from the rural lower classes at the end of the nineteenth century. The real social significance of this way of life, and its relation to the farm servants' eventual chances of marriage, is

*Translated by Cathleen S. Catt.

examined in detail in this paper.

In 1882, 3.5 per cent of the total population of the German Empire worked as farm servants. In Bavaria the figure was higher: 7 per cent of the population were employed as farm servants, and this figure accounted for more than a third of all people employed in agriculture.[2] These male and female farm servants were not so much a separate social group but rather an age group or cohort of the sons and daughters of agricultural day labourers and small farmers. For them, 'service' was a transitional phase. From the statistics gathered in 1882, apparently only 10.8 per cent of the farm servants were older than 40. The average age of the Bavarian female farm servants was 25. Furthermore, 90 per cent of the servants were single.[3] Farm servants married between the ages of 25 and 30 at the earliest, and marriage meant effectively the end of service life. The peasant household, which in Bavaria was usually based on a middle-sized holding, was unable to absorb married couples or families: there was simply not enough land to integrate the labour of servants' offspring into the household economy. In the last analysis, farm servants were only used by peasant farmers when their own families were too small to perform all the necessary labour.[4] The farmers preferred to employ single farm servants because they demanded less — they required only a place to sleep, and they could be dismissed after a year.

Thus in general the years of service covered only the 10–15 years between childhood and marriage. Nevertheless these years were of crucial significance for the future prospects of women from the rural lower classes. The years spent as a farm servant were decisive for a woman's eventual position in village society.

Female farm servants were usually the daughters of agricultural day labourers, cottagers or small farmers.[5] Their parents usually owned less than 10 hectares of land. The productivity of the land could vary enormously according to geographical location, but in general it was probably sufficient to keep one or two cows, several goats and possibly some chickens. In addition there would be a kitchen garden, which in Bavaria usually provided the family with vegetables, fruit and some of the staple foodstuffs. For a small household this amount of land would be sufficient to provide enough basic food for the family. Of course, many of these small concerns depended on some form of supplementary income. Some cottagers were also artisans or craftsmen, and undertook various jobs around the village as shoemakers, carpenters, bricklayers, etc.

Others worked as day labourers for the larger farmers in the village, either harvesting hay and corn in summer, threshing in the autumn, or working in the woods in winter. The draining of marshland and stone-breaking for road construction was also undertaken by agricultural day labourers. If the children were old enough to look after the house and mind younger brothers and sisters, then the wife would also sometimes undertake some form of day labouring.[6]

The female farm servants who came from these small farming and labouring families had mostly grown up sharing in the family's work. They had looked after smaller brothers and sisters, done the lighter housework, tended the livestock, harvested potatoes and gathered berries, and as they grew older and stronger they had also been initiated into the harder farming tasks.[7] After they had left school these children had to leave home and make their own way in the world. The labourers and cottagers were not in a position to be able to feed older children longer than was necessary, and their labour was not needed on the small patch of land belonging to the family. For the sons and daughters of smaller peasants the situation was much the same once there were enough children to work the land: younger sons and daughters would be sent into service.[8]

Thus when young girls of 13 or 14 took their first position on a farm, they had, by and large, already learned many of the tasks they were expected to carry out, and they were already used to a certain degree of responsibility. Probably for many of these girls the memory of their parents' home and way of life served as a pattern on which to model their future.[9] Some, of course, entered service in an industrialising area, or perhaps found a position with a town family, and finally left village life behind.[10] But in Bavaria, at least until the beginning of the twentieth century, the majority of young men and women from a rural background remained firmly tied to village life and agricultural employment. They went into service to ensure an independent existence, and to acquire the material basis for that purpose.

II

The hiring and firing of farm servants followed the cycle of the farming year. The law governing the conditions of service (*Gesindeordnung*) laid down two dates on which farm servants could enter into employment with a farmer: Either in Spring on 2 February, Candlemas Day, before the spring sowing took place (this was a day on which a great migration of farm servants from one farm to another took place); or on 29 September, Michaelmas Day, at the end of the harvest.[11] When a girl went into service this generally meant the beginning of a period of migration between farms, and from village to village, as the majority of them changed their employer annually. If they stayed with the same employer it was generally only for two or three years at the most. Service thus meant that a young farm servant would come into contact with several different-sized farming concerns, different families and different ways of working within a certain area. Farm servants seldom went further afield than one or two hours' walk from their parental home, which they visited on their free Sunday afternoons.[12]

From the moment that a girl left home and took a place in service, her status was no longer defined primarily by her relationship within the household (as it had been at home), but by her position in the work of the farm. 'Belonging' to a farmer's family meant being subject to the patriarchal authority of the household — the farm servant would have to obey the farmer in the same way as his children did.[13] The rules governing service meant that the girl had to live in the same house as the farmer and his wife, share the work and the holidays with them, and finally — and this continued even at the end of the century on middling peasant farms — she had to eat the same food at the same table. In all, this meant complete integration into the hierarchy of the household.[14] Both male and female farm servants were in a similar position to the children of the peasant family on whose farm they were employed; however, their rights and their participation in the work of the farm differed from that of the farmer's own children in a fundamental way: they were employed by him, and stood to inherit no land from him.

The continued complaints of farmers about the negligence and apathy of their farm servants, common enough at any time, were particularly loud and frequent at the end of the nineteenth century.[15] In all probability, the performance of farm servants underwent no real decline during the period. It was simply the fact that they never fulfilled their tasks in the way that farmers could demand of their own children. Of course, the female farm servants undertook the same tasks as the farmer's daughters, but the amount a female farm servant would be able to save during the course of the year bore no relation to the rewards the farmer's daughter would reap eventually for work well done.[16]

Belonging to a peasant household also meant belonging to the village of which it was a part, and the kind of household to which the servants belonged determined her social identity in that village. She was a member of that village only as the farm servant to the mayor or a prosperous farmer. In order to be part of the village outside of this position, she would have to be married and run her own household, which implied a house and a bit of land. This was the only way that she could earn the right to be a *bona fide* member of the village with all the rights which this implied (*Heimatrecht erwerben*), and meant, of course, that she would have to leave her job as a farm servant.

Local court records show the lengths to which a village would go to get rid of an unemployed, possibly sick, farm servant. The case of Anna K. is typical. She was badly injured by an accident involving a threshing machine, and it was also suspected that she was pregnant. She was living temporarily with the foster-mother of her first illegitimate child. The mayor of the village applied to the court in Ebersberg for permission to ban her from the village:

Anna K., single, from the Upper Palatinate, is staying in this village against the will of the undersigned village administration. Since she had an accident while working in the village of Assling she is causing a great deal of work for this village, which we are not legally liable to provide. Also there is the danger that her condition will mean that the local sickness insurance fund will have to pay for her treatment, because she has no work and no relatives in the village. For these reasons we have decided that she should be forced to leave the village within three days starting from today.[17]

Other applications from villages to ban unemployed female farm servants show that village officials regarded the presence of unmarried farm servants as a moral danger. This applied above all to those who had left their previous employers without due notice.[18] Village officials feared that because these women lacked money or relatives they would strain the meagre resources of the village and would also endanger the prevailing code of sexual ethics. And an illegitimate child whose father came from the village would be entitled to support from the village's poor relief fund, or would be an additional burden on some village family. Village officials were always concerned to avoid such extra financial burdens on the community as far as possible.

Thus an unemployed female farm servant did not come under the protection of the village's forms of social control and responsibility, but was regarded as an interloper. This period of service and moving from household to household meant living continually on the borderlines of belonging and alienation. If she failed to follow the rules of service she was very soon beyond the pale, an outsider, an asocial being. Court records show that female farm servants who got on the wrong side of the law were usually convicted of begging, vagrancy or theft. They frequently show to what straits a farm servant could be reduced.[19]

III

The fact that female farm servants 'won't stay longer than two or three years on the same farm' was a frequent cause for complaint from farmers.[20] But for the servant this continual change of employment not only entailed the risk of vagrancy, it was also the only way she could work her way up through the hierarchy of farm servants. Promotion, however, was dependent on physical fitness and experience as well as age:

First, a girl 13–14 years old will be taken on to help the peasant's wife with the household chores and looking after the children. As she grows she is promoted to under-servant (*Unterdirn*) and starts learning farming tasks. Then she gets promoted to middle servant, who milks the cows and feeds them under supervision. Finally she becomes an upper servant, who is responsible for the animals. One or other of the stages can be left out, depending on the size of the farm, what position the farmer wants to fill, the age of the girl when she came into service, and what experience the girl brings with her from her own home.[21]

The classification of the various levels of servants varied in the different regions of Bavaria. In some areas, for instance, a girl's career could begin with the position of gooseherd.[22]

A farm servant's position within the hierarchy of servants prescribed both the kinds of work she had to perform and her function within the economy of the peasant household. It determined what work she would have to undertake in the house and in the cowshed, and especially what she was expected to undertake at harvest time. Ideally a female farm servant was initiated into all aspects of women's work on a farm during her time of service. As a kitchen or scullery maid she would learn, under the supervision of the farmer's wife or the housekeeper, all the skills of household management, how to keep house and kitchen clean, how to prepare food, how to preserve vegetables and meat, how to dry fruit from the garden in autumn. She learnt how to purify honey and how to prepare for the slaughtering of an animal. Stable and dairy maids usually worked in the cowshed in Bavaria. They were in charge of feeding the animals, in particular the calves, mucking out the shed, and later undertook the milking. Pigs, hens and geese were also looked after by the women. Stable maids often spent the entire day in the cowshed. In winter their working day began at 6 a.m., in summer at 3 a.m. The cows had to be milked before breakfast, and the day would only end at 7 or 8 in the evening after the last feed.[23] Most of this work had to be carried out on Sundays as well. When a cow calved this could well mean the maid had to spend the night in the cowshed. This constant presence amongst the animals meant that a maid would get to know the individual animals very well, the way they behaved, their illnesses and their dispositions. This very exact knowledge was the key to successful treatment of sick animals or in dealing with a weak calf. The importance of the maid to the well-being of the animals was recognised by the farmers, and maids regularly received a bonus when an animal was sold.[24] The very great trust farmers placed in their dairy maids is exemplified by the *Sennerinnen*, who often spent the entire summer quite alone (or perhaps accompanied only by a small boy) on the high Alpine pastures looking after the cows, milking them and making the butter and cheese.[25]

The hardest work on a farm was the variable seasonal work in the fields. This was, of course, particularly so at harvest time, dependent on the weather. At certain times every available hand had to get out into the fields to gather in the harvest, and this would include servants whose main work was in the house — sometimes even the cook had to join in.[26] The working day began in summer with the first ray of light and ended late in the evening. Mowing with a sickle and stacking hay and corn were regarded as women's work,[27] despite the strenuousness of these tasks, particularly as most of the harvest work was carried out in dry, often boiling hot weather. Finally, in the autumn, the maids were also expected to help with the threshing, not only that carried out on the farm on which they were employed, but also on the neighbouring farms which required help when the threshing machine was doing the rounds. Thus many maids spent two long weeks working in the noise and dust produced by these dangerous machines.[28]

Agricultural reports are full of complaints about maids who absconded just before harvest time because the work was too hard.[29] It is difficult to ascertain exactly how many were involved in reality. Farmers always feared that at the critical moment that the harvest had to be gathered in, there would suddenly not be enough hands to help, and at harvest time no extra hands could be hired. They feared in particular that their maids would be pregnant at this crucial time. At any rate, a maid who did abscond from a farm before or during the harvest would find it very difficult to obtain a new position. She had thrown away her reputation as a useful and reliable servant, something that was not only important to prospective employers, but also counted for much with a prospective husband. It does not therefore seen reasonable to suppose that the number of maids who absconded from service was very large. The frequency of the complaints probably reflects the seriousness of such a situation for the farmer and the maids themselves.

A hierarchy of servants and the strict division of labour was only possible on farms large enough to require many servants. The middling and smaller peasant farmers were not in a position to employ several maids to undertake the different kinds of tasks, so a maid employed on a smaller farm would almost certainly help both in the house and in the cowshed. She would be responsible for the kitchen garden and quite possibly would have to look after the children too. It there was only one maid on a farm she would have to be able to take over if the farmer's wife was ill or in childbirth, or if she spent a day visiting relatives or shopping in town. These demands on the maids make it clear that a 'good maid' had to be capable of undertaking any household or agricultural task independently and reliably.[30]

The economy of the peasant farm did not lay down strict dividing lines between the work expected of a male farm servant and that expected of a female one. This would have cut across the real needs of this method of production. Stable boys and dairy maids were expected to perform much the same tasks or, at least, their work complemented each others', especially at harvest time. They went to the fields together in the mornings and ended work at the same time. In the cowshed the maid was responsible for feeding and milking the cows, the boy for fetching the feed.[31] The only area of work that was exclusively female was in the house and kitchen, which meant effectively that the maids generally worked longer hours than the men, as in the evening after work in the fields and cowsheds was over they would have to help with the preparation and clearing up of the evening meal. At harvest time the housework had still to be done after returning from the fields. In the winter the maids were also expected to do any darning and sewing. And finally, until the turn of the century, many maids would spend winter evenings with the farmer's wife and daughters at the spinning wheel, in order to spin linen thread to weave into the bales of cloth that the farmer's wife needed for her linen cupboard, the daughters needed for their bottom drawers, and the maid too wished eventually to take with her when she married.[32]

Wages, like work, also varied according to the age and experience of the maid. This was particularly clearly expressed in the money portion of a maid's salary, which was paid annually at Candlemas. In 1890 in Bavaria housekeepers received 240 Marks p.a., cooks 150–80 Marks, and house- and dairy maids, scullery and undermaids 120–80 Marks.[33] In some areas, particularly those near larger towns towards the end of the century, weekly payments became more common.[34] The basic wage was supplemented by certain cash bonuses: sometimes as recognition for their hard work they might receive a bonus when an animal or some crops (for example hops), were sold, or as Christmas, Easter or Whitsun bonuses, or on village festival days. Over the year these bonuses usually amounted to about 12–15 Marks. A dairy maid might make up to an extra 15 Marks in bonuses when animals were sold.[35]

The portion of wages that was paid in kind also took the form of bonuses or gifts, and this was commonly given at Christmas. They usually consisted of flax and linen thread, up to 20 ells (*Ellen*) of linen and cloth, often a '*Wachsstock*', working clothes, aprons, shoes and sometimes kerchiefs and a Sunday dress. As the domestic production of thread, linen and cloth waned, and the spinning-wheels and looms disappeared from winter evening work, and clothing and material were brought in the town, the practice of substituting these payments in kind with money sums grew. This happened first and foremost in those areas near to towns. As the maids usually paid their annual wage into a savings account,[36] the extra payments for feast days and special bonuses allowed them the chance to pay for extra costs that arose without their having to touch their yearly lump-sum, which they needed for their future dowry. Their savings also had to pay for the upkeep of any illegitimate children they had. The payments in kind also served the same function. They provided the clothes the maid needed in the short term, while the linen and flax were a contribution to her future dowry.' Overall, the wages and the payments in kind were made with a future marriage in view.

IV

A maid's existence was entirely oriented towards her future marriage. In the last analysis marriage was the only opportunity she had to achieve a secure position for herself and her children within the village, with financial security, status and prestige. During the period of service maids saved the 'dowries' they needed in order to become attractive marriage partners. Even amongst the poorest sections of the village, the group from which the maids were generally drawn, a potential husband would have to take into account the financial contribution his intended wife could make.

The dowry consisted of several separate elements. The first was money. In order to buy or take over a smallholding — a necessary preliminary to starting a family in this peasant farming world — and in order to buy the necessary household and agricultural equipment and livestock, it was necessary first of all to have a little capital; and the wife had to pay a portion of it. If she stood to inherit nothing from her parents and could only expect at most a small sum of money from her brothers (it was usual in Bavaria for brothers to take over the family smallholding) it was up to the maid to save some money herself.

The gifts which the maid received at the end of the year and at Christmas — the flax and the linen and woollen cloth, which, with the passage of years, could mount up to a sizeable quantity — formed the second part of the dowry. With the money that she had managed to save, the maid had demonstrated her understanding of thrift, an important virtue for a future manager of an agricultural smallholding. The amount and quality of the material she had managed to acquire were proof of her capability in the specifically female areas of the household economy. With this she demonstrated the kind of household she would run. As this would also reflect on the household where she had been employed, the farmer's wife also had an interest in ensuring that her maid had a respectable quantity of linen in her bottom drawer when she married.[37] Other women would judge both the maid and the farmer's wife by the quality and quantity of the cloth — especially her future mother-in-law.

A further, less tangible, but no less important element of a maid's dowry consisted in the domestic and agricultural skills she had learned during her years of service. She would need these in order to run her own household, cultivate her kitchen garden and look after whatever livestock they might have. As a married woman she would also need to be able to undertake some of the field work as well, as the men were usually employed as day-labourers or would have to work at some other kind of supplementary handicraft. Character witnesses of maids in criminal court records given by labourers and male farm servants (potential husbands) show how much they valued these skills. Working together in the fields or the cowshed meant that a maid and a male farm servant would know very well whether the other knew how to pull their weight and work well.[38]

A further important element of a maid's dowry was the network of relations and acquaintances that she brought with her, through her family or through her years of service. It is likely that working with other farm servants, both male and female, created the basis for the individual maid's future network of neighbours and friends on whose co-operation her future might depend. The farm servants were also the bearers of future generations of the lower classes in the villages and thus formed a distinctive group within the village youth who were of marriageable age. The farm servants knew the farms and their owners well, within their own area, and also had personal knowledge of the labouring families from which they themselves had come. They thus had a fairly comprehensive view of their local society in its important features.

Finally, and very important for the reputation of any future family, was the position the maid had established for herself by getting to know her neighbours through gossip in the female society in the village. This was vital, for the women of the village would be her future neighbours and helpers. Thus, when they married, maids were already in some ways integrated into the female community of the village, which, though it wielded its power in an informal way, was nevertheless the way in which women vitally influenced village life.[39]

V

The following letter, sent by Agathe S., shows another side of the life of farm servants — their love affairs, and the care of the illegitimate children that resulted from these affairs.

Spittelsberg, 19th August 1894

Dear Josef,

Once again I take up my pen to write you a short letter, you must believe it is very difficult for me, but I have to as, you know, my parents have no spare money and can't bring up the boy for nothing, and you know they can't wait until he is eleven years old to get something back from him — they might not live that long, you must understand this, you know I wouldn't trouble you if I didn't have to, if I could manage on my own I would, but I can't. Dear Josef, how I have ruined my happiness. It is good that I have left home, that I can stop thinking about it, I was going mad from reproach [?], but now I have no time, there's too much work. Andreas, who works for the miller, will have told you that I went back to my old farm to work, to Spittelsberg, and I should stay until Candlemas, but I don't know for sure. And I have to tell you that if you pay me off, father will let you off half of it, because I know there's no chance that we will get back together again. My father doesn't want to do everything himself, he's already paying something for the boy, as long as my father and mother live, he'll be all right, they are looking after him and they allow me to go where I want to, but they won't let you go there again. They are very happy when I go to see them on Sundays, and even my brothers like it. Anton calls Josef [the child, presumably], a little friend. I must finish writing now, with best wishes, I remain your unforgettable Agathe S. I beg you once again from my heart. . .[40]

The situation Agathe S. found herself in was not ususual. Many farm maids had illegitimate children. Illegitimacy in the lower classes was not a scandal, nor was it even in farming circles if the father was a genuine marriage prospect. In Upper Bavaria the illegitimacy rate was about 15 per cent even at the end of the century,

though this rate varied from region to region within Bavaria.⁴¹
Male and female farm servants frequently had one or even several
children by the time they married. Often the children lived with
their grandparents, like the two children of Agathe S. The mother
paid for their keep out of her wages, and the father also contributed, like the above-mentioned Josef, who finally contributed
about 80 Marks annually towards the boy's keep — approximately
one-third of a male farm servant's wage. There were similar conditions attached when the child was sent to foster-parents, which
happened either if the grandparents were dead or were too old, or
were not themselves willing to take on the illegitimate children of
their own daughters. There was no place for these children on the
farms where their mothers worked. The maids were employed to
work — for them motherhood had to begin with marriage. Unmarried mothers, who brought their children into the world with the
help of the village midwife or their parents, spent scarcely any time
living in the same house as their children. Almost immediately after
the birth the child was given to foster-parents, and the mother
would visit it on their free Sunday afternoons. Under these circumstances, brothers and sisters would often grow up separately. If the
mother finally did get married, her children might themselves
already be in service to another farmer, and the family would never
have the chance of living together.⁴²

The farm maid, Agathe S., who wrote the letter was in a particularly difficult situation. From court records⁴³ it appears that
Josef D., himself a farm servant, whom she had met, like many
other maids had met their future husbands, when they were in
service together, was not prepared to marry her, and had tried to
avoid paying any maintenance for the child. In her next job, she
began a new affair with another farm servant, Michael B., who
again worked on the same farm. She became pregnant again, and
Michael B. refused to acknowledge paternity. Like Josef D. he was
also a farmer's son, with a little land, while Agathe S. was the
daughter of a labourer. She was thus from a lower class that the
fathers of her two illegitimate children; and from the beginning, as
far as the men were concerned, she was not a marriage prospect for
them. In the statements of the two men Agathe S. was described as
'*liderlich*' (a woman of easy virtue) and it seems that she had the
same reputation even in her own class. With two illegitimate
children by two different men, neither of whom, according to
village wisdom, could have been regarded as suitable suitors,

Agathe S. had damaged her reputation with her own people. If a maid had to pay to keep a child she had had by another man, in the eyes of a potential suitor, this meant a reduction in the dowry a maid could bring with her.

In the final analysis, the reputation of an unmarried mother was bound up with her material and familial status within village society. Thus another unmarried mother[44] was regarded as a 'proper and respectable' person, although the father of her first children had ended his relationship with her, and the father of her third illegitimate child had been a stranger to the village with whom she had worked in service for a short while, but who had shortly thereafter disappeared. She was in the position where she could bring up her children without much problem, because, apart from her wages, she stood to inherit a little land and had some capital. With this material background, she was probably still sought-after as a possible spouse. The money which she would be able to contribute, and the reputation of her family, still counted for more than the total savings of a maid from another area, who had no connections with the village.

The life of the farm maids was thus not just a 'transitional' phase: it was also the time of life when the material basis for a future marriage was created, and it was here that the options which village society offered the lower classes at the turn of the century became apparent. The time spent as a farm servant was not only characterised by the pressure to survive and the harsh working conditions on the farm, but also prepared them for the demands which their projected future would make on them. As mothers, and as a farmer's or cottager's wife on a small plot of land, they would have to be able independently to undertake a large part of the domestic and agricultural labour.

Notes

1. Ludwig Thoma, 'Der Wittiber', in idem., *Jubiläumausgabe in sechs Bänden* (Munich, 1978), Vol. 4, pp. 7–171.
2. Wilhelm Kähler, *Gesindewesen und Gesinderecht in Deutschland* (Jena, 1898), p. 100.
3. Ibid., p. 63. Cf. Walter Hartinger, 'Bayerisches Dienstbotenleben auf dem Land vom 16. bis 18. Jahrhundert', *Zeitschrift für bayerische Landesgeschichte* 38 (1975), pp. 598–638. See also Michael Mitterauer, 'Zur Familienstruktur in ländlichen Gebieten Österreichs im 17. Jahrhundert', *Beiträge zur Bevölkerungs- und Sozialgeschichte Österreichs* (1973), pp. 167–222.

4. Cf. Rosa Kempf, *Arbeits- und Lebensverhältnisse der Frauen in der Lan.lwirt-schaft Bayerns* (Schriften des ständigen Ausschusses zur Förderung der Arbeiterinnen-Interesen, Heft 9, Jena, 1918), pp. 8 ff. On the proportion of rural workers who belonged to the farmer's family, see Kähler, *op. cit.*, p. 100.

5. Kempf, *op. cit.*, pp. 74–5.

6. On the situation of the rural lower classes, cf. Axel Schnorbus, 'Die ländlichen Unterschichten in der bayerischen Gesellschaft am Ausgang des 19. Jahrhunderts', *Zeitschrift für bayerische Landesgeschichte*, 30 (1967), pp. 824–52. See also Kempf, *op. cit.*, pp. 55–73; and individual examples in *Untersuchung der wirtschaftlichen Verhältnisse in 24 Gemeinden des Königreiches Bayern* (Munich, 1895), pp.94, 116, 138, 200, 232, 260, 419, 420.

7. Ibid., pp. 59, 169, 200, 231, 260.

8. Ibid., pp. 46, 81, 115; see also Kempf, *op. cit.*, p. 56.

9. Ibid., p. 78.

10. Cf. *Untersuchung in 24 Gemeinden*, pp. 60, 259, 351, 420, 488; also Kempf, *op. cit.*, pp. 38 (for 1907).

11. Hartinger, *loc. cit.*, p. 606.

12. Cf. the portrayal of serving women's daily life in criminal files such as Staatsarchiv München (StAM), Staatsanwaltschaftsakte, St. Anw, 1177.

13. Kähler, *op. cit.*, S. 221.

14. Cf., for example, Franz Schweyer, *Schöffau. Eine oberbayerische Landge-meinde. Eine wirtschaftliche und soziale Studie* (Stuttgart, 1896), p. 126; and the *Untersuchung in 24 Gemeinden*, pp. 45, 60.

15. Ibid., pp. 17, 259, 373, 421, 488–9.

16. On the position of maids in peasant families and households in general, see Edit Fél and Tamas Hofer, *Proper Peasants. Traditional Life in a Hungarian Village* (Budapest, 1969), p. 101; and for a description of the dowry of a peasant's daughter, see Lena Christ, *Werke* (Munich, 1970), pp.247–503; also Karl von Leoprechting, *Bauernbrauch und Volksglaube in Oberbayern* (1885; reprinted Munich, 1975, p. 218).

17. StAM, LRA, 78105.

18. Cf. StAM, LRA, 78101.

19. Cf. for example StAM, St Anw, 840, 1177, 1458.

20. Kempf, *op. cit.*, p. 82.

21. Ibid., p. 76.

22. Cf. *Untersuchung in 24 Gemeinden*, pp. 59, 80, 93, 337; Hans Platzer, *Geschichte der ländlichen Arbeitsverhältnisse in Bayern* (Munich, 1904), p. 207.

23. Kuno Frankenstein, *Die Verhältnisse der Landarbeiter in Deutschland. 2. Bd.* (Schriften des Vereins für Sozialpolitik LIV, Leipzig, 1892), p. 156. For another description of the work situation, see Lena Christ, 'Rumpelhanni', *Werke* (Munich, 1970), pp. 505–672. For a description of the woman's role during the slaughter of a pig, see the fascinating book by Yvonne Verdier, *Façons de dire, façons de faire. La laveuse, la couturière, la cuisinière* (Paris, 1979), pp. 24 ff.

24. Frankenstein, *op. cit.*, p. 156.

25. Cf. Christ, *loc. cit.*, pp. 318–19.

26. Cf. St Anw, 185, 693.

27. Kempf, *op. cit.*, pp. 82, 102; cf. Christ, *loc. cit.*, pp. 516, 553.

28. Cf. StAm, LRA, 78105, Kempf, *op. cit.*, p. 87.

29. Cf. *Untersuchung in 24 Gemeinden*, pp. 511, 373.

30. Cf. StAm, St Anw, 185.

31. Cf. StAm, St Anw, 185, 682, 693.

32. Schweyer, *op. cit.*, p. 79.

33. Frankenstein, *op. cit.*, p. 184.

34. Cf. for example *Untersuchung in 24 Gemeinden*, p. 84.

35. Cf. Frankenstein, *op. cit.*, p. 184; *Untersuchung in 24 Gemeinden*, eg. pp. 17, 45, 80, 94, 260, 36; ibid., pp. 15, 29.

36. Ibid., pp. 15, 29.

37. Cf. Lena Christ, 'Matthias Bichler', pp. 342–3.

38. Cf. for example StAM, St.Anw. 185.

39. Cf. Susan Carol Rogers, 'Les femmes et le pouvoir', in H. Lamarche, S. C. Rogers and C. Karnoouh, *Paysans, femmes et citoyens. Luttes pour le pouvoir dans un village lorrain* (Paris, 1980), here pp. 97–9.

40. StAM, St.Anw. 177.

41. W. R. Lee, 'Bastardy and the Socioeconomic Structure of South Germany', *Journal of Interdisciplinary History* 7 (1977), pp. 403–25, esp. p. 410; on Bavaria see also F. Lindner, *Die unehelichen Geburten als Sozialphänomen* (Leipzig, 1900); see also David Sabean, 'Unehelichkeit: Ein Aspekt sozialer Reproduktion kleinbäuerlicher Produzenten. Zu einer Analyse dörflicher Quellen um 1800', in Robert Berdahl *et al., Klassen und Kultur. Sozialanthropologishce Perspektiven in der Geschichtsschreibung* (Frankfurt, 1982), pp. 54–76. On the situation of domestic servants with unmarried children, see Regina Schulte, 'Kindsmörderinnen auf dem Lande', in H. Medick and D. Sabean (eds), *Emotion und materielle Interessen in Familie und Verwandtschaft. Anthropologische und historische Beiträge zur Familienforschung* (Göttingen, 1983).

42. Cf. StAM, St.Anw. 185, the situation of the three illegitimate children of Anna H. On the actual circumstances of the birth of the illegitimate children of female farm servants, see Schulte, 'Kindsmördinnen', *loc. cit.*

43. StAM, St. Anw. 177.

44. StAM, St.Anw. 682.

THE SINS OF THE FATHERS
Village Society and Social Control in the Weimar
Republic

Gerhard Wilke

I

The village of Körle lies in the valley of the River Fulda in northern
Hesse, about 20 km south of Kassel. The old village centre is
dominated by a Lutheran church which stands elevated on a little
hill. Spread around the church walls are the old timber-framed
wattle-and-daub houses typical of the area. The size and design of
the individual houses depended on the class position and landholding of the inhabitants. They formed the economic and social
base for a large household, or *das ganze Haus'*,[1] rather than a
nuclear family. The household's reputation rather than individual
identity was at the centre of perceptions; both the self and the other
were defined in terms of the household's name and standing in the
village. With one exception, all households of the village were
involved in agricultural production in the 1920s and up to and
including the 1950s. The inhabitants assumed that the cultivation
of land, or seasonal work on one of the larger farms of the village,
was necessary for the maintenance of the household's economy.
Despite the increasing integration into the industrial labour force of
ever larger numbers of villagers, the possession of land and a house
and the ability to do agricultural work remained central to everyday
life in the village during the first half of this century. The
possession of land, and the draught animals necessary to cultivate
it, formed the basis for the local class structure.

A villager who had 'a lot of land' and used horses for cultivation
was classified as a *Pferdebauer* (horse farmer). These were the full-
time professional farmers who owned between 10 and 30 hectares
of land, produced food for the market, and employed both full-
time and casual labour. In terms of status and prestige it was
important that they did not have to earn a supplementary income.
In 1928, there were 14 of these horse farmers in the village.

The owners of, as they saw it, 'less, but still quite a lot of land', who used cows for draught purposes, for breeding and for dairy produce were classified as *Kuhbauern* (cow farmers).[2] Statistics from the Prussian Ministry of Agriculture record that there were 66 of these households in 1928.[3] Oral evidence makes it clear that none of these could live off the land alone, although they did produce varying amounts of agricultural produce for the market. Individual members of these households earned a cash income to contribute to what was essentially a 'dual economy'.[4] The male heads or eldest sons worked as self-employed or wage-earning artisans and made up the bulk of the village craftsmen. The daughters went into service on larger farms in the surrounding area, or with bourgeois or petit-bourgeois families in Kassel.

Those villagers who owned a 'small patch of land', a kitchen garden, or were reduced to renting allotments or parts of country lanes, and possessed no draught animals, but kept goats and pigs, were called *Ziegenbauern* (goat farmers). These households numbered 80 in 1928 and they were primarily dependent on industrial wages, commuting to the factories in nearby towns to work. These industrial workers still spent their 'free time' on the land and continued to derive their identity within the village from the agricultural sphere. In their perception, continued residence in the village and the preservation of 'the whole house' provided them with a minimum of security, self-determination and self-respect. Their households were seen as protection against the incursion of capitalist society into all aspects of their lives. They regarded their additional income from the agricultural sector as indispensable to their household economy and were determined to defend themselves against the poverty and insecurity they associated with the life-style of their urban working-class colleagues. Up to a point, they perceived this life-style as their own calculated and conscious response to industrial society, and interpreted it as a form of resistance to the controlling influence of that society:

There was no sense in moving to Kassel. Where would we have found a place to live? Who would have looked after us when we were ill or needed help? How would we have fed ourselves during periods of unemployment? No . . ., we had to make sure that we grew some food, kept what was ours and we had to help ourselves and each other. All of us pulled together and we all had to do what we had to do.[5]

Though some of the images in this quotation might echo the mythical associations of the 'good old days', its underlying message was repeated so often in interviews and by so many people that I believe it to be accurate.[6] The older villagers' experience of the social and economic catastrophes of war has not receded from their consciousness. Their relationship to industrialisation has remained ambivalent.

The horse farmers were glad to exploit the market opportunities offered by the growth of Kassel, but hated the threat to their authority which this industrial centre posed. The cow farmers were ready to pick up part-time employment in small industrial concerns and from the state, but they also tried to move heaven and earth to avoid sliding into the goat farmer class. The goat farmers were grateful for their industrial jobs which formed the basis of their survival, but also lacked confidence in the ability of industrial society to offer them a secure future. They expressed incomprehension when I asked them why they hadn't abandoned their farms during the earlier part of the century. The key to understanding the behaviour and thinking of all three classes in Weimar village society was agriculture. It remained the central organising principle behind the economic, social, political and cultural patterns which we can reconstruct both with the help of oral accounts and on the basis of documentary evidence, like the *Preussische Viehzählungslisten*, which show that all but one household kept animals and cultivated land.[7]

A price had to be paid in order to maintain this adaptation to industrial society. The goat farmers' households were not just dependent on one industrial employer, instead they entered into a number of dependency relationships in both town and village. They depended on the horse farmers to cultivate their patch of land — the horse farmers ploughed it, and in return, the goat farmers' households provided casual labour (*Arbeitsleute*) throughout the year. Without this labour supply, the horse farmers could not have produced for the market with the given low level of mechanisation. The inequality of this relationship was glaring, but to fit its injustice into the prevailing perception that all villagers were part of a 'community', the parties involved entered, in several instances, fictive kinship relationships. The head of the horse farmer's household and his wife became godfather and godmother to one or more children in the house of 'their' *Arbeitsleute*.[8] The economic link between the horse farmer and goat farmer classes and the social and cultural form in which their relationship was publicly expressed, provided the basis on which the community ideology could be preserved and was indispensable to the maintenance of social order and the containment of social conflict.

During the Weimar period a consciousness based on industrial or state employment began to develop. It started to affect the private and public actions and the thinking of all villagers, but it did not actually dominate the struggle for hegemony. The change expressed itself in the foundation of separate party organisations by the SPD and KPD and the concomitant fragmentation of associational life. The village clubs split into 'German nationalist' and 'workers'' camps. The workers' clubs and party organisations recruited their members, with very few exceptions, from the households of the goat farmers. These cultural and political innovations of the period were an indication of a new form of political consciousness. They allow us to say that the worker-peasants in the village were beginning to create a new identity and sub-culture in terms of a capitalist society. It would, however, be wrong if we concluded that this form of political consciousness was developed to the point where it became the basis for all actions of the households. The economic and social relations between individual households and between the three classes within the village were only marginally affected by these developments during the 1920s. The class struggle within the village did not touch the existing social and economic hierarchy in any fundamental way. The open expression of conflicting interests was confined to casting votes, going to different pubs, organising meetings under different banners and ideas, and splitting the villages' clubs. These divisions themselves were not new, as the dominant horse farmer class had always 'kept to themselves', only the expression of the existing divisions changed. What one can say is that the SPD and KPD established enough of a foothold in the village during the 1920s to prevent the Nazis ever getting an absolute majority in a free election.

The village economy and its social relations continued to be dominated by the horse farmers throughout the Weimar years. In a democratic context this was achieved through the continued exercise of their economic power, based on their ability to provide casual employment for the goat farmers, and through their co-option of most of the cow farmers and their households in the field of politics and associational life. The cow farmers knew they could not be magically transformed into powerful horse farmers but they tried to prevent a drop in their social standing. This made them willing allies of the horse farmers in their efforts to assert their class hegemony. Goat farmers, who also happened to be Communists or Social Democrats, would read their party newspapers and share a class analysis of society, but they would not dream of declaring war on the enemy in the shape of the horse farmers. The symbiotic nature of their economic relationship ensured the continuance of that relationship in its paternalistic form. They perceived each other in non-political terms. The 'worth' of an individual or a household was still judged in terms of the possession of land and house and the use made of them, the way mutual obligations were discharged, and above all the quality of somebody's work. A horse farmer who employed a Communist as one of his *Arbeitsleute* would not let this fact affect his opinion of the person. The Communist would have to refrain from openly condemning 'his' horse farmer as a member of a reactionary political party if he and his household wanted to continue working on the farm. The consequence of this tacit agreement to keep politics out of 'real life' was that conflicts between the different interest groups had to be dealt with in some other way. People continued to enter reciprocal relationships based on inequality and exploitation. The terms were negotiated publicly through the channels of gossip, the use of rough justice against transgressors, the ritualised and highly symbolic consumption of food, and the social and moral diagnosis of illness and disease. In short, seemingly 'traditional' forms of verbal and non-verbal communication and exchange were used to deal with conflicts that arose in this 'modern' version of a moral economy.

Throughout the 1920s most horse farmers and cow farmers continued to argue against the right of everybody freely to choose a political party or an association. The phrases, 'No good could come of this . . .', 'Clubs should be kept free of politics . . .', 'A village and its concerns should not be a matter of party politics . . .', kept being repeated in interviews. Along with everyone else, the interviewers had to come to terms with the fact that, in reality, at a formal, institutional level villagers were beginning to use their right to choose a party or become a member of a club. Nevertheless, the yardstick for the performance of elected members of the village council, right across the political spectrum, remained their willingness to 'act in the interest of the whole village'. The peculiarities of the economic relations within the village endorsed a sense of pragmatism and limited the extent to which ideological differences could come to dominate social relations.

The working-class clubs represented the beginnings of a counter-culture to the nationalist and conservative clubs which had become the 'natural' domain for the horse farmers and their allies, the teachers. However, one should not overestimate their oppositional effect, over and above the fact that they were established on the basis of social and ideological divisions, and thereby acted as landmarks. The Social Democratic handball club and the Communist cycling club in many ways reproduced elements of bourgeois culture. Like the nationalist clubs they were very concerned with respectability, banners, properly-minuted meetings, orderly-conducted affairs, as well as being hierarchical and competitive. All village clubs, irrespective of ideology, excluded women from positions of responsibility. In relation to the outside world all the clubs shared a concern for representing the honour of the village and thereby effectively helped to recreate the myth or reality of the community spirit. In effect, the clubs became an important mechanism for institutionalising existing class antagonisms in a form which was not threatening to the whole economic and social system. The 'dangerous' implications of your neighbour's class position or political beliefs could be contained within the sphere of formalised politics and leisure. Only against this background can the ease with which the Nazis were to dismantle the separate working-class clubs be understood.[9]

Although the impetus for these changes in the cultural and political institutions of the village came from the surrounding industrial towns and the experience of wider society through the First World War, the form these institutions took and the associated patterns of social interaction were not simply a mirror-image of what can be found in urban working-class communities. The adaptation of bourgeois and working-class culture within the village reflected the special needs of village society and the consciousness of its members. Given the relatively poor agricultural land, the small size of the holdings, the low level of mechanisation and the conscious decision to maintain agricultural production within all three classes in Körle, some form of class compromise had to be found. Labour-intensive agriculture could only be kept up by the continued co-operation between different households and between horse and goat farmers. The horse farmers could not have remained independent agricultural producers without the supply of casual labour from the goat farmers' households. The cow farmers could not have maintained their 'middle-class' position without the existence of the two other classes, who supplied them with a market for their artisan skills. The goat farmers, who paid the highest price for the system's survival, saw additional incomes, through agricultural work and self-sufficiency in food, as a defence against the industrial system. If one places these calculations in the historic context in which only the horse famers were well-off and everybody else lived under the threat of poverty, then it begins to make sense that the villagers tried to turn the idea of a community into a working reality. However, one must remember that their idea of community was not the same as that portrayed by theorists like Toennies.[10] As one villager put it to me: 'One should not have any illusions about the old world. People knew that in those days as well. Those at the top, the teachers, the pastors and the big farmers could live, but in that poverty we all depended on each other.'[11] The consequences of this adaptation to industrialisation of the inhabitants of Körle was that household membership remained more central to the perception of the *self* and the *other* than social class allegiance. Conflict, therefore, was also mediated through the household. The relative absence of open political and work conflict must not however be confused with the total absence of conflict and the existence of a stable, timeless and traditional social structure. Social inequality is not timeless. It is created by members of society and as such it does not survive by itself but must be re-enacted and re-negotiated over time. This process always involves a clash of interests and the expression of social conflict.

During the Weimar years, class hegemony pervaded all aspects of everyday life in Körle. It was a period when class differences continued to be expressed through some well-established social channels but also took on new forms in the establishment of separate working-class organisations. The existence of a class structure meant that apparently unconnected aspects of everyday life, like eating, drinking, illness or health served in some way to remind everybody of the existence of inequality, subservience and domination. Conflict and order were permanently 'reconstructed' and 'renegotiated' through interaction in everyday situations. Social order and conflict did not just happen, they were actively 'accomplished'. The drama of everyday life was acted out in the context of existing structural constraints, imposed by inequality, but also involved each village in interpreting the meaning of his or her own role. Every social interaction, every event, was charged with symbolic significance and moral meaning.

II

Class membership in Körle was essentially based on the possession of land and animals. Class position not only allowed fellow-villagers to know how much land a household owned and what type of animals they kept in their stables, but also what position the head of this household occupied in the social, economic and political hierarchy of the village. These possessions also signalled to the rest of the world the respect due to the owner, who sat next to whom in church or at public functions, and who could think of marrying into the household.

Ownership of land and house was an integral part of the consciousness and personal security of most villagers. If a household had little or no property, its members were seen as 'inadequate human beings' who could not expect to be taken 'seriously'. Land-ownership pervaded the whole social system and was a fixed reference-point in all social interaction and in every individual's psychology. However, it was not just the idea of property which served as a measure for status assessment; equal importance was attached to the way in which a household was making use of its agricultural property. In a sense, Körle was an 'occupational community' and the quality of the labour a household put into the land and the way it distributed the annual produce were as important as landownership itself. These ideas are typical of a 'moral economy' based on the whole household, in which not all economic activity can be judged in accountancy terms.[12] To ensure their survival, villagers developed appropriate enforcement rituals. The old men of the village would, on their daily walks through the fields, look out for crooked furrows and other examples of bad husbandry. The older women would look over the garden fences and gossip about the member of the household who had not pulled her weight to get the seasonal work done. This gossip amounted to social control, but it could also enhance the reputation of a person or a household. It was taken for granted that any household which tolerated members who deviated from the norms would collectively lose prestige and suffer damage to its reputation.

The 'name' of a household was a forceful moral instrument.

Most houses had names associated with them that were independent of the family name of the present occupants and could be traced back over many generations. The house, the name and the attached land had *persona* of their own. It was expected of people that they preserve these symbols of social and economic continuity. Attempts were made to nip any deviant behaviour in the bud, or to channel it into socially acceptable forms. It was recognised that young people in the village were liable, in each generation, to question and step across established boundaries of behaviour (*über die Stränge schlagen*). They were encouraged to channel their energy into ritualised forms of pranks (*Streiche*) or rough justice which were, with village approval, carried out against legitimate targets. This served as an instrument of public denunciation when 'common rights' had been wilfully ignored. The pranks were often directed against people with power and authority — favourite targets were teachers, the pastor, and horse farmers with a reputation for meanness — rough justice was also meted out to deviants within the peer group.

Those at the top of the existing class structure tried to present their own order as timeless. Their ideology pervaded all aspects of everyday life. A class society wants to survive beyond tomorrow and inheritance and marriage are key institutions for its perpetuation. The children of horse farmers had to be kept away from the children of the other two classes. When 'inappropriate' romances occurred those concerned could become victims of pranks. If a couple thought they had evaded the ever-present eyes of the rest of the village and escaped to a house, they could find themselves locked in. A popular method was to block the doors with a pile of dung or piles of firewood. Rituals ensured that the marriage politics of the various classes could be pursued as rationally as possible. Because sexuality was seen as an incalculable quantity, the potential sexual partners had to be prevented from enjoying too much privacy and the beginnings of courtship were placed under strict public supervision, although there were couples who ended up 'having to get married'. Nobody married across the class barriers before 1949. Marriage thus remained an effective instrument of class domination.[13]

The best-remembered form of prank or rough justice against horse farmers was a raid on their sausage pantry. The spoils of the raid would be taken to the local inn (not one the horse farmers themselves frequented) and were shared out very ostentatiously

among everyone present. No doubt the consumption of the food
and the stories of more transgressions by the same household fixed
this event firmly in the public mind and restored a belief in the local
system of dealing with injustice. Stealing, therefore, when done at
the appropriate time and by the right person could be an act of
justice. Pranks like this were also a rich source of oral tradition.
The most celebrated prank of all was one aimed at a horse farmer
whose farm was opposite the biggest inn in the village. He had a
reputation for excessive meanness and deviousness, and was considered to work too hard and demand too much of his employees.
One weekend he wanted to spread manure on his fields. To get a
very early start on the Saturday morning, he had decided to load up
his manure wagon on the Friday night. In this way he would not
lose any time on loading up the wagon in the morning and could
proceed, without delay, with the spreading (a very time-consuming
task) in the fields. He was seen doing this by some village youths at
the inn who, after the farmer had gone to bed, started to unload
and dismantle the wagon, which was then reassembled in the
farmer's hayloft and loaded up again. As the morning wore on, the
farmer was seen strutting up and down the village looking in vain
for his vanished dung wagon. By the time he found it, he had lost a
day's work. This seems to have met with universal approval: everyone who relates the story makes it very clear that 'he had it coming
to him'.

Pranks within the peer group usually had to do with controlling
someone's supposed sexual licence or ensuring that the young men
were given a fair chance to meet their sweethearts. A very common
way for boys and girls to meet during the long winter evenings was
for the girls to assemble for a spinning bee, where they were later
joined by the young men. On one occasion when, as sometimes
happened, the girls locked the boys out, the boys decided to take
their revenge. They climbed in through the kitchen window, stole
the waffles that had been baked for the evening and nailed them to
the fence-posts along the streets. As far as ensuring proper courtship was concerned, a favourite prank was to tie a pram to the
chimney of a house when the daughter of the family was pregnant
and 'had to get married'. Peer-group pressure was applied to those
people who tried to get away and have some privacy by the threat
of public exposure through such pranks. As already mentioned,
they were frequently barricaded into the house with piles of firewood or manure. Trails of sawdust arrows publicly linked the

homes of secret lovers or adulterers.

The openness and directness of these pranks were typical of sanctions against the behaviour of villagers. Conflict with official authority figures took on a more private and individualistic form. Memories of teachers and pastors are ambivalent. They are remembered for having been very strict or even brutal and sadistic but at the same time they were 'good for one's future character' or 'one had learned something from them'. These feelings of hatred and gratitude are inextricably linked in the memories of the older generation. Most people tell how they had tried at one time or another to put a Bible in their shorts or under their skirts to take the sting out of the pastor's cane when they went to confirmation classes. The boys unhinged the pastor's front door and carried it to the other end of the village so that he had to go around looking for it. On other occasions, they smeared soap on the steps leading up to the teacher's house in the hope that he would slip. His front doorstep was covered in *Baldriantropfen*, a medicine which was believed to attract cats and induce them to nocturnal caterwauling. In these ways the pupils hoped to repay the teacher or pastor for some of the suffering they inflicted on them. Open defiance only broke out when some pupils had joined the Hitler Youth and perceived their pastor as old-fashioned and an unreliable patriot. The teachers were open sympathisers of the Nazi movement and there was no need to rebel against them.

There was also a policeman in the village who patrolled daily on his bicycle. His role and authority were fully accepted. When he intervened in law and order issues it was usually in an informal way. He expected to control by 'having a word'. When the policeman made an arrest he was exposed to public censure. Such action reflected badly on the community as a whole and constituted a threat to community ideology. However, respect for authority was such that it was the policeman as an individual who was blamed, not the office he held. By contrast the villagers loved to hate the forester. Each household was involved in annual negotiations with the Forestry Commission for their supply of firewood. Though they had a common right to the wood, the forester decided where they could gather it, and what quality they got. Leaves for their stables, twigs for garden use or the manufacture of brooms and baskets also had to be obtained in this way. The horse farmers who went shooting cultivated good relations with the forester. The other classes perceived him as someone who administered supposed concessions which should have been unconditional common rights. These attitudes must have been formed or strongly reinforced during the nineteenth century when common grazing and collecting in the forest were abolished and the rights sold off. In protest against the interfering forester, households tried to steal leaves or wood to supplement their annual allocation. The boys from goat farmer households were encouraged by their parents to poach the odd hare or fish. Only after such acts had been accomplished were they made public and proudly described. In some of these cases the forester seems to have resorted to police investigations.

Pranks against official authorities primarily served to reinforce a sense of community and gave those who committed them the feeling that they belonged — they were part of the village. When directed against the ruling class of the village, these pranks served to define, in a theatrical way, the limits to exploitation; when directed against young people, they served to define the boundaries of courtship and sexual behaviour.[14] In the absence of any formal redress, villagers who worked as casual labourers for horse farmers used such symbolic statements to signal to an employer that he had offended against the common law contained in the moral economy of the village and that, therefore, he had incurred a social debt which he or his household had to repay in the future. These conflicts were an integral part of class relationships within the village. They reinforced both the notion and reality of social order based on inequality. The conflicts suggest that there was a highly developed sense of class position, but this awareness was not translated into class conflict. These 'interaction rituals' served to clarify the social differences and define the boundaries of acceptable and normal behaviour. The symbolic language used to communicate these messages was taken for granted and only rarely questioned. Perhaps this implies that rituals are not unique occasions which serve to reinforce the ordinary by breaking the routine of everydayness. They can be interpreted as exaggerations of normality, as everyday life is generally based on habit and ritual.

III

Food was of great importance for the cosmology of the villagers; consumption of food was seen in cultural, moral and medical terms. The manner in which food was eaten, the occasion and the participants had cultural significance. Moral censure was placed on people who ate too much of the wrong type of food, whereas those who ate properly were 'virtuous'. Food was an essential part of preventative and curative medicine. It could be argued that eating went to the heart of the most deeply-felt cultural values of village society and dealt with complex moral issues that the inhabitants of Körle might have found difficult to express in ordinary language. Apart from work, eating was a way of defining a person's identity, and the perception of the food consumed served as a way of evaluating changes in an individual's standing and role; interpreting the consumption of food was the most important issue in everyone's mind. The symbolism surrounding it served to establish the terms of the village's moral economy. The making, serving and eating of food were central to the negotiation of power relationships and the division of labour within each household and between different social classes. The consumption of the 'right food' could be seen as one of the keys to achieving status, health, normality, happiness and a sense of belonging or of being different. The selection, the quantity and quality of food eaten clearly helped to signify to the onlooker the class membership and self-image of the eater.[15] At mealtimes and on festive occasions children learned the extent and nature of the kinship system and the sexual division of labour. They could also familiarise themselves with the kind of reciprocal and hierarchical relationships which existed between their own house and households in the neighbourhood and in the village. The exchange of labour between households at peak times of the agricultural season was always associated with eating, and often food was the only formal payment. The annual slaughter of a pig involved the ritualistic giving away of food. The sharing-out was not arbitrary, but reflected the social network of the household. Only relatives and those who participated in the annual work of the household were given some meat or sausages, with those most indispensable to the household's division of labour receiving the best cuts. Others, whose help one might need in the future, were given a token share. Even the stock in which the meat and sausages were cooked was carried all round the neighbourhood and handed out. When horse farmers slaughtered a pig the poorest families were entitled to demand a share. These people 'disguised' their identity with masks.

Mealtimes provided a structure to the normal working day. People ate when it 'was time to eat' and the sequence of meals was inseparable from the routine of the day. The breaking of this routine amounted to a breach of custom and was seen to be an act of stupidity or provocation. Normally, a hot meal was eaten at lunch-time even if this meant carrying food into the fields. Agricultural workers regarded it as one of their few fundamental rights to receive a hot meal and understood it to be part of the employment contract. The daily hot meal was part of ensuring the health, normality and well-being of all household members. Not having a hot meal a day was associated with want, poverty and loss of self-respect. The speed of work, the tone of address and the food a worker received during the working day served to define the nature of the relationship between employer and employee. Hiring, firing or giving up a job were often associated with food. The extent of the integration of the workforce into the employer's household and the general attitudes of the employer could be publicly gauged at mealtimes. Most horse farmers made a point of eating meals at the same table as their relatives and workforce. This showed a willingness to adhere to customary practices whilst it also served as a theatrical enactment of differences in authority, status and sex roles, as the serving duties and seating order were clearly defined.

There were two horse farmers who broke these conventions. They ate in a separate room, consumed better food and served up what the locals called 'pig shit' to their employees. Consequently, these farmers became legitimate targets for rough justice and their employees could enforce the moral code without suffering sanctions. The story is told of an employee who left his job on one of those farms during a meal after being served bad food for several days. He threw the hot food at the wall and shouted that they should '. . . eat their own shit and do their own shitty work'. This was, incidentally, the same farmer whose sausage pantry was raided by the village youths, who, as recounted a few paragraphs above, then took their 'spoils' to the local pub, sharing them with everyone present, thus drawing further public attention to his meanness.

Food was important in preventing illness and disease in addition to providing nutritional needs. It was classified according to which illnesses it could prevent and cure. The perception of food as preventative medicine made health the responsibility of each individual. One dictum that was central for socialisation was: you eat what is put in front of you. Eating properly, cleaning the plate and eating what you were given demonstrated your willingness to abide by the rules. As the survival of most village households — with the exception of the horse farmers — was precarious, it is not surprising that the idea of choosing one's food was unknown and the eating of all the food was expected. An example of the way in which the horse farmers reinforced their separate class position was by adopting bourgeois table manners. The inhabitants of Körle believed that eating properly was the route to good health, health was the precondition for good work, and work was the main source of identity and the way to attain Christian immortality. As one villager put it to me: 'The way a man eats is the way he works.'

IV

During the Weimar years doctors were called in to deal with serious diseases such as TB and conditions needing surgery. School children and those members of the goat farmers' households who worked for one of the big industrial firms in Kassel were the first sections of the community to receive professional medical care. In 1923 the village council decided to pay for the training and part-time employment of a village nurse and midwife, and the introduction of a health system eventually transformed the treatment of the sick.[16] Many of the diagnostic practices and ideas have survived in a fragmented form. Villagers will use a combination of orthodox and traditional remedies and the decision to go to the doctor is still a matter of debate within the household and neighbourhood.[17]

The ability to diagnose illness and practise folk medicine was important for the prestige of women in the village. Illness was diagnosed in two ways: the disease was 'named' on the basis of natural and physical causes and an additional analysis of the wider social implications was made. The neighbourhood was consulted in order to reach a consensual social diagnosis so that responsibility was not left solely to the healer, a practice which was intended to prevent false accusations of laziness or moral and social decline. This collective decision-making process also protected women healers from accusations of witchcraft. Although there was a generally recognised body of folk medicine, each individual household believed it had found its own magic formulae. The principal aim was to prevent illness and the villagers hoped to achieve this by several means. They aimed to follow correct dietary and social habits, believed that magical practices could protect them, and looked for warning signals in nature. As people were aware of the fact that many diseases were incurable and that their own health was the most important economic asset they possessed, a considerable amount of time was devoted to preventive measures.

The gathering of teas for tisanes, lotions and poultices, etc. was usually the responsibility of the older women of the household. Girls helped in this and thus began to be initiated into their future caring and healing role. Each herb, leaf or blossom was classified and associated with powers to cure or prevent particular diseases. The mixture was usually brewed by the elder women, but others were involved in order to share this medical knowledge. The most important medical plant was camomile. It was freely available and had the widest application. It could only be collected on certain hallowed days in order to ensure maximum effect — a practice which prevented over-harvesting and reminded people of the fact that medicine and magic were inseparable. With the exception of the old, who regularly drank certain herbal teas to keep them healthy, all other age groups drank the teas only at times when they were particularly susceptible to illness. They were drunk with honey, which was thought to soothe and tranquilise the nerves. At this time the diet was meagre and illness was thought to be caused, in part, by malutrition. Teas and dietary supplements were thought to restore health in the same way as tablets today. Without exception, the teas and foodstuffs associated with magical curing powers were not included in the everyday diet.

Throughout the year there was an overriding concern to prevent TB and pneumonia. Colds and fevers were seen as the first step to these killer diseases and efforts were concentrated on preventing these minor ailments. To this end, people at risk kept warm, avoided draughts, bathed their feet in hot salt water, inhaled an infusion of camomile, and drank an assortment of hot beverages including hot milk and honey, hot juniper juice and boiled onions with candy sugar. In addition, they would wrap themselves up in the special family shawl or blanket, only used on such occasions, which was believed to have protective powers. Usually, these garments had belonged to a woman (one or two generations back) who had a reputation of having had a 'special knack of curing diseases'. When people were confined to bed with colds and 'flu these treatments continued to be applied. In addition, the back and chest were massaged with hot fat, people slept on sheep and cat skins in order to prevent the cold getting 'into their bones', or put unwashed sheep's wool on their chest in the belief that the irritation and warmth would 'drive out' the illness. Sick people confined to bed were kept unusually warm in an attempt to force 'the dirt' out of the body and restore it to its normal 'clean' balance (*Schwitzkur*).[18] High fevers were brought down by soaking towels in cold water and wrapping them around the patients' calves. This process was sometimes repeated for several days. After each treatment, the patient's body was washed down with vinegar water. Only when someone got pneumonia or TB, or when a fever could not be reduced, was a doctor called and, in most cases, the patient was hospitalised.

Though taboos played an important part in normal socialisation, they were broken if this was deemed necessary for the treatment of illness. For instance, dog fat was regarded as the only possible cure for serious lung disease and the few people who survived attacks of TB and pneumonia continued to eat small quantities as a preventative measure. Butter and lard were invested with similar powers and it was believed that the fat was stored by the body for needy days. The more your body saved, the better equipped it was to defend itself against any attack, especially of TB which was thought to 'eat away the body'. The 'saving for a rainy day' idea of prevention of disease, and the significance of fat as a defence against the threat of destruction, were consistent with the social ideal of a healthy body and a secure existence. A slim person was regarded as socially needy, in danger of illness, and either mean or impoverished. Well-built people had wealth and status. It was believed that health, in contrast to inherited land and kinship structures, was the only asset over which a person had some degree of control. Magical beliefs were important in helping the villagers interpret the coincidental nature of disease and formed an integral part of folk medicine and preventive strategies. These beliefs offered the individual the 'comfort' of holding an insurance policy in his or her hands, but they also helped to establish behavioural norms which appeared classless and natural and thereby provided an independent set of rules for evaluating the actions of every household in a seemingly objective way.[19]

Superstitions had a social control function but they also ensured a degree of humanity and defined the difference between reasonable and unreasonable degrees of exploitation and oppression. Curses were the last resort of the down-trodden and an important symbol of resistance and defiance. During pregnancy, for example, women were protected by taboo. They were not allowed to go underneath a washing line otherwise it would be a difficult birth. The washing line was a symbol of hard work and heavy lifting, both of which were taboo during pregnancy. Wife-beating was believed to affect the health of the child, produce a birthmark on the baby's body, and in some cases lead to a stillbirth. Women were not to touch any rodents during pregnancy and had to be protected from any frightening or upsetting situation. The effects of these beliefs was to afford the pregnant woman some protection from the daily workload and the maltreatment of others. When women did not want their baby, they apparently turned all these 'superstitious' beliefs upside down and broke them systematically in order to induce a miscarriage. In addition, they ate household soap to 'make the baby slide out'. Vinegar was believed to cleanse the blood and the body if taken in small quantities and, consequently, some women drank large quantities in the hope that it would trigger off a spontaneous abortion.

The old women, apart from being the most effective healers, could also bring illness, misfortune and strife into a household because their curses were thought to be potent. Senility was not regarded as a disease in the physical but in the social sense. The symptoms could be seen in the bad temper of those affected, who were believed to lack courtesy. In this state, old women (not old men) were thought to be deliberately antisocial. Again, 'superstitions' identified the danger, offered people a defence, and warned them of the likely consequences. On *Walpurgisnacht* (Hallowe'en) people nailed three wreaths to their doors to protect themselves and their animals against witchcraft or the evil eye of old women. On the night before May Day, if older women came to borrow from their neighbours, it was a sign of antisocial intentions. The neighbours were obliged to lend the things out but were not supposed to answer more than one request with a simple 'yes'. They were to think of a counter-curse — usually 'kiss my arse' — with each answer. Throughout the year, old women from other households were kept away from the stables, as they were believed to bring 'bad luck' to the animals.

In relation to the death and illness of people and animals there were omens in nature which had to be interpreted and read correctly in order to avoid the danger. An exceptionally large molehill in the vegetable garden or meadows of the farm signified a death within the year for someone in the household. A barn owl heard at the wrong time of year signalled danger, but swallows nesting in stables or under the roof were a good insurance policy against misfortune. People who destroyed swallows' nests stepped outside the confines of social and natural order. A link between society and nature was central to the cosmology of villagers as they believed that chance, misfortune and unusual natural events constituted supernatural happenings which had to be faced with the help of magic, superstition, ritual and taboo.

Through the treatment of the sick, the social actors 'made statements' about social reality. Medical practices functioned as a focusing mechanism and a control of experience. A link was created between the cosmological principles adhered to by the villagers and the structures of the social world which they inhabited. The ritualistic context in which illness was diagnosed and the sick treated resembled what social anthropologists have called a 'rite of passage'.[20] These rites tended to be structured in three phases: the person was separated from the normal role and status, initiated into a temporary state of abnormality and social marginality, and finally brought back to normal and reintegrated into society. As the illness label amounted to a dispensation from normal work duties, no one could be allowed to define him or herself as ill or healthy. The difference between having just a cough and 'flu was a matter of social definition. Only when there was agreement that the symptoms were serious enough was the patient advised to withdraw to the sickbed. Through visits, the outside world kept in touch and was able to prevent the patient from taking advantage of the situation. The logic of these events remained obscure to most participants, but the rituals of treatment and its associated metaphorical language of folk medicine and 'good' magic, which resembles mythology in pre-industrial society, allowed people to engage in a 'dialogue' about the nature of social relations and order. These ideas about order could not be free of contradictions in a class society. Both the beliefs and the ritualised context of behaviour, such as being ill, were forms of communication through which social controversy could be maintained and a resemblance of 'community' constructed.[21]

Through folk medicine the 'binary principles' of order and disorder in village cosmology were made clear. Health was associated with purity and cleanliness; illness signified danger and pollution. Treatment was perceived as a method of magical transformation. The patient was restored to 'normal' by cleansing the body of its dirt. What also became apparent was the ambivalent role in which women were cast in this patriarchal society. The ambilvalence was made public through the perception of women as practitioners of good and bad magic. Women were associated with care and love, their involvement in reciprocal relationships was believed to be emotionally based. Therefore, women constituted a threat to the male principles of social order which were seen in terms of mutual obligations and contractual duty. Just as sexuality had to be curbed, so women had to be controlled and watched in the public sphere in order to ensure the continuity of class and property. Class collaboration and the 'resolution' of conflicts within the village were inseparably linked with the diagnosis and labelling of disease. Villagers perceived offences against the behavioural code contained in the moral economy as a debt which had to be settled by a process of public discussion and subsequent compensation.[22] The 'inquest' into an illness looked at such questions as: is this person's illness a direct punishment for his or her own deviancy, a repayment of a social debt incurred by previous generations or, in the absence of any other explanation, could fate be responsible?

The predictability of behaviour within the household and in the marriage market were central to the reproduction of the division of labour and class relations within the village. The invocation of supernatural threats to make people 'pull themselves together' (*sich zusammenreissen*) depersonalised social control, but the enforcement of these 'laws' took place in a highly-charged atmosphere as people put curses on each other or their houses. Curses were a last resort and only people who had broken some of the strongest taboos of social conduct became targets: those, for example, who maltreated their parents, cheated siblings out of a 'legitimate' inheritance, refused to work for the household, or married across class lines. Conflicts between siblings were inevitable as the property usually passed into the hands of the eldest son and as the other brothers and sisters were expected to work for the household with equal enthusiasm and accept that their standing in the village depended on their dutiful behaviour. The person who inherited the house and land also had reasons for resentment. He took over the farm on condition that he and his family would take care of the older relatives and offer board and lodging to any unmarried brother and sister. As the one group resented the fact that they had been left empty-handed (*mit leeren Händen dastehen, leer ausgegangen zu sein*) and the heir began to view his siblings as extra mouths to feed, niggling conflicts could turn into internal household feuds. These quarrels were then frequently accompanied by curses.

Some of these curses are reported to have worked. There was always a household within living memory whose string of misfortunes and illnesses could be interpreted in this way to give villagers ground for believing in this system of retribution. It is also possible that tension within an authoritarian and relatively enclosed social order built up to such an extent that it could only be relieved through the hysterical reactions of individuals who genuinely believed in these powers. Heart failure, circulation trouble, cancer and infections signified faulty socialisation of those afflicted. The diagnosis amounted to a lesson in public morality. Too much work could cause mental illness but too little work was thought to bring about a circulation collapse and lead to heart failure. Those suffering from heart disease were suspected of personal weakness and social irresponsibility — their human nature was somehow flawed. The disease made public the life-history of a secret deviant. As heart disease undermined a person's ability to work, it constituted a threat to the household's division of labour. In the eyes of the others, the person affected had to be carried and was labelled as being responsible for his or her failure to pull his or her weight. The inability to work was the ultimate expression of sickness and therefore one of the severest threats to social order and personal self-discipline. Work was the only cure for heart and circulation problems and the way to restore public confidence.

V

The diagnosis of mental illness took account of the dynamics of internal household relationships. Those people within the household 'who had driven a relative to the brink of insanity' were held responsible. Mental disorder was rarely seen as the product of the sick person's psyche; it was viewed in relation to the actions of those who had flouted the principles of seniority and reciprocity which were supposed to regulate the relationships within each household. In Körle, individuals had to affirm both themselves and the collective values of the household and community. Character and reputation depended not solely on birth and class position, but also upon deeds. Deeds and actions defined the quality and character of people in terms of reciprocity, social responsibility and mutual obligation. The network of relationships within the household was fundamental to a determination of what was regarded as natural and unnatural, of what it was to be fully human. The 'appearance' of mental illness was indicative of disorder and 'unnatural' events, it pointed to a separation between appearance and reality within that household. Very often the accusatory finger was pointed at somebody by a relative who was part of the wider network of the household but had left the parental home. At the first sign of mental disorder, this person would name the guilty party and relate the breakdown to a catalogue of grievances and resentments that he or she might harbour against the household. The local dialect contains a number of stock phrases designed to explain mental illness in these environmental terms: 'His parents drove her to it . . .', 'No wonder that she has gone gaga, they treated her worse than their animals . . .', 'The others are not innocent . . .', 'Nobody could bear what she had to put up with in that house . . .', 'He suffers on behalf of all of them . . .', and so on.

In one such case there had been three children in the family, who lived with their mother and two married relatives. Later, the two younger children married and left the house. The eldest son stayed at home and combined building work and farming. People were worried that he would fail to get a wife; they said he was married to his work. Eventually, he did marry, after a long period of having been mocked about his sedentary habits. The wife came from an outside village and was suspected of being 'stupid' and 'not good enough'. By this was meant that she took this unrepentant bachelor because she was unable to get anybody better, and it also implied that she had not brought a sufficient dowry with her. They had a daughter and when the household had shrunk to grandmother, wife, daughter and husband, he began to be picked on in the village for being ruled by a '*Weiberwirtschaft*' (female rule). The village gossips also suspected tensions between the household and the siblings who had 'married out'. Consequently when the husband had a mental breakdown, the village blamed the women in his household and the relatives connected with it for his condition and his failure to control 'his own house'.

In another house, 'the woman of the house' (*Froche*) was committed to an asylum. Her condition was blamed on her husband because he was seen to be too weak and hadn't defended 'his own wife' against the bullying of his 'own mother' and 'his own unmarried brother' who still lived in the house. This system of diagnosis submitted the reputation of the whole household to public scrutiny and enabled villagers, through the channels of gossip, to identify tensions.[23] The tensions were implicit in clashes of interest which were built into the composition of the whole house: generation against generation, own-family against in-laws, husband and wife against mother- and father-in-law, husband and mother-in-law against wife, resident relatives against the rest, and so on. Each person or group could be accused of having driven any of the others mad. The exceptions were people who lived on their own, had declined into destitution, and had no ties with any household. They went mad because they did not have any of these stabilising relationships. Mental illness, therefore, represented both a form of conflict and a legitimate form of escape from a social world that had become unbearable.

Unlike the Azande, where all death and illness had to be explained by reference to misfortune and supernatural intervention, the inhabitants of Körle exempted TB and pneumonia from this interpretative framework.[24] These diseases were seen as personal catastrophes rather than a form of retribution. The threat of TB hung over everybody and the disease's unpredictability and frequent occurrence seemed to make a nonsense of all 'normal' considerations. The Almighty and Nature were perceived to be more orderly and calculable. Too many undeserving cases would have had to be explained and the beliefs in natural and social justice would have lost credibility. 'Getting' TB was a personal and collective disaster. Apart from depriving the household of one of its labourers, TB led to the social isolation of the sufferer and those who cared for him or her. Fatal illnesses — and TB in particular — were a testing-ground for the moral character of both the individual and the household. Death came slowly to the sufferer and the illness exposed the relatives to danger. Consequently, the neighbours had an opportunity to see the virtues of self-discipline and mutual obligation in action and they could make judgements about resilience and social discipline. Death from TB could be a stigma or enhance the reputation and name of the victim and household. These perceptions of lung disease related to more general notions associated with pain and suffering. Patients with serious illnesses and in great pain were expected to suffer stoically. Visits were restricted and conducted in an unassuming manner. These long-term illnesses were threatening to the routine of everyday life and the assumption that the absence of illness was normal. In contrast, those who had minor accidents or suffered from curable diseases were placed in the public's view and their symptoms acted as a focus for the expression of open sympathy and charity.

The perception of TB and pain would, on first impressions, suggest that these villagers were locked into a traditional system of beliefs which had lost nothing in coherence and displayed stability and resilience. However, traditions are not as changeless as they appear. Although it is impossible to reconstruct the origin of the ideas associated with the TB sufferer, it would perhaps not be too speculative to suggest they bear a resemblance to notions we find in the literary tradition of the early nineteenth century. Villagers probably perceived the TB sufferer in the 1920s through a perspective that was, in part, constructed from traditional beliefs in folk medicine but also incorporated influences which had been brought into the villages through contact with doctors, teachers, newspapers, cheap novels and other aspects of bourgeois culture. It is probably no accident that the TB sufferer in the village was shrouded in a very similar mythology to that surrounding the unwordly, refined and over-sensitive poet and member of the nineteenth-century intellectual aristocracy.[25] In both village society in the Weimar period, and in nineteenth-century upper-class circles, TB was an illness that liberated its victims from an oppressing reality. The people afflicted by TB were perceived as 'too good for this world', its hard work, its sexuality, its insensitivity and its injustice. In some sense they were envied their fate and secretly one admired them for having been chosen by Nature, Fate and God to be released from the bondage of everyday life. They were like children who had regained their innocence, progressing through TB towards the spiritual and pure. In a fundamentally Protestant sense, these tubercular victims served as models of purity and spiritual cleanliness. They could be among the elect and achieve immortality without having to pursue the path of hard work, social obedience and duty. TB, as the exception among the diseases, 'taught' villagers that exemption from moral pollution and escape from the cycle of inequality and social debt could only be achieved beyond the confines of the social universe. Help, if it existed, came through death, not the charity of men.

Cancer was seen as a punishment for sexual transgressions committed during adolescence. The victims most frequently labelled in this way were women who were seen to have followed their emotional and sexual impulses rather than social conscience and sense of responsibility. As a socialisation device, the diagnosis of cancer highlighted the importance of the politics of marriage and the evils of independent character development. The class structure and the household economy, based on the uneven distribution of land, survived within Körle through the limitation of marriage across class boundaries. In order to achieve this, sexuality and certain types of social contact had to be associated with a high degree of moral pollution. It was the diagnosis of cancer, besides charivaris and pranks, which dealt with this important aspect of class rule. On a societal level, the cancer metaphor served even more sinister purposes. Both in the nineteenth and twentieth centuries, the image of the cancerous growth was used by the antisemitic movements that ravaged the Hessian countryside to describe the Jewish population. It invoked the idea of 'the threat from within', and the Nazis made full use of it. They equated 'cancer' with 'enemy' and the 'threat from within' with the cause of all social evil. Social and economic factors were recast as a medical problem which required radical surgery and a hygienic solution. The medical metaphor provided an ideal tool for the Nazis to exploit the hidden fears among sections of the rural population and they used it to incite, justify and legitimise violence, murder and genocide.[26] Nazi propaganda linked in with a number of ideas which formed the basis of the dominant village ideology. Those who joined the Nazi movement seized upon this rhetoric and used it ruthlessly against minorities and organised sections of the working class, whom they perceived as posing a threat to the idealised village community. In its early years, the Nazi Party consisted almost entirely of the sons of the horse and cow farmers who hoped that the movement could preserve or restore their class hegemony by reversing trends towards class polarisation. The magic formula was the 'coordination' (*Gleichschaltung*) of social organisations and cultural values and the restoration of 'health' and virility to the *Volk*. The enemies of this order had to be 'cleansed' or 'eradicated' in the same way as disease was expelled from the body of the sick. What becomes apparent is that the illness metaphor could be applied in a 'rational' way to the analysis of social conflict, but that the overall perspective rested on 'irrational' premises, the underlying assumptions being fear, obedience and control. These were the sentiments of class rule, the emotions used to intimidate and control those who were different or wanted to effect fundamental change: '*Wir haben uns doch nicht getraut, was zu sagen. Wir haben früher doch nichts als Angst gekannt.*'[27]

In the 'theatre' of everyday life, the inhabitants of Körle acted out a variety of roles, each of which required the 'presentation' of a different aspect of self. Everyday social interaction involved the negotiation of these images of self and other and implied the reconstruction of social reality. Definitions of illness have been examined in some detail because they enabled me to piece together some of the fundamental cosmological notions which formed the basis for defining the self and other in a context of inequality, poverty and class compromise. The threatening moral symbolism associated with health and illness was a powerful social control mechanism which was linked to the ideology of class and the practice of Protestantism. The key to personal self-discipline and public accountability was individual conscience. By not listening to his or her conscience a person was believed to put the whole household at the mercy of misfortune. The attempt to establish a connection between the victim, the disease and the idea that illness and misfortunes were apt punishments for social, political and economic 'offences' mystified complex and historically specific social and economic issues while, at the same time, trying to make sense of these phenomena.

Luther's dictum 'Let work be the way to salvation', and Hippocrates' prescription 'Let food be your medicine and medicine your food' embodied the struggle by these villagers to make the prevention of illness a social duty and mark of responsible behaviour. This survival strategy depended on the objective of retaining a degree of self-determination and security but also confined the individual to the hierarchical and authoritarian order of each household. By linking disease, collective guilt and individual deviancy with the public reputation of a household, the preservation of the individual and household name became a strategy for maintaining the *status quo*. Health, in the minds of most villagers, represented something desirable, a state of purity and normality. Sickness was a condition of physical and spiritual danger and pollution, and both prevention and cure were seen in terms of magical transformations. The diagnosis and treatment of illness metaphorically restated fundamental assumptions of the ruling ideology and clarified role and authority divisions. The diagnostic model used tackled the problem of 'managing' the social injustice implicit in reciprocal social relationships based on inequality of wealth and power. The process of arriving at a diagnosis of disease by means of public debate, and balancing social debts against individual misfortune created the appearance of 'objective' justice and kept alive the oral history of the village.[28]

The sick suffered on behalf of the social system, their pain served as a focus for the hidden tensions in the class relationships. Disease and misfortune, something beyond human control, were seen as the only legitimate form of disruption permitted within the existing social order. The pain caused by exploitation and internalised resentments was privatised and personalised. The fact that the repressive social system could be the cause of suffering, injustice and actual disease was obscured. Illness could not become a rallying point for wider social discontent. The system of settling accounts, of cancelling out social debts and offences against the moral economy only allowed social scapegoating and provided, at best, temporary relief. Instead of being cathartic, in social terms, the diagnosis of disease became another occasion for the household to keep up a social front and confirmed its position within the existing class structure. The perception of illness and health were a vital ingredient in the perpetuation of class rule and helped to neutralise structural conflict and threats to the ruling ideology of the village community.

From the poorer villagers' point of view, industrialisation confronted them with one overriding existential problem: to feed every member of their household and protect them, as far as humanly possible, from misfortune, poverty and destitution. To this end, all households, but in particular the goat farmers, mobilised whatever resources they could muster: trading, hiring out, wage labour, neighbourliness, barter, exchange of gifts, mutual obligations and last, but not least, politics.

> We earned very little in those days. Compared to now, anyway. . . . We had to make do with whatever came our way. We helped each other, we had to go and work for those horse farmers. . . . That's how it was. . . . Politics alone doesn't feed anyone. . . . Nobody has ever come through my door and given me 10 marks. . . . You have to work for everything, and . . . you have to try to help each other. Who but your fellow villagers could you turn to in the bad days?

In the eyes of this witness, the village community and his household could not have survived without the limitation of open conflict. Given the unequal distribution of land and draught animals and the relatively poor quality of the arable land, the seasonal work in agriculture could not have been accomplished without co-operation and the exchange of labour within each kinship and neighbourhood network and across the class boundaries. This created a 'community' of labour which in no way resembled or could be described as a village idyll. The sense of community was also strengthened by festivities both within the village and among relatives. On festive occasions gifts were exchanged and invitations were issued which served to reinforce existing social relationships. Hospitality and gifts obliged the receivers to cancel out moral and social debt incurred through their acceptance. Last but not least, the mutual antagonism directed at strangers and outsiders was important in restricting access to the village and helped to reinforce the village's own identity. This was taken so far that the worker-peasants commuted in groups from the village to the factories in nearby Kassel. Often the rival groups taunted each other and enacted ritual fights which confirmed the identity of the combatants as 'Körler' or 'Guxenhagener' (the neighbouring village).[29]

It is important to recognise that consciousness is not logically consistent. A person's or a society's cosmology can be constructed from a number of contradictory elements and yet be perceived as a coherent and meaningful system. The people from Körle whom I interviewed saw no problem in reconciling the seemingly contradictory needs for conflict and order. Their community of poverty was not based on fatalism but on the quest for sufficiency. In the context of poverty and insecurity inherent in the capitalist system, this was a struggle for relative self-determination and security. Self-sufficiency in food could only be realised in the poor households of the goat farmers if they co-operated with the ruling class of the village, who owned the draught animals needed for cultivation. Both cow and goat farmers recognised that this system was unjust, in the sense that the agricultural land was distributed unequally. However, as they saw no immediate alternative or new life-style around the corner, they were resigned to the fact that the whole cycle of inequality started at birth. In their view, any real hope of justice and equality lay beyond the grave or could only be realised through divine retribution or the workings of misfortune. The horse farmers themselves could not have survived as independent operators without the supply of cheap casual labour from the goat farmers' households. This explains why conflict had to be excluded from the sphere of agricultural production within the village and why the system was not challenged, despite the increasing rate of change in German society. Nevertheless, as the potential for conflict was still present in the class structure of village society, it had to be expressed through other forms than the open clash of employer and employee. During the Weimar years open political debate increasingly featured in the life of the village as separate working-class organisations were established, but issues of equality and inequality and justice and injustice concerning the moral economy continued to be perceived through the 'traditional' or 'established' metaphors of illness and health.

To the Körler, continuity did not represent traditionalism or a dogged resistance to the forces of change, but symbolised a degree of hope which ensured some protection against natural, economic and social disasters. Apparently contradictory allegiances emerged as a consequence of industrialisation between urban employment and work on the land, affiliation to working-class organisations and continued submission to the rule of the horse farmers. These contradictions were recognised as a part of everyday life, which had to be accepted or faced up to, not overcome. What was seen as changeable were the forces which directly intervened in their daily existence but which were beyond the villagers' control and often their comprehension. These were: the capitalist economy, and the forces of the state, Nature and Fate. Of these Nature and Fate (or fortune) were most accessible to the villagers and were seized by them as modes of explanation. While recognizing that change was the most important factor which industrialisation had brought into their lives, the initial reaction of these villagers was to strengthen their familiar agricultural life-style. In the long run, worker-peasants were to have a very profound effect on the development of the village's social, economic and political structures. However, it took the further upheavals of the Nazi period, the Second World War, and the post-war economic 'miracle' to consolidate these changes. They are still going on today. It was the defeat of the Nazis which was to break the political and cultural stranglehold which the horse farmers had over the village. Only when a certain standard of living had been reached and when industrial employment was deemed to be as secure as land or a job with the state, did the goat farmers and cow farmers abandon farming in large numbers. This radical transformation of the village landscape was not evident before the 1960s. As far as the Weimar years are concerned, therefore, the worker-peasants remained an integral part of the village and their economic dependence on the horse farmers explains the relative stability of the community. In this context it is crucial to analyse patterns of socialisation and social control which were linked to politics and economics. Until recently these have only been studied by social anthropologists or in isolation as part of the domestic world. Yet the domestic world is inseparable from the class structure. It provides one of the keys in helping us understand how class relations are perpetuated and negotiated, and how social order is, in part, created through the socialisation of individual people.

Notes

1. Otto Brunner, 'Das "ganze Haus" und die alteuropäische Ökonomik', in *Neue Wege der Verfassungs- und Sozialgeschichte* (Göttingen, 1968).
2. *Vorratsermittlung des Staates Preussen, 1923: Gemeindeverwaltung, Körle.*
3. *Preussische Viehzählungslisten, 1923–1929: Gemeindeverwaltung, Körle.*
4. P. Kriedte, H. Medick and J. Schlumbohm, *Industrialisierung vor der Industrialisierung* (Göttingen, 1977).
5. Oral evidence.
6. Lutz Niethammer (ed.), *Lebenserfahrung und kollektives Gedächtnis. Die Praxis der 'Oral History'* (Frankfurt, 1980).
7. *Preussische Viehzählungsliste.*
8. These kinds of relationship have also been found by social anthropologists in other parts of the world. For details see E. N. Goody, 'Forms of Pro-Parenthood: The Sharing and Substitution of Parental Roles', in J. Goody (ed.), *Kinship* (Harmondsworth, 1971), pp. 331–45; S. W. Mintz and E. R. Wolf, 'An Analysis of Ritual Co-parenthood (*compadrazgo*)', *Southwestern Journal of Anthropology*, Vol. 6, No. 4, pp. 341–65.
9. Kurt Wagner and Gerhard Wilke, 'Dorfleben im Dritten Reich: Körle in Hessen', in D. Peukert and J. Relecke (eds.), *Die Reihen fast geschlossen, Beiträge zur Geschichte des Alltags unterm Nationalsozialismus* (Wuppertal, 1981), pp. 85–106.
10. F. Tönnies, *Community and Association* (London, 1955).
11. 'Da gab es auch nix zu verschönern an der Welt früher. Das wußten die Leute ja auch. Die eine Schicht, die Lehrer, die Pfarrer und die grossen Bauern, die konnten halt leben, aber in der Not damals waren wir doch auch alle aufeinander angewiesen'.
12. E. P. Thompson, 'The Moral Economy of the English Crowd in the Eighteenth Century', *Past and Present*, No. 50 (1971), pp. 76–136.
13. Gerhard Wilke and Kurt Wagner, 'Family and Household: Social Structures in a German Village between the Two World Wars', in R. J. Evans and W. R. Lee (eds.), *The German Family* (London, 1981), pp. 120–47.
14. E. P. Thompson, ' "Rough Music": Le charivari anglais', *Annales*, No. 2 (1972), p. 308; M. Scharfe, 'Zum Rügenbrauch', *Hessische Blätter für Volkskunde*, Vol. 61, pp. 45–68; Ian Farr, 'Haberfeldtreiben', unpublished paper.

15. Peter Farb and Georg Ammelagos, *Consuming Passions, The Anthropology of Eating* (New York, 1980); J. Goody, *Cooking, Cuisine and Class. A Study in Comparative Sociology* (Cambridge, 1982).

16. *Gemeindeprotokoll, Gemeindeverwaltung, Körle.*

17. Ann Oakley, 'The Family, Marriage and its Relationship to Illness', in David Tuckett (ed.), *Medical Sociology* (London, 1978), pp. 74–99

18. M. Douglas, *Purity and Danger* (Harmondsworth, 1966).

19. Gustav Jahoda, *The Psychology of Superstition* (Harmondsworth, 1971).

20. A. Van Gennep, *Les Rites de Passage* (Paris, 1908); E. R. Leach, *Culture and Communication. The Logic by which Symbols are Connected* (Cambridge, 1976), pp. 29–55.

21. E. R. Leach, *Social Anthropology* (London, 1982); Joe Loudon, 'Religious Order and Mental Disorder, A Study in a South Wales Rural Community', in Michael Banton (ed.), *The Social Anthropology of Complex Societies* (London, 1966).

22. E. R. Leach, *Political Systems of Highland Burma* (London, 1964).

23. Simon Roberts, *Order and Dispute* (Harmondsworth, 1979).

24. E. Evans-Pritchard, *Witchcraft, Oracles and Magic among the Azande* (Oxford, 1937).

25. Susan Sonntag, *Illness as Metaphor* (Harmondsworth, 1983).

26. L. Steinbach, *Ein Volk, Ein Reich, ein Glaube?* (Bonn, 1983).

27. Oral evidence: 'We didn't dare to speak up. We knew nothing but fear in the old days.'

28. Jan Vansina, *Oral Traditions* (London, 1965); Paul Thompson, *The Voice of the Past* (Oxford, 1978).

29. A. P. Cohen (ed.), 'Belonging, Identity and Social Organisation in British Rural Cultures', *Anthropological Studies of Britain*, No. 1 (Manchester, 1982).

8 PEASANTS, POVERTY AND POPULATION
Economic and Political Factors in the Family Structure of the Working Village People in the Magdeburg Region, 1900–39*

Gisela Griepentrog

I

By the beginning of the twentieth century social differentiation had become very marked in the Magdeburg 'black-earth' region.[1] The rich soil and the district's close proximity to major market centres, notably Magdeburg itself, had stimulated the middle and larger farmers to specialise in sugar beet production, while those with too little land to profit from this development had been gradually impoverished. In 1900, 70 per cent of the farms had become so small that they accounted for only 6 per cent of the cultivated land in the area. By contrast, while the capitalist agricultural enterprises made up only 7 per cent of the total number of farms, they had expanded to cover no less than 70 per cent of the district's cultivated land. Some of the biggest landowners of the district could be found among the names listed in the *Handbook of German Millionaires*. The average size of landholdings was: the largest estates, 323 hectares; large peasant-farmers, 40 hectares; middle peasant-farmers, 10.4 hectares; and small peasant-farmers, 3.4 hectares. Those with land of 0.5 hectares were increasingly forced to work in the factories in the nearby towns, especially in Magdeburg, and left the cultivation of the land to their wives.

How was this situation reflected in family life? The Prussian census-takers did not distinguish between different social groups in the rural population, so that questionnaires, interviews and participant observation had to be used to provide some of the basic figures. Some 100 inhabitants of the area, selected in proportion to its former social structure, were interviewed over a period of seven years, and the data make it clear that the nuclear family was shrinking, with a decreasing number of children per marriage,

---

*Translated by Richard J. Evans

while average household size, on the other hand, was growing. The declining family size was most evident among the large and middling peasants, as a direct reaction to the economic situation. Agricultural mechanisation and the availability of cheap labour from seasonal migrant workers, the unemployed and, in 1914–18, prisoners of war, meant that it was no longer necessary to raise a large family to work on the farm. Additionally, the costs of their education and inheritance portion made children expensive. Between 1900 and 1935 the average number of births per marriage decreased from 4 to less than 2. Family size was further reduced by the high infant mortality rate and deaths of sons in the First World War. At the same time, life expectancy increased and led to a growing number of grandparents (and to a lesser extent great-uncles and great-aunts) living on the farm. Although they seldom lived in the farmhouse itself and generally looked after themselves, they were still counted as part of the main household by the census-takers, as were servants, nannies, housekeepers, and the like.

Our interviews revealed above-average numbers of children in working-class families before the First World War. For the post-war period, the variable and, on the whole, smaller numbers of interviewees, do not allow us to make estimates for all the social groups. But as Table 8.1 suggests, there seems to have been a levelling-down process at work. The peasant and worker families had on average between 2 and 3 children. Between 1933 and 1945 the fascist state sought to combat the decline in the birth rate by propagating the idea of the 'master race' and through the glorification and mystification of motherhood, in order to win more people over for the implementation of its expansionist aims. This seems to have led to a slight increase in the birth rate, but it was not large enough to bring about an increase in population. Ideological campaigns were doomed to fail without an improvement in the living standards of families with children. As local officials in the Wanzleben district (*Kreis*) in this region were forced to admit, in responding to an order to report on the 'achievements of the Third Reich' in this field, there were only 779 births in the district in 1933 as compared to 1187 in 1932. Perhaps a few families had hopes of an improvement in living standards after the fascist seizure of power, as Nazi demagogy and propaganda about the German family indeed promised. In 1934 there were more marriages in the district, and 962 children were born. But as early as 1935 the number of births had fallen back to 845, and it remained at roughly

Table 8.1: Average Household and Family Size, by Social Class, in the Magdeburg Region, 1900–61

Period (according to date of birth of interviewees)	Peasants			Artisans and white-collar workers			Working class		
	Household size	Family size	Number of children	Household size	Family size	Number of children	Household size	Family size	Number of children
Before 1915	5.9	5.4	3.4	6.2	5.7	3.7	6.8	6.5	4.5
1915–20	9.5	5.5	3.5	5.3	4.0	1.7	5.0	4.8	2.8
1920–27	3.0	3.0	1.0	5.7	4.7	2.7	5.4	4.4	3.0
1927–33	4.2	4.0	2.6	–	–	–	6.0	4.6	2.6
1933–42	3.3	2.3	1.3	–	–	–	5.0	4.6	2.6
1942–46	7.0	4.5	2.5	–	–	–	–	–	–
1946–52	–	–	–	–	–	–	6.0	4.5	2.5
1952–61	6.0	3.3	2.0	5.0	2.0	1.0	–	–	–

Source: Oral interviews in five selected villages.

this level (1932 = 864; 1937 = 863).[2]

II

In the early years of the twentieth century, doctors and others active in the field of social policy were becoming increasingly concerned with the high infant mortality rate in Germany. They published a number of demands for the investigation of its causes and for an improvement of the situation. In one such document, issued c. 1905, it was pointed out that while Germany's general mortality rate was very 'favourable' compared with the rest of Europe, infant mortality was not; 20 per cent of all infants died before the age of 1 year. Only Austria-Hungary and Russia had worse figures, whereas in countries such as France, with a lower neonatal mortality rate, infant mortality was also lower. Roughly two-thirds of the deaths in Germany, it was claimed, were caused by nutritional deficiencies: infants who were breast-fed, the pamphlet argued, had a lower mortality rate than those who were not.[3] These and other, similar arguments prompted the Prussian government to institute a general inquiry into infant mortality in 1908.[4] Local registry offices had already been required to distribute notices giving advice on infant care and feeding since 1905, in order 'to impress upon the popular mind the high level of infant mortality, and the need to take appropriate counter-measures.'[5] Yet almost the only practical steps to improve the situation were taken by private initiatives and voluntary associations, such as the 'Association for Combatting Infant Mortality and Increasing Milk Consumption'. In the winter of 1908/9 this association reported that infant mortality among a group of working-class families in Halle had been reduced to 10 per cent through modest financial support and supervision by the town's infant welfare services.[6] In combination with improvements in medical science, voluntary efforts do seem indeed to have succeeded in lowering urban infant mortality rates to some extent at this time.

But the situation was very different in the countryside. While there were 192 infant deaths per 1000 live births in Prussian towns in 1904, compared to 179 in the countryside, by 1909 the figures, at 158 and 167 respectively, had been reversed.[7] And on average, in 1904–9, the infant mortality rate in the core district of Wanzleben in the Magdeburg region, the figure stood at 238. This was the second highest rate of any district in the whole administrative area of the Prussian Province of Saxony. (The urban district of Halberstadt, had a rate of 242.[8]) As we can see from Table 8.2, stillbirths and infant mortality were high for the other districts in the Magdeburg region as well, and well above average for the administrative area as a whole. The underlying cause undoubtedly lay in the increasing social antagonisms in the district, which were connected with the complete domination of the capitalist mode of production in agriculture and the corresponding worsening in living standards of the working people. Ruined small peasants forced to give up their farms, disinherited peasant sons and daughters, were all compelled to work in factories in the city and took up residence *en masse* in the small towns of the region and the suburbs of Magdeburg itself. Wanzleben was one such suburban district, as were two of the other districts with the highest infant mortality rates in the Province of Saxony (the rural districts of Erfurt and Zeitz). The local doctor in Wanzleben, Dr Burmeister, wrote in 1911:

> Here in the suburbs . . . a great number of materially badly-situated people, in part factory workers, in part rural labourers, live close together, and in unfavourable hygienic circumstances. They do not yet enjoy such advantages of the big city as mains water or sewage, and are not catered for by urban welfare agencies. . . . On the other hand, they do suffer from the drawbacks of the big city, overcrowding and factory work that is often scarcely advantageous to their health.[9]

Here, then, was the same poverty that had existed in the big cities of Germany half a century before, as the growth of industrial capitalism sucked in masses of workers and subjected them to ruthless exploitation. When extreme weather conditions or epidemics were added to all this, the result could be the decimation of whole birth cohorts of infants. Dr Burmeister reported, for example, that in the hot summer of 1 July to 27 September 1911, deaths exceeded births in the 10,000-strong commune of Gross Ottersleben, just outside the city gates of Magdeburg, where infant mortality reached the level of 56.4 per cent.[10]

Mothers were forced to work in order to feed their families, and since home and workplace were generally separated and nurseries and crèches non-existent, the children were left unsupervised. Girls

Table 8.2: Infant Mortality and Stillbirths in the Magdeburg Region, 1904–10

	Calbe district		Wanzleben district		Wolmirstedt district		Neuhaldensleben district		Magdeburg city centre		Magdeburg administrative area	
	Infant mortality	Stillbirths	Infant mortality	Stillbirths	Infant mortality	Stillbirths	Infant mortality	Stillbirths	Infant mortality	Stillbirths	Infant mortality	Stillbirths
1904	22.0	29.0	26.1	26.0	23.3	37.1	24.7	36.2	25.3	32.2	23.0	31.8
1905	22.4	31.7	25.0	29.9	22.0	26.8	21.6	30.3	24.4	32.7	22.6	32.0
1906	22.0	33.3	25.6	27.2	22.0	25.8	23.4	30.1	21.4	31.9	21.3	31.7
1907	17.2	27.2	21.4	30.8	19.9	22.9	19.1	41.9	21.7	37.3	19.2	31.8
1908	22.9	30.3	24.2	27.0	22.4	38.6	21.4	32.5	21.5	34.5	20.7	33.0
1909	18.3	24.9	21.5	33.3	18.2	35.8	19.1	34.4	18.1	34.4	18.0	30.7
1910	19.2	30.2	20.7	24.7	18.5	37.3	20.1	30.2	18.9	36.9	18.5	31.7

Source: 'Übersicht über die Säuglingssterblichkeit in den einzelenen Kreisen und Regierungsbezirken des preussischen Staates während der Jahre 1904/10' (Staatsarchiv Magdeburg Rep. C 20 I b, 1529 II, Blatt 214–219).

Note: The columns under each district give, respectively, infant deaths (aged 0–1) per 100 live births, and stillbirths per 100 births, p.a.

no longer learned cooking and household management by becom-ing domestic servants, but went straight into the factory, where they earned more and were more independent. 'Although husband and wife, later on the children too, go out to work and earn money', continued Dr Burmeister, 'such a family seldom makes any progress. The home is dirty and very sparsely furnished, the family is undernourished because it mostly lives off coffee and bread, because the housewife cannot cook or manage the household.'[11] Of course, this poverty has in the first place to be explained by the inadequate pay for long hours, and by the exhaustion and apathy that resulted from mind-numbing, physically-debilitating exploitation — what Burmeister called the 'emotional dullness and indifference towards life in general and that of the child in particular.'[12] But women did lack the experience they might have gained in domestic service, even in a subordinate position. They also lacked the model that the petty-bourgeois or peasant household had once provided them. Without a stimulus, without an aim in life, many workers simply vegetated. Former peasant families, torn from their traditional way of life, had to learn how to cope with their new situation; how to come to terms with only working in a part of the productive process instead of producing something complete in itself, on their own responsibility; how to choose from the confusing variety of foodstuffs on sale instead of growing their own food themselves. Food was expensive in the town, and there was no spare time in which to grow it. It took several generations before women could adapt to their new life-style and develop self-help and community institutions to cope.

Infant mortality was also high in the villages of Wanzleben district at the beginning of the century. But as Dr Burmeister pointed out, in two villages, Altbrandsleben and Ampfurth, there were no infant deaths at all. The proportion of infants who were breast-fed for longer than 3 months were 86 and 93 per cent, respectively in the two communities. Yet there must have been other contributing factors, since 31 per cent of infants died in Gross Ottersleben even though 78 per cent were breast-fed for more than 3 months there,[13] while in Eggenstedt only 50 per cent of infants were breast-fed for more than 3 months, of whom only 9 per cent died.[14] Alfred Grotjahn, a leading propagandist for improved public health and medical care at this time, noted in 1902 that the growing demand for food from the cities was encouraging the growth of co-operative dairies and similar institutions which removed an increasing proportion of argicultural produce from the rural markets.[15] Farmers' wives were using the proceeds of sales of dairy produce for investment in the farm, and used coffee or skimmed milk in their own households.[16] While per capita annual consumption of milk increased from 93 to 115 litres between 1896 and 1903, it declined in the countryside from 115 to 54 litres over the period 1890 to 1900.[17] The wife of one large peasant farmer in Zens recorded in her account-book that of a daily average of 190 litres of milk from her cows in January and February 1909, only 3–3.5 litres of milk were consumed by the six people living on the farm.[17] The farm did not even make its own butter; some curd was produced from its daily supply of milk, but one must assume that the former habit of eating milk soup and bread soaked in sour milk for breakfast or supper had been abandoned by this time.[18] It is not likely to have been very different in smaller peasant farms, and was undoubtedly a major contribution to the high infant mortality rates.

Many small peasant farmers by this period had to supplement their income by working in the factories, leaving their wives to look after the farm. But as the local doctor in the Zeitz district wrote in 1912, even when the husband worked the farm, labour shortages and high wage costs forced his wife to work in the fields as well as doing the housework.[19]

> This change in the division of labour places heavy demands on the women's physical resources. It is all the more significant because the nourishment available to many a countrywoman today does not by any means provide her with the energy necessary to maintain her own strength or that of the child that she carries in her womb. For country people, out of an excessive desire for earnings and ready cash, sell any of their produce that they can dispense with to the towns, and content themselves instead with the meagre residue and with skimpy substitutes. Their diet is poor in fat and protein. This is harmful to pregnant women, to unborn infants and to women in childbed. Debility of the newborn, a short breast-feeding period and a premature use of artificial baby foods, with all their disastrous consequences for the infant, are the result.[20]

If we substitute for the reference to 'the excessive desire for earnings and ready cash' the fact that the mere need for survival forced these people to strain every nerve to obtain money, then the doctor's opinion can be endorsed without further comment. Peasant women who took their babies into the fields and fed them during breaks from work were, as he remarked, a rarity. Most infants were left behind, to be looked after by older children, other relatives or neighbours, or were farmed out to baby-minders. The neglect that often resulted was a further threat to their survival.

III

Another consequence of the heavy burden of work placed on women in small and middle-sized peasant farms was the high proportion of stillbirths (see Table 8.2), which rose as the infant mortality rate in the corresponding area and/or year fell. Despite unreliable data collection, it seems reasonable to conclude that still-births and neonatal deaths (due to 'general debility of the newborn') reflected damage done to the foetus *in utero*. A 30–40 per cent stillbirth rate, as in the rural districts of Wolmirstedt and Neuhaldensleben, suggests that the health services were virtually non-existent, and that a role was also played by what the doctors frequently referred to as the 'old-established bad habits, indifference and incomprehension' of the rural population.[21] 'It is well-known', wrote the local doctor for the Zeitz district, 'that a very large proportion of infants in rural areas die without having received medical attention. . . . The family is afraid of the costs of calling a doctor and visiting a chemist, and would rather pay for a sick cow to be seen to than a sick child.'[22] As the doctor pointed out, the lack of state welfare measures and effective employment protection laws for women and children on the land also led to disastrous consequences as women in the small and middling peasant farms had to work increasingly hard. Tables 8.3 and 8.4 indicate that country women had higher death rates than men, and higher death rates than women in the towns too,[23] and these rates were increasing among women between the ages of 20 and 40.[24] E. Gnauck-Kühne, in an investigation of the subject, argued that the higher female death rates were the result of unhealthy factory work.[25] But, as Tables 8.3 and 8.4 also show, increasing overwork had an even more serious effect among women in the countryside.

In the following decades the situation grew worse, despite educative measures by the authorities and individual improvements

Table 8.3: Age- and Sex-specific Mortality in Town and Country, in the Western and Eastern Provinces of Prussia, 1895–1906

Age group	Town				Country			
	male 1895/96	male 1905/06	female 1895/96	female 1905/06	male 1895/96	male 1905/06	female 1895/96	female 1905/06
Eastern provinces								
15–20	4.4	4.6	3.8	3.7	3.6	3.5	3.2	3.1
20–25	5.3	5.3	5.3	5.1	5.7	5.5	4.6	4.3
25–30	7.4	7.1	6.1	5.8	4.9	4.9	5.3	5.2
30–40	11.7	9.3	7.6	7.1	6.2	5.6	6.9	5.9
Western provinces								
15–20	4.5	4.1	3.8	3.3	4.5	3.7	4.4	3.9
20–25	5.8	5.2	4.6	4.4	6.6	5.5	5.2	4.7
25–30	6.5	5.9	5.8	5.3	5.3	4.5	6.5	5.4
30–40	9.4	7.6	7.7	6.6	6.5	5.1	7.8	6.4

Source: I. Kaup, *Ernährung und Lebenskraft der ländlichen Bevölkerung* (Berlin, 1910), pp. 70–1. Deaths per 100 population of the same age.

Table 8.4: Age- and Sex-specific Mortality in Town and Country, in the Prussian Province of Saxony, 1895–1906

Age group (years)	Town				Country			
	male 1895/96	1905/06	female 1895/96	1905/06	male 1895/96	1905/06	female 1895/96	1905/06
15–20	4.2	3.9	3.6	2.8	4.1	3.6	3.6	3.3
20–25	5.6	5.4	5.2	5.3	5.7	5.1	4.4	4.4
25–30	6.0	6.2	5.9	5.7	4.7	3.8	5.7	5.0
30–40	8.0	6.8	7.1	6.8	5.5	4.8	6.2	5.3

Source: I. Kaup, *Ernährung und Lebenskraft der ländlichen Bevölkerung* (Berlin, 1910), p. 159. Deaths per 100 population of the same age.

Table 8.5: Social Characteristics of Individual Communes in the Magdeburg Region, 1939

Commune	Population	Households (Total)	Non-agricultural households	Agricultural households < 0.5 hectares	Agricultural households 0.5–2 hectares	Number of workers	Agriculture and forestry employees	Industry and agriculture employees	Permanent agricultural labour force	Family members in permanent agricultural labour force	Others in permanent agricultural labour force
Ampfurth	660	160	37	16	4	478	470	93	437	206	231
Bahrendorf	877	267	246	0	–	548	456	183	–	–	–
Dodendorf	790	260	246	–	0	552	210	385	–	–	–
Domersleben	1180	325	150	100	61	695	622	266	320	150	170
Eggenstedt	421	–	–	–	–	263	250	92	201	76	125
Etgersleben	1229	351	327	–	–	772	497	421	–	–	–
Gross Germersleben	950	–	–	–	–	590	389	310	290	220	70
Hadmersleben	2598	–	–	–	–	1666	886	1076	731	84	647
Hohendodeleben	1769	511	444	–	–	1042	528	793	–	–	–
Klein Oschersleben	861	229	212	2	3	469	325	261	364	38	326
Osterweddingen	1604	–	–	–	–	–	501	588	348	286	62
Peseckendorf	286	–	–	–	–	233	232	6	180	168	12
Remkersleben	886	285	120	–	18	476	377	249	–	–	–
Sohlen	592	–	–	–	–	432	299	179	–	–	–
Tarthun	1162	–	–	–	–	698	254	474	600	150	450
Unseburg	2038	–	–	–	136	1128	403	966	–	–	–
Wanzleben	4371	1328	1162	82	47(1944)	2181	1220	1184	602	388	114
Welsleben	1991	623	577	58	49(1945)	1169	675	800	–	–	–

Source: StA Mdg, Rep. K Ministerpräsident, No. 1058.

in welfare, such as the appointment of a midwife to every village. The demands made of women in small and middling peasant farms were even more severe during the first world war, and the economic crises and increased agricultural competition of the 1920s and 1930s. The 1939 census showed an untypical excess of men in three age groups of the population of the Wanzleben district. Among 25–30-year-olds there were 2876 men to 2752 women; among 30–35-year-olds the figures were 3171 and 2661; while in the 35–40 age group the figures were 2995 and 2803, respectively. The expected excess of women over men still prevailed in the older age groups.[27] In some individual communes the disproportion was even more marked. Gross Germersleben, for example, showed an excess of men in seven age groups from 30 years upwards; in Etgersleben and Sohlen in six age groups; in Welsleben, Bahrendorf, Hohendodeleben and Klein Oschersleben in five; and in nine other communes in four age groups. In Dodendorf there were 42 men to 30 women aged 25–30, and 43 men to 33 women aged 30–35; in Domersleben there were 47 men to 36 women aged 20–35, and 62 men to 48 women aged 35–40. Extreme examples can be found in Ampfurth (45 to 23) and Peseckendorf (23 to 8) in the 25–30 age group. As Table 8.5 indicates, when one examines the social composition of these communes, those with an excess male population were generally industrial suburbs with a large number of factory workers, or villages with a high proportion of independent small farms and unpaid family workers.

IV

In 1928, Dr Robert Engelsmann, at an international congress on the declining birth rate, declared that Germany offered 'a striking example of the rule that the birth rate is restricted by contraception in the upper classes and abortion in the lower.'[29] Another doctor Dr Vollmann, had told the German medical congress three years earlier in 1925 to compare the miscarriage statistics with the birth rate. In this way they would recognise that 'the major part in lowering the birth rate in the last decade has been played by abortion.'[30] The Prussian Rural Health Council in its published estimates of the same year, stated there had been at least 400,000 abortions in 1923,[31] while for Magdeburg itself, the proportion of pregnancies ending in miscarriage almost doubled from 16.8 per

Table 8.6: Unemployment Benefit Recipients in Germany, 1923–27

Month	1923	1924	1925	1926	1927
January	150,220	1,439,780	535,529	1,498,681	1,748,597
February	190,008	1,167,785	593,024	2,030,646	1,827,200
March	222,410	694,559	540,460	2,055,928	1,695,515
April	266,966	571,783	465,761	1,942,011	1,121,150
May	253,529	401,958	319,656	1,781,152	870,378
June	185,982	426,429	233,463	1,744,126	648,606
July	139,016	526,188	195,099	1,740,754	540,717
August	249,215	588,485	197,248	1,652,281	452,127
September	533,546	513,496	230,727	1,548,138	403,845
October	953,769	435,321	266,078	1,394,062	355,162
November	1,465,670	436,690	363,961	1,308,293	339,982
December	1,533,495	535,654	673,315	1,396,768	604,586

Source: R. Engelsmann, calculations in *Denkschrift über den Geburtenrückgang*, StA Magdeburg, Rep. C 20 Ib, Oberpräs. Magdeburg, 3928, Bl. 42.

cent in 1913 to 30 per cent in 1924,[32] the numbers of miscarriages being 1458 in 1912 and 2068 in 1924.[33] Many doctors considered 'miscarriage' a euphemism for abortion in nearly every case. An investigation carried out in Kiel showed an inverse relationship between the birth rate and the miscarriage statistics.[34] Its author, Dr Engelsmann, also reported a significant correlation between the birth and miscarriage rates and unemployment. The stabilisation of the Mark after the massive inflation of 1923 created a general optimism which led to an increased number of conceptions in 1924 and a correspondingly higher birth rate in 1925. However, he continued,

a large proportion of the pregnancies which began in the months November and December 1925 and January and February 1926 was interrupted because the economic recession, which made itself visible in the increased unemployment figures, robbed the families of all their hope. Hence the renewed decline in births and a fresh rise in miscarriages.

In the rural district around Kiel, he added, this phenomenon occurred about a year later.[35] Magdeburg was roughly comparable to Kiel in size, and it seems reasonable to suppose that these conclusions held for both districts.

Very few unmarried women seem to have suffered miscarriages. On average in Prussia there were 2.2–2.6 illegitimate births per

1000 population.[36] In Wanzleben, however, these figures were much higher: 16.4 per cent of births in the district were illegitimate in 1921, rising to 18.7 per cent in 1922 and 20.3 per cent in 1923, before falling to 17.5 per cent in 1924 and 14.3 per cent in 1925, then rising again in 1926 to 17.5 per cent and again in 1927 to 18.5 per cent. The mothers were mostly female farmworkers and domestic servants.[37] At the end of the First World War many people who had postponed their wedding because of the uncertainties of the war decided finally to take the plunge. There were only 22 weddings in the Wanzleben district in 1918, but no fewer than 68 in 1919, 56 in 1920 and 51 in 1921. But the numbers declined slightly to 45 in 1922 and then fell dramatically to 24 in the crisis year of 1923, remaining low in 1924 (22) and 1925 (25), before rising again in 1926 (32) and 1927 (35). This was more or less comparable to the pre-war average of around 24 weddings a year.[38]

It is likely that these changes reflected improvements in the wages and working conditions of the rural labourers after the 1918 revolution. The deteriorating economic situation and the declining marriage rate from 1921 to 1923 was reflected to some extent in the rise in illegitimate births over the same period from 16.4 to 20.3 per cent , as some expectant couples now postponed their weddings or cancelled them altogether. But these fluctuations in the illegitimacy rate were relatively small. Nor can the decline in marriages account for the very sharp rise in miscarriages over the same period. On the whole, as Dr Engelsmann concluded, miscarriages (i.e. abortions) were mostly sustained by married women who already had two or three children, who, in a time of economic crisis and increasing unemployment, were unable to support or look after any more. Although contraceptives were already widely available and publicised in the press in this period, they were either unknown among rural labourers and small farmers or rejected by them, as Engelsmann observed.[39] However, folk medicine and herbal potions still provided a well-known and widely-applied means of contraception in the villages at this time.

The district President (*Landrat*), the leading local official in the Wanzleben district, was obliged to confess at the end of 1920, in answer to a query from his superior, that illegitimate children in his district were looked after by their grandparents or were in suitable foster family care. At least his counterpart in the Calbe district could point to a day-nursery for 20 infants, provided by the Patriotic Women's Association in Stassfurt and run by a local doctor, as well as orphanages and children's homes in Stassfurt (12 beds) and Gross Salze (26 beds) run by charitable foundations, and one in Schönebeck (20 beds) run by the town council. Some idea of the way such institutions were run can be gained from a report published in 1927 on a 'school for small children' run by the Protestant church in Wanzleben and paid for out of charitable funds. Up to 1924 it had only been open in the summer, but from then on it functioned all year round. A staff of three were in charge of no fewer than 80 small children. There was also a similar institution run by the Catholics.[40] Given the high ratio of children to staff, there could have been no question of anything more elaborate than mere supervision. Such measures were the merest drop in the ocean of poverty in which many of the district's inhabitants lived.

Neither the Royal Prussian authorities nor, under the Weimar Republic, the Social Democratic provincial governments, responded to the many warnings about the seriousness of this situation or the numerous calls for administrative and legislative improvements, such as the introduction of a comprehensive state social welfare scheme.[41] The Imperial Association of Large Families' proposal for a state family welfare scheme to ease the material poverty of large families, fell on deaf ears.[42] The insurance statute introduced in 1924 and the establishment of maternity benefits in 1927 both explicitly excluded female rural labourers, and would not in any case have applied to farmers' wives because they were self-employed.[43] The resentments which accumulated through the persistent refusal to introduce family welfare measures for this group can be seen as one reason for the ease with which the fascist ideology of the 'preservation of the race' and the 'support and encouragement of hereditarily sound large families' found a response in wide circles of the population. It was precisely among the members of families which had to bring up children in the midst of an exhausting struggle for the bare necessities of life, that must have registered with satisfaction and understanding the fascist ideologues' declaration that 'hereditarily sound, large families' were responsible for the future of the race and that 'the nation's ultimate fate would be decided in the stillness of their home, not somewhere in the wide world outside'.[44] This quotation from a speech delivered at a meeting of the Imperial Association of Large Families in 1931 indeed suggests the extent to which representatives of fascist ideology had already found a place in this organisation.

V

Families need suitable conditions in order to fulfil their most important task, the perpetuation of the human species. These conditions are decisively influenced by the stage which social progress has reached. The development of the population is affected by both natural and social circumstances, but in the area and the period with which we are concerned, natural circumstances such as the climate played only a subordinate role. The decisive factors at this stage of the development of capitalism were the low level of medical and sanitary provisions and the lack of welfare institutions for the working masses. The level of infant mortality is one factor that can help characterise the general level of social progress of a society as a whole. The average life-expectancy of a particular generation depends both on the social policies of the ruling class and the state of scientific knowledge in a society. It can also be influenced by economic and political circumstances such as wars, famines and crises of various kinds. In the first half of the present century the intensified exploitation of working people called forth a wide range of different influences acting against population increase and led to a decline in the birth rate of all industrialised European states. These social factors determined the conditions of life of the working population. They also influenced the consciousness of these people and led to a reaction on their part. Through contraception and abortion they sought to find a way out of their impoverished situation, or at least to prevent its further deterioration. These attempts at 'family planning' cost many women their life, but they must be regarded in the last analysis as self-help measures on the part of the working class, and the poor and propertyless on the land against state power and church dogma.

Notes

1. The present paper is part of a larger collective project, the results of which have been published in *Landwirtschaft und Kapitalismus in der Magdeburger Börde* (1. Halbband, Berlin, 1978: Veröff. zur Volkskunde und Kulturgeschichte, Band 66/1); *Landwirtschaft und Kapitalismus in der Magdeburger Börde*. (2. Halbband, Berlin, 1979: Veröff. zur Volkskunde und Kulturgeschichte, Band 66/2); *Bauer und Landarbeiter im Kapitalismus in der Magdeburger Börde* (Teil II. Berlin, 1981: Veröff. zur Volkskunde und Kulturgeschichte, Band 66/3); *Vom Leben der werktätigen Dorfbevölkerung in der Magdeburger Börde* (in press); *Die werktätige Dorfbevölkerung in der Magdeburger Börde* (in press). See also Chapters 4 and 9.

2. 'Antworten der Standesämter des Kreises Wanzleben auf eine Umfrage von 1938', Staatsarchiv Magdeburg (StA Mdg) Rep. C 30. Wanzleben A, No. 41, the figures give officially registered births; they do not tell us how many children survived in the difficult years of unemployment and depression.

3. StA Mdg, Rep. C 20 I b, 1529^I, Bl. 41–9.

4. Ibid., Bl. 122–5 (Ministerial No. II^{b}2538 bzw. 9501/07).

5. Ibid., Bl. 122 (Ministerial No. II^{b}2538 bzw. 9501/07).

6. Ibid., Bl. 182–93.

7. Ibid., 1529^{II}, Bl. 134.

8. Ibid., Bl. 138.

9. Ibid., Bl. 139.

10. Ibid., Bl. 139.

11. Ibid., Bl. 139.

12. Ibid., Bl. 135.

13. The figures in Hohendodeleben were: 67 per cent breast-fed for over 3 months, 36 per cent infant mortality; in Osterweddingen, 55 and 29 per cent; in Wolmirsleben, 97 and 27 per cent; and in Bottmersdorf, 61 and 20 per cent (all for 1907). (StA Mdg, Rep. C 20 I b, 1529^I, Bl. 189.)

14. Ibid., 1529^{II}, Bl. 140. The same source gives comparable figures for Altenweddingen (57 and 8 per cent), Dodendorf (48 and 12 per cent), Hakeborn (48 and 16 per cent), Remkersleben (51 and 11 per cent), Tarthun (58 and 6 per cent) and Welsleben (39 and 17 per cent).

15. StA Mdg, Rep. C 20 I b, 1529^I, Bl. 136.

16. Ibid., Bl. 138.

17. Ibid.

18. *Wirtschaftsbuch für die Landwirtin, geführt von Olga Diesing, Zens* (Kreis Calbe).

19. StA Mdg. Rep. C 20 I b, 1529^{II}, Bl. 135.

20. Ibid.

21. Ibid., Bl. 140.

22. Ibid., Bl. 137.

23. Eingabe an die Staatsregierung, StA Mdg, Rep. C 20 I b, 1529^I, Bl. 141.

24. I. Kaup, *Ernährung und Lebenskraft der ländlichen Bevölkerung* (Berlin, 1910), p. 30. Kaup also noted that the drop in male mortality had been greater in the towns and cities than in the countryside in the previous decade for the 25–40 age group. The decline had been the same in older age groups, but urban mortality among males above the age of 30 remained higher than rural. The urban/rural differential was much smaller in the case of women. Female mortality was higher in the countryside than in the town in the 25–30 age group. 'Precisely these smaller differentials and in part the higher mortality of the female sex in the countryside suggest unfavourable influences on the state of health and the condition of life of rural women', he remarked. 'This has a serious effect on newborn babies and the upbringing of children.'

25. Elisabeth Gnauck-Kühne, *Die deutsche Frau um die Jahrhundertwende*, quoted in Kaup, *op. cit.*, p. 10.

26. Ibid.

27. StA Mgd, Rep. C 30 Wanzleben A, 39, Bl. 77.

28. *Volkszählung 1939*, Tabelle Bz. 4a II, StA Mdg, Rep. C 30 Wanzleben A, Nr. 39, Bl. 51–2. These latter statistics only divide the population by sex into self-employed, family workers, civil servants, white-collar workers, factory workers and people of independent means.

29. StA Mdg, Rep. C 20 I b, 3928, Bl. 40.

30. Ibid., Bl. 41.

31. Ibid.

32. E. Rösslcr, 'Die Magdeburger Fehlgeburtenstatistik vom Jahre 1924', *Archiv für soziale Hygiene und Demographie*, Bd. 1, 1926, in StA Mdg, Rep. C 20 I b, 3928, Bl. 38–9.

33. Ibid. Miscarriages registered by hospitals rose from 385 to 601 (partly because non-inhabitants were counted in 1924 but not in 1912); those registered by doctors rose from 314 to 1203; by midwives they fell from 750 to 264.

34. Ibid., Bl. 41.

35. Ibid., Bl. 42–3 (the printing errors [misdatings] have been corrected).

36. Ibid., Bl. 44.

37. *Bericht über die Verwaltung und den Stand der Gemeindeangelegenheiten der Kreisstadt Wanzleben, 1926–1927*, p. 14; *1927–1928*, p. 15, in StA Mdg, Rep. C 30, Wanzleben A, 93, Bl. 26, 66.

38. *Bericht über die Verwaltung und den Stand der Gemeindeangelegenheiten der Kreisstadt Wanzleben*. 1.4.1927–31.3.1928, p. 17 (StA Mdg, Rep. C30, Wanzleben A neu, Nr. 93; Bl. 27).

39. It is possible to say this even though, according to a listing of 1928, there were only 33 peasant households and 218 rural workers' households in Wanzleben, out of a total of 1069. There were also 304 households of workers, probably employed in Magdeburg. The picture is somewhat obscured by the large number of households imprecisely classified as pensioners and 'other trades' (262), 'white-collar workers' (32) or 'people living on their own with a separate dwelling and own household'. Nonetheless, I think one can reasonably call it a rural community. The civil servants (189) and white-collar workers (162) included not only people employed in Magdeburg but also in the local administration of Wanzleben and in the sugar refinery of Klein Wanzleben.

40. *Bericht über die Verwaltung und den Stand der Gemeindeangelenheiten der Kreisstadt Wanzleben für die Zeit vom 1.4.1926–31.3.1927*, pp. 45–6, in StA Mdg, Rep. C 30 Wanzleben A, 93, Bl. 42; also in the *Bericht vom 1.4.1927–31.3.1928*, pp. 40–1, in the same file, Bl. 39.

41. 'Vorschlag zu einem Gesetzentwurf betreffend die Staatliche Familienversicherung von Martha Starost, Halle', in *Wir Kinderreichen. Nachrichtenblatt für alle Kinderreichen, besonders den Sächsisch-Anhaltisch-Thüringischen Landesverband* (Halle, Vol. 1, No. 8, 1.12.1922), in StA Mdg, Rep. C 20 I b, 3928, Bl. 13.

42. StA Mdg, Rep. C 20 I b, 1529 III, Blatt 197 (pamphlet *Wie erhalte ich mein Kind gesund?*, by E. Piper, Greifswald, 1925).

43. StA Mdg, Rep. C 20 I b, 1529, I, Bl. 41–2.

44. *Rede des Präsidenten der "Reichsbundes der Kinderreichen", Konrad, auf der Kundgebung der kinderreichen Familien am 19.7.1931 in Köln*, in StA Mdg, Rep. C 20 I b, 3928, Bl. 201.

9 PEASANT CUSTOMS AND SOCIAL STRUCTURE
Rural Marriage Festivals in the Magdeburg Region in the 1920s*

Christel Heinrich

This analysis of peasant family festivals is part of the wider research programme conducted into the socio-economic development of the Magdeburger *Börde* in the nineteenth and early twentieth centuries.[1]Although family festivals are a traditional theme of ethnographic research, the intention in this paper is to analyse the complexity of family festivals as an expression of the social infrastructure of village life in the period between 1918 and the 1960s with particular emphasis on marriage festivals in the 1920s.[2]

Economic development during the nineteenth century — in particular the rapid expansion of sugar beet cultivation and sugar refining in the *Börde* — accentuated the existing degree of social differentiation within peasant society. This inevitably affected the nature of family festivals, and their broader social function within individual village communities. On the basis of available literary and archival evidence, together with material collected through a written questionnaire and personal interviews, it has been possible to analyse different aspects of family festivals, including their preparation, the circle of participants, their duration and cost, and the appropriate costume and presents. In every case the process of increasing social differentiation in the long term was very evident. Specific research was confined to three localities which were representative for the region as a whole: a peasant village without a sugar refining factory (Bottmersdorf); an estate village with a sugar factory (Klein Wanzleben); and a group of villages close to an urban centre with a relatively high proportion of industrial workers (Grossmühlingen, Klein Mühlingen, Zens). The following socio-economic classification was adopted: workers (under 2 hectares); cottagers (2–5 hectares); smallholders (5–20 hectares); and large-scale peasants (20–100 hectares).

Marriage festivals are representative of the general function

*Translated by W. R. Lee.

224

which festivals traditionally had in the structuring and management of daily life. However, it is immediately apparent that the conditions necessary for the holding of a marriage festival varied considerably according to the socio-economic status of the rural population. The cramped living quarters of the parents of rural day labourers often restricted the scope of the wedding celebrations. Frequently, the accommodation provided for labourers by estate owners only consisted of one room and a small closet, with the use of a kitchen shared with another family lodged in the same building. Under these circumstances, even if 20 guests were invited to the celebrations, the rooms had to be cleared of all available furniture.[3] For workers employed in sugar factories spatial constraints were not so restrictive. In the case of families accommodated in the workers' barrack of 'Belfort' in Klein Wanzleben, participants in the eve-of-wedding party had to sit down on the staircase.[4] Significantly, working-class celebrations were seldom held in a village inn. Only in exceptional circumstances was a room hired for this purpose, and even then the food for the meal was provided by relatives of the bridal couple, and the meal was simply prepared and served in the inn.[5] In most cases a local inn was only used if the parental income was sufficient to meet the additional cost of hiring a room, or if the innkeeper was a relative. For cottagers therefore, the family living-room was invariably used for all major family festivals, including wedding celebrations. A marked degree of social differentiation within rural society was immediately apparent in the case of medium-sized and large-scale peasants and families who had become shareholders in sugar beet factories. In many cases this stratum of rural society had benefited substantially from the development of capitalist agriculture in the course of the second half of the nineteenth century and had been able to build so-called 'sugar beet palaces'. In stark contrast to the day labourers and agricultural smallholders, these families had a separate room where they could hold wedding celebrations and similar festivities.

Indeed, these festive occasions were deliberately used by wealthy peasants to display their relative affluence. According to a contemporary report, such weddings were regarded as a special event in the village. The whole farm was redecorated, and all sorts of craftsmen, particularly painters, found immediate employment.[6] Increasingly, however, large-scale peasants began to imitate the practice of the estate holders and arranged for the wedding celebrations to take place in the city of Magdeburg, thereby emphasising the existing degree of social differentiation.

Significant divisions within rural society were also evident in relation to the expenditure on the wedding celebrations. Although the bridegroom traditionally had to provide the rings, working-class couples frequently had to pool their resources to buy these, and even then they could only afford the cheapest.[7] Indeed, it was not unusual for a bridal couple from the rural proletariat to pay for their own wedding celebrations, although the majority of guests would be expected to contribute, in cash or in kind, as much as they could. In many cases, however, the young couple had to decide whether to use these cash gifts for their wedding festivities or for the purchase of essential household items. Their relatives and friends, in any case, would contribute what they could in order to ensure the success of the celebrations. They attempted to supply enough cheap meat (usually rabbit or poultry), and provided their own home-made fruit wine. The whole event was characterised by a high degree of self-help and mutual support. All female family members helped with the preparation of the meal, and with the baking, although the wedding cake itself was entrusted to the local baker. Neighbours and members of the so-called 'chorus' (a group of intimate female friends), invariably helped with cooking, or with cleaning the dishes.

Arrangements for wedding celebrations within the upper strata of peasant society were significantly different. The bridegroom was always responsible for paying for all the drinks, although the total cost of the celebrations was often reduced by using foodstuffs from the parental farm. Nevertheless, the total expenditure was frequently considerable, particularly if the number of guests was substantial.[8] On such occasions large-scale peasants often employed the few village women who enjoyed a local reputation as good cooks.

Another aspect of social differentiation within rural society was evident in the wedding festivities of estate owners, both in terms of preparation and expenditure. Even before 1914 their celebrations were frequently held in a good quality restaurant in the city of Magdeburg, with the guests being accommodated in the more expensive hotels. The total cost could sometimes be very substantial: in the case of an estate owner from Domersleben in 1913 expenses were: 1790 Marks for the party on the eve of the wedding, and a further 8,847 Marks for the wedding itself.[9]

According to the chronicle of the Atzendorf community, published in 1928, the eve-of-wedding party was a well-established custom by the mid-eighteenth century. This was when the bride and groom usually exchanged presents.[10] In working-class families, however, financial constraints once again restricted the extent of the party. There were no official invitations, but relatives, friends and acquaintances from local clubs would turn up in the course of the evening. The workers' choral society of Klein Wanzleben would sometimes sing a serenade on such occasions.[11] Children also participated in these parties and traditionally in the late afternoon they smashed to pieces some old dishes which were no longer needed. On the morning of the wedding the bridal pair, or the groom alone, had to clear up the débris. The eve-of-wedding party was also the occasion to display the various presents. Within the working-class milieu, these would be given to enable the couple to set up their own home and usually consisted of practical items such as cooking pots, buckets, crockery, coffee-mills, egg-whisks, washing-lines and baskets. For a bridal couple from the working class such gifts were invaluable, particularly as the bride seldom received a formal dowry from her parents.[12]

In the case of peasant families with extensive landholdings, the nature and form of wedding celebrations reinforced the existing degree of social differentiation. The eve-of-wedding party was an impressive occasion, with a large number of guests presenting gifts, and local clubs or societies providing large quantities of beer. Moreover, in such families the daughter would have traditionally received linen for her future household on her confirmation, or as birthday and Christmas presents. As a result an extensive family dowry enabled the various wedding guests to choose more valuable presents, such as expensive tablecloths, porcelain, glassware and clocks. Furniture dealers in Magdeburg frequently made special offers for such weddings,[13] and in the case of an estate owner from Domersleben the furnishing of the newly-weds' ten-room house led to an order from the firm of Knüppelholz for 21,217 Marks.[14]

Social differentiation within rural society, however, was most clearly apparent in terms of the wedding guests at the celebrations. In the case of rural labourers there was no special form of invitation and guests were only invited from the immediate family circle. If the bride came from a distant village, even her parents were unlikely to be able to attend.[15] Families engaged in rural industry or employed on the railways frequently had a slightly larger circle of guests, which might even include workmates.[16] Peasants on small and medium-sized holdings also invited the godparents of the bridal couple, friends from the choral society,[17] neighbours and the local pastor. Large-scale peasants restricted their guests to people of the same social status.[18] Their relatives could also afford to travel greater distances, and wedding guests often included old regimental comrades, school friends from distant educational institutions, as well as the local pastor.

Broader social and economic considerations influenced the selection of wedding guests. Estate owners, of course. were always keen to include as many members of the local nobility among their list of guests as possible;[19] and social superiors were sometimes invited, if there was the chance of promotion or the favourable settlement of an outstanding problem. If social inferiors were invited, this was solely to enable them to proffer their thanks at a suitable opportunity. The seating arrangements at the wedding celebrations served to underline the guests' social rank and reputation.

Family festivals in general also functioned as occasions for initiating or regulating specific business transactions with invited guests. In particular it was an opportunity for arranging the marriages of other sons and daughters. The list of guests was accordingly structured to include potential marriage partners from within the existing circle of acquaintances. Wedding celebrations therefore fulfilled the function of a marriage market, based on an acute appreciation of the financial circumstances of the families of prospective marriage partners.

A church ceremony represented the official climax of the marriage celebrations, although if the bride was pregnant a civil ceremony was frequently preferred, followed by a religious ceremony at the family home when the child was baptised. The bride in this situation was also subject to certain measures of moral and social censure and was prohibited from carrying the traditional bridal garland in church. This rule was still strictly observed as late as 1945,[20] and is symptomatic of the continued effectiveness of communal influence and control in the sphere of individual behaviour.

Social differentiation could also be seen in the gradual adoption in the *Börde* villages of urban clothing fashions and style. The large-scale peasants had begun to reject traditional dress as early as the 1840s, and this change to urban style clothing was copied in due course by the small and medium-sized peasants. The rural proletariat, however, perhaps because of economic constraints, was more resistant to change, and in any case could only afford to wear cheaper, mass-produced clothing.[21] The social gap within village society in relation to accepted apparel appears to have widened in the 1920s, when many young day-labourers found it difficult to afford the necessary black suit and top hat which was by then almost a social requirement for church attendance.[22] Many rural labourers had to borrow these items of clothing for their own weddings.

For civil marriage in the 1930s the bride would normally wear a dress, and the groom a suit.[23] Up until 1914 a bride from the rural proletariat would normally wear black, although this was gradually replaced by the white bridal gown (*Brutkleed*), which ideally should not have been made by the bride herself. Indeed, by the 1920s, with many girls finding employment as seamstresses, there was a great deal of help and assistance in making the bridal dress.

Other aspects of the marriage ceremony in the inter-war period provide important indications of the nature of village relationships and the persistence of traditional roles. The sisters and female friends of a bride, for example, continued to play an important part in a number of activities connected with the marriage ceremony. They festooned the official notice of the marriage banns with flowers, and prepared garlands to hang on the front door of the house where the wedding festivities were to take place. In the church they surrounded the spot where the bride and groom would stand with flowers arranged in the shape of a heart.

The bridal procession went on foot to the church, and followed a traditional order. The bridal pair were immediately preceded by the *Streukinder* (children scattering flowers), followed in pairs by the various brothers and sisters and friends of the couple; next came older married couples; and the procession was completed by the parents of the bridal pair, who frequently had changed partners.[24] The village as a whole was therefore a witness to the festive events, which also had a wider representational function. On the way back from the church, the path was traditionally blocked by children with a rope. Only after the groom had handed over a few coins was the barrier lifted. By the 1930s this tradition was also being practised in the case of civil marriages.[25] The origins of this custom are probably to be found in the levying of a charge on all newcomers to the district for the general benefit of the community.[26] Equally prominent, even up to our own day, was the symbolic eating of bread, salt and water, which were proffered to the bridal pair when they entered the house where the wedding celebrations were to take place. This reflected the customary wish that there should never be a shortage of food in the new household.

Working-class families, who generally celebrated wedding festivities within a small circle of relatives and friends, would try to provide their guests with better food than was normally possible throughout the rest of the year. Roast meat was followed by traditional cakes (*Topfkuchen, Blechkuchen*), and served with beer, spirits and home-made wine. Sandwiches were provided in the evening. The wedding breakfast of large-scale peasants, by contrast, was invariably more extensive and elaborate. An *hors d'oeuvre* was followed by a choice of different cuts of meat, a dessert, and served with wine or beer. The dancing which followed was interrupted by a break for coffee and cakes, and a full evening meal was provided.[27]

Similar differences existed in the type of entertainment laid on for wedding celebrations. In the families of day-labourers and small-scale peasants, neighbours or friends who played a musical instrument (such as an accordion) provided the music. In Klein Wanzleben the members of the workers' choral society performed a similar function.[28] Families who were better-off financially had already begun to play gramophone records by this date, although factory managers and large-scale peasants more usually engaged professional musicians from the city of Magdeburg, and estate owners hired military bands to provide the musical entertainment for family wedding celebrations.[29]

However, there were a few customs that were observed irrespective of socio-economic status. It was invariably the case that towards midnight the bridal garland was taken from her in a dance, and her head-dress and veil exchanged for an ordinary cap. This practice represented the acceptance of the bride within the community of married women. The bridal garland was supposed to show which couple would follow the newly-weds to the altar steps. The bridal couple were blindfolded and then chose a girl from the group of young couples dancing around them, who would then receive the garland. The bridal veil was either ripped to shreds, with each guest attempting to secure a piece as a lucky token, or was kept for the baptism of the first born and used to wrap the baby on the way to church.

In peasant families it was usual practice to invite friends and acquaintances who had not formally participated in the wedding celebrations, but had nevertheless bought a present for the bridal couple, to a post-wedding party (*Sustarben*).[30] Workers in Klein

Wanzleben, on the other hand, entertained their workmates in the factory with beer and spirits on the following morning.[31] The financial constraints which limited the formal hospitality of working-class families on such occasions were often resented. It was felt that they were not able to celebrate the wedding in an appropriate manner. Indeed, according to oral evidence, later generations tried to make amends for the hardships suffered during the life of their parents by laying on elaborate celebrations of important wedding anniversaries for them.

One further point can usefully be noted. Particularly from the 1920s onwards, there is clear evidence of an increasing assimilation in the *Börde* of urban influences. This was apparent in a broad cultural sense, and could be observed in a whole variety of ways. Nevertheless, the actual pace and extent of this process of cultural assimilation were often limited by financial constraints and by the material living conditions of the *Börde*'s working-class population. A radical change in the nature of family celebrations did not occur until the 1960s, when the final implementation of the socialist mode of production in the primary sector radically affected the economic condition of the rural population, and occasioned a major break with many aspects of the 'traditional' form of family festivals in this region.

Irrespective of social class, marriage festivals in the *Börde*, particularly in the 1920s, retained certain common strands. The formal structure of wedding celebrations, and the eve-of-wedding party continued to follow a common basic pattern. Similarly the innate symbolism associated with particular aspects of the wedding celebrations, such as the removal of the bridal garland, remained central on every occasion. However the nature of economic development in this region from the mid-nineteenth century on wards had an important impact on the nature of such family festivals and the types of social and cultural 'traditions' that were adopted on such occasions. In particular the rapid expansion of sugar beet cultivation and sugar refining exacerbated substantially the level of rural social differentiation. As a result the nature of wedding celebrations, specifically in relation to the circle of participants, the appropriate costume and presents, their scale and cost, began to differ markedly. The development of commercial agricultural practices, therefore, not only affected the class composition of rural society, but also its cultural manifestations. Increasing economic differentiation was accompanied by a similar divergence in the structuring of family festivals, such as marriage celebrations. Moreover the increasing assimilation of urban influences, particularly on the part of large- and medium-sized peasants which the poorer segments of rural society were unable to emulate only served to heighten the growing degree of cultural differentiation in this area.

However it is difficult to evaluate the overall impact of these changes in the actual form of contemporary marriage festivals, in terms of the persistence of common cultural strands. A number of customs associated with marriage celebrations were clearly followed irrespective of socio-economic status, and the continuing role of the local community in most marriage festivals during this period hints at the persistence of traditional role functions well beyond the inter-war period. This in turn reveals a continuing symbiosis between the 'traditional' cultural elements relating to the structure and symbolic function of marriage festivals, and the changing contemporary form of celebration, which was largely determined by increasing socio-economic differentiation within rural society and the growing impact of urban cultural influences. Only on the basis of using all available types of traditional evidence, both archival and literary, together with material collated through a rigorous application of the research techniques associated with oral history, will historians and ethnographers eventually understand both the complexity and dynamics of this process of cultural symbiosis within German rural society in the twentieth century.

Notes

1. Hans-Jürgen Rach and Bernhard Weissel (eds.), *Landwirtschaft und Kapitalismus. Zur Entwicklung der ökonomischen und sozialen Verhältnisse in der Magdeburger Börde vom Ausgang des 18. Jahrhunderts bis zum Ende des ersten Weltkrieges* (Untersuchungen zur Lebensweise und Kultur der werktätigen Dorfbevölkerung in der Magdeburger Börde. Teil I.1 und Teil I.2, Berlin, 1978, 1979); idem., *Bauer und Landarbeiter im Kapitalismus in der Magdeburger Börde. Zur Geschichte des dörflichen Alltags vom Ausgang des 18. Jahrhunderts bis zum Beginn des 20. Jahrhunderts* (Untersuchungen zur Lebensweise und Kultur der werktätigen Dorfbevölkerung in der Magdeburger Börde, Teil II, Berlin, 1982).
2. Christel Heinrich, 'Fest- und Feiergestaltung im Familienleben der werktätigen Dorfbevölkerung in der Magdeburger Börde' (forthcoming, Vol, 4 of the research results of the Magdeburger *Börde* project).
3. Written evidence from a rural day labourer from Domersleben relating to his wedding in 1920. Questionnaire enclosure provided by Hans Hermann Merbt,

Domersleben, No. V/15a-e.

4. Oral evidence of a worker in the sugar refinery at Klein Wanzleben, whose marriage took place in 1921.

5. Oral evidence of a craftsman employed in the sugar refinery in Klein Wanzleben (1928).

6. Questionnaire reply from Walter Finke, Grossmühlingen, No. V/15.

7. Oral evidence of an agricultural labourer from Klein Wanzleben marrying in 1930.

8. Oral evidence of a peasant with a smallholding from Grossmühlingen marrying in 1931. On this occasion, with 30 guests, the cost of purchasing everything for the wedding feast was 95 Marks.

9. Questionnaire enclosure provided by Hans Hermann Merbt, Domersleben, No. V/15a-e.

10. Samuel Benedikt Carsted, *Atzendorfer Chronik* (1761) (Eduard Stegmann (ed.) for the Historische Kommission für die Provinz Sachsen und Anhalt, Magdeburg, 1928).

11. Oral evidence of a craftsman employed in the sugar refinery Klein Wanzleben, married in 1928.

12. Oral evidence of a female agricultural labourer from Klein Wanzleben who married in 1914. If the bride did bring a dowry this was invariably the result of personal savings often undertaken in very difficult circumstances.

13. Oral evidence of a railway worker from Bottmersdorf.

14. Questionnaire enclosure provided by Hans Hermann Merbt, Domersleben, No. V/15a-e.

15. Oral evidence of a female agricultural labourer from Klein Wanzleben marrying in 1923. The additional travelling expenses were simply too great.

16. Questionnaire reply from Walter Finke, Grossmühlingen, No. V/15.

17. A choir was traditionally composed of married women from the same social group who visited each other on a regular basis in the winter months during their limited leisure time. Coffee and cakes were traditionally provided, and the women made handicraft goods and generally amused themselves. Younger single girls also formed their own choral societies.

18. Questionnaire reply from Fritz Cube, Rodensleben, No. V/15.

19. Questionnaire reply from Hans Hermann Merbt, Domersleben, No. V/15. On the marriage of estate owner Lömpcke (28.5.1921) 32 of the 55 guests were members of the nobility.

20. Questionnaire reply from Walter Finke, Grossmühlingen, No. V/15.

21. Hans-Jürgen Rach, 'Zur Lebensweise und Kultur der Baüern unter den Bedingungen des Kapitalismus der freien Konkurrenz', in Rach and Weissel (eds.), *Bauer und Landarbeiter, op. cit.*, pp. 43–78.

22. According to Pastor Seeger this was one of the main reasons why young people were no longer attending church on a regular basis (*Der Sonntagsfreund*, 1.Jg. 1924, No. 29. 19.10.1924, p. 334)).

23. For many female rural labourers, the normal holiday dress also served as their wedding dress. Oral evidence of a female rural labourer from Klein Wanzleben, married in 1930.

24. Oral evidence of several persons in Klein Wanzleben and Bottmersdorf.

25. Wilhelm Garke. *Geburt und Taufe, Hochzeit und Tod im Volksbrauch und Volksglauben des Magdeburger Landes* (Veröffentlichungen der Gesellschaft für Vorgeschichte und Heimatkunde des Kreises Calbe, H.3, Schönebeck 1929, p. 70).

26. Siegmund Musiat, 'Ethnographische Studien zur Familien-Lebensweise der sorbischen und deutschen Werktätigen in der Oberlausitz. Sozialökonomische, rechtliche und ethno-culturelle Aspekte der Eheschliessung und Familiengründung vom Beginn des 16. bis Anfang des 20. Jahrhunderts', unpublished dissertation

(Berlin, 1977), pp. 93–5.

27. A printed invitation to a marriage in Hohendodeleben (1910). The actual menu consisted of crab soup, a chicken fricassée, perch with Hollandaise sauce, asparagus tips (with cold and hot garnish), roast fillet, cheese and butter, ice-cream and cake.

28. Oral evidence of a craftsman in the sugar refinery of Klein Wanzleben, married in 1918.

29. Questionnaire reply from Erich Berchner, Hamersleben, No. V/15.

30. Questionnaire replies from Karl Münchneier, Hundisburg, Bo. V/15, and Ernst Gajewsky, Kleinalsleben. No. V/15.

31. Oral evidence of a craftsman in the sugar refinery at Klein Wanzleben, married in 1928.

10 PEASANTS AND OTHERS
The Historical Contours of Village Class Society*

Wolfgang Kaschuba

I

It is particularly difficult in Germany to deal impartially with village history or the history of rural society in general. The historian is confronted at the outset with a complex web of stereotypes and clichés which has been spun over almost 200 years of work on the village. It is all too easy to become ensnared in academic, literary and ideological traps of various kinds without really noticing it. There exist in the literature innumerable and varied images of village life, rooted in peasant tradition. Above all, perhaps, there is the contradictory combination of a harsh material life and the comforting atmosphere of the village community. To some extent, this carefully stylised 'image of the peasant' deserves acknowledgement as an historical, ideological and cultural achievement of the highest order. However, the overall effect of this stubborn tradition in the historical analysis of the homeland and the village has been unfortunate. It has served in the end to frustrate a deeper analysis of peasant society and barred the way to the historical uncovering of its inner structures. The same can be said of the argument that rural Germany was the fountainhead of Nazism, a view encouraged by the Nazi cliché of 'blood and soil'. Seen in these global, general terms, the view that places the peasant at the heart of Nazism is really so undifferentiated and unhistorical as to negate any possible conclusions. Once again it prevents us from asking who were the agents and who were the victims of Nazism in rural Germany, and what was the cause and effect of the Nazi appeal. I have already discussed these particular problems elsewhere:[1] it remains important, however, to look in more detail at the Nazi image of the village community, the reasons why it was developed, and above all the extent to which it accorded with reality.

---

*Translated by Eric Clare and Richard J. Evans.

235

On the one hand, the village presented itself to the Nazis as an ideal setting, one in which the legendary cycle of the German family and the German race, of blood and soil, of Germanic myth and rural folk culture could be admirably staged. And the village extras usually played along willingly, because for the first time they imagined themselves in a leading role in the social drama. They were probably as flattered, confused and naive as the observer who reported in a south German provincial paper in 1934 on his village harvest festival:

At two in the afternoon a magnificent procession set off from the Three Kings' Inn. At its head rode two strapping carnival riders in brown ceremonial dress. They were followed by the musicians and the band, the young people and the Hitler Youth, and the *Bund deutscher Mädchen* with a beautifully-arranged fruit cart. Behind the cart came the sower, who could not scatter enough. The farmer and his plough were also there of course, simultaneously sowing the grain in the soil. Then came the field watcher with the young mice. Summer was represented by a mowing machine being driven out and by mowers setting off for work. A group of male and female reapers represented the harvest. Autumn and Winter were represented by a cart, on which hemp and flax was being diligently threshed. The flax-comber saw to its thorough cleaning and handed over the tow to the hard-working spinner. A winder wound up the finely-spun thread. At the square in front of the town hall a large rally took place, at which the area leader of the NSDAP and the land farmers' leader gave an address.[2]

Yet behind this folkloric scenario lay another. The village, with its special social framework, was supposed to embody a sort of microcosmic model of the Nazis' 'people's community' (*Volksgemeinschaft*), which was in turn supposed to replicate on a larger scale the idea of the village society as a system of economic, social and cultural integration. Nazi ideologues held in high esteem the apparently innate virtues of village society. It could, they thought, combine non-contemporaneous elements, unite the contradictory, and stifle the causes and development of social conflict under the communal blanket of peasant and village life.

The Nazis also sought to propagate these virtues as a vision of the future national and racial community: a classless society free from conflict, which at the same time remained self-contained. A study published in 1941 on the 'Rural Populace and Industrial Living Space in the Neckar Region' by the *Reichsarbeitsgemeinschaft für Raumforschung* referred to the worker-peasant villages of South Germany as follows:

> The most special achievement of the spatial organisation of life in the Neckar region is the emergence of a completely indigenous body of industrial workers who are embedded in the life-blood of healthy kin and families, and bound to the soil of the homeland by ownership and the use of land: a racially-united group of peasants and workers. It is therefore important not only to maintain this arrangement, but to develop it methodically, to strengthen it and to safeguard it.[3]

What was meant by this can easily be deduced: the village was a preserve of history, in which the workers' existence still followed the pattern of 'peasant' rather than 'proletarian' models of thought and behaviour. 'Peasant' behaviour was held to combine the traditional producer roles, cultural conservatism and political apathy. In short, the village was a 'petrified' area of experience, in which learning processes were blocked by a residue of historical encrustations.

Even if one leaves aside the ideological stage scenery, it is still difficult to contradict this characterisation convincingly. Historically speaking, the village would inevitably seem to represent mental horizons which are socially narrow and locally limited. In many respects it does indeed appear to be exasperatingly close to the Nazi image of the rural community. The history of the Third Reich itself appears to provide essential proof of this proximity, with the traditional image spreading itself so effortlessly over village and countryside. But is this adequate? Does it actually provide confirmation of that all-embracing argument which portrays the village as an area devoid of class and social conflicts, as an association that invariably blocks social experience;[4] as a community in which social and cultural integration is systematically enforced? In short, does it represent the substance of the history of rural society, which is designed to make one simultaneously blind, deaf and incapable of learning? These questions, which represent central historical problems, seem to be worth closer examination. They pertain not only to the Nazi view of the village, but also more generally to the supporting pillars on which the entire mythical conception of rural existence and communal village destiny finally rests. Myths can only be shaken, if at all, through direct confrontation with reality. So let us speak no more about 'the village' in the collective singular, which means too much and proves too little. Let us take instead a concrete piece of historical reality, one village alone and its social history.[5]

II

Kiebingen, the south German community which is the subject of this study, and from which the harvest festival report quoted earlier derives, was in the 1920s a Catholic village of smallholders and workers with barely 740 inhabitants, situated near the small cathedral town of Rottenburg and only a few kilometres from the university town of Tübingen, both of which could easily be reached by rail and, from 1927, by bus. It therefore could not be included in what was at the time disparagingly called 'the flat land' — not one of those purely agricultural regions, still cut off from transport, communications, technology and industry. The inhabitants of that time would certainly have vigorously defended themselves against such an assessment. Indeed, there were already several signs of progress in the village, such as the first private telephones and cars, an electricity station and after 1925 a domestic electricity supply. From 1927 there was a modern water supply system, and even a petrol station, owned by a German-American oil company. Even the cultural scene appeared lively, particularly in the traditional form of village clubs and church activities. Kiebingen boasted a shooting club, a choral society, an ex-servicemen's association, a League of Catholic Women, a newly-founded gymnastic club and a local branch of the Catholic Centre Party, formed in 1922. Equally 'modern', there were cultural offerings and leisure activities, lectures with slides, amateur theatricals, communal radio evenings, village festivals, even film shows, which had their première with the 1927 silent film 'A Victim of the Secret of the Confessional' (*'Ein Opfer des Beicht-Geheimnisses'*).

Kiebingen,[6] as revealed by contemporary employment statistics, was without doubt a workers' village. Almost two-thirds of the 218 gainfully-employed inhabitants were dependent workers in small-scale trades, in industry and in farming. Fifty-four were employed in the building trade, 23 were unskilled workers (frequently on the railways), 19 were factory workers and 14 were farmhands and labourers. The remainder were made up of seamstresses, serving maids or temporary workers in village crafts. The other third, the 'independents', consisted of farmers with 3–8 hectares of arable (49 individuals described themselves as 'farmers'), master crafts- men, widows and some retailers, who at the same time were involved in farming as a supplementary source of income. Employ- ment on the basis of wage labour was therefore predominant. The majority of adult males in Kiebingen, as well as some of the women, worked in factories, in workshops or on building-sites out- side the village. In 1925, during a period of relative prosperity, no less than 140 individuals commuted daily, either on foot or by train, to nearby industrial towns.

This, then, is one aspect of Kiebingen that can be drawn on the basis of local cultural and economic statistics. But one can just as easily draw up a contrasting picture of this village scene, which gives it a quite different, yet still markedly rural appearance, and which apparently corresponds equally well with the contemporary material and cultural reality of village life. Out of the approxi- mately 180 families, 168 lived in their own house or part of it. They all cultivated their own land, and two-thirds still had their own cattle, particularly dairy cows. In almost every house the men, and especially the women during the summer months, were principally employed in farm work. In the elections for professional represen- tation to the agricultural council (*Landwirtschaftskammer*) in 1932, 124 farmers and 12 farm workers had the right to vote — that is, more than three-quarters of the local heads of household. This picture appears to have an even stronger farming flavour if one examines the daily village scene. There was a predominance of farming business. The meetings of the cattle insurance association and the milk producers' association were always well attended, and many villagers came in the evenings to discuss the trend in milk prices, the problems of the reform programme or the regulation of the usage rights of the common pasture and common land, which served all the families as a potato and cabbage field. On the other hand there was little to be heard on the theme of industry and wage labour. There was no workers' inn in the village, no trade union meetings, and hardly any activities at all on the part of the SPD or KPD, which only held sporadic meetings with outside speakers in the period of a Reichstag election.

'Proletarian life', in the form that we know from urban working-class districts, did not therefore appear to exist in Kiebingen. There was hardly a trace of working-class street politics, of 'red houses', or of after-work discussions among industrial workers. However, there were of course a number of 'workers' problems', which affected the situation of most families: low rural wages, job-hunting for the children, short-time working and constant unemployment. In 1929 alone, 71 inhabitants were officially registered as unemployed. The real number was in fact considerably higher, probably representing 50 per cent of those in gainful employment if one includes those women and youths living on social security, but who did not appear in the official statistics. Despite the high unemployment rate, however, the workers' families of Kiebingen apparently remained quiescent. The unemployed did not gather in front of the labour exchanges, town halls and social security offices to demand from society their right to work, wages and support. They silently vacated their jobs in the town and held nobody responsible for their plight save themselves and their families. They appeared to interpret the Depression and the loss of wage income and work from a peasant point of view. Their response to the situation was to withdraw to the village and its opportunities for self-support through farming. They fell back on the old reproductive pattern of agrarian survival based on cutting down personal expenses and relying on the system of family work and support. The reaction was one of agrarian resistance, not of socio-political action. Their meeting-places were in the fields surrounding the village, not the forecourt of the labour exchange; the topics of discussion were field work and the weather, not politics.

These two faces of the village and the everyday life which they reveal, with its socially defensive patterns of reaction, illustrate in perhaps typical fashion the divided nature of village life. Despite problems and structures typical of an industrial society, village life was permeated by a network of peasant traditions and mentality, which on the one hand formed useful channels for the turbulent flood of social change, but on the other hand could also render the villagers impotent, even defenceless, in the face of new and unexpected challenges. Fernand Braudel once described traditions as 'props and obstacles' by which individual bearings and boundaries are drawn, 'which man can scarcely exceed on the basis of his own experiences'.[7] This disposition of experience is clearly true here as well. It seems furthermore characteristic of the orientation problems experienced by worker-peasants, who were peripheral to the agrarian sphere as well as to the industrial. In 1934 a Nazi economic statistician praised this 'Kiebingen' attitude with admirable frankness:

> And so in Württemberg the factory worker is not proletarianised, but has remained as a healthy country-dweller, rooted to the soil as a smallholder. What one is trying to achieve elsewhere with 'suburban housing estates', the creation of a stable worker, who does not become dependent with the onset of unemployment, is to a large extent already in existence in Württemberg.[8]

Yet it is important to ask whether Kiebingen really did represent a 'peasant village community' and an 'integrated village system', which corresponded to the National-Socialist picture. Did workers, who according to their subjective interpretation had remained agrarian producers, continue to exist in a peasant system of reference dominated by local horizons of experience, despite wage income, industrial experience and dependence in an external labour market? Did they really follow the old, but now 'false' social logic of peasant life?

One answer to this question might be that the predominance of non-agricultural wage labour outside the village was still in its infancy at the time of the Weimar Republic and the Third Reich, and that the new circumstances of existence were still not organised into the villagers' own structures of experience and translated into analogous value-systems. But that was clearly not the case with Kiebingen. A century earlier in Kiebingen's history the local economic profile hardly looked any different in its outline: wage labour, external place of work; on the one hand the economic livelihood of the sub-strata of peasant families split between craft employment and subsistence farming, and on the other hand independent farming and artisan families living in and from the village. The basic economic dividing-line in the community was therefore the same; it ran through village society in the late feudal period as well as in the industrial age. And the closer one examines their development and effects, the clearer it finally becomes that this economic dividing-line also constituted a demarcation between an upper and a lower class, almost forming a barrier between two distinct villages within the village. Indeed, the barrier appeared to be almost impenetrable for five or six generations of social history, for in 1820 each of these two Kiebingens already contained the same family names as in 1920. This historical dimension illustrates the degree to which many of the views of the 'modern village' are encumbered with the economic and social burdens of the eighteenth and nineteenth centuries, as a legacy of feudal, rural class history.

The traditional system of partible inheritance has left, perhaps, the most important traces in terms of village boundaries and in its general appearance. Originally this was an example of peasant self-determination and expressed a deeply egalitarian ideology, as described in another context by Martine Segalen.[9] In Kiebingen peasant land could be transferred within the family to all children in equal portions, to both male and female heirs. It therefore provided relatively free use of the family's means of production, without allowing the feudal authority any possibility of intervention. This afforded members of each new generation an equal chance of material existence, and offered them above all the prospect of marriage and setting up their own family. The considerable growth in population in the course of the eighteenth century, however, meant that this principle started having the opposite effect. The family's land holdings became fragmented, the former large-scale peasant farms disintegrated, and instead of ensuring the family's existence from one generation to the next, partible inheritance now seemed to destroy it. The smallholder families thereby affected were forced to seek a second source of income to supplement what was left of their subsistence economy. They either turned to domestic industrial production — particularly weaving, in which they worked for south German or Swiss distributors — or they tried to get by as seasonal migrant workers. Both alternatives effectively meant a dependence on wage labour, with the difference, of course, that the weaver families could at least still work in the village and in their own house. Building workers, migrant artisans and day-labourers, on the other hand, had to search for employment outside the village. The destination of most of them was Upper Swabia, about 100 km to the south-east. This was also a Catholic region, dominated by large-scale peasant farms, with an economy based on the export of cattle and corn and with a correspondingly high need for seasonal workers.

In the middle of this first phase of the local process of pauperisation and proletarianisation, one can observe a striking peasant counter-movement. When a monastery near the village was dissolved in 1786, a group of 39 peasant families purchased its agricultural estates. This takeover of the feudal means of production, which also had a symbolic significance, provided them with an invaluable supplement to their restricted peasant existence and guaranteed moreover to the following generations the prospect of a continuation of their rural peasant life. Finally, the dissolution of the feudal order in the last phase of the process of 'peasant emancipation' led to a substantial redistribution of land within the village after 1849. The poorer families were in many cases forced to sell off plots of arable and pasture land because of outstanding redemption payments. This only served to complete the picture. The better-off peasants followed the feudal path and organised village resources and their own available means of production in terms of the 'old economy', thereby assuming the social roles of power and domination. Already at this stage, crucial turning-points were discernible in Kiebingen's history. They determined in the long term the nature and direction of development both for the sub-stratum of 'proletarians', and for the established peasantry. Both groups, and within them each individual family, were assigned their economic and social positions in the village's framework. The first group subsequently found it almost impossible to abandon this position, while the privileged group was for its part quite unwilling to see any change. Even the later phase of industrialisation did not substantially change this pattern of development. Indeed it prolonged it even further, without opening up new economic possibilities and new horizons of experience to compensate, at least within the confines of the village.

These fixed and static snapshots of the village system of socioeconomic reproduction can be developed further within the context of occupational changes over different generations. Historical occupation data are usually only of limited reliability. Even in relation to nineteenth-century village life they merely indicate one activity out of a broad spectrum of diverse sources of an individual's income and 'occupations'. The importance of these varied greatly according to the season and the trade cycle. At least a quarter of those working in Kiebingen were officially engaged in two or three different occupations — for example, as bricklayer and peasant, as weaver and day-labourer, or as a field-watcher, wine-grower and day-labourer. The declared occupational priorities did not usually accord with economic reality. The nominal artisan frequently turned out to be a building worker or a casual craftsman after a more exact examination of the handicraft *cadastre* and other sources, but to complicate matters further, his principal source of income was often actually derived from day-labouring or from agriculture. Despite these limitations, the main secular trends can still be distinguished on the basis of data from 1823, 1864 and 1914. In 1823, 24 per cent of those in gainful employment still described themselves as farmers: the figures for 1864 and 1914 were 24 and 21 per cent respectively. The group of village crafts, including the smith, butcher and baker, which catered for the local market and were practised in addition to farming, remained relatively constant at just under 20 per cent. These two groups together represented the position of the independent producers in the village, whose proportion in 1823 was still about 50 per cent, although by 1914 it had fallen to well below 40 per cent. If one takes into account the actual wage-earner status of many nominal craftsmen, the proportion was probably nearer 30 per cent.

Correspondingly there was a strong increase in the dependent sector relying on wage-labour on a regular or occasional basis. This sector, however, also witnessed internal regroupings. The quota of day labourers, who worked predominantly for local farmers or for the parish, fell from an initial figure of 19 per cent in 1823 to 14 per cent in 1914. The traditional trade of handloom weaving was a dying occupation. At the latest, with the rise of the Württemberg textile industry in the 1840s, its practitioners found themselves in a hopeless competitive situation. And yet even in 1864 they still formed 11 per cent of the Kiebingen workers, which illustrated in particular the delayed nature of the rural response to industrialisation. This figure represented 20 weaver households, which clung tenaciously to the recesses of the village economic framework on the periphery of the regional market, simply because for these families there was no alternative occupational source of income. In place of weaving, and to some extent of day-labouring, there was an increase in occupations connected with the building trade from the start of the nineteenth century. This was initially the case in relation to bricklayers, followed by carpenters, stonemasons and finally plasterers. Their proportion grew between 1823 and 1914 from 11 to 32 per cent and gradually filled the space vacated by weaving as a wage-earning trade. Not until 1900 did modern wage-earning occupations emerge. In 1914 there were only 18 factory workers in the village employed in the metal-working and textile factories of the nearby towns, and 14 railway workers.

Of course, this occupational profile of the village only represents half of historical reality, for almost all the figures given only relate to male occupations in Kiebingen. Women's work remains largely invisible in historical occupation statistics, which were only compiled for fiscal purposes. The village tax records did not officially recognise women's jobs at all until the end of the nineteenth century. Women did not enjoy equal economic and legal status in the village and in society as a whole until 1918, in spite of the fact that their working efficiency and function were often more central to the family economy than that of the men. In Kiebingen women in particular carried out the supplementary farming work and thereby safeguarded that vitally important margin of the family's economic survival[10] which could never have been achieved through handicraft income alone. Moreover, the majority of the daughters of poorer families took up wage-earning jobs as maids, day labourers or domestic servants, both before their marriage and at times even afterwards. A form of provisional independence was only applicable at that time to widows connected with farming and small-scale craft production, who were able to carry on the family business until they remarried or handed it over to a son. In exceptional cases there were also a few women small-scale retailers in the village. It was only in the Kiebingen tax registers of the 1880s that the first legally and fiscally recognised women's occupation — that of seamstress — was recorded. A little later the job of domestic servant was also accepted for tax purposes as a genuine occupation. And in the 1920s, when the first female factory workers appeared in Kiebingen, every female wage-earning job was finally registered separately, and no longer concealed by the shadow of the husband's or father's occupation.

It is also difficult to recognise from a cursory examination of occupational statistics the high degree of self-recruitment and the marked inter-generational continuity within the individual occupation groups which contributed to a family job tradition over three, four or even more generations. I have already indicated that professional mobility in Kiebingen, even in the industrial period, took place within a limited framework and almost horizontally, as it were. People only changed their occupation when forced to do so, and only into related jobs which were both economically and socially similar to their previous one. Moreover, they were in many cases already familiar with the new occupation through their former job and work experience in the village. In this way the entire occupational framework of cottagers and wage-earners gradually slid down the steep path leading to proletarianisation, taking people away from the local agricultural sphere and into the external sphere of commercial and industrial production. One can no longer talk of a genuine and free choice of occupation, between different job alternatives. Typical of this is the well-known transition from weaver and day-labourer to building worker. Two-thirds of all building workers' sons remained in this occupation well into the twentieth century. A proportion of them finally followed the way indicated by society into the factories and the railway workshops. And so the first generations of factory workers in Kiebingen in the 1920s was composed of the great-grandsons of the weavers, day-labourers and building workers of the mid-nineteenth century not only in a figurative sense, but also as the result of direct family descent. In the case of the peasant families, however, the possibility of earning a living as an independent trader or craftsman became an accepted status-preserving alternative. In particular, second and third sons frequently chose this path. While the elder brothers continued to manage the parental farm, younger brothers became butchers, innkeepers or joiners. They retained in any case an economic base as peasants and remained their own masters.

III

This classification according to status as a wage-earner or an independent producer meant not only different social group affiliations, but also areas of experience which were geographically and socially divided. Those who lived in the 'proletarian' area, or strayed into it, also had their place of work outside the village and to a certain extent outside the rural world. The statistics of rural labour migration also show that especially in the years between 1830 and 1870 more than 10 per cent of the inhabitants of Kiebingen were constantly on the move, some only during the summer months, but many during the whole year. On average that meant at least 80 to 90 people, and in many years, such as 1849, with 129 'outsiders', every sixth Kiebingen inhabitant was either working or looking for work outside the village. The local council of Kiebingen complained in 1842 that

The local community numbers 717 inhabitants and the population is constantly growing. The largest part of the population is sustained by farming, day-labouring and the customary crafts, partly in the village, and partly nearby. Many young people, even children, have to try to earn a living by working in more distant regions. The individual families are not at all well-off and the support of the poor is a heavy burden on the community.

Not until towards the end of the century did the situation change somewhat, when the railway brought about the new phenomenon of commuting to work. The growing number of industrial jobs in the neighbouring region also ensured that absence from the village was gradually limited to the working week, or even only to the working day. But that still meant that on a rough calculation, from families in the poorer half of the village, one or two members of the family lived and worked mainly outside the village at any given time. This represented between a quarter and a third of all working men and women. Their jobs and workplaces have already been listed: domestic servant, day-labourer, bricklayer, carpenter, maidservant and at a later date railway worker or plasterer. By the twentieth century the list also included metal-worker and female textile operatives, without exception dependent on wage-labour.

Inevitably in these periods of living outside the limits of the village, they experienced various needs which clashed with the narrow, traditional framework of family village life. These other modes of thought and behaviour patterns, which were learned in different places, working conditions and social groups, the frequent encounters with the police and the authorities during the tiresome search for work, the experience of begging, petty criminality and vagrancy, as recorded in hundreds of cases of local criminal proceedings, and even the freer forms of sexual relationships and sexual practice — all inevitably brought into question the one-sided, patriarchal and strict system characteristic of Kiebingen. The new mode of thought could not simply be left behind at the village boundary when migrant workers returned home. In the eyes of the village peasants, the new modes of thought naturally seemed to threaten their ideas of work discipline, obedience and morality, and to constitute an erosion of their hierarchical values and general social order. Just like every deviation from traditional behavioural norms, so these new ideas had to be censured and suppressed. Yet there were signs of them everywhere: in the form of illegitimate children, 'whom the young women mainly brought back from other places', in the tendency to 'revels and dances', in the 'insults hurled at the village mayor', in the tendency to 'foolish behaviour, idleness and lavishness'. Everything in village life which exhibited disagreeable features fitted into these stereotypes. And the accusations and punishments are continuously listed in the local council proceedings and parish reports of the nineteenth century. One of the Kiebingen ministers who consistently shared this vision of a well-settled and honourable village, summed up such views (or rather, prejudices) as early as 1830 in a simple formula, which retained its validity for posterity: 'Most excesses', he claimed, 'are caused moreover by totally impoverished people, who prefer begging and its associated dissoluteness, to work, and a quiet, honourable life.'

Clearly the village establishment of the permanent peasant and craftsmen families still responded totally in the style of the old 'peasant society'. Without regard to the important supportive economic function of outside wage-labour for the general village system, it preserved for itself its hermetic horizon of perception by simply blotting out the causes of this existence and the behavioural patterns alien to the village. Anyone who did not fit in with the local peasant code, which was legitimised by custom and tradition, was ostracised and stigmatised. In the marriage certificates issued by the local council, in sermons and commentaries on the 'moral conduct' of migrant workers, there are numerous indications that the status of the outsider was already characterised in negative terms. Taking a job outside the village was equated with personal failure and carried the taint of slovenliness and inferior social morality. The social character of the historical proletarianisation process that had overtaken even Kiebingen was simply ignored. At the same time the inevitable problems of orientation and socio-cultural confusion, even the contradictory views of life with which the affected groups had to grapple, were also ignored. What perhaps may have been acceptable in the case of outsiders — the fact that they behaved 'differently' and lived 'strangely' — could not be tolerated on the part of fellow villagers, even if they occasionally had to spend half their lives 'as foreigners' outside the village. The villager was expected to be able to live in both worlds, or better still, to live in only one, the Kiebingen 'peasant world', with its fixed social order and its clearly articulated cultural grammar.

When one evaluates this conflict, one should doubtless take into account the fact that the work migration of the Kiebingen lower classes, both, under pre-industrial and advanced capitalist conditions, clearly followed the trade cycle. However, the highest migration quotas between 1830 and 1931 were not, as one might have suspected, in crisis years, when economic conditions in the village were particularly bad and external relief especially necessary. On the contrary, they occurred in periods of exceptional prosperity. In fact the majority of workers flooded back into their home village at the onset of an economic recession and attempted to reintegrate themselves into the family subsistence economy, or, if necessary, to obtain support and help from the parish authorities. Thus the minutes of the council proceedings in December 1846 noted for example,

> Today the unmarried and impecunious Wendelin Heim returned home and stated the following: that he could no longer support himself during the present season, as he could find no more work either here or elsewhere, and so he was obliged to turn to the village council for support . . . [It resolved] . . . to provide Wendelin Heim with food at the villagers' expense and according to the tax . . ., whereby Heim was charged that he was to work the same day for the citizen who that day provided him with food. . .

The explanation for this withdrawal to the village and the reversion to old village survival strategies can be found outside Kiebingen at the level of society as a whole. In crisis periods, communities which had been centres of in-migration, took care that they did not have a community of needy, unsettled and unemployed strangers. It was specifically the country workers who were driven back to their home villages and treated as an 'industrial reserve army' with strict refusals of support and official residence prohibitions. This policy continued until the economic barometer rose again. Even in the economic crisis in the years following 1929 this remained a customary and legal practice in Württemberg.

For communities like Kiebingen this pattern of in-migration during crisis had serious consequences. The two camps in the village — the farmers and worker-peasants — were constantly opposed to each other in the same points and on the same fronts at times of economic depression, when things were tense anyway. There was always discussion about the common rights of those returning home, about claims for financial support, about measures for providing work in the village wood or in road construction, and consequently there was always discussion about the same demands as before on the parish budget and communal social policy. The farmers, as controllers of the village purse-strings, objected to such expenditure as vehemently as they had done previously. The conflict was as old as Kiebingen's class society itself, because the causes were also the same. In a crisis it was still the limited resources of the village which provided the only safety net. Yet one cannot explain the seasonal migratory behaviour of the Kiebingen workers solely on the basis of economic motives and constraints. Despite the coming of the railway and the encroachment of industry, the migration pattern preserved its pre-industrial form right up to the years before the First World War, remaining characterised by 6 or 12 month periods of absence from the village. The reasons for this can probably be seen in the special intergenerational rhythm of succession in cottager and small peasant families, which followed its own dynamic. It is no coincidence that the juvenile and young adult members of the family preferred to seek out distant places of work outside the village, whereas the older and married inhabitants remained as close as possible to the village. The younger generation represented to a certain extent the surplus workforce, whose absence on the one hand contributed a material relief to the family budget, as well as helping minimise inter-generational emotional conflicts and role problems. On the other hand their earnings were a substantial contribution to the continued maintenance of the family subsistence economy. Only on this basis was cash periodically available for taxes, mortgage payments and for production costs, such as the purchase of tools, cattle or seed corn, necessary to the cultivation of their own land or for the family share of the common.

In its basic characteristics this family-based economic system still fully represented the traditional linear sequence of generational succession to the family's hereditary position within the village's economic and social framework. One can see the persistence of patriarchal and pre-industrial concepts according to which the individual workers were naturally only organs of the communal work capacity of the family. On this basis, individual views of life were 'naturally' subordinate to those of the family. External work was not considered as a springboard for a gradual weaning away from the family, or as the foundation for an independent existence outside Kiebingen. On the contrary, this inter-generational sharing of roles and division of labour was supposed to facilitate the continuance of a generative rotation system, in which the material basis of the children's existence was not contrasted and parallel to that of the parents, but conceived of as something additional and dependent. Not until after the economic withdrawal of the parents because of age or illness, and frequently only after their death, was there room for an independent existence and the setting-up of one's own family. Without home-ownership, a plot of land and the family's share of the village common, this seems to have been scarcely possible even for young factory workers in the 1920s, and one can still detect something of the 'homeostatic equilibrium' in the structure of family generations, which the historian David Levine has described as characteristic of pre-industrial life-styles.[12] This close connection between economic and generative reproduction was confirmed in the very high age of marriage in Kiebingen. For men, the average age at marriage only dipped below 30 after 1875. In the years 1920 to 1929 it was still 28.9 years. Building workers had a marginally higher age at marriage, and factory workers were somewhat below this figure. On average, women in the post-war period married at an age of 25.8 years, whereas previously the average had rarely been below 27 years. Incidentally these figures also support the supposition that rural proletarianisation did not automatically lead to a lowering in the age at marriage.[13]

Throughout the nineteenth century and, with certain limitations, in the early twentieth century as well, the period of continuous work away from the village corresponded to a special phase in the life-cycle. This period of migratory work, which often lasted 10 to 20 years, represented a distinctive period of transitional adulthood for the sons and daughters of small peasant families, when they were still single and not yet fully independent. Their first escape from the family and the village to look for work, which most experienced between the ages of 13 and 15, was like an initiation rite into this new life-style. It symbolised a farewell to childhood status and provided confirmation of their recognition by their family and society as fully-fledged workers. With the step outside the village, they entered at the same time into a pre-adult status and into what was literally a 'strange' world. This constituted a completely different socialisation context from that experienced by the peasant children of the same age who remained within the village sphere of production, and stayed as 'children' for a longer period under parental control. It was at this point that what had previously been a largely common horizon of experience with a gradual assimilation of definite child and age-specific roles and abilities came to an end. It broke down into separate spheres and systems of experience. Opportunities for further education, or for vocational training, became very unequal. The experience of work and everyday life differed considerably, depending on whether the young person remained within the village, or sought work in Upper Swabia, Switzerland or in one of the factory towns of northern Württemberg. The relatively secure life-chances for a peasant contrasted markedly with the absolute insecurity which faced the sub-peasant stratum. Two separate worlds now emerged, with their own discrete social and biographical structures of experience. The one stayed in the village and was 'the village'. For the other, for the children from the families of day-labourers and building workers, probably only the period of childhood and then the later period of adulthood constituted an individual life-cycle phase which was experienced during a longer and enclosed period in the village.

IV

Many elements of this worker-peasant world must seem rather strange, according to present-day standards, revealing a society dominated by economic forces, social powerlessness, and traditional, mostly reactive, modes of behaviour. This is certainly largely true in the sphere of material production. But it is not the whole picture. We must also enquire into those areas in which the men and women of this other Kiebingen confront us more clearly as subjects of their own history, who consciously and actively shaped their lives differently. Where can one find such elements of self-determination, of autonomous social and emotional experience, perhaps even of stances of resistance towards the system of peasant norms, which can provide some support for the marginal existence of the other Kiebingen, and reveal evidence of its separate identity? These elements certainly did exist, although in a locality with such limited material, social and cultural means of living they could often only survive in small freedoms and in modest forms of self-assertion. Moreover many of them inevitably remained unseen, as the written sources of village history are almost exclusively official documents which only portray the daily life of the lower strata as a history of objects — objects of disciplinary measures, of administrative acts, of punishment, of welfare — or more accurately, guardianship.

How much stubbornness, and how much conscious experience of the 'governed' is simultaneously contained in a situation can only be gleaned from a reconstruction of its own social logic, if one reads between the lines and changes approach. When there is smoke, there is fire; where there is control and punishment, there are people and groups who contravene the prevailing rules when they try to live according to their own conflicting precepts. 'Foolish behaviour', vagrancy, the 'desecration of the sabbath' by drinking in inns, the 'immorality' of migrant workers and their families — all these little norm infringements are simply a photographic negative torn out of the context of a positive, self-contained system of everyday attitudes. They provide a breath of fresh air, they circumvent restrictive norms and satisfy their own social and emotional needs. In adhering to such 'illegal' forms of individual and group behaviour, there is a definite expression of self-understanding and a feeling of self-esteem, which selectively provided a sub-cultural group commentary on the accepted social attitudes of the village. One creates and assumes a (limited) 'freedom of necessity'.

In the history of Kiebingen, on the basis of the available sources, this type of freedom only appears episodically. The farm servant who felt himself unjustly dismissed by his farmer in 1833 ('. . . which I won't stand for because I had to run around for 10 to 12 days until I found a capable employer again') and who claimed compensation and his remaining wages from the village council, provides evidence of its existence. There are other cases, too: A weaver, who would not let his sons be ordered into school by the teacher, declared 'with bold and wild defiance that he would not allow his sons to go to school because he needed them now for threshing.' In 1840 a day labourer and cottager refused to submit silently when his field was used as access by a rich farmer, who was also a local councillor and field judge. He protested in exasperation:

It is particularly bad that a field judge, who should maintain public order, should ruin and destroy another citizen's property; from this one can see that no field judge has any conscience . . . because they themselves only go onto the fields to place boundary stones so that they can earn a lot of money.

In 1860 a railway worker refused to perform the customary labour services required by the village community, because he could not and would not give up his wages for the lost days. A young family was ordered by the village council to go to the local poorhouse, but when they were due to be removed, they objected, and insisted on their 'right to poverty'. Finally we must not forget the everyday events: card-playing and dancing, drinking after hours in the inn, the rebellious gestures against the authorities, and above all the numerous thefts from the fields and woodland. In the crisis year of 1929 these thefts were just as common as they had been in 1847, and were clearly regarded by both men and women as a form of private self-help, when family survival could not be assured by legal and practical means.

Certainly, seen individually, these could never be regarded as great acts of emancipation. The actual infringement of written laws and unwritten rules was unremarkable. What appears to be much more critical is the attitude behind the incidents, which revealed a definite consistency of thought and action. In it were expressed precise ideas as to when the limits of 'fair' economic and social relations were exceeded, and as to whether people's social rights, honour, dignity and feelings had been offended. This attitude reflected a fixed level of expectation: although certain social inequalities and bourgeois laws were accepted as realities, underneath the surface there lay communal ideas of what was right for guiding people's experiences and actions. The villagers may not always have had the law on their side, but there were situations where, independently of the law, they felt 'in the right' in a deeply moral way.

Another area of village experience illustrates some of these points and takes them further.[14] Love and marriage were never a private matter in Kiebingen, but always a matter of complex family and village decision-making processes. Between 1833 and 1871, they also posed considerable legal and political implications. During these years the Württemberg law of civil rights not only demanded that those wishing to marry must have reached the traditional age of majority (21 years), but the prospective bridegroom also had to prove that he had 'adequate means of subsistence'. Proof of this, which the village council, as the decision-making body, officially examined, had to be furnished in the form of money, property, or through the 'ability to carry on an independent trade'. If this proof was not considered adequate, the parish council had the right to refuse approval for the marriage. The council, which was dominated by bourgeois and craft interests, applied the law rigorously, particularly in all those cases where it feared that the future family could later become a burden on council funds. In the case of suitors with negligible property or dependent entirely on wage-income, such an assumption was invariably made. The law itself, moreover, expressly declared that, for example, 'an ordinary factory worker is not allowed to marry'. In these 38 years, 20 of the marriage petitioners were turned down, including 8 building workers, 6 day-labourers, 4 wage-earning village craftsmen and 2 railway workers, together with their respective brides. The peasant and artisan couples, on the other hand, with their larger property holdings, invariably got over this hurdle with ease. Nevertheless, almost 10 per cent of all planned marriages in the village were blocked. The additional deterrent effect of this degrading procedure almost certainly ruined other wedding plans at an early stage.

Let us examine just one of these cases of refusal, that of a 40-year-old railway worker and former weaver, Josef Heim, and a 39-year-old railway worker, Regina Kunstle, from a village not far from Kiebingen, who wanted to marry in 1860. To do this, it was necessary for the bride first to be granted Kiebingen citizenship. Their total cash savings and personal possessions just sufficed to fulfil the legal requirements in this case. The village authorities, however, after examining the application, became convinced that

the alleged available savings, as well as the prospect of his earnings as a railway worker, did not provide them with a secure livelihood, and that it should be taken into consideration as to whether or not Heim would sooner or later become a burden on the community and this fact makes it all the more necessary to subject this case to a careful examination, as Heim has already worked for 14 years as a single man on the railway and has only saved 115 florins and a single bed out of an allegedly good wage.

The parish council . . . further notes, that Josef Heim in earlier years when he lived here, was not known as a good householder; and even if the reference for Josef Heim and his bride from the railway engineering office had been favourably written, this reference could not be accorded any great credence as proof of a secure livelihood . . .

The application for citizenship and for permission to marry were refused. Three years later the two betrothed made another attempt to marry in Kiebingen and when this was once again refused, they appealed to a higher authority. But this was also without success, not least because Josef Heim, enraged at the second refusal, had loudly declared in local inns 'in the presence of two village councillors that he would easily get money as an advance from his employers, if he needed 300–400 florins to present as cash.'

Even on the basis of this single example, one can at least suspect how radically the marriage laws and their local application could affect the courses and plans of people's lives. The village council's line of argument very clearly shows that refusal did not depend on purely economic factors. As in other cases, a regular pattern emerged, portraying as it were the prototype of a negative social character, according to which the applicant was described: already absent from the village for a long time, 'insecure livelihood', 'an alleged existence of cash', 'an incompetent householder'; in short neither a solid livelihood nor a trustworthy character. The village councillors certainly showed no trace of any special personal antipathy or prejudice. They conducted this process of social and character discrimination purely on the basis of principle. For this was a systematic procedure, the expression of an economic and socio-political defence strategy of the village ruling class against socially marginal village groups, which they automatically tried to repel. Apparently with success too: the railway worker, with his inn talk about the money swindle which was not meant to be taken very seriously, but was only an attempt to vent his anger, impotence and scorn, was finally his own undoing. He thus confirmed the existence of a particular and coherent course of action in the village — not the normative power of the real person, but the real power of the normative person: one became, in the end, the person one was alleged to be. There was never any talk about love or feelings in the attitudes adopted by local authorities, because for them this was no way to view marriage.

Many of those affected by the ban, however, resisted surrounding pressures, warnings and punishments, and carried on their relationship illicitly. The resulting illegitimate children confirmed, yet again, their loose morals and seemed to justify the original refusal. Between 1849 and 1869, 15 cases of 'concubinage' or illegitimate cohabitation were officially recorded. The number of illegitimate births also clearly increased in this period, and between 1860 and 1864 reached its peak of 18.5 per cent p.a. of all births. These facts together do not simply indicate excessive sexuality, or indeed anything beyond the scope of legal relationships. In many years almost half of the bridal couples went to the altar with a child conceived out of wedlock. They rather seem to me to indicate the intensity of the emotional need for union, which was so brutally declared illegal, or had to remain totally unfulfilled. And many of these stories of relationships finally take on an almost symbolic character, as, for example, the day-labourer couple who came to the minister at the ages of 49 and 53 in 1871, when the restrictive marriage laws were finally lifted, with their three illegitimate children. Defiant and proud, so one can assume, they had finally defeated the law of the village.

There was a tendency during the second half of the nineteenth century for the lower peasantry in terms of relationships and marriage to develop a definite counter-model to the rules of peasant endogamy, which traditionally limited in advance the local choice of marriage partner on socio-economic grounds. It laid down that marriage should take place within the village. The affinity of family property ('field to field') was clearly of more importance than emotional affinity. These rules apparently had increasingly less validity for the worker-peasant families. Property, family lineage, and an economically strategic choice of marriage partner were for them no longer exclusive life co-ordinates which continued to envelop the peasants' existence in what Charles and Richard Tilly have described as 'an iron chain of reproduction and inheritance'. They began to enjoy, within specific limits, a certain freedom of choice of marriage partner, both within Kiebingen and, more importantly, beyond its boundaries. There was also a general trend towards a more modern concept of marriage. One should not speak at once of 'love', because this is difficult to prove; but one may at least assume that marriages in these circles began to possess more initial emotional capital than in the case of many model peasant marriages, whose capital could only be measured in the number of hectares. What of course remained in force almost unaltered was the traditional rule of social endogamy: poor married poor, and rich joined with rich. This prop of Kiebingen's social structure did not totter nor fall for generations. An investigation of the village marriage circle carried out by means of family reconstitution and an analysis of the village social structure showed that property-ownership in the nineteenth century and at the start of the twentieth century remained the structural determining factor in the choice of partner, because it decided the present and future social standing of the family generations.[15] The choice of a marriage partner also impinged on family and kin relationships and affected social standing. Indeed, this could not be left to chance especially in peasant families, but had to be arranged through regulated marriage strategies.

If we divide the local society of Kiebingen into three social groups, on the basis of definite criteria relating to property-ownership, occupation and income, which do not need to be elucidated at this juncture, we can distinguish a proletarian lower class, a middle or intermediary class composed of cottagers and small-scale craftsmen, and an upper class of peasants and artisans. For once the available figures provide a very clear message: from 1810 to 1920 three-quarters of the upper-class males married women from the same class. In the lower class the corresponding figure was about 60 per cent, and only the more open, intermediary class fell marginally below 50 per cent, with approximately half of all cases revealing either upward or downward social mobility in the choice of marriage partner. The high level of class consistency in local marriage practices was in fact a piece of social class reality in Kiebingen. For the upper class it meant a controlled transfer of their material and socio-cultural capital,[16] and therefore they resolved to make this practice a line of demarcation between themselves and the propertyless lower class. However, at the same time, it becomes clear why this dichotomic (property) class structure[17] constantly revealed a socially rather blurred profile at its economic core. The close marriage circles ensured that the village class structure would remain almost perfectly hidden for generations behind the pattern of kin relationships. It was, on the surface, not economic and social differences which divided the village but family ties, affiliation to one or another kin group, and private animosity between clans. Conflicts seemed to reflect family relationships and not class relationships. It was difficult to realise that the structural and political lines of conflict were analogous to the patrimonially-divided kin superstructure. Thus kinship networks served to disguise the exercise of power and domination in the village along social class lines.

V

These power structures can even be exposed at the purely political level, if we take a closer look at the village council as the central institutionalised organ of power in village society. Externally this body, concerned with both decision-making and representation, initially represented a kinship scenario in which the good 'peasant-bourgeois' family names were dominant, and specific 'lineage principles'[18] ensured a seat on the council for generations, almost on the basis of hereditary tenure. Over 87 per cent of all Kiebingen village councillors who held office between 1820 and 1940 had a father or a father-in-law who had held a seat either on the council itself or on its controlling body in the village, the citizens' committee. The names of individual relatives occur in the list of councillors up to 14 times during these 120 years. With an average period of office of 13 years, this means that, from a statistical point of view, there were always one or two representatives of these clans in office. In terms of occupation, the peasants (47 per cent) were ranked above the building craftsmen (23 per cent) and the village artisans (15 per cent). To this extent the scene did not seem to be socially balanced, but that was, after all, 'normal' for the village. The well-organised network and property and power structures concealed behind them are only revealed if one enlists the aid of the previously-constructed economic three-class model as a key to the code. Of the 72 councillors who 'ruled' Kiebingen in the 120 years between 1820 and 1940, a mere two belonged to the lower class (to the families of day-labourers, weavers, building workers and factory workers) who nevertheless composed almost two-thirds of the village population. The upper class, on the other hand, which represented just 10 per cent of the village, had 31 office holders — that is, almost every other councillor. In addition, of course, it also usually provided the mayor.

It is clear that institutionalised politics, in this context, were carried out in the village according to the everyday structures and rules of domination. Politics offered no prospect of a democratic, grassroots political culture, but were a carbon copy of the village hierarchy, devoid of any special standards. This is of course probably the case nowadays in many places too. The jurisdiction of the village council remained comprehensive until 1933 and basically represented control of all local means of production and resources. It stretched from the organisation of the field system to the use of common land, from tax collection to the many small community services and their associated earnings potential, which the council could mobilise as it wished. Its greatest significance lay in the field of social and welfare policy, which in Germany remained predominantly a local matter until 1927, and in the subsequent possibility of social and moral control of all private and public aspects of life. The council could decide who received a marriage licence (at least until 1871), which forms of unemployment and public relief were to be granted, who received a tax deferment, and who was publicly criticised for his life-style and housekeeping. In addition to these economic and political means of power, this furnished the council with social and emotional forms of control. As property, tradition and office provided the basis of legitimation, forms of power which had a patriarchal stamp continued to operate and the weapons of 'honour' and 'shame', 'pride' and 'humiliation' remained important. There was probably no villager who could totally escape the operation of these methods of 'moral chastisement' which almost recalled the medieval pillory. They were a shadow and reflection of their own particular history, from which it proved very difficult to escape.

In view of this hermetic system of village politics, it is hardly surprising that there were actually only two occasions in Kiebingen's history when social conflict was played out on the open political stage. Within the context of the receding revolutionary and republican activity of 1918/19, a building worker suddenly came forward in the mayoral elections of 1921 in opposition to the designated candidate of the village élite, who was the son of the former mayor. The building worker stood for election expressly as the man of 'the workers and cottagers', and demanded that from now on 'there will be impartial dealings at the town hall'. Although the establishment was clearly irritated and adopted publicity tactics in local newspapers ('The worker too always got his due'), the village élite won the election. Not until seven years later, in 1928, did an opposition group finally succeed in winning two seats in the council elections, and they achieved this with a slogan taken almost directly from the class struggle: 'Elect nobody who is only out for his own interest, and is not at all concerned with the lower class.' But these were the exceptions which could only be interpreted with difficulty as incipient trends towards politicisation, or even democratisation, against the general background of the break in political development of 1933. Otherwise conflicts and politics in Kiebingen continued to be settled within a traditional and symbolic framework. Confronted with a perceptible change within society of conflict awareness, the face-to-face nature of patterns of conflict, on a personalised and localised basis, remained largely in force. Displeasure, resistance and social criticism from below did not express themselves according to the rules of bourgeois public opinion. They were expressed through the village's system of morally-based reprimand and punishment, based on rumours, abuse, specific damage carried out to fields, and the deliberate breaking of rules.

A custom which had clearly developed in the context of the 1848 revolution was used time and time again right up to the 1920s as a symbolic act of protest against unpopular local office-holders. From the council minutes of the year 1922: 'Council members Christian Geiger, Paul Raidt and Bernard Wittel each had two productive fruit-trees sawn down as an act of revenge in the night of 22/23 February.' This bizarre form of social protest had a symbolic meaning: each Kiebingen citizen formerly had to plant two trees on the common when he came of age and entered the community, as a sign of his 'naturalisation'. The sawing-down symbolised to that extent a reversal, a kind of expatriation, an excommunication from the village community of people who had misused their power in the estimation of the lower class. Social conflict in Kiebingen could hardly be carried out in anything more than this anonymous, covert form. The economic and social dependence of the village lower class was still too strong and the struggle for the distribution of the village resources was too unequally organised. There was also the lack of a suitably self-contained, active group-awareness of the underprivileged, which would have been able to create collective forms of expression.

And so 'the other Kiebingen' must finally remain in parenthesis. It cannot be described as a village counter-society in the full sense, because social alliance and social conflict, and the elements binding it to the peasant village and those separating it from it, were still too similar to the hotch-potch situation of the village fields. The life of workers and peasants also remained largely centred on the axis of the family's property, on the rhythm of agricultural production and also on specific peasant values, which now of course had a proletarian village meaning. Ownership of their own house and land was for the rural workers, then as before, the essential criterion of economic and social independence. This was deeply rooted in the consciousness of families who had always lived with the threat of unemployment, and whose grandfathers and grandmothers had both known and often carried the little tin sign which legitimised the begging of poor families in the village up until the middle of the nineteenth century. And it was hardly any different in relation to the strong fixation on marriage and the family, which now represented, in addition to their economic significance, an era of justice and autonomy after the degrading marriage restrictions of the nineteenth century. Marriage provided security, which was perhaps not old-established enough to be automatic, and naturally also confirmed village standards of respectability and ideas of status.

Edward Shorter, referring to specific areas of Bavarian village life in the nineteenth century, has mentioned a gradual 'dissolution of traditional cultural models', which 'however leave behind no normative vacuum'.[19] One can use this formula quite generally in relation to Kiebingen's development process, if by 'dissolution' one does not presuppose any radical split in the peasant village culture matrix, but a modification and reconstruction within the sphere of behaviour and significance. The worker-peasants of Kiebingen, in whom the 'workers' soul' wrestled with the 'soil soul', as a Württemberg economic statistician expressed it very graphically in 1919,[20] had to master two contradictory elements at this period. On the one hand they had to develop and implement new methods of production within an old, self-contained system of reproduction, and on the other hand, they had to defend considerable elements of the home-spun logic of their village against the systematic logic of industrial capitalism.[21] Although the dilemma appeared almost insoluble, those affected by it in history are by no means to be viewed as losers and victims. They asserted their specific needs in a determined and unspectacular way, in opposition to the village élite and society as a whole. Consider again the long-standing caution of the first Kiebingen wage-earners with regard to factory work. Not only did this preserve them from the contemporary susceptibility to crisis and the uncertainty of industrial employment in Württemberg; it also enabled them to avoid the associated process of total estrangement and alienation from their family, their village and their familiar cultural world. For this generation, at least, a cautious attitude towards factory work contained a quite decisive element of self-determination. It was not prepared to comply with every demand of society but organised its work primarily around home values — farming, day-labouring and building work in the agricultural context. Industrial work was only accepted when the social costs of the factory worker's existence had diminished, and when commuting offered him the possibility of continuing to live in his home village without being totally uprooted. The earliest factory workers in Kiebingen therefore apparently had very clear ideas about which types of mobility could be married to their needs, and only accepted mild forms of professional and regional mobility.

This attitude ultimately casts a special light on their ties to family and village. Until 1871 the fixed village nexus had been mandatory, as all social security claims and the rights to citizenship and marriage were restricted to the home village. Now a rural existence appeared much more as a possibility than a necessity, as a question of deciding for or against the home village. The majority of workers' families in Kiebingen decided for the village; in the end they did not move to the towns. It certainly was not because village life had offered them, for example, security and safety and had ceased to reflect earlier patterns of social control, discrimination and suppression. It is more likely that the social alternatives apparently still seemed to them more unattractive and more uneconomic than life in Kiebingen. Here at least one knew the rules and laws of everyday life as the whole way of conflict. One had learned to discover and to uphold one's place in it, one's little freedoms and identity. One was not 'blind, deaf and incapable of learning' — to take up again the introductory catch-words — in the processes of experience and learning of many generations. I believe that one should take this decision as a historical plea to take the village, its history and its forms of cultural life seriously.

Notes

1. Wolfgang Kaschuba and Carola Lipp, 'Kein Volk steht auf, kein Sturm bricht los. Stationen dörflichen Lebens auf dem Weg in den Faschismus', in J. Beck *et al.* (eds.), *Terror und Hoffnung in Deutschland 1933–1945* (Reinbek, 1980), pp. 111–55.
2. *Rottenburger Zeitung* 3 October 1934.
3. Gunther Ipsen, 'Landvolk und industrieller Lebensraum im Neckarland', *Raumforschung und Raumordnung*, vol. 5 (1941), pp. 243–57, esp. p. 256.
4. Oskar Negt and Alexander Kluge, *Öffentlichkeit und Erfahrung* (Frankfurt, 1973), p. 79.
5. The following anecdotes and data are the result of a village study carried out

some years ago with my colleague, Carola Lipp. Here we try to link the socio-historical and folk views of the rural process of history. (Wolfgang Kaschuba and Carola Lipp, *Dörfliches Überleben. Zur Geschichte materieller und sozialer Reproduktion ländlicher Gesellschaft im 19. und frühen 20. Jahrhundert,* (Tübingen, 1982).) We have therefore dispensed with citing individual sources in the following sections.

6. See also the contribution of Utz Jeggle in this volume (Chapter 11) as well as his investigation in *Kiebingen — eine Heimatgeschichte. Zum Prozess der Zivilisation in einem schwäbischen Dorf* (Tübingen, 1977).

7. Fernand Braudel, 'Geschichte und Sozialwissenschaften. Die *longue durée'*, in M. Bloch *et al., Schrift und Materie der Geschichte* (Frankfurt, 1977), pp. 47–85, esp. p. 55 *et seq.*

8. Otto Trüdinger, 'Die Wechselwirkungen von Industrie und Landwirtschaft im Wirtschaftsaufbau Württembergs', *Württembergische Jahrbücher für Statistik und Landeskunde* (1934/35), pp. 111–29, esp. p. 112.

9. Martine Segalen, ' "Sein Teil haben": Geschwisterbeziehungen in einem egalitären Vererbungssystem', in H. Medick and D. Sabean (eds.), *Emotionen und materielle Interessen* (Göttingen, 1984), pp. 181–98.

10. Hans Medick, 'Zur strukturellen Funktion von Haushalt und Familie im Übergang von der traditionellen Agrargesellschaft zum industriellen Kapitalismus: die protoindustrielle Familienwirtschaft', in W. Conze (ed.), *Sozialgeschichte der Familie in der Neuzeit Europas* (Stuttgart, 1976), pp. 254–82.

11. Karl Marx, *Das Kapital,* Vol. I (Berlin, 1969), p. 92.

12. David Levine, 'Proletarianisation, Economic Opportunity and Population Growth', in W. Conze (ed.), *Sozialgeschichte,* pp. 247–53, esp. p. 247.

13. Ibid., p. 247.

14. The attitude to marriage, the demographic processes, and their significance in Kiebingen's history have been thoroughly investigated and documented by Carola Lipp in the second part of the joint village study: 'Dörfliche Formen generativer und sozialer Reproduktion', in Kaschuba and Lipp, *op. cit.,* pp. 287–598.

15. Heinz Reif, 'Theoretischer Kontext, Ziele, Methoden und Eingrenzung der Untersuchung', in J. Kocka *et al., Familie und soziale Plazierung* (Opladen, 1980), p. 45 *et seq.*

16. Hans Medick and David Sabean, 'Emotionen und materielle Interessen in Familie und Verwandtschaft' in ibid,m *Emotionen,* pp. 27–54.

17. Josef Mooser, 'Gleichheit und Ungieichheit in der ländlichen Gemeinde', *Archiv für Sozialgeschichte,* Vol. 19 (1976), pp. 231–62.

18. Georges Balandier, *Politische Anthropologie* (Munich, 1976), p. 64.

19. Edward Shorter, 'La vie intime', in C. Ludz (ed.), *Soziologie und Sozialgeschichte* (Opladen, 1972), pp. 531–49, esp. p. 538.

20. Hermann Losch, 'Lohnhöhe und Lebenskosten', in *Württembergische Jahrbücher für Statistik und Landeskunde* (1919/20), pp. 246–58, esp. p. 257.

21. Jürgen Habermas used this category in his *Theorie des kommunikativen Handelns,* (Frankfurt, 1982).

11 THE RULES OF THE VILLAGE
On the Cultural History of the Peasant World in the Last 150 Years*

Utz Jeggle

I

The traditional village is on the retreat, not simply as an economic unit but in other respects too. Where it once created order, it is now confronted with the prospect of upheaval. The situation is ripe with dangers as well as with opportunities. A choice has to be made between those traditions worth preserving and practices better abandoned. But there is little hope that the right decisions will be made. Small-scale farming now only makes a minimal contribution to the West German economy. The village no longer functions as a social and economic sphere that can satisfy most of the needs of its inhabitants.[1] As the world has grown bigger, time for the village has retreated, proximity to nature has become attenuated, and the community which once necessarily gave the villagers their social cohesiveness is less compelling. The village as a way of life and experience has not only changed its external appearance in the last 30 years; within its boundaries, the ordering of society and the structure of its mental outlook have changed too. Yet during the course of many centuries the village created traditions which have not simply disappeared with the new conditions of life. Certain ways of experiencing the world can continue in a social sub-culture far longer than a simple stimulus-and-response theory can comprehend. Education and socialisation are not merely oriented towards direct social needs, but also respond to the abilities of parents and grandparents. The possibility of experiencing happiness, of surviving partings, of feeling secure, of trusting, the whole spectrum of ways of feeling and the richness of the emotional qualities that form the basis of mental outlook, all evolve in a long and crisis-ridden developmental process, in which the bearers of older traditions feed in their attitudes and views of the world even before the

---

*Translated by Richard J. Evans.

child has learned how to speak, and so become deeply embedded in the unconscious and subconscious aspects of human existence in the community.[2] It is possible — as my friend Albert Ilien once put it — that villagers today still suffer from the hunger and under-nourishment of their ancestors.[3] He meant by this, that it is not only possible, but to a certain extent it is actually inevitable, that collective experiences continue to influence the individual even when these experiences no longer seem necessary for the material existence of the group. With changing conditions some attitudes do change, but not all, and it is possible that the continuation of old world-views in new conditions is sometimes painful to experience.

The history of *mentalités*[4] is a subject that has received attention not only from social historians, but also from those who, like my-self, work within the conventions of *Volkskunde* — a discipline that represents a mixture of folklore studies, cultural anthropology and ethnology. The point of departure for our work is generally the daily consciousness of ordinary people, their normal experience of everyday life; and where this consciousness is incomplete, or where people have preferred to repress their insights into the real nature of things because it is painful to maintain a clear view of them at the forefront of their minds, problems of understanding and portrayal obviously arise for the researcher. Thus what people order and control themselves is clearly visible, but what is imposed on them from above is more obscure. We can get a relatively faith-ful picture of the internal structures of village life, but the connec-tions that undoubtedly exist between the village and the outside world can only be sketched in outline. A microscopically exact portrayal of the village makes it seem like a world in itself, and it is not easy to reflect adequately the village's external determinants and orientations. The discipline of *Volkskunde* looks at the world in a specific way, and from a different vantage point, than that of social history, sociology and other related disciplines, and it there-fore requires complementing and extending. The same could be said, of course, of all academic disciplines — some have simply not realised it yet.

The history of *mentalités*, as practised within the discipline of *Volkskunde*, seeks to interpret the possibilities and dangers that arise when the equilibrium of collective ties and individual freedom is disturbed or enters a period of crisis. This is why I have called this paper 'The Rules of the Village'. By this I intend putting for-ward an ideal-typical model in which security is created at the cost of freedom of choice. We would find such a way of life suffocatingly restrictive today; but for those who experienced it, it made possible feelings of happiness and unhappiness, joy and sadness, which we ourselves seek with more urgency but not always with more success. The peasant village constituted not only a form of settlement but also a way of life, which characterised society in south-west Germany alongside urban artisan culture well into the industrial era. It was the result of a differentiated economy which was so constructed as to build bridges between small-scale agriculture and hungry bellies that would be acceptable to as many as possible. The ordering of village life that resulted was not regionally or even nationally specific. Comparable laws of the village are observable elsewhere, as far afield, for example, as Hungary.[5]

We began our reconstruction of the ordering principles of peasant life[6] by attempting a sociography of a village in south-west Germany. We were interested only in the present. We wanted to uncover the internal power structures of the village, to find out by a series of interviews of the local inhabitants how decisions were made and who took part in them. We chose Kiebingen for practical reasons. We wanted a Catholic village with a population mostly engaged in industry, and we wanted a village close to our Institute in Tübingen because we began the project with student participation and so needed to keep the costs and travelling time to a minimum. Beginning in 1970 we asked a representative sample of the villagers who they thought had power in Kiebingen: 'Who in your opinion are the most important people in deciding things in the community?' was the question we put to some 70 villagers, along with a whole battery of other issues. The results were as platitudinous as they were predictable: the mayor was the most important, then the priest, and after him the local schoolteacher. It seemed as if the villagers had read the same books on rural sociology as we had, for in the second round of interviews, when we questioned the members of the village council, we obtained precisely the same, standardised answers. The 10 councillors described in long and open conversations and in great detail how harmonious, rational and democratic the council proceedings were, and how conscientious they were in following the dictates of reason and in meeting the demands of the public good. We encountered nothing but responsible local politicians, who seemingly did the best they could according to their knowledge and their conscience, within the letter of the law. It all seemed happy and harmless, an impression strengthened by our investigation of the village's clubs and societies, which were also — it could no longer surprise us — run by co-operative and responsible functionaries, who painted for us a picture of the village that no romantic novelist of the nineteenth century could have bettered.

One day, however, we got to know Albert Ilien, who was not a native of Kiebingen but lived there and gave Catholic religious instruction at the grammar school in nearby Rottenburg. His wife taught in the primary school in Kiebingen, and the village they knew was another one altogether from the one we had so far encountered, a darker, less unified community, a place in which the sun did not always shine, a village in which there were conflicting power-groups perpetually trying to put their own specific interests into effect through the local council: for the main work of the council at this time consisted in the allocation of farming land for building plots, and every power clique in the village was anxious that the building plots should be sited on their own fields, in order to benefit from the consequent rise in land values. At first we hardly believed this startling revelation. Not only did it show all our previous investigations to be worthless, but it also made us seem rather foolish and naive. But as we were introduced to Albert Ilien's acquaintances, this time not as investigators from outside but as 'friends of Albert', and went over a number of points with them again, we were given, as 'insiders', a new and more ambivalent picture of the village. At first we were inclined to throw our initial investigations into the dustbin, but we gradually realised that in this village, as elsewhere, two separate realities could exist, one regulating the internal life of the community, the other held in readiness for representing the community to the outside world. As ethnologists we are always tempted to treat the inner truth as the real one, and it was not easy for us to accept that these were not two competing belief-systems but two sides of the same — the inner and the outer world of the village of Kiebingen.

Our existing theories of local sociology had sufficed to understand the outer world, but they were inadequate for comprehending the inner. Again and again we encountered processes and relationships which we were unable to explain on the basis of studying the present situation of the village and its inhabitants. In its social structure Kiebingen is fully adapted to the modern world: there is only one full-time farmer left, who has — with difficulty —

amassed or leased enough land to make it worth while farming as a going concern within the Common Market norms. Most of the adult inhabitants work in the surrounding industrial centres. Altogether there are 500 commuters, more than one in four of the entire population of the village. Even large numbers of the children go to school outside; some classes of the middle school have been moved to the neighbouring village of Bühl, and the more senior schools are all in Rottenburg. Even the physical appearance of the village has changed: the centre is mainly inhabited by old people, foreign workers and students, and anyone who thinks anything of himself builds a new house on the outskirts, mostly with the help of relatives, who in their turn demand help with the construction of their own modern homes. For adult men this means spending every summer weekend on a building site for eight to ten years of their life.

This contrast between the physical appearance of the village and its inner world was for long a source of irritation to us. Everything in Kiebingen looked just as it did in other villages: the villagers watched the same television programmes, drove the same cars, and worked in the same factories. Yet despite all these levelling factors there evidently existed secret forces which bound the villagers and did not allow them the untrammelled operation of their free will. As a striking proof of this, Albert Ilien was able to predict with astonishing accuracy the result of the mayoral election of 1971. With the help of a handful of trusted informants we were able to work out not merely who would vote for whom, but also why. Mostly this had to do with traditional client relations — blood relationships, societies or clubs — and with common knowledge or gossip (X had talked about the candidates in the village inn; Y had said this or that to Z, and so on). The village suddenly revealed itself as a manifest protective and offensive association, which shocked us as outsiders so much that we spoke of a 'structure of terror'[7] and thought that nobody could do what they wanted in the village, but that many more situations were programmed in advance than was the case in the urban life we knew ourselves. We learned that these binding forces in village life did not draw their energy from the present but from the past, and that the forces of the past continued to exist beneath the surface of the present that was to some extent 'cryptic', but was still of the greatest importance for the architecture of the village's present social structure. This was a decisive moment of recognition. From this point onwards we divided our efforts. I began with one group of researchers to reconstruct the village's historical development; Albert Ilien carried on with the analysis and description of the structure of communication in the village today.

II

The village of Kiebingen belonged to the province of Hohenberg, which fell, through inheritance, under Austrian rule in the fifteenth century. Its population then was about 300, but during the nineteenth century it began to grow, and had doubled by 1900. To the south of the village lay a monastery of the order of St Paul, which cared for the souls of the community but added little to its material wealth. In 1786 the monastery was dissolved and its estates sold off as a part of the reforms of the Emperor Joseph II. This event forced Kiebingen into a new world in which it was no longer protected from above, but was now responsible for its own actions. It was one of the decisive impulses that pushed the village towards the new era, which, perhaps, it has still only partially reached. The other impulse was the 'taming of the Neckar', the attempt, lasting almost the whole of the nineteenth century, to end the damaging and unpredictable spring floods and to confine the river into a regular and ordered course. Apart from these influences, there were also important changes in the legal situation of the villagers with the abolition of feudal dues, and in the economic opportunities open to them, as the beginning of industrialisation allowed construction workers from the village to earn money in Switzerland over the summer, at the price of being away from home and placing a corresponding extra burden on wife and family. Of course, these developments were gradual and affected different groups and families at an uneven pace. We were very careful, therefore, to describe the traditional rural structure as accurately as possible. We had to bear in mind that this was itself far from static, but it changed at a snail's pace compared with the developments of the late nineteenth century, and so it seemed permissible to portray the situation of peasant labour as in a snapshot, so as to find in it clues to the mental outlook of the villagers, for their mentality is, even today, not only open to new behavioural expectations, but is also conditioned by the demands of a peasant economy which was dominant for centuries and so inevitably rooted itself deep in their psyche.

The traditional peasant village is a community of settlement that organises itself in such a way that the cultivable land within its boundaries is farmed to the limits of its fertility. This simple fact conditions the spatial organisation of the village and the subordination of its inhabitants to the demands of this organisation, of course in their own best interests. The three-field system, which was customary in this region, was considerate to the land: it accepted that it would become exhausted and needed rest and enrichment, that nothing came from nothing, and that the land, as the basis of life, needed and deserved care and attention; that, like human beings, it would remain shrivelled and impotent if it was stinted or denied food and nourishment. This alliance of people and land varied according to the form of settlement. In south-west Germany the people were housed close together and so enjoyed the advantage of greater security, or at least of diminished fear. But they were obliged to pay for the advantage of a close and intensive common life the price of a more restrictive social order. Land was scarce, so every metre was exploited; there were rules determining who could enter whose fields for purposes of harvesting, sowing or muck-spreading, the division of the three fields was rigidly maintained, the grazing rights to the meadow were pedantically prescribed, even the right of exploiting the few public footpaths across the fields for agricultural purposes was given to the village official as a part of his wages. Space was narrowly defined and precisely distributed. It was a house of many chambers, each with its own quality, determined not only by the fertility of the soil but also by the rights of access that attached to it; even the places where carts could be kept were fixed and there were farmers who ploughed their furrows with curves that were not only elegant in themselves but also had the incidental effect of exploiting the straight lines of the field boundaries for their own very practical benefit.

Fences, hedges, gates and boundaries played a dramatic role in the life of the village. Invisible but by no means imaginary lines divided the space; just as the way over the fields, which could be trodden only after the harvest had been gathered in, was visible to the villagers the whole year round, so too were the unmarked pews in the church, allotted to the village families according to their current ranking in the village hierarchy. At funerals the whole village lined up in a long procession led by the local notables and the relatives of the deceased and so down through the different steps of the social ladder to the village paupers, who, on this day, were provided with bread from the deceased's house. As in the village and its fields, so too in every individual house there was no free disposition over space. Everything had its place; the garden was structured and programmed, not only in the use of fruits and vegetables, but even in the flowers grown there: certain families are praised in Kiebingen even today for growing simple country flowers, while others are condemned for their arrogance because they insist on growing showy roses in front of their houses. The division of the rooms was preordained, as was the nature of their furnishings. Even if there was no strict division between the parts of the sitting-room used on workdays and the parts used on holidays (as there was, for example, in the Hungarian village of Atányi studied by Edit Fél and Tomás Hofer) still, it was clear which part of the room was to be used for which task, who sat where at mealtimes, and who gave the command to be seated or to rise at the end of the meal. In the Hungarian village of Atányi, for instance, the table was a particularly revered piece of furniture at which no task involving dirt or mess could be performed and where, consequently, children were not allowed to sit. Thus a local farmer could say, 'We loved our daughter so much that we even let her sit at table.'[8] The table did not play this role in Kiebingen, but signals were given to cease using it, such as putting on the tablecloth or a crotcheted covering, which announced that this particular piece of furniture was not suitable for daily use. Thus every piece of furniture had its fixed disposition, and the space within the room was divided into small zones, distinct and distinguishable in function and task, which constituted an order in the minds of the inhabitants, and assigned each thing, each beast, each person a particular place.

In south-west Germany forms of common property and work had not really emerged: instead whatever had been gathered up and held together despite all obstacles in one generation had to be divided up every time among the next. Every child received the same portion of fixed and moveable property as an inheritance. Binding together and tearing apart was the perpetual motion that shook these families to their foundations with a force that was often hard to bear. If the spatial system was oriented towards having and holding, binding and sealing, the generational system was larded with the bitter compulsion of tearing it all asunder.[9] Being a citizen of the village meant having property. Property was inherited from parents and in-laws, but it went to brother and sisters too, and, with old age, to the children once more. 'Have you divided up your property then?' was the question that was asked in Kiebingen of every family whose members appeared to get on with one another reasonably well. Jealousy and ill-will have not departed even today; there are still parents who only communicate with their children through a lawyer, and brothers in the same line of business who poach each other's customers by lowering their prices, even at the risk of their own financial collapse. Nowadays one might be justified in calling such behaviour neurotic: in rural society it was far from irrational, however: it was rightly said that 'a brother is a brother and a field a field'. Such a sentiment was one of the main rules of the practical philosophy of social action: generosity was too expensive to afford, mistrust was better. Boundaries were drawn between people as sharp as those on the ground, and they did not stop short of feelings and emotions, but regulated and ordered them through utilitarian calculation. With 10 hectares, so goes another saying, you don't need love; others say, with 10 hectares love will come unasked-for.

The village is strict, it cannot afford to show mercy. It needs order so that it can regulate the intercourse of its meagre space and its teeming inhabitants. The village has devised elaborate systems for ordering its affairs, taken them into service and maintained their existence. To the three-field system, which organised the space within its boundaries, corresponded a code of behaviour in the village and within the home, a code which, for all its rigidities, none the less holds for us today a certain dignity, even a seductive degree of security. Like the village land, so too the life that depended on it was a whole, knit together by innumerable threads of custom and order. Everything had its measure and stood in an observable relation to the measure of other things:[10] the size of the table to the size of the family; the number of milk-churns standing in the yard to the number of cows standing in the stall; the height of the hay-rick to the potential number of calves to be raised; the logs in the woodshed to the cold of the winter; the flour in the sacks to the number and size of the family's hungry bellies; the number of children to the number of fields and to the hopes or fears of the farmer and his wife at the prospect of a perilous and uncertain old age.[11]

Just as space was divided by boundary lines, so too was time. The course of the day, of the year, of life itself, was structured by boundaries. Isolated experiences and perceptions were impossibilities: bad weather in the morning accounted for anger the next evening, despondency the next month and the danger of hunger the next year. The rules of the village were thus not — as the discipline of *Volkskunde* once maintained — the interplay of customs performed by peasants in traditional costume like picturesque folk-dances; they were choreographed by poverty and fear, and led by cold, sickness, hunger and death. The strictness of the rules was a necessity of life: no one could sit out this particular dance or any part of it. It was called to the tune of economic circumstances, even if long practice had given it cultivated forms, which at key moments of life, such as baptism, marriage and death, found modalities of emphasis and depth which we observe with admiration today, which bound individual memories into the collective experience. They gave meaning to a life which was exhausted itself within the bounds of a simple village existence, but which none the less was experienced by some as rich and beautiful despite all its harshness. Whether or not this village life was less complex than our own less closely-knit, more open world of experience, it was certainly taken as a matter of course, as self-evident as bicycling is for us, a skill which, once learned, is automatically exercised by body and brain, and only surfaces to consciousness when we meet an obstacle or fall off.

The system of rules which governed life in the peasant village was thus not separate from life or observable as something discrete, but was part of life itself, as natural as the air we breathe. The certainty of appropriate social behaviour was like a sixth sense; the order imposed by village society was carried out as naturally as smelling or hearing. For this reason, it was necessary for the people who moved in this social landscape continually to take stock of their position and report it to their fellows. The current meaning and importance of a moment in time or a social space were transparent to the eyes of the villagers. The almost supernatural significance possessed by boundary marks even today has its expression in the condemnation of those who transgress them.[12] Such people commonly suffered a fate in fairy-tales far worse than that of mothers who killed their infant children. Similarly, there were marked and easily-definable boundaries set to the use of time, so that the working day, the working month and the working year were clearly structured and set in an observable relationship to periods of rest and breaks, which were most commonly announced by visible or audible signs, such as the ringing of a bell, the saying of a prayer, the position of the sun, or the appearance of children bringing supper out to the fields.

The material world was also filled with such signifiers of order. As in the Schwalm district of Hesse,[13] so too in the Tübingen area the clothes a person wore presented their own form of social appropriateness. A girl's status and age, but also her possible state of mind, whether sorrow or joy, would be announced to all by what she wore. Traditional peasant costume was at its most elaborate in the form it took when the wearer went to Mass. As late as the 1960s the ethnographer Martha Bringemeier had difficulties in obtaining access to these dresses even though it was only for research purposes, for they had, as the peasant women said, 'experienced so much blessing' that it was impermissible to desacralise them by profane study. Clothes were inextricably associated with the occasions on which they were worn. These associations determined the outward appearance of the village and the physical expression of its rules in many situations. The honour of the house demanded that the house wife wear an especially elaborate costume on Sundays, just as a relatively poor artisan in the Hungarian village of Atányi said to his sons: 'Mark you well, you can save money on your stomach, but not on your clothing, everyone sees that.'[15] Such an order of priorities is difficult for us to grasp, so closely bound are we to the idea of 'eat first, then think about morality'. But one can easily imagine that in Atányi and similar places, the hunger of people's eyes for the visible world exceeded that of their stomachs for that which could be eaten.

Martha Bringemeier has described how in the Schaumburg area wedding dresses and mourning dresses came with the same trimmings. How the bridal procession trod the same path as funerals took; and how the same neighbour whose duty it was to drive the hearse was also expected to take charge of the bridal cart.[16] Life's grandest moment, the ceremony that brought the quality of life to its highest point and property and possessions to their greatest extent, was placed in a clear and self-evident relationship to the moment when the amplitude of maturity, and indeed of life itself, came to an end. Material objects were not only representations of needs but also guides through life, to a certain extent a catalogue of collective memories, bringing before people's eyes the prospect of how life would proceed and how it would eventually come to an end. A particularly striking example is the trousseau which girls made for themselves in preparation for their own life's destiny. On their wedding day it was displayed in an open cupboard or trunk, and it was not just there as a sign that all was well and ready, for next to it were also placed the clothes of the as yet unconceived and unborn child and the fittings for the funeral bier.[17] These objects were mute appeals for an appropriate attitude to the different stages and situations of life: the trousseau, for example, was to a degree the programme for the role which a woman was expected to perform. The wedding guests inspected these goods not because they wanted to know how wealthy the farmer's daughter was — they knew that already; they inspected them because they wanted to know whether she had as much as they knew she should have.[18] The peasants saw in this ensemble of bedclothes and table linen, bonnets and mourning clothes, the whole of their common life's course laid out before them, a course, that ran from point to point without deviation, and could only be changed or frustrated by accident or disaster. Of course, these signs were planted out in a bed of obligations that left little room for independent decisions. Such obligations were exercised not only in the degree and organisation of labour demanded by the division of the fields, or in the tasks that were to be done when the weather was good or bad; they appeared also in the tools used in these tasks, in the clothes worn for them, even in the hours of leisure, which were also filled with orders and rules.

III

All this gave a high degree of similarity to the life-histories of all the village's inhabitants. It also gave them security. The predictability of life was the best insurance against shocks and surprises. Membership of a particular family was already a prediction of a certain specific future for a child: knowledge of its parenthood gave every villager the ability to make prophecies, the accuracy of which would be the envy of every fortune-teller. They knew how much land the child would one day own, how rich he or she would be, into which social group he or she would marry; the occult powers of the Eve of St Thomas when, standing naked and throwing a log behind her, allowed a village girl to see the future,[19] were seldom frustrated, for the choice of possible suitors was not large and if the log could never conjure up a fairy prince, it could at least conjure up her own subconscious preference for Müller's Fritz or Meier's

Franz. Naming him was to name a known degree of satiety, the fatness of the body, the number of pearls on the necklace, the pew in the church, the chances of being elected to the local council and even, finally, the sentiments to be expressed in the funeral oration. The certainties of life's plan affected all in equal degree: every villager's life depended on the family he or she was born into, and that in turn determined the size of the fields and the richness or poverty of the farm.

The village universe had two dimensions, that of the citizen who belonged to the village and had equal rights and duties as such, and that of the property owner, which was not really a single dimension but rather an extraordinarily fragmented and splintered terrain. However similar the activities the villagers undertook, however great the communality of legal practices, it made a decisive difference in the end whether someone had five cows to milk or only one, whether he could drive one cow or five onto the common to graze. While there was a collective Kiebingen mentality, formed by shared experiences in the struggle with nature, in the sufferings of war, in the fear of illness and death, there were also sub-cultural mentalities within it, which did not of course overturn this collective dimension, but none the less broke it down to fairly small proportions. There was a peasant way of life, but for the internal structure of the village it was only of secondary importance: property was the decisive factor. Just as the nature and division of the land speaks volumes about the character of the village, so the extent of landed property gives the essential information about its village owner. Landed property was the central, determining feature of life, it laid down how large the house and outbuildings were to be, so that all the produce of the land could be stored in them, it controlled whom a man married — a woman with a large dowry or a small one — it determined if a farmer could hire a horse to draw his plough and cart or not, if his family was well fed, if the living-room was warm in winter, if his children could be attended to or whether they had to be neglected, if meat could be served on Sundays or whether vegetables or broth had to do. In Kiebingen there were three main groups: those who owned more than 3 hectares of land, who never had to worry for the basic necessities of life, and formed a kind of village élite; those who owned between 1 and 3 hectares or earned an equivalent living through artisan production and domestic industry, who may be described as the middling group of villagers; and the large number of the village poor, with less than 1 hectare a piece, who lived in perpetual hardship and uncertainty, and often had no idea where their next meal was coming from. These three groups to some extent formed separate social milieux within the village; the barriers between the lowest level and the rest were very real and even grew harder as the nineteenth century progressed; while the village élite married almost exclusively among themselves, at least until the late 1860s.[21] Property relations thus divided the villagers into separate groups who found it far from easy to integrate one with another.

In south-west Germany, indeed, the poorer peasants so clearly lived below the poverty line that it would have been surprising that the villagers kept the peace for so long had they not experienced the social hierarchy of the village as something preordained. Social differences appeared to them as natural as sexual differences: or, to put it another way, having was a decisive aspect of being, possession of existence; a villager might perhaps filch a furrow from a neighbour's field for a time, but to ask why he had more land was unthinkable. Questioning the system of land distribution in a fundamental way was as absurd as questioning the weather. Such a rigorous ordering of society could only be sustained by strictness. It seems, at first sight at least, as if the village children had no difficulty in accustoming themselves to the village order, though they had reason enough to rebel. There were occasional flare-ups, but they were not regarded as genuine rebellions by the village, rather as suckers on a rose, or untidy growth on a bush, to be clipped back into order at the earliest opportunity. Yet to my mind it must have been far from easy to have been pulled through a needle's eye of this kind, and our impression now, after two village studies, is that the placid surface of everyday life concealed violent eddies and turbulences of the psyche whose number was far from insignificant.[22]

The peasant village found an interesting way of creating distance from some of its members while keeping them within the community in the case of the village idiots. They may have been mocked and stigmatised — though no villager would admit it — but they were always supported by the community. They were classified as nature's mistakes; they were not regarded as sick, and because of this they were not carted off to the asylum. A grain of madness had its place in everyday village life too: village stories indicate how demoniacal and supernatural forces led an accepted existence within the community alongside ultilitarian and reasoned, causal interpretations of the world.[23] What Max Weber called the 'demystification of the world' enthroned rationality in the place of magic, but it also necessitated the drawing of sharp boundaries between the rational and the irrational. In the cosmic universe of the village these boundaries were vaguer and less severe. Some fears and tensions at least were allowed, just as religion spun a web of belief over the world that gave life if not security, then at least an unquestionable meaning and importance.

Much of what appears nonsensical to us had a function of its own in the old village life. The obsessional interest and engagement that appear even today when the question of how land is divided is a burdensome and continuing bequest of the three-field system. It has become as problematical today as the traditional relations of the sexes, which rested on the belief that only one person could have the say in running a farm, that this person had to be a man, and that only he could be a citizen with voting rights in the community. Women had rights to accompany their duties, but these were subordinate to those of men, a fact reflected in the place they occupied at table[24] as it was in the time they got up in the morning. Villagers interacted with their children — on a level less conscious and more apparently natural than that of deliberate education, a level perhaps even more decisive for the development of future generations — in such a way as to ensure the reproduction of the ability to master the numerous ambivalences of village life: thus certain ways of behaving could be experienced as completely discrete and separate from one another, demanding no fully consistent personal reaction. A peasant child had to learn how to accept a brother or sister as a working partner and at the same time fear him or her as a competitor for the inheritance. Such a splitting-up of the personality was necessary in many situations. In a long term perspective this mixture of demands from the social environment and dependence on it for a particularised character structure appeared 'normal'; these ambivalences constituted the consistent element in the peasant character. A life-history in our sense did not need to form a logical whole; rather, the vicissitudes of the surrounding environment, of weather and season, provided the mould in which such a life took on what only we regard as a contradictory, inconsistent shape.

Indeed, remarkedly enough, the strict rules of the village could only be maintained by transgressions. As soon as we begin to look through village archives, we find an extraordinarily striking number of offences recorded in the files:[25] quarrels and feuds, and property and sexual offences are in the great majority. They are not the outcome of pranks, follies or a free-floating communal mentality. They are the product of the most bitter poverty and distress; and sexuality, in these straitened and legally-restricted circumstances, was sometimes no less hungry for gratification than the appetite was for food. Destitution of whatever kind called forth its auxiliary troops, whose transgressions set in motion a whole process of investigation, prosecution and expiation that continually reinforced the correctness and validity of the rules they sought to break. Even those who lived on the margins of village society took part in this process; they acted as living examples of what could happen if the rules were disobeyed. Kiebingen's paupers, for example, were permitted to go from farm to farm on Fridays, — 'beggar's day' — to kneel at the door and intone the Lord's Prayer in return for a bowl of soup or a piece of bread: they were not merely the bit-players in the social drama of the richer farmers' charitable deeds, they were also a lesson to children in the home who were inclined to put a pretty face above a well-manured field when it came to choosing a marriage partner. The village paupers also documented the consequences of idleness and depravity. They were maintained in the community as living witnesses of these things, as warnings to deter others from becoming like themselves.

Compassion could thus be maintained in the village according to rules established by custom. On the other hand, so too could the severity with which a day-labourer's wife, caught pulling a few handfuls of grass from the meadow's edge to feed her hares, was denounced to the authorities. Charity was one thing, property another. In its dealings with outsiders the village displayed all the roughness of its hierarchy of values in a way as far removed as possible from comradeship, sensitivity or community spirit. This system of values had developed in such a way that spontaneous, independent-minded compassion was possible only at an unacceptable cost for the individual who chose to exercise it. The villagers said, 'I can't harvest a good heart',[26] and the present-day observer must learn to understand such a statement in a sense disassociated from morality, for the armies of beggars that invaded the village, the numberless thefts that despoiled its fields, made property owners all the more avaricious in the fear that they would themselves sink down into the ranks of those who were forced to glean food for their animals at the dead of night, or even to wander from house to house collecting stale bread and leftovers for their own sustenance. It was the danger of falling into such an abyss that made the barriers between the different kin-groups — or in our own parlance, social strata — in the village so watertight. Those who nevertheless fell through the occasional gaps in them served as a permanent warning to others not to suffer the same fate. The propertied inhabitants of the village knew at the bottom of their hearts that these social failures were basically the same as they were, they had just made a fatal mistake, and this knowledge inflated their fear to vast proportions, overcoming every temptation to break the rules even for a moment, even if they would have enjoyed doing so.

This function of those who otherwise had no function in village society was generally accepted and maintained. Village outcasts and drop-outs were treated harshly, but they were not abandoned. The village idiot, the village whore, the thief and the beggar were socially despised and could be badly treated, but they were not banished from sight, as occurred with the institutionalisation of the poor, the criminal and the handicapped in the city. The village accepted them as a kind of counter-image of the proper order of things. Just as the trousseau cupboard of the farmer's daughter confirmed this life as a good one, so too did the face, furrowed with the effects of drink and worry, of the beggar who was maintained in the poorhouse with his wife and children at the expense of the community. Like holy untouchables, the despised in the village community were honoured, they were useful for the experience of their uselessness, their shattered existence enabled the more prosperous to contain their own secret desire to break out of the mould of village life, and to connect this desire in their minds with the unhappy fate of those outcasts who seemed to have succumbed to it.

Perhaps this also helps explain why rebellion within the village was invariably interpreted as the outcome of unhappy fate and failed ambition, so that rebels were rendered harmless because their rebellion could never become a model, but always, in this scheme of interpretation, remained a warning and a deterrent. The inherited 'right' way of doing things did not allow the emergence of new 'alternative' ways; those who refused to tread the known paths of village life could only be thought of as having lost their way. This open rebellion could only find satisfaction through emigration to the city or across the ocean. 'Inner' rebellion, the way to self-destruction through suicide, was so strongly despised within the village that one might almost suspect that the temptation to take this way out was very widespread, and had to be countered by especially strict taboos. We encountered suicides again and again in the archives and the memories of the villagers. In the end, however, these radical outsiders, who were serious in their criticism of the narrowness and violence of the village rules, were themselves evidence for the strength of village orthodoxy, which continually demanded new sacrifices in order to prevent the emergence of heresy.

IV

The fear of deviance from the village norms called forth such rigorous preventive measures because, in the end, the danger of deviance was growing steadily greater. The decline of village life could already be observed in the nineteenth century: today it has been shaken to its foundations, and little remains of the earlier order of things in the villages of our own time. The ties that once bound life and work so tightly together have been broken, and only fragments remain, often with a significance that bears little relation to their former meaning. Humanity has changed the environment more rapidly than it can itself adapt to it. There are different rhythms in history; the world is not everywhere turned upside down at the same pace or at the same time. Such irregularities can create problems of course, but they can also help and protect those whose lives are subject to such drastic changes by allowing them gradually to alter the direction of their journey when it threatens to go the wrong way.

The integrity of village life has been broken, and an element of closeness, familiarity and security of intercourse has been lost. Yet there has been a corresponding gain in freedom of choice as well. The old system of village rules was not the product of chance, but the creation of the village economy — in this case based on the requirements of the three-field system. The material productive and reproductive conditions of village life have been revolutionised: very few of the villagers are engaged in agriculture today, the off-spring of once-prominent farming families now work in factories and the few remaining full-time farmers have put their farms on a business footing and have long since ceased to be the undisputed leaders of the village community. The spatial divisions of the village are no longer sacred: every field can now be reached by a made-up road, and no one is outraged nowadays when one of the part-time farmers exhausts the soil with a two-crop rotation such as wheat and maize because it is easy to harvest with a combine and only needs making up with chemical fertilisers until such time as it can be sold for a housing development. There is no longer any village court to prosecute such transgressions — if such they still are — and disapproving looks glare today only from older eyes. The new landowners, who have often consolidated their holdings or even bought them where possible, are in any case beyond this measure of good and evil. The field-watcher has gone to work in the factory, and the disruption of the rhythms of the soil is cured by chemistry, rather as the villagers now treat their own troubles with pills. The fields have changed their appearance. Land is no longer an obsession, a god before whom all bend the knee; it is a possession, cultivated with new, less intense, more diffuse emotions.

At the same time, the principle of profit and loss has not proved completely victorious. The part-time farms are uneconomic not only by European Community standards but even by the concrete measure of the hourly income they generate. Indeed, as business propositions they are an absurdity. Yet everyone who possesses one strives to retain it, even, if possible, to extend it. If one has land, then it cannot simply be left untended. New forms of loan or mutual aid have evolved to cope with this situation. A seed-drill or a tractor can be borrowed in exchange for help in building a house or in harvesting the corn, a cartload of dung is available at the price of a day's work in digging up the turnips. The contempt of the traditional village inhabitants is still visited on anyone who neglects his land; the general view is that he would do better to rent it out to someone who would make better use of it. Of course, no one tells him so to his face, instead, the opinion of the village is expressed in his absence, in the village inn, where, it is assumed, there are sufficient prying ears and loose tongues to carry it further, until it eventually gets back to its object. Yet even village gossip — the necessary instrument by which transgressions of the village rules are recorded and in this way simultaneously punished — no longer functions as directly as it used to. It is now possible to live in the village without belonging to it, though only for outsiders. The villagers themselves still leave for other parts if they want to be different and live in another way than the rules prescribe; but the new immigrants cannot be harmed by gossip and intrigue; they never even get to hear of it.

Of course, there are villages that have lost their character by increasing immigration, but as we later began to study another village near Tübingen, we were surprised to find that here too, just as in Kiebingen, the old mechanisms of inclusion and exclusion, of belonging and not belonging, were still in working order. We conceived the idea of basing an exhibition on this new project, in cooperation with the village inhabitants along the lines of other local history studies.[27] We deliberately chose not to work with a preselected group. We were deterred from this course by our experiences in Kiebingen, where we had run around in circles for a year because one kin-group had sent us from one relation to another without our noticing it, so that we were quickly put down as supporters of this particular family network and only received information from other groups in the village in a form directed at and filtered by the one into whose hands we had inadvertently fallen. At the beginning of the new project, therefore, we put up informal green notices and issued an invitation in the parish magazine announcing an open meeting in the fire station, which everyone was welcome to attend. About 15 people turned up, but only two of them obviously belonged to the 'old' village: one, a financial civil servant, who looked after the local archive, regarded our project with some mistrust as a rival undertaking to his own; while the other, who had been wounded in the war and retired early from his job with a war pension, was a kind of janitor who was there to watch over us, our actions, and the information provided by his fellow-villagers. The rest were all marginal figures, standing between the village and the world beyond, who saw in us a chance to enter the village community through co-operating in our project.

For example, one of our informants was a German refugee who had fled from Yugoslavia at the end of the war. He would not have dared come on his own but the war pensioner brought him along and so he felt able to join us two 'chiefs' on the table at the end of the hall, facing the audience — although he was all too easily pushed aside from this rather small piece of furniture by our elbows. He described with pride how, on his arrival from Yugoslavia, he had learned the names of all the villagers off by heart, and claimed that he thus knew more than many an old villager and was therefore indistinguishable from the original inhabitants in every respect. This declaration occasioned a glance at me from the war pensioner, Herr Walter, which refuted it completely, though without causing any upset to the refugee, who did not notice it. The look told me that no one could learn their way into the village community, it could only be joined through a lifetime's experience. A village woman who worked with us was apparently able to do so only as an appendage of Herr Walter. Whenever she gave us some information, it was always with the words '. . . wasn't that so, Walter?' He was the notary who had to seal her every word with the stamp of approval, and was thus always able to reject it. When we met one evening in the village inn to discuss possible new collaborators, every name suggested by the woman was rejected by the men under the leadership of Herr Walter: the selection of the informants was clearly the men's job.

Even as we had begun to arrange this meeting in the inn, there had been curious confusion. We had chosen the place, and no one had objected at first, but all of a sudden we were told that Herr Walter could not come on the evening in question, he had another appointment. The woman, who knew Herr Walter's pietistic disinclination for evenings in the inn, then added, 'I don't much like going into pubs.' She could, of course, say this as a woman, but it was difficult for a man to utter such a sentiment without becoming known as a 'Holy Joe'. So Herr Walter immediately denied any aversion on his part, and declared himself willing to arrange another time for a meeting. This he did, and turned up at the inn with two old people from a neighbouring village as companions. They were both well-regarded figures in the village; one was the son of an innkeeper. This demonstrated that Herr Walter had nothing against pubs, but nevertheless he spent the whole evening drinking fruit juice, thus indicating his inner distance from pub life. While his right hand was raised to confirm the oath, his left, in other words, remained with fingers crossed behind his back.

A certain ambivalence was obviously necessary in this business because we researchers were requesting co-operation on the one hand, while the village was requiring solidarity on the other, and had to agree on what to tell us and what not, and why some things had to be kept secret while others could be revealed. To begin with only Herr Walter was prepared to accord us an individual interview: otherwise everyone was accompanied by a witness, for safety's sake, as the villagers must have seen it. So we experienced right from the beginning the continued presence and control of the suspicious village super-ego, watching jealously over the boundaries between the community's inner life and the outside world. Our most spectacular experience of this was with Herr Werner, a German refugee from the East who had married into a well-respected village family. In the very first meeting in the fire station he boasted of 3000 slides he had taken of the village, and we urged him to show a selection from them in public — we wanted to use the visual memories they would conjure up as a means of stimulating better and more detailed discussions of the old days than we had so far managed to evoke. The refugee agreed straight away, though I imagine the other villagers at the meeting cast all sorts of warning glances that we were unable at the time to notice or interpret.

We announced the slide-show in grand style, along the lines of the first meeting, but when the day came Herr Werner said he could not come, and so we were unable to do anything; the fire station was embarrassingly full, and we had little to offer save excuses. As we promised to show the slides at the next meeting, someone from the audience said no one had seen them (an assertion which, idiotically, stimulated our ambition to show them still further). We were also told that if we wanted to have Herr Werner appear on time, we had to fetch him from his house an hour in advance — a coded warning which we were also unable to pick up. Instead, I was foolish enough to take this literally, and sent a student collaborator to get Herr Werner as suggested, an hour before the meeting — once more widely advertised, and even better attended than before. Just before the show was due to begin, the student appeared in dismay to inform us that Herr Werner was sitting at home, half-dressed and as drunk as a lord, surrounded by heaps of slides and obviously incapable of doing anything with them. We had disregarded the warning signals given to us and demanded of him far more than he could deliver. I went to his home and made him come to the meeting.

The evening was a complete fiasco. To begin with the projector could not be plugged in because there was no extension lead, then the carousel box for the slides could not be found. Finally, when all the technical details had been arranged, it became clear that Herr Werner was no longer capable of working out which way up to put the slides in. I tried — like a typical town-dwelling academic, I would say today — to rescue our project by trying to put the blame on our victim: Werner had let us down, would have kept us waiting had we not gone to fetch him and so on. But the atmosphere in the fire station was hostile: we had made one of the villagers appear ridiculous. In the village people enjoy observing the weaknesses of others, especially when they come from outside, and they had indeed come for just such a purpose; but the weak are protected at the same time from the eyes of strangers, whom such matters, it is felt, do not in the end concern. The village — even this village, where there were scarcely any farmers left and people worked mostly in the surrounding towns — still possesses the strength to defend itself against inquisitive strangers and pushy newcomers. The village still exists, now as before, as a communicative structure with its own domestic and foreign policies, and even if the latter is more pacifically inclined than was our experience in the second village we studied, one should still have no illusions about its effectiveness.

These may not be 'facts' as far as historians are concerned, they are not even the products of the conventional methods of oral history, but are experiences emerging from the confrontation between a researcher and his field. They are to a certain extent just the accidental by-product of a researcher's misfortune and incomprehension. The rules of village life nowadays are no longer confined to the village itself, they are to be found in Common Market regulations, Education Acts, industrial relations, church policies and the like, in far more amplitude, detail and consistency. But if we want to find out how village people live within the rules, and how they deal with them, then we need to employ, I believe not only the tools of social history, but also the methods of ethnological research.

Notes

1. Ina Maria Greverus, *Der territoriale Mensch* (Frankfurt, 1972).
2. Mario Erdheim, *Die gesellschaftliche Produktion von Unbewusstheit* (Frankfurt, 1983).
3. Albert Ilien and Utz Jeggle, *Leben auf dem Dorf* (Wiesbaden, 1978), p. 98.
4. Wolfgang Kaschuba and Carola Lipp, *Dörfliches Überleben* (Tübingen, 1982).
5. Edit Fél and Tamás Hofer, *Bäuerliche Denkweise in Wirtschaft und Haushalt* (Göttingen, 1972); and idem., *Geräte der Atányer Bauern* (Copenhagen, 1974).
6. Ilien and Jeggle, *op. cit.*; see also Utz Jeggle, *Kiebingen — eine Heimatgeschichte* (Tübingen, 1978); and Albert Ilien, *Prestige in dörflicher Lebenswelt* (Tübingen, 1977).
7. Ilien and Jeggle, *op. cit.* The concept would not be sufficiently ethnological for me today, it denies the double character of these ties that not only bind but also secure, and so possess not so much a terroristic as a protective nature.

8. Fél and Hofer, *op. cit.*, p. 350.

9. It would be very useful to undertake a parallel project to our Kiebingen study in an area of primogeniture, where there are suggestions that the mental structure of sibling relations and generational conflicts are difficult. Se Otto Baer, *Die bäuerliche Familie im Realteilungsgebiet und ihre soziale Sicherung*, (PhD thesis, Tübingen, 1956); and Helmut Röhm, *Die Vererbung des landwirtschaftlichen Grundeigentums in Baden-Württemberg. Forschungen zur deutschen Landeskunde* (Remagen, 1957). The latest and very exact community study by Kurt Wagner on the north Hessian village of Körle also deals with an area of partible inheritance and comes to comparable conclusions (PhD thesis, unpublished Kassel, 1984).

10. Many examples of this are in Fél and Hofer, *op. cit.*

11. Utz Jeggle, 'Vom richtigen Wetter', *Kursbuch*, 64 (1981), pp. 115–32.

12. E.g. Friedrich H. Schmidt-Ebhausen (ed.), *Schwäbische Volssagen* (Struttgart, n.d.), pp. 104–13.

13. Martha Bringemeier, *Mode und Tracht* (Münster, 1980), pp. 40–72.

14. Ibid., p. 66.

15. Fél and Hofer, *op. cit.*, pp. 332–3.

16. Bringemeier, *op. cit.*, pp. 63, 60. On wedding dresses in general, see Martha Bringemeier, 'Die Brautkleidung im 19. Jahrhundert', in Martha Bringemeier *et al.*, (eds.), *Museum und Kulturgeschichte. Festschrift für Wilhelm Hansen* (Münster, 1978), pp. 299–320.

17. On the trousseau, see Fél and Hofer, *op. cit.*, pp. 328–9.

18. The importance of the measure is made clear by Hofer and Fél, ibid. See also Max Bartels, 'Volks-Anthropometrie', *Zeitschrift für Volkskunde* 13, pp. 353–68.

19. Karl Bohnenberger (ed.), *Volkstümliche Überlieferungen in Württemberg* (Stuttgart, 1961), pp. 300–1.

20. For further, more detailed information, see Kaschuba and Lipp, *op. cit.*

21. On the general development of agriculture in this period, see H. Haushofer, *Die deutsche Landwirtschaft im technischen Zeitalter* (Stuttgart, 1972).

22. Unfortunately we have no statistical information on the number of psychologically-disturbed people in the village, and though we constantly encountered them in the files, it is not easy to make an historical diagnosis. It is probable all the same that the strict rules of the village often prevented the emergence of true psychoses.

23. The theories of folk-tales that interpret ghosts as aspects of persecution mania must be tested again to discover the extent to which ghosts can be understood as the incorporation of a moment of insanity into everyday life. This is not without its dangers, but neither is the sharp division of mortality and immortality as practised in present-day western cultures. Cf. Friedrich Ranke, 'Sage', in John Meier (ed.), *Deutsche Volkskunde* (Berlin, 1926), p. 208.

24. For two such seating orders, see Scharfe *et al.*, *Heitere Gefühle bei der Ankunft auf dem Lande* (Exhibition catalogue, Tübingen, 1983), p. 37.

25. There were 370 offences in Kiebingen between 1826 and 1871. The number of offenders involved was 148. Up to 4 or 5 separate cases involving the same person are common above all in begging and sexual offences. Comparing this with an estimate of the village population gives a figure of 15 per cent, or on in seven, involved in conflicts with the law in this period. One might say this was one in every family, if we did not know that most families contained no offenders, and a minority consisted of nothing but offenders. Cf. Jeggle, *op. cit.*, p. 266.

26. This saying was told us by an older villager; such formulae are very common in the village. Speech itself is standardised in many respects, because the frequent recurrence of the same situations allow appropriate verbalisations to be transmitted from generation to generation.

27. Utz Jeggle, 'Geheimnisse der Feldforschung', in Heide Nixdorff and Thomas

Hauschild (eds.), *Europäische Ethnologie* (Berlin, 1982), pp. 187-204. On recent problems of ethnological field studies, see Utz Jeggle (ed.), *Feldforschung* (Untersuchungen des Ludwig-Uhland-Instituts, 62, Tübingen, 1984).

NOTES ON CONTRIBUTORS

Cathleen S. Catt was born in 1953 and studied European History at the University of East Anglia, where she is currently preparing a doctoral dissertation on 'Family, Land and Occupation: German Rural Society in the late Nineteenth Century — the Example of Maudach in the Lower Palatinate, 1840–1900'. In 1984 she gained her Diploma of Education. She now teaches History at an Upper School in Bury St Edmunds.

Ian Farr was born in 1951 and studied Modern History at the University of Durham. In 1972/73 he was Research Assistant at University College, Lampeter. Since 1976 he has been Lecturer in European History at the University of East Anglia. His publications on Bavarian peasant society and politics in the nineteenth century have included articles on the Peasant Leagues and on 'Haberfeldtreiben', the German charivari.

Gisela Griepentrog was born in 1935 in Fürstenwalde on the Spree and took a degree in Enthology at the Humboldt University in Berlin in 1957. She is the author of *Historische Volkssagen aus dem 13.–19. Jahrhundert* (Berlin, 1975) and of a contribution on family life in the Magdeburger *Börde*, written as part of the collaborative project on the area in progress at the Central Institute for History, at the Department of Cultural History and Ethnology, in the Academy of Sciences of the GDR, Berlin, where she has been on the staff since 1975.

Willian W. Hagen was born in 1942 and studied at Harvard and the University of Chicago. He is the author of *Germans, Poles and Jews: the Nationality Conflict in the Prussian East 1772–1914* (Chicago, 1980) and a number of articles on aspects of the rural social history of early modern Brandenburg. He is currently preparing a book on manor and village in Brandenburg from the sixteenth to the nineteenth centuries. Since 1970 he has been teaching at the University of California, Davis, where he is currently Professor of History.

Hartmut Harnisch was born in 1934 and studied Geography,

History and Archival Science at the University of Greifswald and the Humboldt University, Berlin. He gained his doctorates from the University of Rostock in 1964 and 1978. After working as an archivist from 1959 to 1973, he moved to the Academy of Sciences of the GDR, where he is currently on the staff of the Institute for Economic History. His work, for which he was awarded the René Kuczynski Prize in 1978, has included *Die Herrschaft Boitzenburg* (Weimar, 1968) and other studies of agrarian history in the eighteenth and early nineteenth centuries. His most recent book is *Kapitalistische Agrarreformen und Industrielle Revolution* (Weimar, 1984).

Christel Heinrich was born in Bernau, near Berlin, in 1931 and has been on the staff of the Academy of Sciences of the GDR, where she is currently a member of the Department of Cultural History and Ethnology in the Central Institute for History. She holds a degree in Ethnology from the Humboldt University and is the author of contributions on migrant labourers and on family life and festivals in the multi-volume study of the Magdeburger *Börde* currently in progress at the Institute.

Utz Jeggle was born in 1941 and studied at the Universities of Tübingen, Bonn and Vienna. In 1968 he gained his doctorate with a thesis on Jewish villages in Württemberg, and ten years later was awarded his second doctorate for *Kiebingen — eine Heimatgeschichte* (Tübingen, 1977). Since 1981 he has been Professor of Empirical Cultural Studies at the Ludwig Uhland Institute, University of Tübingen.

Wolfgang Kaschuba was born in 1950 and studied political science and empirical cultural studies at the University of Tübingen, where he gained his doctorate and is currently a member of the Ludwig Uhland Institute. His work on community studies has included collaboration on a book about the 'red' village of Mössingen and its general strike against Hitler, *Da ist nirgends nichts gewesen ausser hier* (Berlin, 1982), and two books co-authored with Carola Lipp, *1848 — Provinz und Revolution* (Tübingen, 1979) and *Dörfliches Überleben* (Tübingen, 1982).

Hainer Plaul was born in 1937 and studied Philosophy and Ethnology at the Humboldt University, Berlin. He gained doctorates in

1966 and 1981 and has published studies of trivial literature in eighteenth- and nineteenth-century Germany, *Illustrierte Geschichte der Trivialliteratur* (Leipzig, 1983) and rural society in the Magdeburg region, *Landarbeiterleben im 19. Jahrhundert* (Berlin, 1979). Since 1966 he has been a member of the Central Institute for History of the Academy of Sciences of the German Democratic Republic, in the Department for Cultural History and Ethnology. He has contributed a number of articles to the collective work in progress on the history of the Magdeburger *Börde*.

Regina Schulte was born in 1949 and studied History, German and Sociology at the Universities of Bonn and Munich. In 1977 she gained her doctorate with a dissertation on prostitution in nineteenth-century Germany, *Sperrbezirke: Tugendhaftigkeit und Prostitution in der bürgerlichen Welt* (Syndikat Verlag, 1979). From 1982 to 1984 she held a Research Fellowship at the German Historical Institute, London, and she is currently Assistant in the Institute for History of the Technical University of Berlin. Her work on peasant society in Bavaria has appeared in a number of journals and collections.

Gerhard Wilke was born in Körle, Hesse in 1948, left school in 1962 and served an apprenticeship as a butcher. He went to Ruskin College, Oxford in 1969 and studied Sociology and Social Anthropology at King's College, Cambridge from 1971 to 1974. He is at present Lecturer in Sociology at a College of Further Education in London. Together with Ernst Parkin he published a study of the major plays of Samuel Beckett, 'Schluss mit Warten', in *Das Werk von Samuel Beckett* (Suhrkamp, 1975). His research on the oral history and historical anthropology of the village in which he grew up has been presented in a number of articles and contributions, including radio and television broadcasts for the Open University.

INDEX

293